Causation and Universals

Causation and Universals

Evan Fales

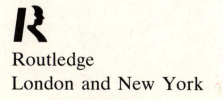

Routledge
London and New York

First published 1990
by Routledge
11 New Fetter Lane, London EC4P 4EE

Simultaneously published in the USA and Canada
by Routledge
a division of Routledge, Chapman and Hall, Inc.
29 West 35th Street, New York, NY 10001

Typeset in 10/12 Times by Columns of Reading
Printed in Great Britain by T.J. Press (Padstow) Ltd, Padstow Cornwall

British Library Cataloguing in Publication Data

Fales, Evan
 Causation and universals.
 1. Causation
 I. Title
 122

Library of Congress Cataloging in Publication Data

Fales, Evan
 Causation and universals / Evan Fales.
  p.   cm.
 Includes bibliographical references.
 1. Causation. 2. Universals (Philosophy) 3. Realism.
 4. Knowledge, Theory of. I. Title.
 BD541.F35   1990
 110—dc20   89–10902
                                                         CIP

ISBN 0–415–04438–3

To Ruth W. Fales and the memory of Walter Fales, without whom I would never have begun thinking about these matters

Contents

Overview

This book is an essay in systematic ontology. Part one sets forth a realist and non-Humean theory of the causal relation. Part two integrates that conception of causation with a theory of universals that might not unjustly be described as Platonic. In Part three, the focus shifts to epistemology; in it, some epistemological consequences are drawn from the ontology developed in Parts one and two.

One of the motivations for this project was to see whether the phenomenal foundationalism with which the investigation begins must lead inevitably to either skepticism or idealism: could such a foundationalism, if it has available to it a sufficiently robust conception of causation, escape from these seemingly unavoidable alternatives? The epistemology sketched quite summarily in Part three would reasonably qualify, I think, as a version of scientific realism.

Those, in the broadest terms, are the themes of this essay. Because the argument is a long one, and because the connections between the various topics taken up may sometimes be difficult to anticipate or remember, the reader may find it helpful to embark provisioned with a brief summary that maps the terrain, indicating both the argument's architectonic and the chief relationships among its parts. Arming the reader with such a guide will, I hope, help to illumine the path.

Chapter 1 is focal to the project. In it, I argue that Hume was right to regard causation itself as the ontologically fundamental notion in that cluster of concepts that also includes the notions of law, disposition, counterfactual, and induction; and, like Hume, I adopt (both for dialectical purposes and out of conviction) a foundationalism whose basis is phenomenal. But Hume was wrong in claiming that there cannot be found within sense experience an "original" for the "idea" of a non-logical "necessary connection" between events: just such an "original" exists in the sensation of tactile pressure. That claim is defended against various objections, including (what I take to be the most serious ones) Hume's own. One problem, the peculiar phenomenal elusiveness of the causal relation, is shown to be characteristic of relations in general, for they are perceptually diaphanous; but this problem is not fully disposed of until Chapter 10, where it is taken up again in the context of a general treatment of relations.

Even if successful, this defense of causation would be of little interest to ontology, or to a realist epistemology, unless the causal notion thus unearthed could be instantiated by events outside of experience. The chapter closes with an argument to this effect; and the issue is taken up again in Chapter 11, where further arguments are given.

Chapter 2 argues that causal relations are dyadic relations between events (or states of affairs) that have, as their ontological ground, a tetradic second-order relation that holds between a pair of first-order properties or relations, a temporal relation, and a spatial relation. This chapter and the next, which discusses the relation of causation to causal laws and the logical form of such laws, raise a number of formal and semantical issues: the individuation of events, the extensionality of causal contexts, and the modality of causal laws. Much of the argumentation in these chapters reflects the style of most contemporary discussions of these issues, which approach ontology via semantics. Those who, like myself, have doubts about how much direct light linguistic analysis can shed on ontology, may wish to skim or pass over these sections, keeping in mind that the way events are individuated will be of importance subsequently.

Chapter 4 investigates the implications of a robust conception of causation for the traditional problem of induction; as such, it explores one central connection between ontology and epistemology.

Chapter 5 argues for two theses concerning the relation between causality and time: (1) that causal sequences are temporally dense (i.e., that between every two events in a causal chain there stand other events that are members of the chain); and (2) that backwards causation is possible only if backward-directed causal sequences are completely isolated, causally, from forward-directed ones. The latter thesis has certain implications for the ontology of time – a problem explored more fully in Chapters 7, 10, and 11. There I deny that time and the temporal order are parasitic upon, or supervenient upon, events and the causal order. The view of time (and of space) developed in those chapters is consequently one that assigns to them a kind of independent existence. The argument for thesis (2) above hinges on an analysis of certain counterfactuals, to which end a novel theory of the truth conditions for counterfactuals is introduced, one that presupposes a realist conception of causation.

Part two commences with Chapter 6, in which various nominalist theories are surveyed and criticized. Of these, Stout's view is the one whose rejection raises the most interesting question for the realist: in individuating what Stout calls 'abstract particulars' in terms of their spatiotemporal location, one is confronted by the problem of how to individuate (instances of) spatial and temporal relations themselves, construed as abstract particulars. A regress analogous to the one that threatens Stout must be confronted by the realist who individuates ordinary particulars by relying on spatio-temporal position. Chapter 7 is largely devoted to this question.

Chapter 8, which is pivotal to the epistemology developed in Chapter 12, integrates the realist conception of causation developed in Part one with a species of Platonic realism. The central theses of this chapter are (1) that the causal relations that connect first-order physical universals to one another are essential to those universals, and provide the only means we have of identifying and distinguishing them; (2) that such identification via causal relations shows that a disposition term, if it designates any property at all, designates an occurrent property – but identifies it in terms of the causal relations it has to some other universals; (3) that the kind of verificationism implicit in scientific procedure is not (as positivists thought) a semantic principle, but an ontological one – it is causal relations (which, though necessary, are not knowable *a priori*) that determine which features of the world it is possible to identify; and that to postulate further, causally inaccessible features would be ontologic-ally idle, though not meaningless; (4) that ultimately, entry into the system of causally related universals requires that we identify some universals directly, in a way unmediated by causal relations; and (5) that a physical universal exists if and only if it is a member of the causal "web": if it is, then it exists whether or not it is ever instantiated. (Hence, my characterization of this realism as Platonic.)

Chapter 9 discusses and rejects a theory once held by David Armstrong according to which there are no generic universals. Armstrong explained the phenomenon of determinates falling under a common determinable by holding that the determinate universals are complex ones that share constituent universals. An alternative theory is proposed, one that does admit generic universals. Finally, I explore the possibility of understanding the necessary connection between a determinable and its determinate species in terms of the hypothesis that the determinates have a certain subset of their causal relations in common, and that this set is the set associated with the determinable.

Chapter 10 treats relations. On the view I defend, there are no internal relations (as distinct from their relata), and it may well be that the only pure external relations there are, are spatial, temporal, and causal. Causal relations do not themselves have causal essences; they do not stand in (higher-order) causal relations to anything. Thus they cannot be perceived (since external perception is a causal process), except directly or immediately. This is why there is not (as Hume observed) a distinct perception of causal relation in our ordinary perception of causally related physical events.

Chapter 11, which initiates the development in Part three of a realist epistemology, attempts to establish the objective existence of time, space, and causal relations. The objective existence of these three is required by any realist conception of the material world: they form the necessary framework of any such conception. Here the reader will find a discussion of the A and B theories of time and of McTaggart's paradox, of the relation between phenomenal spaces and physical space, and of arguments for the existence of unexperienced causal relations.

In Chapter 12, finally, I attempt to defend a realist epistemology. The chief antagonist here is Hilary Putnam, who rejects metaphysical realism, as he calls it, in favor of an "internal" realism. Putnam's view, as I analyze it, hinges on the claim that no univocal relation can be established between language (or thought) and the world: no such relation can be both epistemically accessible to us and serve to underwrite an objective conception of truth. The hope (entertained by Putnam in his earlier writings) was that causation, by grounding reference, would provide the required objective word/world relation. But this assumes that an objective referent for the term 'cause' (and with it, for 'reference') can be established; as Putnam sees it, this re-raises the very problem that the appeal to a causal theory was meant to solve. The only way out, I believe, is to show that we have direct cognitive access to the notions crucial for a realist semantics (or more fundamentally, for a realist conception of the objects of thought). But it was the burden of Chapter 1 to demonstrate that we do have such access to at least one of the required notions: that of cause. The remainder of this chapter is devoted to an exploration of the further consequences for epistemology of the ontology previously set out. The most important implication is that, because of the way universals are cemented together into an interlocking system by causal relations, warranted empirical belief converges, in the long run, to truth – where truth is understood realistically, in terms of correspondence.

There are two features of the essay's trajectory that deserve emphasis. First, it adopts an undefended phenomenal foundationalism. This is, in part, so that I may meet Hume on his own ground. But, at the same time, the label 'phenomenal' may, in this context, be quite misleading. The argument does presuppose that we have warranted noninferential empirical beliefs, but it does not require any commitment as to the infallibility of such beliefs in general, nor any commitment to a particular ontology of perceptual experience – for example, as to whether there are sense data, mental states, or the like. Second, the web of causally linked universals that unifies the physical world requires a holistic approach to empirical knowledge: sure identification of a universal requires knowing all its causal relations. This has an advantage and a disadvantage. The advantage is that no part of the world is "in principle" inaccessible to perceptual investigation. The disadvantage is that knowledge of any part of the system (other than what is "given") requires, apparently, knowledge of all of it – and this, practically speaking, seems to invite skepticism after all. The reader will have to judge for him- or herself whether I have provided a satisfactory response to this difficulty.

Preface

The world, as I see it, contains objective causal relations. It also contains universals. The first fact and the second are intimately connected. These claims, if they are correct, must have profound and far-reaching consequences. I shall try both to justify the claims and to trace some of their consequences for ontology. Such an investigation, moreover, cannot leave epistemology untouched. Throughout, I shall raise epistemological issues, though they do not become the central concern until Part three. There, I shall try to show how these three features, causes, universals, and the connection between them, breathe new life into a certain theory of empirical knowledge: how, in particular, they undergird epistemological realism. Without them, I believe that realism is a forlorn hope, and idealism or skepticism wins the game.

Empiricists have almost universally felt themselves forced to adopt a leaner ontology than mine. As a result, they find themselves hard-pressed to explain many of our most fundamental beliefs; in the end, many of these beliefs are either abandoned or disguised – as in Berkeley's characterization of our belief in material objects. I admire the intellectual heroism which such philosophical asceticism breeds; and also the methodological credo of empiricism, to which I aspire to adhere to throughout. But it is a mistake (I shall argue) to suppose that this credo deprives us of the right to assert the existence of causation and of universals. It is equally a mistake to suppose that it forces some form of idealism upon us.

Since I am by temperament (are not most of us?) a realist, this outcome of the richer ontology is welcome. But the victory, as always with such matters, is partial, tentative, disputatious, and not easily won. In many places I fear I have sacrificed detail in favor of scope. It is my hope that this sketchiness does not damage the argument irretrievably, and that more is to be gained by providing a certain systematic closure.

It is here necessary to say a further word about my general epistemological orientation. It will be evident immediately at the beginning of this essay and throughout, that I take for granted the knowability, indeed the foundational status, of certain introspective contents of awareness. On many issues it is the "given" which constitutes my ultimate court of appeal. If this methodology constitutes an embarrassment, it is not one which I shall attempt to relieve by confronting head-on the philosophical lessons which Wittgenstein and others have supposedly taught us. (I save my head-on confrontation for Hume, with whom I am in agreement on at least this issue. For the time has come, I believe, to re-examine the problem of causation in the terms in which he posed it. It is largely because the Humean skeptic has seemed to win so decisively when the problem and the conditions for its solution are stated in these terms, that philosophers since Hume have so consistently attempted to shift the terms of the debate. I suggest that this is a mistake.)

The "given" has, over the past few decades, received an increasingly bad press. I believe that some doubts about the given must be taken seriously; but on the other hand I do not believe that the reasons for such legitimate doubt entail the conclusion commonly drawn, that there are no contents of experience which are not inseparably suffused with concepts, with linguistic categories, or with culturally determined understanding and interpretation. Indeed I believe that, in recent history at least, the attractiveness of the thesis that all experience is "theory-laden" has been significantly motivated by the failure of foundational programs to deliver what was promised: a constructive account of our knowledge (or of what we take to be known), and a refutation of skepticism. This – and the fact that this is primarily an essay in metaphysics rather than epistemology, determine my strategy. Rather than confront directly the arguments of Wittgenstein, or of Heidegger, or of Kuhn (among others), I aim at a constructive proposal with the ultimate intention of showing (on the epistemological front) that foundationalism is by no means dead.

Indeed there are hard – it seems to me insurmountable – problems with relativism, internal realism, and the like. For one thing, no one has successfully shown, so far as I can see, how such theories can account for the acquisition of cultural and linguistic knowledge in the first place, without that account reducing these capacities to plastically reactive noise-making behavior, neuronal patterning, or the activities of conditionable robots. What is wanted is not this, but an account of how we obtain the concepts, publicly endorsed rules, conventions, and beliefs, which constitute the alleged framework of our cognitive enterprises. Relativism, it seems to me, fails to block the slide toward skepticism, whatever its rhetoric. Those who reject the given or its foundational role are not like sailors attempting plank by plank to reconstruct their leaky boat, but rather like sailors who do not even know they are at sea; nor what can serve as a plank.

In speaking of the given, I use at various times the expressions 'phenomenal' and 'directly experienced.' I feel somewhat handi-capped by the historical associations which have accreted around these terms, not all of which I welcome; and the more so as I do not propose to offer any analysis here of *what* are the items of which we are directly aware. Constrained to use the common terms, I nevertheless attempt to steer clear so far as possible of any positive ontology of perception itself. I do not think this cripples the account. For I should agree thus far with the enemies of the given: that no philosophical theory of the nature of the given is itself given to us, vouchsafed before our philosophical labors have begun. And I try at all times to respect the principle that what is given is not, in virtue of that alone, automatically guaranteed to be philosophically transparent or understood.

That there are manifold puzzles about sense data (and also about the alternative theories of the given); that we learn to describe how things *are* before we learn to speak of how they look; that there are problems about the relation between sensing and knowing – all of these facts ought to be acknowledged; and none of them ought to deter us from an epistemological enterprise which takes the given as its starting point. For the givenness of the given is certainly not something made secure only after we have answered such philoso-phical questions about it. A philosopher of the given cannot avoid the profound difficulties which attend theorizing about the given; but no genuine philosopher of the given could allow that these difficulties are sufficient to cast a fog of doubt over the existence of the given: to concede that would be already to abandon the very claim of givenness. Were a sophisticated account required at the outset, one which locates the given within the general scheme of things, then too it would automatically forfeit its status and its distinctive epistemological role. That is not to say that we have no right ultimately to demand an accounting which allows and responds to the perplexities engendered by philosophical thought about the nature of the foundations of knowledge. This latter task will not be undertaken here. This will not impair my present strategy, however, which is to re-examine the resources of foundationalism as a defense against skepticism, in the conviction that philosophical programs, like prophets, are ultimately known among men by the fruit they bear.

Acknowledgments

To two people I owe a preeminent debt for assistance and inspiration: Professor David Armstrong and Professor Panayot Butchvarov. Armstrong's contribution is twofold, partly unwitting and partly witting. As for the first, a seminar in which I used his two-volume work on universals was "the" proximate cause of the writing of this essay. Subsequently, Armstrong generously read the manuscript and offered many criticisms and comments which have been a great help. Though Armstrong and I differ on many fundamental issues, the persistence with which his name appears in this text will I hope bear adequate testimony to the extent of his influence upon my thinking.

I owe an equal debt to Professor Butchvarov, whose incisive criticisms (and many conversations over several years) have forced me to see and think about these problems with more care than I might otherwise have managed. I have also benefitted greatly from remarks made by Professors Michael Tooley and Richard Fumerton, and by members of the philosophy department of the London School of Economics, especially Professors Colin Howson, Peter Urbach, and John Watkins. The LSE was a very hospitable home away from home during my sabbatical year in 1981–2. If I had been able to satisfy all these critics, this would I am sure have been a better book by far.

Earlier versions of Chapters 4 and 12 appeared in *Midwest Studies in Philosophy*, Volumes IX (1984) and XII (1988), respectively. An earlier version of Chapter 9 was published in the *Australasian Journal of Philosophy* (1982), and some of the material of Chapter 2 overlaps my discussion of events in "Davidson's Compatiblism," *Philosophy and Phenomenological Research* (1984). My thanks to the editors of these publications for permission to use these materials.

To Jean Graham and Chris Ahn, whose fingers are far faster than mine, I give my heartfelt gratitude; with intelligence and Sisyphusian patience they translated my pen-scratchings into bytes.

In a more personal vein, I wish to thank Sandy West, who extended to me an invitation to live and write for three weeks in complete isolation in a unique and extraordinary environment, Ossabaw Island. In that peaceful setting, a crucial phase in the composition of the book was completed.

This project taught both my wife and me the meaning of that special forbearance that is demanded of the one when the other is gestating a book. To her, Stuyvie Eagle, a special word of thanks. Parturition has its pains and joys: my last gesture of appreciation goes to Ishi, our son, who kindly waited until this task was done before demanding entry into this world.

Part one
Causal realism

1 Natural necessity

1. METHODOLOGICAL PROLOGUE

It has been one of the most generally agreed upon doctrines of empiricism that there is no such thing as natural necessity. It is also one of the most universally troublesome doctrines. For, although the details are likely to be complicated, there is little doubt that a great many philosophical problems could be brought much closer to solution, if not actually solved, by means of the assumption that there are necessary connections in nature. Among these problems are: the problem of induction, the problem of providing a satisfactory analysis of the logical form of many of the laws of nature and of scientific explanations, the problem of providing a semantics for many of the subjunctive conditionals and disposition statements we use, and the provision of a sufficiently full-bodied conception of causation to sustain causal theories of reference, perception, and knowledge.

Abstinence from natural necessity has been largely responsible for the chronic anemia suffered by empiricist treatments of all these problems. This situation has led some philosophers, notably Arthur Burks, to attempt the construction of formal systems incorporating a causal operator. Others have investigated the related problem of formalizing subjunctive conditionals.[1] But such systems are empty unless they can be provided with an adequate semantics. Talk of physically possible worlds, and the like, only defers the day of reckoning. Sense must be made of such talk. Of course the dialectical desirability of having a notion of natural necessity is one thing; getting such a notion into the philosophical arsenal without cheating is quite another. Much effort has been invested in seeking ways to avoid the essentially skeptical conclusions of Hume while remaining true to the spirit of his objections to natural necessity.

3

But in the end, we are forced, I think, to confront directly the central issue in terms of which Hume's destructive analysis of causal claims is cast. That is to say, we must confront the nature of those experiences from which our idea of causal connections derives indirectly – as a matter of theoretical inference or – as I shall maintain – "directly." So this is where I propose to begin. Because I will be disagreeing with Hume – indeed, disagreeing with him on phenomenological grounds – it will be necessary to make a number of methodological observations before proceeding to the main task.

First, a terminological point of some importance. In his treatment of causation, Hume often speaks of the problem as that of finding some necessity in nature; and in these opening remarks, I myself have adopted this usage. However, for reasons which will presently emerge, I believe the notion of causal relation to be more fundamental than that of natural necessity, and not, strictly used, equivalent to it. Thus my initial and primary focus will be on this relation. Necessary connection – if by this one means the necessity of one event's following upon another – will occupy a back seat. More generally, it is my view that a grasp of causal relations underlies our understanding of both necessary and sufficient conditions for the occurrence of an event, of (some, not all types of) natural law, of many counterfactuals, subjunctives, and disposition statements, and of the notion that (some) laws of nature are defeasible. In all of these related cases, I believe the ontologically and semantically fundamental notion is causation itself. Thus I am out of sympathy with attempts to reduce this notion to one of the others.[2] I shall not attempt to develop in detail a semantics for subjunctive and dispositional statements[3] but I shall have some things to say about laws and about the related problem of induction.

My first methodological point concerns the role of phenomenological appeals in philosophy. Like Hume, I hold that the contents of sensory experience provide the starting point (or more precisely, one of the starting points)[4] for our thinking about the world. Therefore, that which we find in experience represents a court of last appeal with respect to those questions which are, or ought to be, decidable on such grounds. Distinct from their claim to epistemic fundamentality, however, is the claim that sense experiences provide us with knowledge. That further claim requires – and has traditionally been supported by – the view that the contents of experience are themselves known. And this must be distinguished from the claim that there is nothing more fundamental to be appealed to, should disputes arise as to what we are taught by experience.

I intend to engage in just such a dispute with Humeans; yet I should agree with Hume that there are some things about the contents of one's own sense experience which can be known with certainty. But I also wish to insist that not all sensory content is cognitively transparent; and that it is not easy to articulate a general formula for just what it is that can be known in this way; certainly not as easy as some empiricists have supposed: though Hume himself, at times, is suitably cautious on this score. After all there are, embarrassingly, disagreements about the nature of sense experience; and it is incumbent upon the foundationalist to provide an explanation for this.

Moreover, whatever it is that may be known directly on the basis of sense experience must be independent of any philosophical theory of perception, and of any theory about the ontological status of the constituents of experience. For we surely have no business claiming that any particular philosophical analysis of this sort is known to be true (by philosophers, let alone by lay perceivers), whether it be a sense-datum theory, an adverbial theory, or a mental-state theory. Thus in making phenomenological appeals I shall try to state my disagreement with Hume, so far as is possible, in a way which does not presuppose any commitment to particular philosophical theories.

At the same time, I shall adopt an idiom – 'sense content' is a case in point – which may suggest or appear to favor a sense-datum theory. I do so partially for expository convenience, and what I say is, or ought to be, translatable into an idiom congenial to alternative theories of perception. Any theory must be able to provide an analysis of ordinary descriptions of perceptual awareness; and my goal is not to deviate from normal or natural usage. Eventually – but only in Part three – I shall provisionally adopt a sense-datum theory; so my present terminology also presages that provisional commitment. (I say provisional because I am far from convinced that the analysis of perception requires the positing of such entities as sense data.)

There is a rather cavalier way of dealing with disagreements at the level of sensation; and it is perhaps initially rather surprising that it is not more frequently mobilized to explain such differences. It consists simply of arguing that where such differences of opinion exist, it is because there are corresponding differences between the contents of the inner sensoria of the differing parties. We make this kind of move without hesitation when, for example, the difference occurs between a person who is physically blind and one who has normal eyes. Yet we are extremely hesitant to attribute such differences in experiential content to persons all of whose sense organs appear to be in good working order. From a philosophical perspective, this is rather puzzling, since it is not clear that the high confidence we attach to experiential congruence is justified. Nevertheless, it is sound philosophical strategy, in adjudicating or explaining phenomenological disagreements, to resist the temptation offered by this maneuver. Not only would this be a weak strategy dialectically – the Humean is unlikely to be moved by the claim that one has perceptual powers which differ systematically and pervasively from his own – but, used without independent justification, it would concede at the outset to skepticism more than we wish ultimately to concede. On the strategy I am forswearing, it would be alleged that Hume and all his followers have been equipped with impoverished inner sensoria: though they could see, hear, and smell, they have had no direct experience of causal connection – a defect which no doubt would cripple one (from the perspective of those endowed with this power) far more than blindness or deafness. Instead, it is my view that a sufficiently careful analysis of his own experience would have led Hume to change his mind – or at least exercise greater caution – in supposing there to be no "original" of the concept of causation to be found there.

Such boldness on my part needs to be supported by some words about the perils of phenomenological analysis. These problems are of at least three overlapping sorts. There are problems arising in the effective communication of phenomenological discoveries to others; I shall call these language-related problems. There are problems arising from the extraordinary complexity and wealth of detail which characterizes many experiences. Finally, there is the difficulty that the phenomenal character of many experiences, even fairly simple ones, is genuinely unclear. For example, it is often unclear into how many constituents an experience can be analyzed.[5]

The language-related problems include the likelihood that experience is too rich to be fully described by any actually existing natural language; and the fact that there is not very much one can say, at least of a philosophically enlightening sort, about sensations which are sufficiently elementary. When description and analysis fail, the best one can sometimes do for those who do not grasp what one is talking about is to try to get them into the situation of having that experience in a relatively salient way, and then, proceeding by means of the various devices of ostension and elimination, to get them to focus on what one has in mind. Arguing, as I shall, that we have identifiable experiences of causal relation will require in part resorting to this kind of strategy.

The problem of complexity has, as its corollary, the problem of deciding what is phenomenologically simple, and is in this respect a problem which is one among several which force us to admit that even what is "given" can be puzzling; its intrinsic nature is far from transparent to reflection. Take simplicity. If one gazes at a uniformly red wall, covering the entire visual field, it is tempting to say that the color is phenomenologically simple. Dismissing the suggestion that the color which is seen has spatial parts, and is on that account complex, we encounter a further objection which must be taken more seriously. It is possible to show that color perception is analyzable into three independently variable characteristics, to wit, brilliance, saturation, and hue. Arguably, these are the phenomenally simple constituents of color perception. Even such a trivial example suffices to show that judgments of simplicity and complexity are not so apodeictic as to brook no disagreement. Similar disputes are bound to arise, as indeed they have, over the analysis of experienced events and their relations.

Another locus of phenomenological unclarity is the phenomenon of inattention. Everyone recognizes what it is to focus upon certain items within a visual or auditory field, so as to have the other items recede into the background. But how are we to understand this difference between what is attended to and what is not? Metaphorical descriptions of relative vividness, and the like, may be suggestive, but they are not really accurate and are apt to mislead. That which is "out of focus" is still present in the perceptual field, and hence present to consciousness, yet in a sense it is also absent from consciousness. For example, let two qualitatively identical spheres be present within one's visual field, and let attention be focussed upon the right one and not upon the left one. Then is the difference between the experience of them a phenomenal difference in the sensory images which one has – that is, in the objects of perception – or is it to be found in the nature of the act(s) of consciousness? Or, indeed, is the act/object distinction itself misguided? I believe it would be foolhardy to claim certainty with respect to this question or the others which I have mentioned. It should become sufficiently obvious presently how these remarks variously bear upon the problem of analyzing putative candidates for the experience of causal relation.

2. NATURAL NECESSITY AND LOGICAL NECESSITY

An essential feature of Hume's skepticism about natural necessity is his denial of the reducibility of natural necessity to logical necessity. Most philosophers have found Hume's arguments convincing in this regard, but some have not. The thesis that causal relations are logical relations or something closely akin has been advocated, for example, by Stout (1935), Ewing (1935), Harré and Madden (1975), and Blanshard (1962).[6] This theory is one which I reject. We do not in the first instance acquire our knowledge that one event causes another by having such a sufficiently detailed knowledge of the first that we are able, by standard deductive procedures, to infer the occurrence of the second. Although it is possible to construct a description of an event which has causal implications, making sense of such a description presupposes that we have a prior understanding of causal connections. Nevertheless, it will be useful to examine some of the arguments put forward on behalf of the logical relation thesis. The arguments I shall discuss are due to Blanshard and Madden.

Blanshard's main arguments are to be found in his *Reason and Analysis*.[7] He argues, to begin with, that there are various relations of necessity which we find in experience, though not within the sensory content of experience. This just shows, he claims, that our experience of nature is not exhausted by its sensory content. And in particular, it shows that we have some knowledge of necessary connections which is grounded in our experience of objects, even though the necessity is not a distinct constituent of the sensory experience of those objects. Here are some of Blanshard's examples: that this scarlet patch is more like this crimson patch than like that azure one; that this surface cannot at once be both blue and red; that this pink shade is a color; that the space between the ends of this ruler can be divided without limit; that this sweet taste is different from that sour taste. I have excluded a few of Blanshard's examples which are essentially mathematical. The rest cannot, I think, be construed as involving logical necessity, at least not in a narrow sense. However the examples are quite disparate, and it is not easy to find a single element common to them all, which accounts for their necessity (or appearance of necessity – it may, for example, be false that the physical space between the ends of a ruler can be divided without limit). Common to many of them, however, seems to be the fact that the necessary relation they exemplify is an internal relation. That sweet and sour are different tastes, for example, is entailed by their natures. But does this not mean that we have here a case of logical necessity? And if so, should it not be unsurprising that there is no constituent of experience which can be singled out as the experience of the relevant relation? Yet there is some justice in replying on Blanshard's behalf that if we wish to speak here of logical necessity, we are dealing with a relation of a very different kind than those deductive relations between propositions which depend upon the truth-functional operators and quantifiers. For in the former case but not in the latter, our apprehension of the relation is dependent upon a recognition of the sensuous content of certain experiences. Thus in the former case, the relation is in a sense to be found in sensory experience: we plausibly speak of tasting the difference between sweet and sour.

Secondly, Blanshard makes a distinction between imagination and conception. Conception, it seems, is for Blanshard stronger than the Cartesian notion of forming a clear and distinct idea of a thing, for it appears to require in addition that this idea reflect a complete understanding of its object. With this distinction in hand, Blanshard argues that although conceivability is a sufficient condition of possibility, imaginability is not even a necessary condition. (For example, the inability of a blind person to imagine colors is no proof of their impossibility; conversely, an ability to imagine an electron simultaneously having a precise position and velocity does not entail its possibility.) Thus, it does not follow from our ability to imagine any sequence of events whatever, that any sequence is possible. Blanshard argues that the *conceivability* of an arbitrary sequence is far harder to attain, for to achieve it, we should have to know that we had a complete and adequate comprehension of each member of the sequence. These arguments, whatever their cogency, are at best negative: they may serve to establish the non-triviality of a proof that there are no necessary causal relations. They do little to dislodge the skepticism of Hume, which rests content with proving the unknowability of such connections.

But perhaps more interesting is Blanshard's argument that a specific kind of necessity – namely logical entailment – plays a causal role in the connection between certain events. For Blanshard believes we need to assign a causal role to logical entailments to account for the connection between a rational agent's thoughts when he reasons – for example, when he constructs a mathematical proof. Blanshard's claim is that we cannot account for the content of a man's thoughts – the fact that he has just those thoughts in just that order – except by appealing to the entailments which he apprehends; that is, to the propositions which he entertains, and to the entailments which hold between them. These form a part, though not all, of the total cause of each successive thought. So if a man's reasoning is guided by the rules of logic, these rules play a causal role in determining his thought. Blanshard says:

> It may be replied that what determined the acceptance was not the necessity apprehended but the apprehension of it. This might mean . . . that when a thought works casually, it is the bare contentless act of apprehension that works, and hence that it makes no difference what the thought is about. I do not think this is plausible . . . If what works in the mind is the apprehension of necessity, then the necessity apprehended must be one element of what works. Without this element the apprehension would neither be what it is nor work as it does.
>
> (Blanshard 1962: 463–4)

The first thing to say about this argument is that a great deal may depend upon what sort of analysis one gives of mental acts. An adverbial theory will dispense with mental objects – hence, in this case, can deny that timeless propositions and their entailments are constituents of the sequence. There will be something about the mental acts – some characteristics they have which reflect the fact that a certain proof is being created – and these characteristics will play a causal role in the adverbial theorist's explanation of why one thought follows upon another. But these characteristics are characteristics of temporal entities.

If, on the other hand, one's view of mental acts is an act-object view (as Blanshard's is), then everything hinges upon how the relation between the mental act and its object is to be understood. Supposing timeless propositions and logical relations to be the objects of these mental acts, it is not clear what role they play in the relations between the mental acts in which they are apprehended. Even if we concede that their content partially determines the content of succeeding mental acts, this is consistent with holding that this determining role is not a causal role. For it would be either begging the question, or else trivializing the causal claim, to assume that every determining relation between events is causal, if by 'causal' we mean that relation for which collisions between billiard balls is paradigmatic. Blanshard simply assumes that every event-determining relation is causal.[8]

Edward Madden and Rom Harré hold a somewhat different, though allied, view.[9] According to them, our descriptions of the world embed a conception of particulars as having natures or essences that involve causal powers. The world is composed of powerful particulars; to be a particular of a certain kind entails having certain abilities and capacities. The ascription of these powers is built into our conceptions of that kind, by a linguistic process according to which these conceptions evolve so as to reflect our growing empirical knowledge of natural necessities.

Thus on Madden and Harré's view, conceptual necessity is a product of the recognition of natural necessity. But they deny that our experience of forces and muscular exertion are primary to this knowledge of physical powers, for they believe, with James and Whitehead, that the attempt to locate our concept of causality in these experiences leads to panpsychism.[10] This is a consequence at which James balked, but which Whitehead accepted. Madden and Harre prefer instead to appeal to our visual experience of collision processes – the very cases upon which Hume mainly focuses. In particular, they appeal to the experiments of the psychologist A. Michotte (1963), who has demonstrated that when people are shown "collisions" between moving, colored spots, arranged so as to represent in an idealized manner collisions between moving bodies, they make judgments of causal interaction quite spontaneously. Michotte's experiments are not without interest, but it must be noted that all his "collisions" were confined to a single axis of motion, and the judgments of causality were undoubtedly associated with judgments of the solidity of the moving spots. Now there is an especially evident sort of necessity which constrains the motion of impenetrable objects when they meet, provided that they both persist. Where motion is restricted to a single axis, the possibilities are particularly few in number. But even this special case requires that the subjects in Michotte's experiments had already acquired the notion of solidity. Although the tactile sensations upon which our notion of solidity is founded are not to be identified with the sensation of force, they require and involve the sensation of force – a matter to which I shall devote some attention below. Thus the judgments made by Michotte's subjects presuppose the very concept upon which Madden and Harré wish to avoid founding the concept of causation.[11]

3. EXPERIENCING CAUSAL RELATIONS

The main task which now confronts us is to describe the nature of our knowledge of causal relations. This project divides into two not entirely disjoint parts. The first task is negative; it is to show that Hume's arguments are not sufficient to demonstrate that we do not experience causation. The second task is positive: it is to give an analysis of experience which is adequate to show that we do experience causal relations. The two tasks are not entirely disjoint because one part – the strongest part – of Hume's destructive argument can be adequately refuted only once the positive account has been developed.

There is one type of experience to which we are commonly subjected, which must strike us as one of the most natural starting points for any discussion of our concept of causal connection. It is the type of experience we have when our own bodies are pushing or pulling, or being pushed or pulled by, other bodies. It is this sort of experience upon which I shall focus, when I give a phenomenological account of the nature of the causal relation, as part of the positive account of our knowledge of causation.[12] In so doing, it is my intention to prescind from any commitment to the existence of physical bodies. My procedure, therefore, will be foundationalist in a rather traditional sense. Thus such a description should in principle be cast in the terms of a phenomenological language. But because such an explicitly phenomenological description would be verbally awkward, I shall use terms which are ordinarily used to refer to physical objects. It must be understood, therefore, that as I use them here, these terms are intended to refer to the relevant actually occurring sensory experiences.

What, then, is Hume's analysis of these experiences? It is a cause of some astonishment to find, when one examines the writings of Hume, that he discusses the bodily experience of force in exactly two places; and both these discussions occur in footnotes to Section 7 of the *Inquiry*.[13] They are long footnotes to be sure; and it will be worth quoting in full the first of them.[14]

> It may be pretended, that the resistance which we meet with in bodies, obliging us frequently to exert our force and call up all our power, this gives us the idea of force and power. It is this *nisus* or strong endeavor of which we are conscious, that is the original impression from which this idea is copied. But, *first*, we attribute power to a vast number of objects where we never can suppose this resistance or exertion of force to take place: to the Supreme Being, who never meets with any resistance; to the mind in its command over its ideas and limbs, in common thinking and motion, where the effect follows immediately upon the will,

without any exertion or summoning up of force; to inanimate matter, which is not capable of this sentiment. *Secondly*, this sentiment of an endeavor to overcome resistance has no known connection with any event: What follows it we know by experience, but could not know it *a priori*. It must, however, be confessed that the animal *nisus* which we experience, though it can afford no accurate precise idea of power, enters very much into that vulgar, inaccurate idea which is formed of it.

The relevant passage from the second footnote is:[15]

No animal can put external bodies in motion without the sentiment of a *nisus* or endeavor; and every animal has a sentiment or feeling from the stroke or blow of an external object that is in motion. These sensations, which are merely animal, we are apt to transfer to inanimate objects, and to suppose that they have some such feelings whenever they transfer or receive motion.

None of the points Hume makes is decisive. Recapitulating, his arguments are: (1) that many of the circumstances to which we apply the concepts of power or causation are ones in which force, or the sensation of force, are absent; (2) that our error in attributing to forces a role in the natural order of physical events arises from our projecting into the inanimate world certain sensations, which are "merely animal," that is, which are impressions of sense to which nothing external to sense corresponds; and (3) that feelings of force are not related by means of necessary connections to subsequent events, so that their outcome could not be predicted *a priori*. Of these, points (1) and (2) can be disposed of in fairly short order; (3) requires more careful treatment, as we shall see.

As regards (1), it should be readily admitted that there is a generic conception of causation or production which embraces each of the cases Hume mentions, and no doubt more as well. How this generic idea is formed, and what its limits of application are, is a matter of great interest; but nothing in what Hume says refutes the conjecture that our primary idea of causation derives from sensations of bodily force, or that the other examples mentioned by Hume represent distinct species of one genus. Perhaps we arrive at notions corresponding to these distinct species, and of a genus which embraces them all, by a process of abstraction and addition – that is, by subtracting from our primary concept of causal connection certain components, and/or by adding to it others. For example, to arrive at the idea of psychophysical causation, we may need – as Hume does – to subtract the requirement of spatial contiguity from our primary notion. This, too, is required for the notion of action at a distance; other extensions or revisions of the notion are clearly required to adapt the notion of causality to the peculiar features of quantum mechanics. Each of these extensions places certain strains upon our conception of causation.[16] If we stray too far from the concept or set of allied concepts derived from experience, it becomes unclear whether what remains is an intelligible concept. (Thus for example, creation *ex nihilo* is something which many find difficult to comprehend.)

On the other hand, we must be prepared to allow the possibility that, as scientific investigation may show, nothing in nature corresponds *exactly* to our primary and naive concept of causal connection. This would not be terribly disturbing, so long as several conditions were met: (1) that the scientifically sophisticated concept is not too drastic an extension of the ordinary one;[17] (2) that the sophisticated conception be integrated into a theory which enables us to explain, among other things, why ordinary sensory awareness of causal connections is defective or inadequate in the relevant respects; and (3) that some instances of what science countenances as causal relations can be referentially identified with instances of causation which common sense picks out as paradigmatic. In this respect, I believe our notion of causation is no different than our notions of space and time. Each of these may have to be revised as science advances; but in order to get started upon the journey, we need some notion of each of them derived from naive experience.

Hume's second objection is ambiguous. In saying that feelings of force are "merely animal" sensations, Hume might mean to be saying that they are sensations of secondary qualities, qualities which characterize the content of conscious experiences, but which are fallaciously ascribed to material objects. So Hume might have in mind the contrast exemplified by color and shape. But on the other hand, he might have in mind the contrast between qualities which can be distinguished from the acts of consciousness in which they are apprehended, and those which cannot. On this latter interpretation, the distinction Hume has in mind is that which some take to be exemplified by color and shape on the one hand, and pain on the other. In that case, the mistake Hume is accusing us of making is the kind of mistake one would be making if one thought that inanimate objects, or nonconscious animals, could feel pain. However, Hume supplies no argument which supports the suggestion that perceptions of force are analogous to feelings of pain rather than to perceptions of color or shape. And no one – or almost no one – supposes that billiard balls *feel* a force when they collide, any more than they suppose that billiard balls perceive each other's shape and color. What we suppose is that force, like color, can exist in objects even when they are unperceived. We may be wrong about this, with respect to force as well as with respect to color. But if, as I shall presently argue, force is a primary quality (i.e., relation), then we are not mistaken in this way either. This argument will not, to be sure, solve the problem of how in general we can acquire justification for believing that force is present or absent "in the objects." That is the problem of induction; and it will be addressed separately.

However, one need not at this stage of the argument be committed in any case to the view that force is a primary relation. What first must be shown is only that force, as we feel it, establishes a non-accidental connection of some kind between distinct occurrences which are given in experience. This will provide an explanation of the origin of the concept of force, and a (partial) understanding of what force is, without requiring any assumption that forces exist unperceived.

The third of Hume's objections has two related parts. The first is that force is experienced as an isolable sensation or event. The second is that this event has no necessary connection with what follows it; which can be shown by seeing that we are quite unable, from the experience of a force, to deduce *a priori* what will follow it. I shall argue that Hume is partly mistaken on both scores, and that the way he is mistaken undermines the force of the objection. But to do this requires turning now to a more exact examination of our sensations of physical force.

4. THE POSITIVE ARGUMENT

It will be sufficient for my purpose to consider an everyday circumstance in which sensations of force are induced in us. Suppose, therefore, that someone pushes steadily against my forehead with his hand. I have the visual sensations which accompany the approach and contact of the hand; then I experience a combination of sensations, among them tactile, kinaesthetic, and visual sensations, as well as those arising from my organs of balance. What these sensations are will, as we ordinarily speak, depend upon the motion and degree of solidity of hand and forehead, the pressure exerted by the hand, and the degree of muscular resistance exerted by me. Is it possible to isolate from this complex of sensations those elements which are described as the experience of force? Are these elements isolable from those perceptual elements which constitute the perceptual events of the hand's motion, and that of the head? And what is the intrinsic character of the sensation of force?

The sensation of force is primarily identified, insofar as we are patients, with the feeling of pressure; and insofar as we are agents, with muscular tension. I shall concentrate upon the feeling of pressure.[18] I want first to bring out five characteristics of this feeling. The first of these is that like pain, color, or shape, it has a spatial location. This location often covers some area of the surface of our bodies.[19] In our example, the location is identical, or nearly so, to the points of contact between hand and forehead. The second characteristic is that the force is experienced as having a magnitude. The third characteristic is that a force is experienced as having a direction in space. The fourth characteristic is that forces, even when several of them are applied to more or less the same portion of the body, can sometimes be individuated. Such individuation frequently relies upon differences in the spatial directedness of the distinct forces, or upon differences in the points of application. The fifth characteristic is the fact that felt forces form what I shall call an algebra. That is, they can be felt to add together in a certain way which depends upon their respective magnitudes and directions. This is most obvious when the forces are directed along the same line; but we are also able to sensorily compare the combined result of two differently directed forces with the sensation associated with a single force whose direction is intermediate between these.[20]

None of these characteristics should occasion surprise; in fact, it will be immediately noticed that they are exactly those which have been taken over into physics and given a precise representation there by means of a vector calculus. My first major point is that each of these characteristics is an actual element in the content of our experience of pressure, not merely a theoretical construct or a feature introduced by physics to facilitate mathematical representation. Does this list then exhaust the characteristics of felt forces? I think it is clear that it does not. For, in the first place, there are other qualities or relations which can be characterized in these five ways. Motion, for example, has magnitude, location, and direction, and hence can also be given a vector representation. Hence the vectorial features of force are not sufficient to distinguish it from everything which is not a force. Secondly, supposing forces to mediate or constitute the connection between causes and effects, we must remark that there is lacking in the vector representation any asymmetry which can serve to identify causes as causes, effects as effects. The direction of the vector indicates the direction of the force; but the force may point either toward or away from those objects which are its source (i.e., the force may be either attractive or repulsive). Moreover, we are able to distinguish cause from effect in many practical circumstances in which there is no *observed* distinction in time between the occurrence of the one and the occurrence of the other. This suggests that there must be some additional element in our experience of force which is characterized by an asymmetry of a sort fit to distinguish cause from effect.

This further component, which is perhaps the most elusive one, I shall call *production*. It represents what is the most generic feature of causation, for every instance of causation, whether experienced as a felt force or not, involves it. Indeed the term 'production' can be taken to be a synonym of 'causation,' where the latter term is understood in its broadest sense. Hence in using 'production' to isolate the most essential feature of causal relations, I do not purport to be shedding new light on that relation – much less offering a definition. Nevertheless I am in agreement with certain other philosophers that here we arrive at the "core" of our conception of causality.[21] That production is an asymmetric relation is something we experience. We do not merely experience forces as having location, magnitude, and direction. We experience them as acting upon something – in the case at hand, upon our bodies. We are able to distinguish in perception between active agency on our part and the passive reception of force, between an impressed force and the resistance of our bodies, between self-initiated motion and the passive transmission of motion, as when someone pushes our arm, which in turn pushes a third object. And we do not infer any of these distinctions; rather they are perceptual discriminations.

I shall now draw out what seem to me to be some of the consequences of this analysis of pressure sensations. Is the sensation of force a distinct sensation from those sensations by means of which we identify the causing event and/or its effect? Certainly the shape and motion (though not the mass or inertia) of the hand can be identified by means of visual perception; and the visual sensations are distinct from the sensation of pressure. But the motion and shape of the hand can also be discerned by means of tactile perception (indeed are so discerned at the time of contact);

and the objects of these tactile sensations are identified with the spatial qualities of the hand which visual perception ascertains.[22] But the tactile sensations – for example, the tactile sensations by means of which we can identify the position of the hand at the moment of contact with the body – are precisely sensations of pressure. Sensations of pressure are also implicated in the tactile perception of the mass or inertia of the hand, its degree of solidity, and its elasticity. It does not follow, of course, that all these objects of tactile perception are identical, are one and the same quality. But the tactile perception of each of them is connected with the sensation of pressure or force, for that is the medium, as it were, through which they are represented to us.[23] Tactile location of an object, for example, is possible precisely because force is experienced as located in space. Mass, solidity, and elasticity are all detected as functions of the time-dependence of felt force and location. It is plausible to maintain, therefore, that the connection between tactual perception of force and tactual perception of the spatial location of objects is not a contingent connection but a necessary one. An analogy to this would be the connection between the perception of color and the visual perception of spatial extension. As in the color/extension case, we see that the tactile qualities are distinct but not separable. Or, they are separable, but only by means of the intellect, by means of a process which, for want of a better name, I shall call abstraction.

Thus, the tactually perceived force which in this instance constitutes the causal relation between two events both is, in a sense, and is not, in another sense, separate from the causing event. On the other hand, the analogy to the necessary relation between visual color and extension is intended as no more than an analogy. For example, I shall argue presently that causal relations are to be understood as ontologically grounded in the existence of second-order relations; that is, relations between properties. That view has also been proposed independently by Michael Tooley, David Armstrong, and Fred Dretske.[24] I argue this thesis on both phenomenological and other grounds; but the analogy cited above to color and extension is one which seems to me to be independent of the order of the properties and relations involved.

Next, what of the connection in experience between perceived force and that perceptually given event – in our case, the motion of the head – which we take to be the effect? Hume asks whether we can find any necessary connection between cause and effect. Hume's demand, applied to our example, is that a necessary connection be

found either between the motion, etc. of the hand and the motion of
the head, or – because Hume conceives the sensation of force to be
itself a distinct event – between the felt force and the motion of the
head. In speaking of a necessary connection, Hume clearly has
logical entailment as his conceptual model. I, like Hume, fail to find
any connection of this sort between the perceived events. But
Hume's way of posing the question is importantly misleading in two
respects, and question-begging in a third.

First, Hume's terminology can be misleading in that he speaks of
the fundamental causal relation as a necessary relation. Clearly,
there appears to be a conceptual connection between the ideas of
causation and necessity. We can express this (alleged) connection as
follows: Whenever an event in nature is caused, some set of events
will be causally sufficient for its occurrence. It is therefore
necessarily true that, if the first set occur, the second will follow.
But as we have seen, causal relations, conceived as forces, can act in
concert. This is to say that the total cause of a given event can
sometimes be – and almost always will be – composed of distinct
component events which are associated with distinct forces. These
forces, as noted, add together in a way expressable by a vector
algebra.[25] But if this is so, not every *individual* exercise of force of a
given type is, as such, necessarily followed by the same specific type
of event. What happens all depends on what other forces are
present in such a way as to combine with it. It follows that the
notion of necessary connection is not ontologically fundamental, but
rather derivative. Thus, it is false that, if one experiences a single
force, one should be led, from this fact alone, to the expectation of
any given effect. That depends upon whether other forces are
present. Clearly such forces might be present without being
experienced; often they are present. For this reason if for no other,
it is not merely conceivable but actually true that what follows upon
the experience of a force on one occasion is not what invariably
follows upon the exactly similar experience of a force upon another.
If we could know that upon both occasions no other force was
present, then we would have an experiment of the sort Hume
envisions when he raises the issue of conceivability, but how to
know this is one of the more dicey problems in epistemology.[26] And
even if that problem were solved, there is a further one which must
be given due consideration, namely, that an imperceptible difference between two forces can produce a perceptible difference in
their effects.

We can however envision an experiment of the sort Hume had in mind at least in thought; and this brings me to the other difficulties with his statement of the problem. The first of these concerns the criterion of conceivability to which Hume repeatedly appeals as a test for possibility. Hume says that we know that any two distinct events are independent because we know that they are distinct existences, with neither one "contained in" the other. And we know that there is no such containment, because there is no difficulty in conceiving either event's happening without the other.

William Kneale (1949, pp. 78–89) has pointed out, rightly, that conceivability is not, as such, an adequate criterion of logical possibility. Kneale notes that when one considers a mathematical conjecture such as Goldbach's conjecture, which has neither been proven nor disproven, one can understand perfectly well what the conjecture asserts, and conceive both its coming to be proved and its coming to be disproved. If the conjecture is true, it is necessarily true; if false, necessarily false. Therefore one can conceive what is necessarily false.

This argument hinges upon a certain looseness in the notion of what it is to conceive something. It must be granted that we understand the propositions expressed by 'Goldbach's conjecture has been proven (is true)' and by 'Goldbach's conjecture has been disproven (is false).' As we contemplate each of these propositions, no apparent contradiction arises before the mind, even though one of them is contradictory. There is a reply that might be made on Hume's behalf to this argument. It is that (1) *if* these propositions come to be held before the mind with adequate clarity and distinctness, then the truth of the false one will become inconceivable; and (2) that whether any proposition of this type is beheld with adequate clarity is itself something which can be known. In support of (1), it can be argued that sufficient clarity requires the possession, and comprehension, of a proof of either the proposition or its negation; and in support of (2) it would be argued that we can know whether we possess, and comprehend, such a proof.[27]

How does all this bear on Hume's problem? I think it likely that Hume would have offered a defense suggested by the above remarks against Kneale's criticism. Hume felt that the problem of ascertaining the truth-value of statements about the content of our own sensations was at least as transparently open to solution as that of proving mathematical hypotheses. A mathematical conjecture, for example, can be extremely complex; or its proof, if one exists, may be obscure; whereas the inspection of those sensations which attend any putative example of causation can be completed in a finite – indeed a relatively small – number of steps. There is little doubt that Hume held that we are fully acquainted with those contents of sensation to which we properly attend; moreover he claims to have established with at least moral certainty that, in regard to the analysis of causation, we can know whether or not we have properly attended to all of the relevant sensations. Hume's own efforts at so attending yielded nothing, he says, which renders inconceivable the following of any event by some event other than the one which did in fact follow it.[28]

Thus Kneale's objection is not decisive, though there are perhaps grounds for doubting either of Hume's claims, or both. Rather than pursue that question further, I wish to bring out another difficulty with the criterion of conceivability. This difficulty results from the fact that there appear to be different species of inconceivability; and indeed there are some cases where it is unclear whether what is being considered is inconceivable or not. The following list includes some familiar examples: a round square, that $2 + 2 = 5$, the existence of a four-dimensional space, the existence of an everywhere non-differentiable curve, something simultaneously green and red all over, pink's being darker than red, two material objects occupying the same place at the same time, time-travel, that space and time are "curved" in the way specified by General Relativity, that space and time are quantized in the way some quantum physicists have speculated, that Julius Caesar could have been a teacup rather than a man. Here I have deliberately chosen a rag-bag of examples, for I wish to illustrate the point that it is exceedingly implausible, *prima facie*, to suppose that a unified account can be given of all the states of affairs which someone or other might find genuinely to exceed his powers of conception. To be sure, there have been strenuous efforts to achieve such unification – discarding certain examples as spurious, and giving a single explanation for the remainder. I shall not criticize these attempts, for I think it is sufficient for my purpose if it be admitted that no such program can claim to have achieved unqualified success. This being so, there are good grounds for holding that inconceivability comes in different species – and *perhaps*, even, in something like different grades (compare the conceivability of a four-dimensional space with that of an infinite-dimensional space). This shows, I think, that we would be rash to rely upon inconceivability as an exclusive mark of *logical* impossibility, unless we could specify some further distinguishing characteristic that separates this species of inconceivability. If there are in fact distinct species of inconceivability, this constitutes *some* evidence that there exist distinct species of necessity as well. But it is not clear, even for those species of necessity which might be identified *via* the exercise of our powers of conception, that the relevant type of inconceivability constitutes an adequate criterion for it. Conversely, inconceivability may sometimes signal the limits of our powers of conception rather than impossibility in any sense. Moreover, the multiplication of necessities in itself makes more risky the assumption that every species of necessity is epistemically linked to some species of inconceivability. This consideration is damaging to Hume's argument; for that argument rests upon the supposition that where we find no inconceivability, we can have no grounds for claiming impossibility. This, then, is the second difficulty with Hume's case.

The third difficulty is that Hume actually provides two distinct criteria for assaying the existence of necessities in nature. The first of these is the inconceivability test just discussed. The second criterion is this. If, upon experiencing an event A for the first time, we are unable, by *a priori* means, to predict (with knowledge) that it will be followed by an event of type B, then there is no necessary connection between events of types A and B. Once again, in proposing this criterion, Hume has logical necessity as his model. The occurrence of A supplies the "premise" from which, by purely *a priori* means, the occurrence of a B is to be inferred. Hume can find no rule of inference which fills this gap. Hume's argument clearly proceeds as if this criterion and the inconceivability test were equivalent and interchangeable. If one believes, as Hume did, that logical necessity is the only necessity, then it is quite natural to conflate the two tests. But it is far from self-evident that the only noninductive basis one might have for making a prediction is the inconceivability of its contrary. And to make that assumption at this juncture is precisely to beg the question at issue. If we do not make that assumption, then it is not clear why the two tests ought to be regarded as equivalent. In fact I shall argue that the conflation of these two criteria is a mistake. I have already agreed with Hume that occurrences of distinct events are logically independent of one another, so that any sequence of them is conceivable without logical contradiction. It does not follow, however, that Hume is right in supposing that first-instance justified predictions are impossible. I hold that they are possible.

It must be said at once that I have not so much an argument as a strong intuition about this, for in the final analysis, we arrive here at a point at which we must each examine the character of our own sensations. An introspective appeal of the sort upon which I must rest my case can only hope to elicit agreement by pointing out certain aspects of these sensations, by displaying them in a certain light. Unfortunately it is very nearly impossible to settle experimentally the question before us, namely whether first-instance predictions grounded in perception of antecedent events are possible. Since Hume takes the sensation of force to be a separable event, one would pose the question experimentally as follows: could a subject who had *never before* experienced the relevant sensations and who was then subjected to a blow on the forehead, confidently predict what would ensue? There are no fewer than three things which make the execution of such an experiment impracticable. The first, and surely the least significant reason, is that the effects of an impressed force begin to occur immediately. Thus the subject would not have any time to consider the question and make his prediction. This difficulty could be reasonably side-stepped by allowing the subject to experience the effect of a blow just once, and asking him to predict what would ensue were he to experience an exactly similar blow in the future. Presumably, one such experience could hardly suffice to form in the subject the habitual expectation (as Hume would put it) that his head would move in a certain way. If there is *no* reason, derivable from the nature of the sensations themselves, to expect one result over another, then a guess made after a single trial is essentially as hazardous as one made before any trials.[29]

The second difficulty has already been mentioned: the subject must have grounds for believing, not only that the *experienced* force will be exactly similar during the second trial, but that no unexperienced forces are present during either trial. It is hard to see how this can be actually known; but we may still perform the thought-experiment which results from the assumption that it is known. On the other hand, this difficulty suggests what may be considered by some to be an improvement in the design of our thought-experiment. As before, the subject is allowed to experience a single force such as that produced by a blow to his head. Only, let this first trial be so arranged that, simultaneously with the felt blow, another force is applied to the subject's head in such a way as to produce no sensation of force (i.e. by pressing on an anesthetized region). The subject is informed of this fact, and then asked how he believes his head *would* have moved, had only the experienced force been present.

The third difficulty is that human infants presumably experience forces, having a low-grade consciousness of them and reacting to them, even before they are born. Even if the special experience of a blow on the forehead is entirely novel to a subject, we would be unable to rule out the possibility that he performs an induction whose basis is previous encounters with forces exerted elsewhere upon his body.

Thus our thought experiment is significantly idealized – and to that extent, at least, conceptually problematic. We must imagine for ourselves a subject whose literally first encounter with the sensation of force is the cranial blow; and we must imagine that no unknown forces are wreaking havoc with the experiment. If one can perform this act of imagination, then the question becomes: if one were the subject, would one's guess as to the outcome of a second trial be, in some significant sense, a non-accidental guess – a justified prediction? I think it is rather clear what one would predict. I shall say in a moment why I think the prediction would not be a random guess. But first, a further *caveat* must be issued. We must consider how specific a prediction would have to be offered by a subject in order for his reply to count as significant evidence against Hume. On this point, Hume's position is quite clear. He believes that, for all the evidence tells us, *any* coherently imaginable event might follow, or fail to follow, the experienced force. So, any significant restriction of the field will count as a significant prediction. If the subject is unable to describe precisely the predicted event – for example, if he cannot precisely specify the recoil velocity of his head, this fact should not surprise us. It would no more count against the subject's claim to have discerned a non-accidental connection between his experiences, than his inability to determine, without a ruler, the exact length of a line in centimeters would count as evidence that he could not see the line.

In fact, I am reasonably confident that our subject could make the following sort of prediction: (a) he could predict that his head, not some other part of his body, will be the portion most significantly affected; (b) he could predict that one effect will be a movement of his head; (c) he could predict with considerable accuracy (within a few degrees of arc) the initial direction of motion of his head; and (d) he could give at least a very rough estimate of the speed of motion – or lacking that, at least predict greater speed to accompany greater force.[30]

Why should such a prediction not be a random guess? The grounds for this are not far to seek. (a) The force is felt as being applied to the head. (b) The force is felt to move the head. (c) The force is experienced as having a direction. (What would it be for one to have a sensation of force, aimed in a certain direction, without any connected feeling of the item to which it is applied being forced to move in that direction, no other forces being present? To experience a force as spatially directed is not to simply observe the subsequent motion of that item; nor is it to observe something unrelated to the direction of that motion.) (d) The force is experienced as having a magnitude. (To judge that one force upon an object is more forceful than another is to judge that it is more of that which makes for motion than the other. The inference that it will therefore make for more motion is, if not deductive, not plausibly held to be arbitrary either.)

I readily agree, to repeat, that these inferences are not narrowly logical inferences. Not only is any sequence of events conceivable without contradiction, but, indeed, sometimes predictions based on the experience of force actually are badly mistaken. But if this were a regular occurrence, it would be astonishing and entirely inexplicable, were it not for the possibility of postulating hidden forces.[31]

5. OBJECTIONS CONSIDERED

I shall now discuss a number of objections to these claims. The objections are offered in the spirit of Hume, whom I have taken as my principal antagonist. Thus I shall imagine my interlocutor here to be a Humean philosopher.

First, I imagine the Humean objecting: Why should it be supposed that, for example, a cranially felt pressure will be followed by cranial motion? What necessity is there in this, since it is admitted that the one does not logically entail the other? But here, I confess, we seem to have reached precisely the point at which little more can be said, beyond asking such a skeptic to re-examine the character of his sensations of force. Certainly, it will be difficult for him to deny that there are similar *a priori* but non-logical inferences; for example the inference from something being colored to its being extended; and concerning these inferences also, little further could be said to someone not convinced that they are justified.

Contrasting sorts of cases of causal interaction may perhaps help to highlight the phenomenological features upon which these inferences depend. The reflex withdrawal of a limb suddenly brought into contact with a hot flame, and the blinking of an eyelid in response to a threat to the eye, are incidents which everyone judges to be paradigmatic cases of causal interaction. These cases may also admit of prediction on the basis of a single experience – I am almost certain that they do – but in neither of them is a felt force a necessary part of the causing phenomena which impinge upon us. (I am regarding the muscular tension which results in motion as part of the effect.) Thus the character of the inferences in those cases is quite different. Whatever expectations we may be able to form regarding the direction and velocity of the motion of the affected bodily parts, the felt connection between these latter and the impinging heat or eye-directed motion is not of the same character as it is with pushes and pulls. Indeed in these cases, even if we can be quite certain about the existence of the causal connection after a single experience, I think we would be at a loss to explain, except in teleological terms, why the effect has the character it is found to have.

There is a second objection that I imagine a Humean might make. The impossibility of a prediction after the first trial is sufficient to establish the *falsity* of the knowledge-of-necessary-connection thesis. But if, conversely, it is agreed that first-trial predictions are possible, this is not yet sufficient to establish the *truth* of that thesis. In order to explain the conviction that causal necessities exist in nature, Hume invokes the theory that a suitable schedule of observed conjunctions so acts upon the intellect that it invariably forms that habit which projects past coincidence into future expectation. This is due, Hume claims, to a natural tendency or disposition of the human mind. But surely a disposition could be invoked to explain even the alleged result of our thought-experiment. In that case, the disposition could not be one whose triggering required a series of conjunctions. But as long as we are in the business of invoking explanatory belief-dispositions, there seems to be nothing preventing our postulating a natural or instinctive inclination to believe, upon even the first occasion on which a pressure-sensation occurs, that motion will be communicated to an object at the place and in the direction in which the force itself is felt to be directed.

There are two replies to this objection. The first is that it would be perverse to invoke such a hidden disposition as this when an explanation is available to us directly from the surface character of the phenomena. Suppose a man blind from birth were to be given sight, and shown a red surface. Suppose also that on this occasion he somehow succeeds in learning the meaning of 'red' and to associate his tactile understanding of extension with visual extension. Then he is blindfolded and asked: Will the next red thing you see be extended? It does not seem to me that our strong inclination to believe that a sufficiently reflective subject's answer would be 'yes' involves our invoking or supposing the existence of any innate dispositions to do so in the subject. Surely, we think the subject would answer affirmatively, if we do think this, because we suppose him to be able to see the connection between color and extension in *what he sees* upon being presented with a single instance of red. We should apply the same reasoning to my thought experiment.

One might be tempted to suppose that the requisite disposition would have significant survival value, and that therefore it is not far-fetched to imagine biological evolution bestowing upon us an ability to form expectations based upon single experiences of certain kinds. But however that may be, the existence of such a disposition can hardly be invoked to explain our own inclination to predict that a hypothetical subject of this thought experiment other than ourselves would make the predictions which we attribute to *him*. For it is not plausible to suppose that such a disposition would be triggered by vicarious consideration of a third party. Nor could we be reasoning by analogy to ourselves, for none of us can remember how we in fact formed our inductive beliefs about the outcomes of blows.[32]

On the other hand someone might well hesitate to deliver *any* verdict upon the results of this thought experiment, on the not unreasonable grounds that the conditions of the experiment are so unusual and removed from common experience as to vitiate any application of intuition to the case. For this sort of caution I have some sympathy. Indeed my main purpose in developing the details of this experiment at such length is really heuristic. It is one way to get in focus those aspects of pushes and pulls, as we all commonly *do* experience them, which are philosophically crucial. Nevertheless it is important to recognize the implications of the cautious reply I have just considered. Someone who remains uncertain here must in all consistency allow at least that he is not in a position to resolve the dispute between Hume and myself in either direction. He can remain unconvinced of the necessitarian position, but he must also remain in doubt concerning the regularity theory. For any grounds he has for confidence in the correctness of the regularity theory are *a fortiori* grounds for a confident prediction as to the outcome of our experiment. Or rather, they are grounds for confidence if the innate-disposition hypothesis can be ruled out. If someone is inclined to agree with my prediction of the subject's response, therefore, he must examine whether this conclusion is based upon any positive evidence he has as to the existence of such a disposition; or contrariwise, whether it is based upon his own perception of the intrinsic nature of forces.

Secondly, it may be useful to reflect upon the really extreme form of skepticism which this line of argument suggests. For a quite parallel argument could be mounted against our belief in logical necessity, in the following way: we can construct a first-trial test for cognition of logical necessity. To do this, we present a subject with the premises and conclusion of an argument whose logical form he has not previously encountered, and ask him whether it is valid. I believe we are quite confident about the results of such an experiment, given sufficient intelligence on the part of the subject and sufficient simplicity on the part of the inference. Again a degree of idealization is involved, for it is perhaps unlikely that we can find an inference-pattern of reasonable simplicity which is unlike any which the subject will have already used, simply in learning a language. But even granting the idealization and a correct judgment on the part of the subject, why should a skeptic not invoke a natural tendency or disposition, triggered by the premises in question, which causes the subject to answer as he does? Why, further, must the existence of such a disposition have any bearing upon whether the subject's judgment is actually justified? Any feelings or intuitions which the subject invokes may be dismissed as simply psychological states which accompany the triggering of the disposition. Against such a skeptic's argument, the only defense I can think of is to appeal to the skeptic to examine with sufficient care the character of his own logical intuitions. If he cannot find there some intrinsic character which vouchsafes the connection to validity, I believe one would be at a loss as to what to say to him.

As I have said, such an appeal can hardly be considered decisive, and perhaps a skeptic will remain unconvinced. I draw this parallel to the debate about causation only to point out that philosophical understanding must begin somewhere. Our logical intuitions, and the character of our sensations are, in the end, as fundamental as any data we have.

Next, it may be objected that my thought experiment is quite misconceived. Even if there is a causal connection between the sensations of hand motion and subsequent head motion, the former never could be causally sufficient for the latter, and the remaining causal factors include ones which always lie outside experience: for they include certain brain states without which the experiences in question could not occur. And further, it might be argued that these bodily events are in themselves quite sufficient to produce both the earlier sensation and the later one. If so, it would be quite gratuitous to invoke the earlier sensory state in a causal explanation of the later one; and in any case, since the causally relevant brain states are entirely unknown to the subject of my thought experiment, he will have no justification for making the prediction I have ascribed to him, even if the one sensation is a partial cause of the other.

Now to answer this objection, it will be convenient to introduce a bit of terminology. Let us say that a list of the conditions causally responsible for an event E gives *sufficient* conditions for E if and only if it lists all of the existing events which are partial causes of E, *and* also specifies the non-existence of all those events which, had they obtained as well, would have prevented E in the circumstances. The latter part of this list is almost certain to be infinitely long; and in any case I shall want some way of speaking which reflects my view that lack of a causal factor is not itself a causal factor in the production of E. Because non-existent potential preventers of E bear no actual causal relation to E, I shall call a set of conditions existing at a given time which together actually produce E, an adequate cause of E. Now ordinarily, an adequate cause of E will be a total cause of E; but if E is causally overdetermined, then more than one adequate cause of E will exist at some time prior to it. So I shall say that the *total* cause of E is the union of all those sets of existing conditions which are separately adequate to cause it.

Armed with these distinctions, we may address the foregoing objection as follows. In our thought experiment, the sensations S associated with the motion of the hand are – and can be perceived to be – an adequate cause of the sensations S^* associated with a certain kind of head motion. It may well be (indeed we ordinarily believe this, though at this stage of the argument we are in no position to assert it) that the hand-sensations are caused by some external physical event P (i.e. the motion of a hand); and that the sensations of head motion are also caused by a physical event P^* (motion of the head) – both relations being mediated by brain states of some sort. Moreover, it may be that these two *physical* events are causally connected. Let us suppose that, in fact, P is an adequate cause of both S and of P^*, and that P^* is an adequate cause of S^*. By hypothesis, the subject himself knows that S is an adequate cause of S^*. Assuming then that no further independent causal chains run to S^*, it follows that P is a total cause of S^*; yet at the same time, S^* is causally overdetermined, for there are two causal chains emanating from P, each of which runs to S^* – one via S, the other via P^*. So in cases of this kind (and variations on it) a sensation will be causally overdetermined, with an adequate cause which is "given," and one which is not. This result is interesting and perhaps surprising; but I do not see that it constitutes an objection to the view here advanced. Certainly we should not deny the phenomenological facts simply in order to avoid instances of causal overdetermination. Of course, whether such overdetermination obtains depends upon the details of the physical processes which attend perception; and any theories we develop about *that* will not bear upon the present, much more fundamental, level of investigation. But nevertheless we can feel assured that we have nothing to fear from the present objection: nothing in our analysis of causation conflicts with the envisioned role of physical causes in perception.

There is a fifth objection I wish to consider, which is of a different sort. According to this objection, the concept of causation at which we have arrived is a deterministic one. But if the idea of cause which we derive from experience is that of a deterministic relation, then irreducibly statistical laws become conceptually opaque. Yet quantum mechanics contains such laws.

I am eager to concede the force of this objection. For it enables one to explain in part why the statistical character of quantum mechanics seems to us so unnatural, so counterintuitive. This is not, I suggest, the local result of the intellectual climate historically engendered by the success of Newtonian mechanics. Yet 'conceptually opaque' is too strong a phrase. The statistical character of causation ordinarily lies below the threshold of detection of those perceptual processes involved in our common experience. It seems likely, therefore, that our primordial concept of the causal relation is of a relation which is deterministic. Yet this primordial conception would not preclude extension to relations which are both explanatory and statistical. For at this naive level of experience, the existence of a significant degree of perceptual inaccuracy in regard to estimates of magnitudes leaves scope for statistical variation, without thereby undermining the productive relation between cause and effect.

6. THE ARGUMENT FROM PERCEPTUAL ATOMISM

It is necessary now to consider the third of Hume's own objections against identifying perceptions of force with perceptions of a kind of relation. This objection has already been mentioned, but I have not yet adequately met it. I shall state it in the form of a dilemma.[33] Either our perception of physical force is not distinguishable from our other perceptions, or it is. If it is not distinguishable, then there is no impression which can form the "original" of our idea of cause, and hence no way of making intelligible the claim that this idea corresponds to some element in experience. If it is distinguishable, then it, like every element of experience, can be imagined to exist independently of any other element, and hence cannot forge a necessary connection between two perceptions. If the experience of force is a distinct experience, then a perception of a causal sequence which involves an impression of force is really constituted by three perceptual events bearing certain temporal relations: the perception of the cause, of the force, and of the effect. But whatever the temporal relations between these, they constitute a sequence of distinct elements like any other; the alleged element of "connection" evaporates. Although I have already attempted to elucidate the sense in which the experience of force is given to us as connecting events, I am sure that what I have said will lack conviction if this dilemma is not more carefully addressed. In particular, a failure to solve it would surely undermine any intuitive confidence one might be tempted to place in the alleged results of the foregoing Gedankenexperiment.

The purport of the dilemma is to make nonsense of the appeal to experienced forces as experienced causal relations. Some philosophers have sought to evade it by attacking Hume's perceptual atomism.[34] In effect, these philosophers are seeking to destroy the first horn of the dilemma, by denying the distinguishability of cause and effect. Unfortunately, they sometimes make the mistake of supposing that Hume's position requires a *temporal* atomism, a possibility of cutting the flow of experience into discrete temporal "chunks" which correspond to actual joints in that flow.[35] As I see it, there is no reason why Hume's view should be interpreted as requiring that experience exhibit this kind of temporal segmentation. All the Humean requires is that experience be constituted by distinguishable elements. Such elements might include simultaneously occurring events; but whatever their temporal relation, the only question is whether they exhibit any necessary connectedness.

My strategy will rather be to examine the second horn of the dilemma. To do this, it will be necessary to consider quite generally the nature of our experience of relations, and of necessary relations in particular. Of course Hume himself acknowledges that there are relations among our ideas and impressions, relations which are empirically given to us.[36] But there are two apparently universal features of empirical relations which create puzzles concerning our knowledge of them.

The first puzzle about relations concerns the nature of their instantiation. When a monadic property such as a color, a taste, or even a sound is experienced, we are able to assign a spatial location, at least a rough location, to that instance. There is, moreover, a strong intuition that empirical properties could not be apprehended unless concretely realized in time and space – that is, unless they have instances to which it makes sense to assign spatiotemporal location. Instances of monadic empirical properties seem to be individuals in at least the following minimal sense: although a monadic property-instance may be an entity whose existence is parasitic upon, or partially reducible to, the existence of concrete (i.e. material) individuals, nevertheless we are able to apprehend and individuate such instances as having spatiotemporal location, at any rate sometimes, even when we are unable to identify or individuate their owners. Perhaps this is especially evident in the case of sounds. (I believe we have sufficient preanalytic familiarity with instances of properties to make the discussion which follows intelligible regardless of what ontological theory one adopts with regard to them.)

There are reasons for saying that instances of empirical relations lack individuality in this minimal sense. It seems, first, quite unclear how or whether to assign spatial or temporal location to empirical relations. Second, it does not seem possible to identify instances of empirical relations without identifying their relata. It is these facts which, I believe, largely underlie Hume's denial that perceptions of force are perceptions of a causal relation. For he seems to have thought, with some reason, that the perception of force is isolable from, and independent of, a perception of those events which would plausibly be taken as related by the force. Moreover, it does seem possible to assign to forces a spatiotemporal location.

The first puzzle about relations becomes especially evident when we consider spatial and temporal relations. Suppose that *a* is one meter to the north of *b*. There is no problem to assigning a time or temporal region to this instance of *being one meter to the north of*. But there is a problem about assigning it a spatial location. Shall we say the instance is located at *a* and *b*? Or between them? Or both? There seems to be no obvious way of settling the matter. A similar difficulty bedevils all other spatial relations (e.g. *being between*).

Instances of temporal relations seem not to admit in general of either spatial or temporal location.

But this difficulty extends to empirical relations generally. In what way should spatiotemporal locations be assigned to instances of *being a father of, being heavier than, containing more atoms than, being similar to, or being darker than?* (The last of these relations may plausibly be held to be a second-order relation, more explicitly rendered by the predicate 'being a darker color than.' If the relata of such a second-order relation are universals, and if universals are not as such in space and time, this might seem to constitute an independent explanation for the unassignability to spatiotemporal location to instances of *being darker than.* But, if red is darker than pink, it follows that every instance of red is darker than each instance of pink; and these color-instances can be given spatio-temporal location. In this case, it is not necessary to identify the concrete particulars which are red and pink respectively; but we must at least be aware of the existence of a patch of pink and a patch of red.)

The relevance of these considerations to our problem will be evident. On the one hand, there *does* seem to be an assignable spatial and temporal location to every experienced instance of force. What is worse, it seems that one can experience a force without identifying one at any rate of the relata of that instance of causal relatedness. A pervasive example of this is the experience of gravitational force. When someone experiences the force of gravity pulling his arm down, there is no event he experiences which he normally would be able to identify as the cause of his arm's dropping. These facts weigh heavily against the claim that an experience of force is an experience of an instance of a relation of any kind, to say nothing of a relation which connects events non-accidentally.

On the other hand, if the above objection can be disarmed, the same facts about relations may help explain some of the obscurity which surrounds attempts to characterize causation.

Although the assignment of spatial and temporal locations to instances of empirical relations is unquestionably problematic, it is not entirely arbitrary to locate such instances at the locations of their relata, and/or in the spatial and temporal intervals between those relata. Certainly this is where we have to look in order to become aware that the relations obtain. If a relation obtains between two things at a time when they are in contact, and especially if the obtaining of the relation *requires* such contact,[37] it seems reasonable to locate that relation where they are, or more precisely, at their point(s) of contact.[38] Hence it should be less surprising that when one receives a blow, one is aware of the application of force at the point of contact. Here, to be sure, there is little arbitrariness in the matter: that is where we *feel* the blow. Other forces are more diffuse – once again gravity offers a prime example – and it is correspondingly less natural to assign a location to the force, unless it be located throughout the body. Thus I do not think the difficulty about assigning locations to instances of relations is decisive against the view that an experience of force is an experience of (an instance of) a relation.

The second objection is in my opinion less tractable. It seems possible to perceive a force without perceiving one of the events it purportedly relates, namely, that event which would be designated the cause. When does this happen? Not, to be sure, when one is struck from behind without seeing what administers the blow. For in being tactually aware of the blow, one is *ipso facto* tactually aware of the item which produces the blow. Feeling the blow in this case *constitutes* one's tactual awareness of the object. And in being tactually aware of the object, one is aware in this case of certain of its properties – its motion and solidity in particular.[39] But I do not think one can similarly be said to be identifyingly aware of any causing event or object or properties of an object when one experiences gravitational force. Since, in the case of gravitational attraction, one can be aware of a force without being at the same time aware of (or able to identify) one of its alleged relata, evidently an awareness of force is not an awareness of a relation at all. One way of resisting this conclusion would be to argue, using as grounds the other phenomenological features which suggest that force *is* a relation, that in this respect the causal relation is simply unique. One can be aware of instances of it without being aware of one of the relata. But a Humean is likely to view this tactic, and rightly so, as a kind of special pleading. At the very best, it can only be expected to produce a standoff.

My response to the objection will consist instead of a defense of three theses. These theses are (a) that sometimes we are aware of there being a relation of a given sort between particulars, even though we are identifyingly aware of only some of the relata of the relation; (b) that certain spatial relations provide instances of this; and (c) that the experience of gravitational force also provides instances of it.

That one or more instances of a relation can be known to obtain on perceptual grounds, even though not all of the relata are identified objects of awareness, requires, first, that at least *some* of the relata be so identified. Second, it must be known in some indirect way that these particulars stand in the relevant relation(s) to (some) other particulars. Then even though the latter may not be identified – or may not be recognized to be so related to anything – still one can be aware that on a given occasion the relation is instantiated. I shall illustrate the sense in which instances of a relation are thus partially "identified" by means of an example involving a spatial relation. Then I shall turn to causal relations.

The example is this. There are many spatial locations which are ten meters from here. One can uniquely specify such a point by considering the one which lies along a certain direction. One's relation to that point is an instance of *being ten meters from*. There may be nothing in that region of space which one can identify, nor may one be able to visually locate that region of empty space; at least not independently of a visual estimate as to how far away ten meters is. But it seems that one can, roughly, identify the correct region of space precisely by means of one's ability to make such an estimate. So here, it appears that identification of one of the relata depends upon recognition of the fact that the surrounding space instantiates the relation. This recognition is visual; and it is not a matter, I believe, of our making an inference from the recognition of objects which are further away than ten meters, to the existence of a location ten meters distant. For it seems that we could make this judgment if presented with a blank expanse of empty space. However true it is that we fix our bearings in the world by locating ourselves in relation to other identifiable objects, it is also the case that we have a general sense of the spatiality of the world that does not depend upon the identification of objects or points in space, but rather on the visual apprehension of a system of spatial relations that imply such points.

Now our experience of generalized forces such as that of gravity is analogous to the example just analyzed. We are aware of one relatum of the relation – namely, kinaesthetically felt motions of our bodies. And, because we can feel the exertion of force upon ourselves, we are in a position to know that a causal relation is being instantiated. But we may not be – indeed we typically are not – in any position to identify that instance, or to know whether just one or several such instances are being instantiated. For it is entirely possible – in fact it is invariably the case – that more than one object is exerting a gravitational force upon us. What we feel is the resultant vector-sum of those forces – that is, a summing of the causal relations present – without our ever being able to individuate perceptually the distinct components of force which enter into the total relation. In this respect, such experiences contrast with our tactile experiences of pressure, which do in some instances allow the resolution of the total pressure applied to a region into discriminable components individually felt.

Although the awareness of force has a phenomenal content which is richer than that of our experience of, say, spatial relations, there is one aspect of the experience of force which I believe to be decidedly analogous to our perceptual awareness of most relations. The element of production, the element which I have said constitutes the generic feature of all causal relations, is clearly central to the constitution of causation as a relation. There does not seem to correspond to it any isolable impression, in Hume's sense, even when we are directly aware of a force. But in this respect, I do not believe that our awareness of the element of production is in any different case than is our awareness of instances of most relations – for example, the relation *being between*. There is nothing like an isolable impression here either – nothing strictly distinct from our impressions of the relata of the relation. Yet when we are aware of the relational fact, we are certainly aware of something over and above the existence of those relata. Similarly, when we are aware of the production of motion in our bodies through collision with another, we are aware of something more than the two motions. I shall have something more to say about the special nature of our perceptual apprehension of the causal relation in Chapter 10, Section 4. There I shall argue that the special role which this relation occupies in the structure of the world explains exactly why Hume's demand for a separate impression of causation in our perception of physical events is a demand which could not *in principle* be satisfied.

Although Hume's atomism does not require the temporal distinctness of cause and effect, it is at least tempting to suppose that temporal distinctness is a sufficient condition for the absence of necessary connection. For any species of necessity for which inconceivability of the contrary may serve as a criterion, distinctness in time of the relata may seem to be a sufficient condition of contingency. We can always conceive the occurrence of the one relatum without that of the other. A possible exception to this principle arises if temporal moments are themselves accorded independent existence. For, if it is impossible for time to come to an end, this may be because the existence of the present moment necessitates the existence of the subsequent moment. However, as concerns ordinary events, the Humean is on safe ground. All this establishes, of course, is that inconceivability of the contrary is not a criterion of causal relatedness. But we have a right, then, to be puzzled as to how an element of necessity enters into our conception of causal relations.

Is there any other necessary relation whose relata are temporally distinct? It seems not. No mathematical or geometrical relations are of that sort. Nor are the following: that red is darker than pink, that red excludes green, and the rest of the usually proffered examples. Yet we ought to consider the following case: this instance of red is necessarily darker than that instance of pink, where the former exists before the latter does. But this necessity is merely parasitic upon the necessity of red's being darker than pink. There is nothing intrinsic to the relation *darker than* which requires any particular temporal relation between *instances* of its relata. Perhaps then the causal relation is the single relation, other than temporal relations themselves, which necessarily involves a temporal relation, and which is therefore a necessary relation between temporally distinct entities.[40] How can this apparently exceptional species of necessary relation be assimilated to the others? There is a way of achieving this result, a way indirectly suggested by the red/pink case. The idea is that event-pairs which are the temporally localized relata of instances of causal relations, are necessarily connected because instances of causation are parasitic upon a fact which implies generality. The fact which ontologically grounds causation is a second-order relation whose relata are two event-*types* (that is, first-order properties) and a third property, namely, a temporal relation. Then causal relations would be grounded in a fact which was not itself a temporal fact, for the existence of a second-order relation between three universals, themselves not temporal entities, is no more a temporal fact than is the obtaining of the relation *darker than* between red and pink. I shall shortly examine in detail the arguments which favor this strategy.

For the present, it is helpful to reflect upon the nature of our awareness of necessity in connection with the other examples cited. Whereas we clearly understand that red excludes green, that red is darker than pink, and so on, it can hardly be claimed that, in any of these cases, there is a discriminable perceptual element which gives rise to the idea of necessity. That is, there is no component of our experience of red, green, pink, and so on, which is isolable as the experience of necessity. Yet there is no doubt that necessary relations obtain between them. Moreover, I think it is evident that this necessity, and our knowledge of it, does not derive from any linguistic facts whatsoever – for example, from any conventions of language. An awareness of the fact that these relations obtain is open to someone who has no language. A deaf-mute who knows no sign language can be as easily aware of them as a normal language-user. Linguistic conventions may indeed determine the limits of application of our terms – and thus determine that 'red' cannot be correctly used to denote shades of green. That fact alone cannot explain the necessary incompatibility between red and green. If it did, similar linguistic facts would entail that a bell cannot simultaneously emit two tones. But clearly, two tones, whether we give them distinct names or not, do not exclude one another. It is no part of my concern of course to deny that the relevant linguistic "conventions" may exist: but I maintain that the institution of those conventions, so far from being a matter of arbitrary stipulation, derives from the observation of the facts in question. It should not be surprising, therefore, that the awareness of necessity which attends our perception of causal relations is equally mysterious, at least by Humean lights. For here, too, there is no isolable experience which corresponds to the element of necessity.

However, it is of limited usefulness to reflect upon the non-causal non-logical necessities which I have been citing. For even if these are not logically necessary, their contraries appear to be inconceivable. This fact will naturally be pointed out by those who insist that the causal relation is not analogous to the other relations mentioned. It should not be surprising if the awareness of necessity which attends our perception of causal relations is as mysterious as it is in these other relations, in the sense of not affording us a distinct impression; but because it is not impossible to conceive a cause without its effect, the necessity of the alleged relation seems far more mysterious.

Perhaps causal necessity is closely linked to the most generic feature of causal relations, namely the relation of production. But whether, and in what sense, production as such involves necessary connection, is a vexed question. It is not self-evident that it does. Some alleged counterexamples have been suggested. Dretske and Snyder (1972), using an example analogous to Schroedinger's cat, claim that an effect can be produced even though its total cause did not necessitate it. Dretske and Snyder imagine a cat which has the misfortune of being placed by a Mr *A* for one minute in front of a gun which can be triggered by the decay of an alpha source. The probability that the source will produce a triggering alpha particle in that minute is, let us say, only one in a hundred. Nevertheless, let us suppose that the cat is unlucky. In that case, Dretske and Snyder argue, Mr *A* can correctly be said to have produced, or caused, the death of the cat.[41] This example relies upon the ultimate indeterminacy of the process of alpha particle emission. In a reply to Dretske and Snyder, Beauchamp and Rosenberg (1981, pp. 99–101) argue that for this very reason, the nuclear decay which leads to the cat's death was not itself caused. Yet, such decay is describable by laws which show that the phenomenon is connected to certain antecedent conditions in the nucleus; and it is natural enough to say here that these conditions produced the decay.

It is at any rate not easy to show that whenever *A* produces *B*, *A* must be sufficient for the occurrence of *B*. In the case of events connected by felt forces, however, I think we are sometimes perceptually aware of such sufficiency. That is, we can become aware of what it is for an unopposed force to be *enough* to produce a given effect, of when a force is not strong enough, and of when it more than suffices. It is clear that there is no distinct sensation of "enoughness," but because forces have felt magnitudes, we can know, for example, what it is for one of two opposing forces to overcome the other – as when we press our two hands together. And in this sense, it *can* be said that we are able in experience to recognize the necessity of the bringing about of an effect – for we are able to recognize the sufficiency of the cause. This, together with the remarks previously made concerning the complexities associated with the criterion of conceivability[42] constitute my answer to this central aspect of Hume's argument. Distinctness in time, then, does not entail that a cause and its effect are only contingently related, even though it may suffice to guarantee that they can be separately conceived or imagined.

7. THAT CAUSATION IS A PRIMARY QUALITY

Norman Kemp Smith (1941) has emphasized the fact that Hume did not deny the existence within us of an idea of natural necessity. Hume allows that we do have such an idea, but that we have no legitimate grounds for projecting such necessities upon the objects of sensory perception. For the origin of this idea of necessity is not to be found among sense impressions; rather it originates in a feeling (of expectation) which inevitably arises within us as a result of our human constitution, when experience presents us with constant conjunctions of sufficient regularity and salience. This feeling of expectation accompanies the mental habit which is formed, of bringing to mind an idea of the consequent, whenever we are presented with the antecedent of an associated pair of events. Moreover we then (mistakenly) project this feeling onto the events themselves. Hume's location of "necessity" in a human attitude toward events has many modern descendants – for example, in J. L. Mackie's analysis of causation, and in Nelson Goodman's and A. J. Ayer's analyses of natural law. For both Hume and those who have inherited his legacy, necessity is not to be found among the sensory contents of "outer" experience, either among the secondary qualities or among the primary ones. The first stage of my argument has been concerned to refute this thesis, and by implication, to refute Hume's positive account of the source of our idea of causal necessity. But this refutation, even if sound, leaves it open as to whether causation is a primary or a secondary relation. However, the very intelligibility of the primary/secondary distinction, at least as it is often understood, is brought into question when we raise this issue.[43] For the occurrence of secondary qualities is often characterized as being explained by the action upon us of external objects whose qualities are the primary ones. If causation is itself a secondary relation, then on this showing its occurrence in perception must be explained, if at all, in terms of some more fundamental, primary properties of the world. But obviously, this explanation cannot then be a *causal* one. Moreover, we shall have to give up the characteristic lines upon which it has been hoped that explanations of the other secondary qualities might eventually be formulated. For these explanatory strategies all presuppose some version of a causal theory of perception. Such theories require that causation be a primary relation.

The second stage of my argument therefore undertakes to show that, provided the conclusion of the first stage be granted, we must further hold that causation is a primary, not a secondary relation. In support of this claim I shall here offer just one argument. Additional arguments appear in Chapter 11, Section 5. Two of these depend upon the results obtained there concerning our knowledge of space.

It might be thought that the immediately foregoing considerations suffice already to establish the desired conclusion. Surely causation is fundamental to explanation if any property or relation is; and if it is required to explain the secondary qualities, the very existence of the primary/secondary distinction rests upon the primary nature of causation. But this conclusion does not follow, if we take as our definition of primary and secondary qualities that the latter are qualities whose instantiation is dependent upon the existence of conscious mental phenomena, whereas the former are not. Unless additional premises are supplied about the nature of the relation between mental and non-mental phenomena, this primary/secondary distinction can be maintained without supposing causation to be present in mind-independent phenomena. In that case there will simply be no causal relations between the mental and the non-mental. What needs to be shown, therefore, is that causal relations could be and are instantiated in non-mental events.

The denial that force is a primary quality can be understood in different ways. Hume himself acknowledges a common distinction between three classes of properties.[44] One class is the class of primary qualities – extension, solidity, motion; a second is the qualities commonly recognized as secondary – color, sounds, flavors; and the third are private sensations – for example, pains and pleasures. When Hume asserts that we mistakenly "transfer" sensations of force to material objects, what sort of a mistake is he accusing us of? Would it be analogous to the mistake we allegedly make when we attribute colors to objects; or more like the kind of mistake we would make if we thought material objects felt pain? Hume's use of the expression "feeling of force" in this connection certainly gives color to the latter interpretation. Yet, Hume's explicit position is that all sensations of quality are on an equal footing as regards their mind-dependence.[45]

It is, indeed, a difficult question how the distinction between the second and third classes is to be understood, supposing it to be genuine. At any rate, Hume's explanation of the origin of our belief in the persistence of unperceived material objects suggests that the mistake made in connection with forces is of the following sort. We ascribe persistence to material objects (with their ascribed qualities) because of their constancy, and because so doing affords us an especially simple explanation of the patterns of coherence of our impressions of them. No similar explanatory power is gained by accepting the hypothesis that pains or pleasures persist unperceived.

The relevant question in the light of this argument is whether the supposition that forces can exist unperceived affords us explanatory simplification of the sort which belief in material objects does. It is a sufficient answer to Hume, therefore, to point out that *if* the idea of force affords us the idea of a non-accidental connection between the motions of bodies, it affords us an explanatory hypothesis of the utmost power and unifying effect. For then the supposition that bodies exert forces upon each other provides us with a schema for explaining their motion, and perhaps much else.

Most contemporary empiricists would not, however, accept the full implications of Hume's epistemology. What can be said to them? One thing which can be said is that to perceive a push is to perceive being pushed by something or to feel that one is pushing something. The something in question has always the character of a material body; and it is one's own body which serves as a locus for the perceived force. Force therefore is perceived as a relation; and nothing about that perception suggests that the bodies between which a force is exerted need be animate bodies. What pushes me need not be animate; and if an inanimate body can push an animate one, there is no reason to suppose that it could not push another inanimate one. Thus the "prejudice" Hume finds in us is by no means an irrational or unfounded belief. But there is a more detailed argument which will serve to reinforce this conclusion.

The argument to be presented here has three stages. Stage 1 establishes that forces – hence causal relations – are directly experienced via more than one perceptual mode. Stage 2 argues that these forces all enter into a single system – that is, a common algebra. In stage 3, I argue that this result entails a common spatial framework in which these forces operate, and the existence of causal relations, and/or relata of causal relations, which are unperceived.

I have heretofore been discussing primarily those tactile perceptions of force which accompany the impingement upon our bodies of other bodies. But this tactile modality is not the only one through which we experience forces. (I shall set aside here certain relations between our thoughts which might be regarded as causal, and relations between acts of the will (if there be such) and bodily movement or thought, which might also be so regarded. For I believe that if these two latter sorts of relations are to be classed under some general concept of causation, they are at least distinct species of it – too distinct to serve my present purpose.) At least two other sensory modes are modes through which (I shall argue) we are given instances of the same species of force as that which we perceive tactually as pressure. These two sensory modes are our kinaesthetic sense and our sense of balance, whose organ is the vestibular apparatus of the inner ear. Our kinaesthetic sense is sensitive to relative motion between different parts of our bodies, produced (or at least accompanied by) the extension of skeletal muscles. But of course I shall not make use of these physiological facts; and all reference to bodies in what follows is to be understood phenomenologically.

There is a felt difference between passive motion (produced by an external force) and active motion, produced by muscular tension. Such tension (the animal *nisus* of which Hume speaks) is also experienced as a force, whether accompanied by bodily motion or not. Like tactile forces, muscular forces are experienced as being applied to spatially located parts of our bodies; like them, they have perceived direction and a perceived magnitude. They have, among themselves, similar additive and subtractive properties – that is, they obey a vector algebra which is formally identical to that governing tactile forces (at least up to the degree of accuracy with which unaided sensation can supply us). All of the arguments which we have given for supposing a necessary connection between tactile forces and bodily motion apply *mutatis mutandis* to the connection between kinaesthetic forces and bodily motion.

The sense of balance enables us to detect such generalized forces as gravitational and centrifugal forces; I shall however omit this sensory mode from my discussion. Considering just tactile and kinaesthetic forces, as I shall call them, a natural question which arises is: what relationship do they bear to one another?

I shall argue for what seems intuitively to be the right answer to this question – namely, that tactile and kinaesthetic perception are sensory modes through both of which we perceive one and the same type of force. (To avoid possible misunderstanding, let me make it clear that I am not arguing that we always, or ever, perceive one and the same instance of force via both modes; I am arguing that we experience instances of the same causal relation in both ways.) Some evidence for this claim has already been given, in the "structural" parallels between tactile and kinaesthetic forces.

But there is an additional fact whose implications are of great importance. I have spoken of the vector algebra which governs the combined action of multiple tactile forces, and the formally identical calculus which governs the combined action of multiple kinaesthetic forces. We know more than this, however. Neither of these systems is a closed system, providing causal sufficiency for every motion detected through the correlated sensory mode. Experience teaches us that tactile and kinaesthetic forces can combine, and that when they do so combine, the result is once again determined by the same vector algebra, counting each force in terms of its magnitude, direction, and point of application, but indifferently as to whether it is tactile or kinaesthetic. Moreover, the construct which we call the resultant force cannot in these instances be characterized as either tactile or kinaesthetic.

This feature of our perception of forces is easily illustrated. For example, consider this case. I place my hand against a brick on a table and push. There is a kinaesthetic force which I feel my arm applying to the surface of the brick, and a pressure upon my hand. If the muscular force is light enough, it and the pressure are exerted equally but in opposite directions – and the brick remains stationary. If the muscular force becomes great enough, there comes a point at which the backwards frictional pressure on the brick no longer keeps pace, and my hand and the brick begin to move. These results can be suitably varied by changing the direction of the forces, having a moving brick collide with a resisting hand, and so on. It will be evident that the kinaesthetic force and the pressure can oppose each other; and that the resulting motion of the hand is proportional to a force obtained by summing over both tactile and kinaesthetic forces using the vector algebra. The point of application (in our example) of both types of forces is identical, and their directions and magnitudes can be compared. This surely would be difficult to explain, if it were not the case that the space in which tactile and kinaesthetic forces exist is the same space; and that the forces themselves, abstracted from their respective modes of perception, are of the same type.

Next consider this further example. I place the palm of one hand against the palm of the other, and press both palms together. I will have the following perceptions of force: an exertion or muscle tension in the right arm, applied at the position of the left hand and directed toward my left, a similar exertion in my left arm, applied at the same location but directed toward the right, a felt pressure on the surface of my left hand directed left, and upon the palm of my right hand directed right. If the tensions in my two arms are equally strong and directed in exactly opposed directions, no motion of the hands ensues. If the tensions are unequal, or not aligned, there is a resultant motion whose direction and magnitude are once more calculable using the vector algebra; only with the proviso that we do so by adding *either* the two kinaesthetic forces *or* the two tactile pressures, but not *both*. There are but two ways I can think of to explain this result. One is that the muscular tension of each arm is part of a causal sequence which, directly or indirectly, produces the occurrence of that causal relation registered as the felt pressure by the opposite hand. The other explanation is that the muscular force of each arm is to be *identified* with the pressure upon the opposite hand: both, after all, have the same magnitude, location, and direction. In that case, we are perceiving, through two different sensory modes, one and the same force.

Now the first of these two possibilities yields directly the result that causation is a primary quality. For if we have causal relations which operate across sensory modes, then they themselves must be primary relations. The reason for this claim is as follows. We can say that the event of *a* causing *b* to move (by pushing it) causes the event of *b* causing *c* to move. Thus one causal relation in a chain of causes can be said to cause the occurrences of the subsequent causings: which is just to say more simply that it causes events which in turn cause later events. Now a kinaesthetically felt force can cause the existence of a force felt tactually, in the sense that the former force is a causal relation between two events, the later of which is the distant or proximate cause, via the tactually felt force, of some third event. In the case of the two hands pressing together, the second event in this series is not one of which we are directly aware. We are aware of the kinaesthetic force and of the tactile force upon the opposite hand, but not of any intervening event.[46] Since one of the relata of each of the two causal relations is an extra-perceptual event, the relations themselves are primary, according to our definition. Or at least we can say that the relation is such that at least one of its relata, either the cause or the effect, can be non-mental.

The other alternative is that the two felt forces may be one and the same force, directly experienced through two distinct sensory modalities. How on that analysis can we use this experiment to show that forces can exist unperceived, or can relate events which are unperceived? One argument is that if the same force is perceived through two distinct sensory modalities, then that force cannot be identified with either a tactual awareness or a kinaesthetic one. A further argument rests on facts of which we may be quickly reminded. Every tactile awareness of a force is necessarily associated with a tactile awareness of (some degree of) solidity or hardness. Yet hardness is not to be identified with force. It is not a relation, does not have spatial direction, and its magnitude varies independently of the magnitude of felt force. Similarly, kinaesthetic sensations of force are necessarily associated with what, for want of a better expression, I shall call feelings of (some degree of) muscular exertion. Again, the two sensations are not to be identified. Muscular exertion does not have a direction; in extreme cases, it is felt as a kind of pain in the muscle. Yet, it appears to be a truth – indeed a necessary truth – that muscular exertion is not felt tactually, and that hardness is not felt kinaesthetically, just as phenomenal sounds cannot be detected visually.

Now if pressure on the left hand is an experience of one and the same force as that registered kinaesthetically in the right arm, then the same force which the right arm and hand exert, by virtue of their solidity and muscular effort, is perceived by the left hand as a force, without any perception of a part of the cause, namely, the muscular effort. What is not perceived in the left hand is perceived in the right arm; but clearly there is no reason to believe that whenever a tactually perceived force is produced by muscular exertion, there must be an accompanying experience of that muscular exertion. Thus an experienced force can have as one of its relata an event, or part of an event, which is unperceived. If this is so, then at least one of the relata of a causal relation can be mind-independent. Given that concession, there are no grounds for supposing that both relata, and the relation itself, cannot be mind-independent. But then, it follows that the causal relation is a primary relation.

2 An ontological analysis of causation

1. ARE CAUSAL RELATIONS DYADIC?

Thus far, I have argued that causal relations are perceptually given to us; that we are sometimes directly aware of them. These experiences are the fundamental source of our conception of causation. I have argued that Hume was mistaken in supposing that the idea of necessary connection arises as a kind of feeling founded upon habits of mental association. These results, if sound, apply as well to modern descendants of Hume's theory – namely, all those analyses of causation, of subjunctive conditionals, of lawlike statements, and of disposition statements, which seek to locate their special feature of "necessity" in human habits, in attitudes or inclinations which accompany their use, or in various pragmatic aspects of their conditions of appropriate utterance. The second thing I have argued is that causal relations are primary qualities, not secondary ones. Thus they do, or can, have unexperienced instances, and take unexperienced entities as their relata. We have now to consider what sort of entities these relata are, and what sorts of relations causal relations are. Whereas our direct experience of causal relations may be insufficient to provide answers to every question we wish to pose, we shall consider how far it can carry us.

I think it has not generally been disputed that causality is, or involves, relations of some sort; and that some or all of the involved relations are dyadic. But is this correct? The main reason, perhaps, for disputing dyadicity is that an event may be said to have multiple causes, and a cause may be said to have multiple effects. Indeed I have said that we may be aware of several forces applied at the same time to essentially the same place, and contributing to a single motion. But this very fact suggests that such cases are to be analyzed as cases of multiple causation – that is, as cases involving a more than one dyadic causal relation. For each force is given to us as dyadic: as having a source and a point of application. Thus I shall assume that all causal relations are dyadic relations, or are analyzable into a plurality of dyadic relations, though other possibilities have not been strictly ruled out.

2. HOW MANY DISTINCT CAUSAL RELATIONS ARE THERE?

If we take the ordinary term 'cause' to correspond, at least roughly, to some class of relations bearing genuine kinship, then it is apparent that the term denotes what biologists would call a family – a group of genera, each of which has a number of species ranged under it. It is of some importance to determine what, philosophically speaking, the taxonomy of causal relations is.

Thus far, I have focused attention upon what emerges as one genus of causal relations. These are those which can be represented by force vectors. I should not wish to hazard a guess whether, ultimately, the *only* causal relations required by physics will prove to be of this sort. In any case it is evident that we must speak here of a genus, not a species, for forces can vary in magnitude. Instances of force can moreover be distinguished by differences in their directions; but it would be implausible to take spatial direction as a differentia of species of force, just as it would be implausible to take spatial location as such a differentia. Both of these distinguish instances of such a species, just as they distinguish instances of a given length, for example, one meter. Since both spatial position and spatial direction are reference-frame relative, and do not modify, *per se*, the operation of a force, they are not intrinsic to the causal relation. The only intrinsic qualification with respect to which forces vary appears to be their magnitude. Forces, therefore, form a genus whose species are forces of specific magnitudes.

A different distinction among forces may be required, should it emerge that some forces require spatiotemporal contiguity between cause and effect, whereas other forces are able to act at a distance. I shall argue in Chapter 5 that the temporal relation between cause and effect is either one of contiguity (in case time is not infinitely divisible) or that causes and their effects form a temporal continuum. But I leave open the question of spatial contiguity. Our paradigm conception of causal relations is one which involves the cause being either spatially contiguous to or continuous with its effect. This is doubtless because of the way in which we experience the causal relations – pushes and pulls – which I have suggested are central to the formation of that conception. Thus when a cause gives the appearance of producing a distant effect, we tend to posit a continuous chain of intermediate causes to span the gap. Indeed *if* causes and their effects are, as will be argued, temporally contiguous or continuous, and if (as is well supported by current physics) action at a distance always requires an elapse of time, then it follows that action at a distance is action mediated by a chain of spatially contiguous or continuous causes and effects. For otherwise there would be temporal gaps in the sequence. But the proposition that causal influence cannot be transmitted through space at a velocity exceeding that of light (i.e. a finite velocity) is empirical – and may conceivably be found to be false. If so, then it may be necessary to admit action at a distance. Such action would still clearly count as causal, for our concept of causation is surely elastic enough to be stretched this far away from the paradigm.

A further classifying principle for physical forces is in terms of the kinds of causes and effects which they relate. Physics currently recognizes four kinds of forces in this sense. On the other hand, the successful development of a unified field theory would perhaps show that this fourfold distinction is superficial, that all physical forces are of one underlying kind. In any event, it is evident that the three classifying principles mentioned cut across one another, or may do so. Hence, arguably, physical forces cannot be classified in terms of a traditional hierarchical taxonomy.

There are three other relations, or types of relation, which strike me as falling within the purview of the general concept of causation. If there are irreducible relations of these three sorts, then I believe they must be classified as distinct genera under the general heading. These three classifications are: (1) causal relations between mental events and physical events; (2) those relations between mental events and other mental events which fall under the heading of reasoning; and (3) relations of production between pairs of mental events which do not constitute reasoning. Clearly, whether these represent distinguishable categories depends upon the sustainability of some form of dualism.[1]

With respect to each of these types of relations, there are philosophers who have maintained that we are sometimes aware of their instances. However, I believe it is fair to say that in no instances of these types of which we are directly aware are we aware of anything which could be represented by a spatial vector, in the way in which forces may be. I do not have any detailed taxonomy to offer of the species of relations within these genera, though it may be worth remarking that if type (2) represents a distinct genus, a natural principle of classification would be in terms of the rules of inference which guide reasoning from one thought to the next.[2]

I should like next to ask: what is it that binds all of these relations together into a single family? To know this would be to know what is essential to our conception of causation (and perhaps to the causal relation itself), taken in the most general sense. It is evident that spatial direction, location, and contiguity are not essential in this way, for we can conceive of relations of types (1), (2), and (3) as having relata which are non-spatial. Similarly, it is doubtful that constant conjunction is an essential element of the relation, or implied by it. I have argued that our knowledge of "body–body" causal relations is not, fundamentally, arrived at via the observation of constant conjunctions. It is likewise arguable that our knowledge of causal relations of types (1)–(3) is not come by through the observation, in one's own mental life or in that of others, of constant conjunctions.[3] This, however, is an epistemological point, and in no way affects the question whether the existence of such relations implies a corresponding constant conjunction.

One consideration which prevents a facile drawing of the conclusion that the implication holds is the apparent existence of irreducibly statistical laws of nature. If such laws do describe physical nature, how are we to understand them? I suggest that the best available model we have is to understand them as obtaining in virtue of causal relations of the "body–body" sort.[4] The impression of force with which experience supplies us involves a necessary connection, which does imply invariant conjunction in the absence of disturbing forces.[5] But with respect to the forces underlying quantum mechanical laws, this impression (or rather the extension of it to this case) is evidently incorrect. I shall not enter the controversy over how quantum mechanics is to be interpreted. I shall venture to say only that, crudely speaking, we may perhaps think of the causal relations described by quantum mechanics as a kind of mixture of necessity and chance. There is necessity (and hence constant conjunction) in two senses: first, because certain state-transitions are strictly forbidden, and secondly, because among the allowed transitions, each can be assigned a definite law-ordained probability of occurring when the antecedent conditions are fulfilled. In fact, these two types of necessity reduce to one, the cases of forbidden transitions being just those for which the probability is zero. However these probability assignments are to be interpreted, they must be taken to be invariant. It is not, I believe, entirely clear whether quantum phenomena are, in some sense, partly causal and partly acausal, whether they involve a non-deterministic form of causal relation, or whether some third analysis must be given.[6]

If the family of causal relations includes members which require neither spatial contiguity nor constant conjunction, what remains as essential to causality? Two characteristics, I believe. First, temporal contiguity, in a sense to be specified in Chapter 5. And secondly, a notion of non-accidental connection between cause and effect which is the relation, discussed earlier, of *production*.[7] I do not think it is possible to define this general relation, except circularly in terms of causation. It is a relation which is, ontologically, not analyzable or reducible into something else.

Do then temporal contiguity, non-accidentality, and production uniquely characterize causal relations, distinguishing them from other kinds of necessary connection? Logical necessity is excluded by our definition, for it involves no temporal contiguity. There are, however, other plausible candidates, non-causal necessities which may not be excluded by the criteria suggested. I cannot claim to have an exhaustive list of these. A number of the more promising cases can be derived from a list of non-causal counterfactuals proposed by Kim (1973b). The following modal claims are inspired by Kim's examples.

1. Necessarily, if I write 'Larry' then I write 'r' twice in succession.
2. Necessarily, if I flip the switch, then I turn on the light.
3. Necessarily, if my sister gives birth at t, then I become an uncle at t.

As Kim points out, my flipping the switch causes the light to go on; but it does not cause my turning on the light. The other two cases are similarly non-causal. These examples appear to suggest that additional criteria are necessary to distinguish causal necessity from other species of necessity. (1) suggests the criterion that the effect must not be part of the cause, nor the cause part of the effect. This condition is automatically satisfied, however, if temporal contiguity is construed in such a way that no part of a cause and its effect coincide temporally. Temporal contiguity, so construed, also excludes (2) and (3); for it rules out simultaneity. My turning on the light is, entirely or in part, simultaneous with my flipping the switch; and I become an uncle simultaneously with the birth of my sister's child. In Chapter 5 I shall argue on independent grounds that the requirement of temporal contiguity needs to be construed in such a way as to exclude simultaneity. This survey gives us reason to believe, then, that the distinguishing features of the genus of causal relations are non-accidentality, production, and temporal contiguity in the sense yet to be specified.

3. WHAT ARE THE RELATA OF CAUSAL RELATIONS?

We turn now to a matter which is central to our inquiry: in which ontological category do causes and their effects fall? Four proposals may be considered. Of these, the most commonly held is that the relata are events. But some have thought that they are states of affairs. It also has been proposed that at least one of the relata of a causal relation may be a particular. Chisholm (1976), for example, holds that the distinguishing mark of human agency is that the agent himself is a cause of his actions. Harré and Madden (1973), Fisk (1965) and Lamprecht (1929) have argued that in physical causation one of the relata is a physical object. Certain locutions in ordinary language give color to these claims. We say: Hitler caused the destruction of Germany; Mt Etna caused the destruction of Pompeii. Of course, statements of this sort may really be ellipses.

Fourthly, the view that causal relations relate properties is suggested by the independently developed views of Michael Tooley (1977), David Armstrong (1978b), and Fred Dretske (1977).[8] At the same time, none of these three philosophers would wish to deny that events can be causally related. Thus their view must be interpreted as to be consistent with the event-view. The two theses can be shown to be consistent if we make the distinction between properties, understood as universals, and their instances. In making this distinction, we need not be committed to the existence of property-instances as particulars of some sort. We may hold that a property-instance is nothing over and above a special combination of a particular and a universal. Nevertheless, this combination has a kind of particularity: in the case of physical properties, at least, it is locatable in space and time.

If we make this distinction, then we may distinguish between the causal relation understood as a second-order relation between first-order *universals*, and (derivatively) its instances which obtain between the instances of these universals.

What would it be for an event to instantiate a second-order relation? In a preliminary way we may say that an event must be taken in the present context to involve the exemplification of at least one first-order universal by at least one particular; if the universal instantiates a second-order property then each of its instances must do so as well. Thus the second-order property (or relation) will figure as a constituent of the event. In what sense can a second-order relation relate two events, if each event is viewed as the exemplification of a first-order property by a particular? Let there be two first-order universals A and B, and two particulars x and y, and let us say that A and B are causally related by the second-order universal 'causes': C (A,B). If Ax and By are events in our sense, then their constituent properties A and B will be related by C. But how can this relation relate the specific event Ax to the *specific* event By? For B may well be exemplified elsewhere and at many different times. Since C relates the universal A to the universal B, it can hardly serve to single out any *special* instance of B to which some particular instance of A is related, in a way in which it is not related to any other instance of B. A way out of this difficulty is to regard C as a relation which always takes some spatial and some temporal interval as components of the relation. Then C is actually a four-place relation: C $(A, B, \delta s, \delta t)$ and δs and δt can serve to identify that instance of B to which any instance of A is uniquely related by C. We shall presently give independent reasons for construing C in this way.[9] It emerges then that C is not, strictly speaking, a dyadic relation. Yet to speak as if it were, when we are speaking somewhat loosely, would not be unjustified, if the relata δs and δt are always relations of fixed magnitude. Whether that is so is a question which will be examined presently.

Tooley, Armstrong, and Dretske do not employ the above reasoning; but they do all take the existence of events related by causal relations to suggest an ontology of universals structured by causal relations. Causal relations are, therefore, taken to be second-order relations. This view has the attraction, for those who believe that causal relations entail universal laws, of explaining immediately why this should be so. Crudely, if two universals are related by causal connection, then *a fortiori* all of their instances must be.

I shall defend a version of the Tooley–Armstrong–Dretske view. Naturally, much that needs to be said about it needs to be postponed until a theory of universals has been developed. We may, however, investigate here whether particulars are sometimes causes or effects, and the causal status of states of affairs. I shall reject the first claim on both phenomenological and systematic grounds. This will lead in turn to a discussion of the identity-criteria for events and states of affairs.

The phenomenological grounds for favoring events over particulars are straightforward. When an object affects one in some way – say by striking one – it is never merely the object as such which one perceives as producing the effect. What is perceived is that certain of the object's qualities, and not others, are involved. Motion and relative location, for example, are among the qualities which enable an object that strikes me to affect my own motion. A distant object or one not moving in that particular way does not produce that effect. Similarly, the effect does not consist simply of a particular, but of some specific change in or qualification of a particular, or of the creation or annihilation of a particular of a certain kind. A force, as I have argued, causally connects the motion of one object with the motion of another; and we perceive this to be the case.

If, as we typically believe, physical individuals persist through time and through change, then it is senseless to speak of a particular *simpliciter* as a cause; for it is at one time involved in a causal interaction and at another time no longer involved in it. There would be no way to explain this fact if we could not refer to the differing properties had by that individual at various times during its existence. Nor could we explain why certain particulars enter into certain causal relations and not others.

It may happen that one has good grounds for believing an individual or a quantity of stuff to be causally responsible for some change, but not know which property of that individual it is, by virtue of which the effect is produced. When sugar dissolves upon immersion, we are quite certain that the water is causally involved; yet we may understand nothing about the causal mechanism or the properties of water which make this occur. Nevertheless we can be morally certain that it is something about the water and the sugar – some of their properties – that explain this change.

This brings us to the systematic grounds for taking events to be the relata of causal relations. If those relata were particulars it would not be possible to formulate causal laws, for the universality of laws is achieved by specifying, not a list of particulars, but the properties they must satisfy, the kinds of things they are. And if we say that the particular must be of a certain kind, the claim that causes or effects are particulars becomes indistinguishable from the one which takes causal relations to relate individuals "in virtue of" certain of their properties. But the latter phrase can reasonably be understood as expressing what are events or states of affairs.

These considerations suggest in a natural way a criterion for the individuation of events. Since it is the property/individual complexes that instances of a causal relation relate, we may take a single event to be constituted by the instantiation of a single property or relation by a single individual or ordered n-tuple of individuals. Such an instantiation will necessarily occur at or during some time, and if the individuals are spatial individuals, it may generally be said to be located where they are located. Because the terms 'property' and 'particular' are not count-nouns, there is no unique way of individuating events. But if there are simple properties and particulars, it follows that there will be atomic events.

But the individuation of events is only one concern. An essential result of this way of construing events is that it provides a criterion of event identity. This we can formulate as follows:

(EI): If 'a' and 'b' name events, then $a = b$ iff a and b occur[10] at the same time and location, and have the same constitution.

Two events are said to have the same constitution if and only if each involves the same particulars having the same properties and relations, as the other. To be sure, these criteria make event individuation and identity conditions heir to all the vagaries and difficulties attending the individuation and identity conditions for individuals and their properties. But this is as it should be. The identity conditions for properties will presently come under scrutiny.[11]

As I shall speak, both events and states of affairs admit, broadly speaking, of the same analysis. The constituents of both these entities are particulars and their properties and relations. Perhaps this is partly a matter of stipulating a certain use for these terms; however, such stipulation does not stray too far from ordinary usage, which may not be entirely univocal in any case.

Nevertheless, there are several reasons for taking events to constitute a proper subclass of the class of states of affairs. First, it is plausible to allow such things as two plus two being four to count as a state of affairs; but such a state could not be regarded as an event. Secondly, it is arguable that there are such things as general states of affairs – for example, the state of affairs of all crows being black. But there are not in any case general events. Thirdly, the term 'state' is often used to designate relatively fixed, permanent, or stable conditions; contrastively, we normally use 'event' to designate changes or processes. But this last distinction is for our purposes not significant and will be largely ignored. It reflects the general belief that part of every set of conditions which cause some effect must include a change which precedes the effect. This latter is the sort of thing most naturally called an event; and changes are also, in most contexts, the features most naturally singled out from the complex of causally relevant circumstances as causes. Unchanging background conditions, by contrast, may be described as states of affairs. Yet when such conditions are causally relevant to the production of an effect, there is no distinction between the causal relation which links them to that effect, and the relation which links a preceding change to this effect. Hence, standing conditions are also causes – and, in terms of the present analysis, events. The terms 'event' and 'state' will therefore be used interchangeably, as the context permits.

Given these considerations, I shall take the term 'event' to designate those states of affairs (complexes of properties and particulars) which are not general and which can be assigned some location in time. What sorts of particulars can figure in events? Included will be material particulars, quantities of stuff, minds, objects of sensation, and things which might themselves in other contexts be regarded as events or processes involving the above categories (e.g., a fountain, a river, a bolt of lightning). More problematic are such items as rainbows, shadows, and regions of physical space-time. As for shadows and rainbows, they and their vicissitudes can be analyzed in terms of the properties and changes of material particulars; and spatiotemporal regions, even if taken to be entity-like, do not as such play a causal role. Thus things of these sorts need not be considered. It will be clear, I hope, that in formulating this definition it is not my intention to make any commitment as to the ontological status of the sorts of items mentioned. If, for example, there are no such things as minds, or if mental events are identical to physical events, then that category must be either eliminated or regarded as redundant.

Our criterion for event-identity has been stated, quite properly, in ontological rather than linguistic terms. A number of difficult problems arise when we try to analyze the relation between events and the linguistic conventions we use to speak about them. Those conventions and the difficulties associated with them are not, properly speaking, our present concern. Nevertheless, since we cannot speak of events without using language, a digression into some of these semantical issues is necessary.

4. THE EXTENSIONALITY OF CAUSAL CLAIMS

If one event, *A*, causes another, *B*, then the claim that *A* causes *B* remains true, however *A* and *B* are identified. So if expressions '*A*' and '*A**' are used in such a way that '*A* = *A**' is true, then evidently it will be true that *A** causes *B*. Nevertheless, there are reasons for regarding claims such as '*A* causes *B*' as non-extensional. I shall not examine every argument which has been advanced for this view; rather I shall concentrate upon certain central puzzles which attend the way in which we use language to specify and describe events. The expectation, or at any rate the hope, is that when these essentially linguistic facts are accounted for, the extensionality thesis can be defended against the counterarguments.

Two such counterarguments are these. First, the sentence '*A* caused *B*' can be used to explain, or partially explain, the occurrence of *B*. Yet it may be false that an equivalent explanation is supplied by '*A** caused *B*.' This is hard to square with the fact that both sentences make the same claim. A second counterargument would have us regard the expressions '*A*,' '*B*' and '*A**' as representing propositions, and 'caused' as a propositional connective. If we regard 'caused' as an operator, it is clear that it is not a truth-functional one. But suppose that an extensional context is taken to be any context which permits substitution of co-referring expressions, and of logically equivalent propositions, *salva veritate*. Then there is an argument (to be given below) which shows that every compound sentence which is extensional in this sense is also truth-functional. Hence '*A* caused *B*' cannot be extensional in this sense.

The first of these objections relies upon the notion of explanation. Understood in one way, this notion is one which has pragmatic dimensions. What will serve as an explanation depends upon context-relative conditions of appropriateness, hearer's background information, and so on. With 'explains' understood this way, the fact that '*A* caused *B*' serves to explain *B* upon some occasion upon which '*A** caused *B*' fails, has no bearing upon the extensionality of '*A* caused B*,' for explanatory power in this sense is not a necessary condition of the truth of the explanation. However, by explanation we might mean a deductive-nomological explanation such that '*p* caused *q*' is true just in case there is a correct explanation of *q* whose premises are '*p*' and a law. Now suppose there is a law, '(It is a law that) all *A*-like events are followed by *B*-like events' which may be regarded as justifying '*A* caused *B*.' Then if '*A* occurred' is true there exists a D–N explanation for '*B* occurred' of the required kind. But does it follow that there is a correct explanation of this kind which warrants '*A** caused *B*'? This depends upon whether, if '(It is a law that) all A-like events are followed by *B*-like events' is true, it is also a law that all *A**-like events are followed by *B*-like events. But under the criterion EI, $A = A^*$ only if A and A^* have the same constituents; hence A-likeness and A^*-likeness must involve the same set of properties, regardless of how those properties may be designated. Hence if there is a law whose statement mentions the property A-likeness, there is a law whose statement involves the substitution of the expression '*A**-likeness' for '*A*-likeness' – whether anyone has formulated that law or not. This deflects the first objection. Presenting the second in detail, and answering it, introduces a more detailed consideration of the varieties and vagaries of the linguistic devices we use to speak about events.

There are a number of grammatical constructions which can be used in English to refer to, and sometimes to describe, events. These include proper names, definite descriptions, nominalized sentences, and entire sentences of subject-predicate form. For the moment I shall restrict attention to the latter.[12]

Our ontological criterion suggests the following linguistic parallels:

(E) A sentence S is used as an event-specifying sentence *only* if:
(1) It is of subject-predicate form;
(2) The noun-phrases are singular referring expressions, used to refer to nonabstract particulars.
(3) The verb phrases are used to denote properties or relations of nonabstract particulars;

(I) Two sentences S and S' are used to specify the same event iff:
(1) They are both event-specifying sentences;
(2) Their noun-phrases are used to refer to the same set of nonabstract particulars;
(3) Their verb phrases are used to denote the same properties or relations; and
(4) They assign the same extensions to these properties and relations, among the particulars referred to.[13]

The last condition, I(4), allows for the fact that 'John bit the dog' specifies the same event as 'The dog was bitten by John' does, but not the same event as 'The dog bit John' does.

Several points need to be made about the application of (E) and (I). On criterion (EI) 'John bit something' does not specify an event, since 'something' is not used as a singular referring expression. Similarly, 'John bit the black St Bernard' is not an event-specifying sentence *if* 'the black St Bernard' is construed in Russellian fashion as '$(\imath x)(Bx)$', since, so construed, it is not a singular referring expression. I believe, however, that Russell was wrong: definite descriptions can (and usually are) used as genuine referring expressions.[14]

Secondly, I believe that a predicate can be meaningful even though it denotes no property. In this I agree with David Armstrong. Hence, a sentence can satisfy E(1) and E(2) and be meaningful, but not specify an event or state of affairs. For example, arguably

'David Armstrong is identical to David Armstrong'

does not specify an event, and surely

'That is a round square', and 'That is dephlogisticated air'

do not do so.

Thirdly, it is not necessary to specify the time of occurrence of an event in order to specify the event, provided that the particulars and properties involved are known to have that particular configuration upon only one occasion. Otherwise, it is necessary, or must be understood from the linguistic context. I shall discuss briefly below the use of spatio-temporal criteria for the individuation of events.

Fourthly, non-synonymous verb phrases may be used to predicate one and the same property of an individual. 'Blue' and 'my favorite color' may, for example, be used to denote the same property. This suggests the following principle:

(I') Two sentences *S* and *S'* are used to specify the same event if one sentence can be obtained from the other through substitution of co-referring noun-phrases and co-denoting verb phrases.

Thus '$P(a_1, \dots a_n)$' and '$Q(b_1, \dots b_n)$' are used to describe the same event just in case '$P = Q$', '$a_1 = b_1$', ... and '$a_n = b_n$' are all true. A different criterion is suggested by the deductive-nomological model for the explanation of single events. According to that model, an event *e* is explained by a law *L* and a set of boundary conditions *c* provided there exist statements '*C*' and '*E*' specifying *c* and *e* respectively, such that '*C*' and *L* together deductively entail '*E*', while neither '*C*' nor *L* alone does so. Suppose '*E*' and '*E**' are logically equivalent. Then any D–N explanation whose premises entail '*E*' is one which also entails '*E**' It is natural to conclude that

(I″) If S and S' are logically equivalent event-specifying state-ments, they specify the same event.

Although (I′) and (I″) seem reasonable, taken together they encounter serious objections.[15] For example, Jaegwon Kim (1969) suggests that it is natural to extend (I″) as follows:

(I*) If S implies S', the event specified by S *includes* the event specified by S'; if the events specified by S and S' include each other, then S and S' specify the same event.

Using this principle, consider the statements

   (A) a is F.
   (B) b is G.
   (C) $(\imath x)(x = a$ and b is $G)$ is F.
   (D) $(\imath x)(x = b$ and a is $F)$ is G.

Now $a = (\imath x)(x = a$ and b is $G)$, and $b = (\imath x)(x = b$ and a is $F)$. Hence, by (I′), (A) and (C) specify the same event, and (B) and (D) specify the same event. But (C) implies (B) and (D) implies (A). Thus, the event specified by (A) includes, and is included by the event specified by (B). Thus, by (I*), (A) and (B) specify the same event. Yet (A) and (B) can be arbitrarily chosen as any two true singular statements.

The above argument shows that there is something wrong with jointly holding (I′), (I″), and (I*). It is easy to see that the argument turns upon the use of the artificially constructed definite descriptions of (C) and (D). Our objection to this argument is that although '$a = (\imath x)(x = a$ and b is $G)$' and '$b = (\imath x)(x = b$ and a is $F)$' are both true, 'a' and '$(\imath x)(x = a$ and b is $G)$' are not co-referring singular terms, for '$(\imath x)(x = a$ and b is $G)$' is not a referring expression at all, though it contains referring expressions. Moreover, the entailment from (C) to (B) relies upon the fact that the noun phrase of (C) contains an event description which specifies an event (that b is G) which is not specified by (C). On the other hand, suppose the noun phrase is construed in non-Russellian fashion as a singular referring expression – that is, suppose its linguistic role is simply that of picking out the item a. In that case, it is not clear whether the sentence 'b is G' is detachable from the noun phrase of (C). If it is detachable, then (C) implies (B); but then by (I′), (C) and (A) do not specify the same event. If on the other hand it is not detachable, it may be correct to say that (C) and (A) specify the same event – but then (C) does not entail (B).

The difficulty illustrated by this example is symptomatic of more far-ranging features of our use of language, features which I think are bound to frustrate efforts to formalize criteria for event identity. Once these features are identified, however, we have the tools for applying (I'), which I take to be the most general and informative criterion (though it provides only a sufficient, not a necessary, condition of event-identity).

The features of language which are of key significance here are two. With respect to a singular sentence it can happen that:

(i) The noun-phrase does some of the "work" usually assigned to verb-phrases; that is has in part a predicative function; and
(ii) The verb-phrase does some of the "work" usually assigned to noun-phrases; that is helps to single out one or more of the individuals being referred to.

Both of these phenomena, which formal semantics has tended to ignore, can wreak havoc with judgments as to what individuals, and especially what properties, the use of a sentence *S* indicates as *constituents* of the event it specifies. A predicate which occurs in a noun phrase merely for the purpose of helping to identify an individual does not denote such a constituent; but if it also plays a predicative role, it does.

Here then are a pair of examples, of (i) and (ii) respectively:

(i) The context: *A* wishes to single out *B*, doing so in such a way as to convey an estimate of *B*'s character which serves to elucidate the import of the verb phrase. *A* says:
    That two-timing chiseler got caught last night at his own game.
(ii) The context: *A* is lecturing in an aviary to neophytes who know nothing about identifying birds; consider the dual function of the first occurrence of 'orange' when *A* says:
    The Cocks-of-the-Rock are orange and black; the orange is a vegetable pigment derived from their diet.

These observations enable us also to elude trouble that comes from the direction of sentences which include relative clauses. Thus consider both

(1) Randi, who is a professional magician, exposed Uri Geller.
and (2) The man in the black hat, who has entertained kings, exposed Uri Geller.

Let us suppose that, in fact, Randi = the man in the black hat. Now (1) entails both

(1′) Randi is a professional magician.
and (1″) Randi exposed Uri Geller;

whereas (2) entails

(2′) The man in the black hat has entertained kings.
and (2″) The man in the black hat exposed Uri Geller.

As they would ordinarily be used, (1) and (2) specify the same event, namely, that event also specified by both (1″) and (2″). This claim is licensed by (I′), provided that the singular referring expressions in both (1) and (2) are taken to include the clauses introduced by the relative pronoun 'who.' But then, we are not entitled to infer that the event specified by (1) includes the event specified by (1′); or that the event specified by (2) includes that specified by (2′). If we did, we should be forced to conclude, by "subtraction" of the event specified by both (1″) and (2″) from that specified by both (1) and (2), that (1′) and (2′) specify the same event. If, on the other hand, the relative clauses in (1) and (2) are understood to specify detachable events, then they each specify two events; and the first pair, given (I′), is not identical to the second. Hence, co-referentiality must be understood in (I′) as applying only to singular referring expressions taken as a whole, and (I″) is correct only if S and S' are both event-specifying sentences in the sense of (E).

We now have the materials with which to address the second of the objections originally presented to the thesis that causal contexts are extensional. This objection, it will be recalled, rests upon an argument which purports to show that all contexts extensional in a certain sense are truth-functional. This sense of 'extensional' is one which permits substitution of co-referring expressions and of logically equivalent statements, *salve veritate*. Here, then, is the argument; or rather, a special case of that argument which applies it to causal statements. Let '$P \to Q$' be read: 'That P was the case caused it to be the case that Q.' Suppose, further, that 'P,' 'Q' and '$P \to Q$' are all true, and let 'S' be any other true statement. Then we have:

(1) $P \to Q$ Assumption
(2) $[\hat{x}(x=x \text{ and } P) = \hat{x}(x=x)] \equiv P$ Tautology
(3) $[\hat{x}(x=x \text{ and } P) = \hat{x}(x=x)] \to Q$ Substitution
(4) $[\hat{x}(x=x \text{ and } S) = \hat{x}(x=x)] \to Q$ Substitution
(5) $[\hat{x}(x=x \text{ and } S) = \hat{x}(x=x)] \equiv S$ Tautology
(6) $S \to Q$ Substitution

Clearly, (6) does not follow from (1), for S can be arbitrarily chosen. Hence – so the objection runs – we must give up the view that '$P \to Q$' is extensional. This objection is sound. But at the same time, it illustrates the often baneful influence of linguistic analysis upon the solution to ontological puzzles. The characteristic of extensionality, as I have defined it in accordance with traditional usage, has nothing to do with whether causal facts are somehow description-relative. As long as we confine ourselves to singular referring expressions which designate states of affairs or their constituents, substitution into causal contexts will preserve truth value. But definite descriptions are not singular referring expressions (if treated in Russellian fashion), and can be expected to cause trouble. And the fact that two sentences are logically equivalent does not guarantee that they designate or specify the same state of affairs. Hence such substitutions do not always preserve the identity of the states said to be causally related. The argument just cited teaches this lesson.

Thus anyone who takes criterion (EI) seriously will reject the inference from (1) to (6). Granted that (2) is a tautology, does it follow that '$\hat{x}(x=x$ and $P) = \hat{x}(x=x)$' and 'P' signify the same state of affairs? Not, surely, if the former of these signifies the same state of affairs as '$\hat{x}(x=x$ and $S) = \hat{x}(x=x)$'. For in that case these two statements are "about" the self-identity of a certain class, variously identified. If, on the other hand, '$\hat{x}(x=x$ and $P) = \hat{x}(x=x)$' is understood to specify the same state of affairs specified by 'P', then '$\hat{x}(x=x$ and $S) = \hat{x}(x=x)$' does not specify that state of affairs, and the restriction imposed upon substitution by (EI) is violated. How we understand these expressions turns, clearly, on whether we take the predicates which appear in 'P' and 'S' to specify the properties which are constituents of the states of affairs being identified in the antecedents of (3) and (4) respectively. This, as we have seen, cannot be decided on purely formal grounds. But either way, the argument fails: if they do, then the step from (3) to (4) is illegitimate; if they do not, then (2) does not warrant the inference from (1) to (3).

Finally, here is an example which troubles Kim.[16] Kim thinks that

(3) Wilbur intentionally married Edith who intentionally married him.

and (4) Edith intentionally married Wilbur who intentionally married her.

specify distinct events, even though they are logically equivalent.

Now suppose (3) and (4) are both used as event-specifying sentences in the sense of (E). Then, according to us, they should specify the same event, namely, Wilbur and Edith's marriage. But, Kim points out, we would not normally suppose the question, 'What caused Edith to marry Wilbur?' to have the same answer as the question, 'What caused Wilbur to marry Edith?' Different causes; therefore different events. I think this argument is deceptive. 'What caused Wilbur to marry Edith?' is elliptical for 'What caused Wilbur to play his part in the performance of his marriage to Edith?'; similarly 'What caused Edith . . .?' is an ellipsis for 'What caused Edith to play her part . . .?' But Wilbur's playing his part, and Edith's playing hers, are distinct events, and hence may have different causes. Though distinct, they are both sub-events of the event of their marriage, and each is partly constitutive of it. Since each of these sub-events is a necessary condition for the occurrence of the marriage, the total cause of the marriage must embrace the causes of both sub-events. It is the marriage which is specified by both of our original sentences; hence the total cause of the event so specified includes Wilbur's motives and Edith's as well.

5. FURTHER SEMANTIC ISSUES

Thus far we have considered difficulties which arise in connection with the identification of the particulars that enter into events. There are also a number of problems which concern the specification of properties. These problems do not fundamentally concern the relation between language and properties, but nevertheless it will be appropriate to treat them here. Consider

> (5) Xantippe's only husband died at *t*.

and　(6) Xantippe became a widow at *t*.

Now (5) specifies the same event, by criterion (I), as

> (7) Socrates died at *t*.

Yet it is not evident that (5) and (6) specify the same event, although they seem to be logically equivalent event-specifying sentences. If they do specify the same event, then so do (6) and (7). Part of the difficulty here is that some of the descriptive content of the definite description 'Xantippe's husband' in (5) has been shifted into the verb phrase 'became a widow' in (6). For the husbandhood of Socrates to Xantippe is a logical precondition of her being widowed by his death. We have already seen that such predicative use of the content of singular referring expressions can lead to trouble. A second point is that (6) is an implicitly relational statement, one of whose relata is not specified by any singular referring expression. Thus (6) should be analyzed as

(6′) (Ǝx) Xantippe became a widow of x at t.

Our criterion (E) requires that each of the relata of a relation be identified by means of a singular referring expression. Thus, (6) is not an event-specifying sentence by criterion (E). To be sure,

(6″) Xantippe became a widow of Socrates at t.

is an event-specifying sentence. However it is not so implausible to hold that (6″) specifies the same event as (5). Nevertheless, (6″) and (7) do not specify the same event, for (6″) contains a relational property as a constituent and makes reference to two individuals whereas (7) does not.

Comparison of (6″) and (7) raises three further issues, which concern the treatment of relational events. The first of these is: where does an event which involves relations between two or more individuals occur? When an event involves only a single individual and its monadic properties, it is natural to say that the event occurs in the spatiotemporal region occupied by that individual. With relations, the situation is far less clear, and mirrors the difficulty about where the instantiation of the relation occurs. It will be useful to consider here a few examples.

(8) a is lighter in weight than b.
(9) a is the father of b.
(10) a is 5 feet to the left of b.
(11) Event a occurred before event b.
(12) Event a caused event b.

In some cases – for example, (10) – it is not unreasonable to count the space occupied by a, by b, and perhaps the space between them as the location of the event or state of affairs. But with (8), (9), and (11) it is much harder to motivate this view. Similar remarks apply to temporal location where the histories of the relata do not temporally coincide. This is one reason, though not the only one, why the use of spatiotemporal location as a general criterion for individuating events is problematic. We can nevertheless say that events occur "in" space and/or time in at least a weak sense; namely, that their occurrence is logically dependent upon the existence of spatial and/or temporally located particulars.

The second point concerns the distinction between external and internal relations. An internal relation is one which is such that its obtaining between a set of particulars is logically entailed by those particulars having the monadic properties they have. *Being lighter (in weight) than* is an example of an internal relation. Events such as *a*'s being lighter than *b* have therefore no existence over and above the existence of the event of *a*'s being the weight that it is, and *b*'s being the weight that it is. Nor can the relational event be brought about, except by bringing about certain monadic states of affairs in the related particulars.

When relational events are brought about by means of a change in just one of the related particulars, and especially when the relation in question is an internal relation, it is tempting to say that the relational event occurs, or is located at, the location of the changing relatum. It may even be tempting to say that there is no such relational event. We have already mentioned such a case, the widowing of Xantippe. This case involves external relations. Another case, involving an internal relation, is *a*'s becoming heavier than *b* by virtue of *a*'s weight being caused to increase while *b*'s weight remains constant. It would be a mistake here to take the total cause of *a*'s weight change to be the total cause of this event, for the total cause must include those conditions causally sufficient for the stability of *b*'s weight during the time-interval in question. Since *a*'s becoming heavier than *b* does not involve any events over and above the non-relational histories of *a* and *b*, it is perhaps misleading to say that it is a relational event.

The third issue concerns relational predicates which denote species of causation. Sometimes we construe an entire causally connected process as a single event, which may be in turn causally related to other events. Here two questions need to be addressed. Can causal relations themselves be among the constituents of events which are related by still other causal relations? And how shall we assign temporal location to events involving causal predicates? The answer to the first of these questions is 'no.' The correct ontological parsing of '*a* caused *b* to cause *c*' is '*a* caused *b*, which in turn caused *c*.' In connection with the second, let us focus on this example:

(13) The avalanche killed Oscar.

Let us suppose that (13) is true by virtue of the avalanche having critically injured Oscar, causing him to die a week later. By our lights, (13) can be used as an event-specifying sentence. But when did the event in question occur? It would seem that among its constituent events are

(13a) The avalanche occurred, and
(13b) Oscar died.

Even though circumstances sufficient for the death of Oscar were present when the avalanche was over, one might take the view that the avalanche did not finish killing him until he was dead, thus the killing was a process which lasted a week. Or one might locate the avalanche's killing of Oscar at just the beginning, or at just the end, of the week. Action theorists, for example, are wont to say that, although the light does not go on until a short time after the switch has been flipped, someone's turning on the light is simultaneous with his flipping the switch. But (13) logically entails that Oscar dies, whereas what goes on during the avalanche does not logically entail this. The semantics of (13) must therefore be understood in one of two ways. We can take (13) to specify an event which *includes* Oscar's death; or we can take (13) to specify an event which coincides with the occurrence of the avalanche, but which is (retrospectively) identified in terms of some of its effects. On the latter construal, the killing of Oscar is identical with the injuring of Oscar by the avalanche; and to describe it as a killing is to describe it as an event which (as a matter of fact) eventuated in a death. I shall not attempt to settle here the semantic question of how (13) is to be understood. It is not important for my purpose to do so. (In fact, it seems to me that (13) *could* be used with either semantic intention.) Such obscurities or ambiguities, however, should alert us that some care is required when our aim is the perspicuous specification of events as relata of causal relations. So if Oscar's being killed by the avalanche caused his wife to grieve, this could mean either of two things. Perhaps what Oscar's wife grieves over is simply his demise; in that case, his death is the proximate cause of her grief, the avalanche a more distant cause. But perhaps it is not Oscar's death as such which perturbs his wife; perhaps what upsets her is the particular form of his death, namely, his destruction by snow. In that case, it is a relational fact, a causal process, which is the proximate cause of uxorial grief.

There are two other problems with our criteria for event identity which must be mentioned. The first problem is whether our criteria are adequate to correctly distinguish between events related by what Alvin Goldman (1970) calls level-generation. The event of someone's flipping the switch, in Goldman's terminology, generates the (higher-level) event of his turning on the light. Turning on the light is not identical with the light's going on, and the latter, but not the former, is caused by the flipping of the switch. However, an analysis of Goldman's notion of level-generation is beyond the scope of this work, though the preceding remarks about (13) are relevant. The second problem concerns the relation between an event whose specification involves mention of a generic property, and an event involving the same particulars and temporal location, which is specified in terms of a property which is a species of that genus. Some examples will make the difficulty clear. Consider the following pairs of event-specifying statements:

(14)   That leaf changed color overnight.
(14′) That leaf turned red overnight.

(15)   Brutus killed Caesar.
(15′) Brutus assassinated Caesar.

(16)   Matilda dried herself.
(16′) Matilda dried herself thoughtfully on the beach with a towel at 2.30 p.m.

In each of these examples, the primed member of the pair mentions a property which stands to the property mentioned by the unprimed statement as determiner of a subclass to determiner of a class. Things turning red, for example, form a subclass of the class of things changing color. Also, the primed member of each pair entails the unprimed member. In the case of (16) and (16′), the entailment is "pure" logical entailment; in the other two, it is logical entailment more broadly construed, since each inference involves a premise which, though *a priori*, is not a truth of formal logic (e.g., 'Red is a color'). I shall argue that these examples are heterogeneous, (16) and (16′) requiring a different analysis than the other pairs.

Do (14) and (14′) – similarly, (15 and (15′) – specify distinct events, or do they specify the same event under different descriptions? Davidson (1967, 1969) advocates the latter view. Our criterion of event-identity (I) requires the former. Thus we need to clarify the relations between the members of each event-pair, and to do so in a way which sanctions the inferences from primed to unprimed statement. It is evident that this relationship is dependent upon the relationship between *being colored* and *being red*, in the one instance, and between *being killed* and *being assassinated* in the other – hence, between a generic property and its species. We give an account of this relationship in Chapter 9; thus the solution to this problem depends upon the discussion there. In Chapter 9, I conclude that a genus and each of its species are distinct properties. Hence, by (EI), it follows that (14) and (14′) – (similarly (15) and (15′) – do not specify the same event.

(16′) presents a different sort of case, for it can be analyzed into the following conjunction:

(16″) Matilda dried herself with a towel at 2.30 p.m. and Matilda was on the beach at 2.30 p.m.

The fact that (16″) is equivalent to (16′) indicates that (16′) specifies a compound event, whose subevents are given by the conjuncts of (16′). Thus (16′) entails that Matilda was on the beach at 2.30 p.m. in straightforward fashion. One should note, too, that the adverbial modifier 'thoughtfully' can be detached from the verb as in (16″); this suggests that a thoughtful drying is not a species of drying, but a drying accompanied by another sort of event. Many adverbs cannot be detached in this way – compare 'dried slowly'. The time-specifier 'at 2.30 p.m.' does not denote another property of Matilda, but a property of the entire complex event which (16′) specifies. The temporal coordinate, therefore, is not a constituent of an event which enters into it in the same way as the properties which modify its constituent particulars. It enters rather as a relation between events.

The above discussion, though incomplete, will serve our purpose. The essential points, then, are (1) that events are to be individuated in terms of their constituent properties, and particulars and times of occurrence; (2) that both properties and particulars are such that a given one can be picked out by non-synonymous linguistic expressions; (3) that substitution of co-designating expressions for constituent properties and particulars preserves reference to an event; and (4) that 'event' is not a count-noun; hence complex events can be compounded from simpler ones. We may now turn to the way in which events are linked by causal relations, and to certain further challenges to (E) and (I).

6. THE INDIVIDUATION OF EVENTS

Earlier on I took causality to be a dyadic relation, on the grounds that, for example, a compound force could always in principle be non-arbitrarily resolved into the actual constituent forces which composed it, and that each of these forces (or forcings) is a dyadic relation. On the other hand, it is clear that a single causal relation – for example, a single force, may occur as the joint action of several properties of a particular, or of more than one particular. Joint action in *this* sense is not resolvable in terms of individual component forces. For example, the forces exerted by two colliding bodies *a* and *b* upon each other are a function of their relative velocity, their respective masses, their shapes, and their degrees of elasticity. These jointly combine to determine the (single) force in question; there is no question here of resolving the force into one due to relative velocity, another due to mass, and so forth. Yet, if we individuate the constituent events as *a*'s having velocity *v* relative to *b*, *a*'s having mass m_a, *b*'s having mass m_b, etc., then it is clear that "the cause" is not one event but many – and hence the relation is not dyadic in this instance. Indeed there will be no number *n* such that we would have any reason to believe causality to be always *n*-adic.

On the other hand, we can construe the relation as dyadic by allowing the relata to be compound events. There is an obvious reason for using the latter strategy. It is that the masses, initial velocities, etc. are all simultaneous and contributing factors to what we discern as a single force, just as the particulars and properties constituting what is described as the effect are all parts of what this force produces. Since events can be more or less complex by our criterion, we can effect a suitable gerrymandering by taking the cause (in our present example) to be the instantiation, by bodies *a* and *b*, of the complex property, *being composed of a body of mass* m_a, *etc., bearing relative velocity v to a body of mass* m_b, *etc.* This is how Armstrong (1978b) characterizes the situation. But it is not entirely satisfactory as it stands even if we make room for such complex properties as the one mentioned. It may be just a brute fact that (usually) it is only complex events of this sort which stand in causal relations. But it would be more satisfying if we could see how the simpler events which constitute these complex ones contribute individually to the causal relation. For it seems obvious that the causal relations into which a complex event enters are some function of the simpler properties which make up its character. If, for example, we vary the relative velocity, or the value of one of the masses, we find a corresponding change in the nature of the effect, which is a smooth function of these changes in the cause.

The circumstance just noted is not unique to causation. Other relations illustrate the distinction between a compound dyadic relation analyzable into component relational facts, and a simple relation whose relata are complex. For example, if *a* is in the same place as *b*, then for every partitioning of *a* there exists a partitioning of *b* such that it is possible to construct an isomorphism between *a*-parts and *b*-parts which obeys the relation *being in the same place as*. Thus this is a "compound" relation. *Being more beautiful than* is not in general compound in this sense, though its relata can be complex; if *a* is more beautiful than *b*, it will not in general be the case that there exists any decomposition of *a* and *b* such that an isomorphic mapping from *a*-parts to *b*-parts can be constructed which obeys the relation *being more beautiful than*.

Causal relations between events can be compound in both senses. They can be compound through involving distinct component forces, summable according to a vector algebra. Or they may involve a single force only, yet be such that the related events are constituted by more than one individual and more than one property. The question whether some ontological ground exists which explains the fact that a given complex of properties results in a particular force, can be considered only when an analysis has been provided of what it is to be a property. This task is taken up in Part two.

The difficulties over finding suitable criteria for the individuation of events might be taken to support the view that events are indefinitely complex particulars, as houses and trees are. Let us use the expression 'concrete particular' to denote a particular which is such that, however it might be described or referred to there are indefinitely many other properties than those mentioned, which that particular has, and by means of which it might be identified. Donald Davidson (1969) has defended the view that events are concrete particulars in this sense. He also takes such events to be the relata of causal relations. Davidson says:

> Mill . . . was wrong in thinking we have not specified the whole cause of an event when we have not wholly specified it . . . Mill's critics are no doubt justified in contending that we may correctly give the cause without saying enough about it to demonstrate that it was sufficient; but they share Mill's confusion if they think every deletion from the description of an event represents something deleted from the event described.
>
> (Davidson 1969: 698)

In this Davidson is partly right, but in the main mistaken. He is right in implying that 'event' is not a count-noun. This helps to explain a semantic fact which Davidson correctly notices. Language being made for man and not vice versa, it is not surprising that we have linguistic devices for referring to both particulars and properties which fall well short of naming or describing all of their constituents or characteristics. One can use a definite description to pick out a table without mentioning, or even knowing, most of the things which are true of it. So too, *a fortiori*, with reference to events. A partial description of an event need not constitute a reference to only part of that event.

But, *pace* Davidson, the above points have no bearing upon the question of how events, insofar as they are the relata of causal relations, are to be individuated. On this score, I accept Kim's view and reject Davidson's for two reasons: (1) Davidson's analysis does not adequately account for the connection between causal relations and causal laws, and (2) the analysis leads to a criterion for event-individuation which is either viciously circular or viciously regressive. I proceed to support these two criticisms.

Let there be two events, *A* and *B*, each of which is described, partly or completely, as involving material particulars of such-and-such types, in so-and-so numbers, and having certain properties and relations. Let us suppose, for simplicity, that the occurrence of *A* is the sole and causally sufficient condition for the occurrence of *B*. Suppose, moreover, that *A*, while including a sufficient condition for *B*, includes also some constituents causally irrelevant to the occurrence of *B*. Perhaps one of the constituents of A is some particular *a*'s having property *P*, where *a*'s being *P* is not in any way involved in the causal relation between *A* and *B*. Then, it seems obvious, *that* "part" of A is not part of one of the relata of the causal connection between *A* and *B*. Strictly speaking, the cause is not all of *A*, but that part of *A* actually relevant to the production of *B*. Since 'event' is not a count-noun, there is no reason why we should not be able to individuate that relevant portion of *A* as a distinct event; and there are good systematic reasons for so doing.

Consider this simple analogy. We have two wooden spheres, one painted white and the other brown. As we ordinarily speak, it is quite proper to say that the second sphere bears the relation 'darker than' to the first. Suppose, however, that the first sphere is made of walnut (a brown wood) and the second of maple (a white wood). Clearly, we would not wish to invite confusion by averring straightforwardly that the first sphere is darker than the second. Rather, it would be clear that more precision is required: both statements are ellipses. It is parts of each of the spheres – their surfaces – which are such that surface of the second is darker than that of the first. Similarly, we may speak loosely of *A* as being the cause of *B* but precision requires us to say that it is a certain part of *A* that is causally responsible for *B*.

Moreover, Davidson's account of event-identity and laws leads to difficulties over what it is for an event to be subsumed under a law. Davidson's view is that events are concrete particulars which, like tables and toadstools, are describable or specifiable in indefinitely less or greater detail. The trouble is due to the fact that one can invent descriptions which are such as to allow any event to be subsumed under any law. Davidson subscribes to the following principle:

> Law *L* subsumes events *e* and *e'* (in that order) provided there are specifying sentences *D* and *D'* of *e* and *e'* respectively such that *L* and *D* jointly imply *D'*, without *L* or *D* alone implying *D'*.

> (Davidson 1967: 701)

Now suppose we have a law whose logical form is given by *L*: $(\forall x)(Fx \rightarrow Gx)$.[17] It is natural to take *L* to subsume the event-pair specified by '*c* is *F*' and '*c* is *G*' respectively. But take any other event, specifiable by say, '*b* is *H*'. Then '*b* is *H*' and '*c* is *G*' specify an event-pair subsumed by *L*, for the event specified by '*b* is *H*' is also specified by '$(\iota x)(x=b$ and *c* is *F*) is *H*' and this, together with *L*, entails '*c* is *G*.'

Finally, we may consider Davidson's own criterion of event identity. Davidson suggests that, if *x* and *y* are events,

$$x = y \text{ iff } [(\forall z)(z \text{ caused } x \supset z \text{ caused } y) \text{ and}$$
$$(\forall z)(x \text{ caused } z \supset y \text{ caused } z)].$$

Davidson remarks about this criterion that it

> may seem to have an air of circularity about it, but if there is circularity it certainly is not formal. . . . No identities appear on the right of the biconditional.

> (Davidson 1969: 231)

Whence, then, the "air of circularity"? Its source is easily found. It is immediately evident that Davidson's criterion presupposes the notion of event-identity, for if we are to determine that an event *z* caused (or was caused by) events *x* and/or *y*, we first must be able to identify these events, and to distinguish them from causally irrelevant events. Though the criterion involves no "formal" circularity, it is a criterion whose application presupposes an answer to the question it was introduced to answer; and such a criterion is no criterion at all, in the sense of enabling us to determine whether the identity holds, even though what it says may be true. It should further be noted that Davidson's criterion commits one to the view that every event is causally related to other events. In so doing, it prejudges some substantive ontological issues – for example, whether all mental events are causes or have causes.

Although anticipating results presented later, it may be mentioned here that a similar circularity threatens principle (EI). In Part two, I develop a causal criterion of property-identity. In formulating that criterion, I am forced to use the notion of an event, since events are the relata of singular causal relations. It will therefore be necessary to show that the air of circularity which haunts (EI), taken in conjunction with the criterion of property-identity, is a mere appearance, and can be eluded. That is done in Chapter 8, Section 9.

7. CAUSATION AS A SECOND-ORDER RELATION: FURTHER ARGUMENTS

Our analysis of events has the consequence that events allow a natural classification into types. The properties whose instances are constituents of a particular event determine the type to which it belongs. Since, moreover, causal laws relate event-types, a natural way of explaining the universality of causal laws is to take causal relations to be relations between event-types or properties. It is, in other words, to take causal relations as relations between properties. This is one way to develop the Tooley–Armstrong–Dretske view previously mentioned. Before accepting this view, I shall briefly consider an argument against it. Our arguments in favor of the view, excepting the immediately preceding one, have been phenomenological. The contrary argument I wish to consider also begins with what is given phenomenologically.

If causal relations are second-order relations, then properties of causal relations must be third-order properties. But the causal relations which we experience as forces are experienced, we said, to have the properties of magnitude, spatial location, and spatial direction. Yet spatial location and direction are, certainly, first-order properties. Could they be third-order properties as well? To ask this is to ask whether a principle Armstrong (1978b: 141–2) calls the Principle of Order Invariance is true. According to this principle, if a property is ever instantiated by a particular, all of its instantiations are by particulars; if it is ever instantiated by an nth-order property, all of its instantions are by nth-order properties. More succinctly: Every property has a unique order. Armstrong holds that there are counterexamples to this principle. The counter example he gives is *having just m parts*. This property is one of those properties Armstrong calls *formal* properties. Although he does not offer a definition of 'formal,' Armstrong offers 'topic-neutral' as a synonym, and states that he has in mind purely logical, mathematical, and mereological properties as his paradigms. It does seem that such properties as *having magnitude m, being complex*, and *being structured*, which Armstrong would count as formal properties, all can plausibly be held to provide counterexamples to the Principle of Order Invariance. At least this is plausible if there are any properties of order two and higher, failing which the principle is vacuous. This observation suggests a restricted form of the Principle of Order Invariance. The restricted principle is

(R) Every non-formal property has a unique order.

Vague though the notion of topic-neutrality or formality is, it seems reasonable to hold that magnitude is such a property, but that spatial location and direction are not. Would an acceptance of (R) cast doubt upon our phenomenological claims about causal relations? Fortunately, it would not. I previously argued (Chapter 2, Section 2) that spatial location and direction are not characteristics of the causal relation as such, but are rather properties which necessarily characterize any instance of such a relation – just as spatial location necessarily characterizes any instance of redness, though not a property of redness. Thus, causal relations provide no evidence against (R).[18]

Apart from phenomenological considerations, are there any arguments which favor the second-order relational view? One such argument can be drawn from the apparent failure of neo-Humean attempts to explicate the notion of causality and its conceptual siblings. The lesson which this failure appears to teach is that the modal character of causal assertions is neither eliminable nor reducible to psychological facts about cognizing agents. But whence can we hope to find a source of non-logical, objective necessity? The most promising candidates seem to be relational facts about properties. Since a solution along these lines commits one to Platonism – or at any rate to some form of realism about properties – it would be incomplete without the development of a theory of universals. This will be attended to in Part two; for the present I shall assume that such a theory can be produced and defended. With that promissory note in mind, I turn next to several topics closely connected with causation: laws of nature, the problem of induction and finally, the temporal relation between cause and effect.

3 Causation and laws of nature

1. THE PRIMACY OF CAUSATION

The notion of causality is but one of a pool of cognate notions, a pool which contains central uses for such related concepts as these: laws of nature, subjunctive conditionals, dispositions, powers, necessary and/or sufficient conditions, explanation, and projectibility. There is a reasonable presumption that various of these notions are interreducible. If one could give a philosophically adequate account of any one of them, then each of the others could in principle be either defined or explicated in terms of that one. The central problem, therefore, has been to give an analysis of some member of the set. To be sure, such notions as those of causality, law of nature, subjunctive conditional, etc. intersect, as it were, but do not entirely overlap. Not every law of nature is, directly or derivatively, a causal law; not every subjunctive conditional depends upon the existence of a causal relation; not every case of necessity is a case of causal necessity. Causality does not exhaust modality. Causal relations ground a species of modality.

There has been substantial disagreement as to which of these semi-cognate notions is philosophically the most transparent or the most likely to yield up its content upon analysis, thereby providing an entry to the rest of this field of concepts. Here is one point upon which I am in agreement with Hume; for Hume seems to have thought that the causal relation itself was the key to an understanding of the related notions. Hume was right, I believe, in focusing upon causality as fundamental with respect to the related notions of causal laws, causal subjunctive conditionals, and dispositions. That is why I have begun with causality. Insofar as reduction is possible among the notions cognate with causality, it is they which must be analyzed in terms of causal relations, not vice versa. The reasons for this are both epistemological and ontological. Epistemological, because our basic epistemic access to these notions comes via our acquaintance with instances of causation; and ontological, because the facts which constitute the truth-conditions for statements of causal laws of nature, causal subjunctive conditionals, etc. consist in the existence of certain causal relations.

A full discussion of the notions cognate to the notion of causation would require the completion of two tasks. First, it is necessary to distinguish between the properly causal notions and others falling under the rubric – for example, causal laws vs. non-causal laws. Second, each causal notion must be analyzed in such a way as to exhibit the proper logical form, and the factual content, of statements employing that notion. Each of these tasks, in my opinion, will prove to be very difficult and very complex, even if it be allowed that the central problem, the problem of understanding causal relations, is solved.

These matters are, in the main, beyond the scope of this essay. Nevertheless, something ought to be said about them. I shall confine myself therefore to some rather schematic remarks concerning laws of nature, subjunctive conditionals, and the problem of induction. My hope is to exhibit some of the complexities, but also to provide enough in the way of constructive analysis to make reasonable the supposition that the program could be carried out.

The first topic will be to explore the connection between the existence of causal relations and the truth-conditions for laws of nature. This topic I shall divide into four problems, which are treated in the four sections following. These are:

1. The problem of distinguishing causal from non-causal laws;
2. The problem of determining the logical form of causal laws, and of reasoning which employs them;
3. The problem of explaining why and in what sense causal laws are universal; and
4. The problem of explaining the sense in which causal laws are necessary.

2. CAUSAL VS. NON-CAUSAL LAWS

It may be that all laws of nature are ultimately causal. However, it is not entirely a straightforward matter to establish whether or not a law is causal. Because we understand the relata of causal relations to be events, it is tempting to hold that only laws which relate events are causal laws. However, many of the laws of physics, especially basic laws, are not directly about events. Typically, they express one physical magnitude as a mathematical function of other magnitudes. Many such laws describe the ways in which forces depend upon other physical parameters. Clearly such a law helps to determine causal relations between events, although additional laws may be involved in the computation of a given effect from a given cause. That many laws assume this form should hardly be surprising. For one thing, the basic laws of physics abstract from, or tease apart, the complex features of concrete events into components, in such a way as to provide a general algorithm for determining the effect of any permissible combination of these. This result is neatly achieved by combining laws which tell us what forces are produced by events (as a function of features of those events) with laws which tell us how any given force will affect things of a given type, and a law for adding forces. This device is implicit in laws which make no explicit mention of force but are formulated in terms of cognate or closely related concepts – for example, energy, momentum, work, Hamiltonians, and so forth.

Russell (1917), however, drew a different moral from the prevalence in modern physics of abstract functional laws. Supposing functional laws to be non-causal, he went so far as to foresee a time when physics would entirely abandon causal concepts and causal laws. Physics has not, however, abandoned these concepts, and it is hard to see how it could. The existence of a functional law is no token that some causal claim has been superseded.[1] Let us call a law *directly* causal if it is explicitly about types of events, and asserts some causal relation to hold between them, or explicitly concerns forces. Laws which are about such relations or derive from them, but make no explicit reference to causes, effects, or forces may be called *indirectly* causal. Many functional laws are indirectly causal, for example the Boyle-Charles gas law. This law expresses the fact that a variation in any one of the pressure, temperature, or volume of a gas will cause a constrained shift in the values of the other two variables. Nevertheless, there are laws of nature which are, at least arguably, non-causal. If causation implies determinism, then laws which are irreducibly statistical are not causal laws. Hence if the laws of quantum mechanics, as standardly interpreted, are true, there remains little scope for causal laws. I have argued already that our acquaintance with causal relations is not such as to exclude statistical processes from falling under the concept. Another class of laws which are, arguably, non-causal are classificatory laws – laws which reflect the way in which entities within the domain of a given theory are classified. An example of such a law would be the law that electrons have a charge of 4.8×10^{-10} esu. The status of such laws is a matter of dispute. Some philosophers have viewed them as merely definitional for a (nominal) kind. On this view they are called 'laws' by courtesy only, being analytically true. A second view – one to which I subscribe – is that these laws purport to specify the essential properties of natural kinds. Neither of these interpretations appears to support a causal analysis. On the other hand, one might argue that such laws should be replaced by existential statements to the effect that there are entities which co-instantiate a certain group of properties, that is, the "defining" properties of electrons. It *might* be that this fact is ultimately to be explained in terms of the causal relations between the properties in question. Thus 'Electrons have a charge of 4.8×10^{-10} esu' might prove to be an example of a law which is indirectly causal.

3. THE LOGICAL FORM OF CAUSAL LAWS

The simplest laws which are directly causal are force-laws. Such laws are simple in structure in that they isolate specific causal relata; because they are not concerned to connect total causes with their effects, they achieve generality without sacrificing strict truth: they are non-defeasible. Some of these laws specify the magnitude, etc. of a force as a function of features of a causing event, others as a function of features of an effect. An example of the former is Newton's law of gravity; and example of the latter is Newton's second law:

$$F = d(mv)/dt.$$

Force-laws are "incomplete" in that they do not fully specify both terms of a causal relation. A law describing a full cause/effect relation is obtained by setting a cause-determined force equal to an effect-determining force, and adding a *ceteris paribus* condition. This reflects the fact that when a cause is related to an effect by a force of a certain magnitude, both "incomplete" laws must be satisfied.

The form of the law '$F = d(mv)/dt$' indicates that anything which exerts a force changes motion continuously through time; it implies that the initial mass and velocity of an object are among the constituents of the circumstances which produce the final mass and velocity; and it specifies the cumulative effect as the product of the values acquired by these quantities after any period of operation of the cause.

Next, there is a class of laws which state that if a (usually complex) set of initial conditions obtains, and no interfering factors are present, then a certain final state will ensue. Such laws are often derivable from the force-laws just discussed. They must specify the causally sufficient condition for a given effect. Such a total condition will, in the generation of an effect, typically involve more than one binary causal relation. On our account, the truth of such a law depends upon the relevant causal relations obtaining between the constituent properties of the cause and effect. But, moreover, a given such relation can be multiply implicated in the relation between a cause and its effect. Two forces which are of distinct types – for example a gravitational and an electrostatic force – may combine to produce an effect. But also, two forces of the same type – for example, two gravitational attractions – may so combine. The distinction between the former can be made in terms of the distinct relevant properties constitutive of the total cause. In the latter case, the distinction must be made by distinguishing the "sources" of force – that is, by individuating distinct particulars which are constituents of the total cause.

Indirect causal laws have a form such that their causal truth-conditions are to a greater or lesser degree not as obvious. In many cases, such laws are shown to be causal once it is realized that one or more of their terms is definitionally related to some expression which denotes a force. Thus the Boyle-Charles gas law '$PV = nRT$' contains the term 'P' which denotes pressure. But pressure is just force per unit area. Thus the Boyle-Charles law is really a force-law. The temptation to think that it is not is compounded by the fact that it appears to describe a static or co-varying relationship between pressure, volume, and temperature. There is no explicit reference to any temporal sequence of causally related events, nor any suggestion as to which of the three parameters may be manipulated to produce a change in the others. But these appearances are misleading. In the first place, force-laws do not explicitly describe an event-sequence; yet they are causal laws. The Boyle-Charles law governs the way in which a gas can assume successive states as any one or two of the three parameters is independently varied. This does not show that the direction of causation is arbitrary, for in any given case, it is not arbitrary which parameter(s) it is that is causally influenced "from the outside". Moreover, the facts which make the Boyle-Charles law true (of an "ideal" gas) are not facts which involve a *direct* causal connection between pressure, volume, and temperature, but rather facts causally relating the properties of the constituent molecules of the gas. It is often only by looking at the microscopic process operating within the gas that one can ascertain the "direction" of causal influence. Finally, the fact that the Boyle-Charles law describes a "static" relation between three parameters does not show that its truth-conditions are not causal. For, since those truth-conditions consist in facts about the nature of molecular interactions, the macroscopic equilibrium states are a derived feature of the gas, and in fact due to the very busy activity of its molecules. This observation is confirmed by the fact that, if one of the three parameters is changed, the resultant adjustment of the other two is not simultaneous, but propagates through the gas at the velocity of sound for that gas.

Some indirect causal laws are not converted into direct causal laws simply by more explicit definition of contained terms. The philosopher's favorite 'All ravens are black' (were it but true) would be of this ilk. So is Snell's law of refraction. In these sorts of cases, the exhibiting of the causal character of the law typically requires the kind of microreduction just discussed in connection with the Boyle-Charles law. Thus the blackness of ravens derives from causal facts about genes; and Snell's law can be derived from causal facts about wave propagation.

The conservation-laws of physics constitute another class of indirect causal laws. They are true by virtue of the fact that physical forces operate in such a way that, in an isolated system, the magnitudes of certain physical parameters remain constant through time. On our analysis, therefore, a great many laws of nature turn out to rest upon the existence of causal relations.

It would perhaps be too sanguine to expect all laws of nature – or even all causal laws – to possess a single logical form. A more realistic hope is that the fundamental causal laws, from which all other causal laws derive, can be stated in terms of a single schema. Our view is that all such laws are grounded in second-order relational facts which have the form:

(1) $C(P, Q, \delta t, \delta s)$

where 'C' denotes a four-place second-order causal relation, 'P' and 'Q' denote first-order properties, and 'δt' and 'δs' denote temporal and spatial distances, respectively.

A word is in order concerning the role of the spatial and temporal relations δs and δt. The fact expressed by (1) grounds the fact that wherever and whenever the property P is exemplified, the property Q will be exemplified at a spatiotemporal distance (δs, δt) from there. I take the magnitudes of δs and δt to be fixed for a given P and Q. In Chapter 5 I shall discuss the question whether some single value of δt is common to all causal processes. Certainly, our direct experiences of causal processes involve experiences of certain spatial and temporal relations between cause and effect, as Hume himself noted. In the examples I have relied upon, such processes appear spatiotemporally continuous. But this does not by itself settle the ontological issue.

A fundamental causal law, however, is either a force-law or a law relating events. What then is the logical form of causal laws themselves? For these are not second-order singular statements such as (1). Two options suggest themselves. One is to treat the causal relation between events as a relation, and to treat events as particulars. The second suggestion is to denote events by means of singular statements, and to treat the causal relation as a sentential operator.

The first option most nearly parallels (1). Given an instance of schema (1), the corresponding law would be derived by replacing reference to properties with quantification over events of certain types, and replacing reference to a second-order relation with reference to a cognate relation between events, which I shall write 'C^*.' Let e and e' be variables ranging over events, and define the following predicates which apply to events. '$P^*(e)$' is true just in case e is constituted by some particular(s) being P. '$Q^*(e)$' is true just in case e is constituted by some particular(s) being Q. '$T^*(e)$' is true just in case e occurs at time T and '$S^*(e)$' is true just in case e occurs at location S^*. Then we may express the causal law corresponding to (1) thus:

(2) $(\forall e)(\exists e')\{[P^*(e) \ \& \ T^*(e) \ \& \ S^*(e)] \supset [Q^*(e') \ \&$
$(T^* + \delta T^*)(e') \ \& \ (S^* + \delta S^*)(e') \ \& \ C^*(e,e)]\}$
(In English: If anything is P at time T and place S, then something is caused to be Q at time $T + \delta T$ and place $S + \delta S$.)

Ontologically speaking, (2) is far more artificial that (1); but it is more nearly in accord with the way we speak about causes.

However the second option mentioned is more linguistically natural still. To express it, we need variables 'x,' 'y' ranging over the concrete particulars which are constituents of events, and a causal conditional operator '$\rightarrow$' which has modal strength. We further let 't' and 's' be variables ranging over times and locations respectively, and construct from '*Px*' and '*Qx*' the relations '*P(x,t,s)*' and '*Q(x,t,s)*.' The former is read: '*x* has property *P* at time *t* and location *s*.' Then we have:

(3) $(\forall x)(\exists y)[P(x,t,s) \rightarrow Q(y,t+\delta t, s+\delta s)]$
   (In English: If anything were *P* at *t* and *s*, then it would make something be *Q* at $t + \delta t$ and $s + \delta s$.)

None of these three schemas yet exhibits a salient feature of most physical laws, namely, the fact that they express a functional relation between the magnitudes of determinate properties falling under certain determinables. Where *P* and *Q* are determinate properties which can be assigned magnitudes, we may introduce a magnitude function on them: $\mu[P,t,s]$ gives the magnitude of *P* at time *t* and location *s*. Then the fact that the causal relation between *P* and *Q* assumes the functional form *f* (relative to the units of measurement for *P* and *Q*) can be expressed, making use of (1), by:

(4) $[C(P,Q, \delta t, \delta s)] \equiv \{f(\mu\,[P,t,s]) = \mu[Q,t+\delta t, s+\delta s]\}$
   (In English: The causal relation obtains between *P* and *Q* just in case the magnitude of *Q* is function *f* of the magnitude of *P*.)

If *P* is a complex property, its magnitude will be some function *g* of the magnitudes of its constituent properties, $\{p_1, \ldots, p_n\}$:

(5) $\mu[P,t,s] = g\{\mu[p_1,t,s,], \ldots, \mu[p_n,t,s]\}$

The fact that forces have magnitudes suggests the intelligibility, further, of placing the relation '*C*' in the range of the magnitude function. In that case, we may represent the force associated with a given cause by:

(6) $\mu[C(P,Q, \delta t, \delta s)] = f(\mu\,[P])$
   (In English: The magnitude of the force involved in the production of a *Q* by a *P* is a function *f* of the magnitude of *P*.)

and the force associated with a given effect by:

(7) $\mu[C(P,Q, \delta t, \delta s)] = h(\mu\,[Q])$

4. THE UNIVERSALITY OF CAUSAL LAWS

We note next a difficulty which attends the fact that we have produced three schemas, (1), (2), and (3), for expressing causal facts. If the same causal fact can be expressed in any of the three ways, then it should be possible to show that (1), (2), and (3) are formally, or at least "metaphysically," equivalent. But how is this to be done? For example, (1) is the schema of a second-order singular statement, whereas (3) is the schema of a first-order general statement. Moreover, (3) is a type of conditional, whereas (1) is not. The operator '→', which appears in (3) must be interpreted in such a way that (3) entails

(8) $(\forall x)(\exists y)[P(x,t,s) \supset Q(y,t+\delta t, s+\delta s)]$

It is not clear why (1) ought to entail (3). In a closely related objection, Hochberg (1981) has challenged the claim that (1) entails (8). Hochberg's point, which derives from an argument of Gustav Bergmann's, is that (1) is atomic whereas (8) is not. Thus (1) cannot entail (8) according to any standard pattern of formal entailment. As Hochberg says, one should be prepared to introduce a new pattern of entailment to warrant the inference from (1) to (3).

I think we should agree with Bergmann and Hochberg that the pattern of reasoning which takes us from (1) to (8) is not one which should be characterized as a formal inference. But this does not show at all that there is not a necessary connection between the truth of (1) and the truth of (8). The supposition that there is such a connection is hard to escape and indeed not without close analogues. For such analogues (I do not say exact parallels) we do not have far to seek. Thus the fact that red is darker than pink has the consequence that each instance of red is darker than any instance of pink; and hence that red-colored things are darker in color than pink things. And similarly the fact that being a spherical surface is necessarily connected to the property of enclosing a spatial volume, has the consequence that every such surface encloses a volume. As noted, my analogues are not exact parallels: for example, (8) involves an existential quantifier; the first-order proposition about red and pink things does not. Moreover, not every second-order predicate which can be truly applied to properties can be applied, even derivatively, to the instances of these properties or to the particulars which instantiate them: witness the second-order predicate 'being multiply instantiable.' This alone makes it unlikely that there is any purely formal representation of such inferences as the ones just mentioned. However, it casts no doubt upon the propriety of those inferences. The inference from the existence of a second-order causal relation between properties to the existence of causal relations, in a derivative sense, between events has equally unblemished credentials.

In view of such putative examples, someone who analyzes causation as founded upon a second-order relation has ample reason to affirm the connection between (1) and (3), and hence between (1) and (8). If causation is a second-order relation, it must be a relation in virtue of which instances of one property bring into being instances of another. For, what would be understood by the claim that two universals, *P* and *Q*, stood in a causal relation to each other? Certainly not that the one universal produces or creates the other. Most realists have held that universals cannot be created or destroyed; and in any case this is not the intention of those who have put forward the thesis in question. Rather, they understand the causal relation to be such that the instantiation of *P* results in the instantiation of *Q*. Appeal to a second-order relation reflects the fact that it makes no difference *which* instantiation of *P* we have: the very fact that it is an instantiation of *P* is what results in an instance of *Q*. Thus it is part of the nature of *P* that its instances produces instances of *Q*. Conceived in this way, the analysis represented by (1) entails a commitment to (E) (see p. 58).[2]

5. THE MODALITY OF CAUSAL LAWS

Most realists have believed that truths about universals are not merely timelessly true, but that they are necessarily true as well. They have believed that if a universal has any characteristic, other than relations to particulars, that characteristic is part of its nature. The universal in question would not be the universal that it is if it did not have that characteristic. I shall not attempt a defense of any thesis as general as this one. But in Chapter 8, I shall defend the claim that the causal relations into which a physical universal enters constitute part of its nature. If the truths which satisfy schema (1) are necessary truths, then it follows that causal laws are necessary truths, and we will have accounted for the modal element in the connective '$\rightarrow$', provided that (1) and (3) are equivalent.

At present I shall consider the contrary thesis – namely, the claim that truths satisfying (1) are contingent truths. It is surprising that both Dretske (1977) and Armstrong (1977, 1983) make this claim, which they suppose to be compatible with their claim that causal laws are in some sense necessary. That is, both Dretske and Armstrong take truths of the form of (1) to entail truths of the form of (3), where '$\rightarrow$' is interpreted modally; yet they also take the former truths to be contingent truths. I do not believe that these two positions are consistent.

Unfortunately neither Dretske nor Armstrong provide much defense for their view. Armstrong speaks of one property necessitating another; he even speaks of this being an aspect of the natures of properties. His primary reason for denying the necessity of these relational truths seems to be an adherence to the empiricist doctrine that all necessary truths are *a priori* truths.[3] For Armstrong holds – correctly – that nomic and causal connections cannot be known *a priori*. This however is weak ground upon which to build the denial of the necessity of causal relations. Serious questions have been raised in recent years concerning the coextensivity of necessity and *aprioricity*.[4]

Dretske argues that a contingent connection between two properties P and Q can yield a non-contingent universal connection between instances of being P and instances of being Q because the relation between P and Q transcends the contingent fact that these properties are instantiated where they are. Putting it in terms of possible worlds, Dretske's argument is that '$C(P,Q, \delta t, \delta s)$' if true, asserts something true in possible worlds other than the actual world as well as in the actual one; whereas a mere universal statement, e.g., '$(\forall x)(Px \supset Qx)$' says something only about the extension of 'P' and 'Q' in the actual world. This shows why causal laws can support counterfactuals whereas accidental generalizations cannot.

This argument does not establish the conclusion it seeks to establish. '$C(P,Q, \delta t, \delta s)$' is true in possible worlds in which the extensions of P and Q differ from their actual-world extensions; but this is also the case with '$(\forall x)(Px \supset Qx)$.' Each is true in possible worlds in which other contingent propositions, true in the actual world, are false. But each is, on Dretske's account, false in some possible worlds. If there is a possible world in which '$C(P,Q, \delta t, \delta s)$' is false, then what is the truth-value, in the actual world, of the statement that, if a thing were P at t, s, then something would be Q at $t+\delta t$, $s+\delta s$? Standardly, in possible world semantics, subjunctive conditionals are taken to assert that their consequent holds in every possible world of a certain class in which the antecedent holds. But what is that class? Perhaps Dretske means to assert that the class of possible worlds in which '$C(P,Q, \delta t, \delta s)$' is true is a proper subclass of the possible worlds at which all P's are Q's; that is that there are worlds in which P's are only accidentally Q's. The actual world (and certain others) then are ones in which all P's are Q's, but something more is true as well: namely there being a relation between P and Q. But now it is still entirely mysterious why '$C(P,Q, \delta t, \delta s)$' should sustain counterfactuals, whereas '$(\forall x)(Px \supset Qx)$' does not. Failing the specification of a relevant class of possible worlds in which a conditional's consequent must be true whenever its antecedent is, what remains of Dretske's claim? If '$C(P,Q,\delta t,\delta s)$' is true but contingent, then there is a possible world at which '$C(P,Q,\delta t,\delta s)$' is false, a world at which it is false that if a thing were P at t, s, then something would be Q at $t+\delta t$, $s+\delta s$. But this is (in any standard S5 modal system) to say that the latter is actually, not just possibly, false. Thus I believe it imperative to maintain that truths such as '$C(P,Q,\delta t,\delta s)$' are necessary truths, true in every possible world in which the relevant universals exist, though they are not, of course, truths of logic.[5] That claim I shall argue for at length in Chapter 8.

4 Causation and induction

1. POST-HUMEAN APPROACHES

The connection between views about causation and attempts to justify inductive reasoning is sufficiently close that some philosophers[1] have taken success at the latter as a litmus-test for the truth of the former. I do not agree with this approach. Like Hume, I believe that the nature of causal connections must be understood prior to, and independently of, solutions to the problem of induction. Like Hume, I also hold that the problem of induction cannot be solved if Hume's analysis of causal connections is correct. But that analysis is one I have rejected. It is natural, therefore, to inquire whether and to what extent a necessitarian can justify inductive inference.

Not everyone, of course, is convinced that Hume's analysis renders the problem of induction insoluble. Some, such as Ayer and Goodman, adopt modernized versions of Hume's own solution. This is the We-Do-It-Anyway view. Perhaps one can formulate rules, as Goodman has valiantly striven to do, which govern the entrenchment of predicates. But why should entrenchment bear on justified projectibility? In reality, justification is abandoned in favor of human psychology and practice. Or rather, the former is seen as inseparable from, or reducible to, the latter. But this does not mesh well with the conception of justification which we in fact have; one that is linked to a realistic conception of truth. If human psychology and actual practice are to be philosophical touchstones, then the claims of these ordinary conceptions of truth and justification cannot be lightly dismissed.

A second approach is to admit that the problem is insoluble, but cheerfully to claim that it does not need to be solved – at least not for the purposes of scientific inquiry. Popper introduced this line of thought, which I call the Sour-Grapes view. It has at least three defects. First: most of us want to know how it *is* with the world, not merely lots of ways it isn't. Second, even falsifying observation-statements are in Popper's own view not certain. They require – and can supposedly achieve – confirmation. An inspection of the ways in which observation-statements are justified and confirmed easily reveals, I think, that their confirmation involves inductive reasoning. For observation statements concerning material objects are reliable only insofar as the perceptual processes which lead to them are "normal" and in "good order." To justify the latter claims requires causal knowledge of various sorts – knowledge for which our only evidence is indirect. Third, even Popperians admit the need, from a practical or action-guiding standpoint, of inductive predictions.[2]

Thirdly, we have the The-Buck-Stops-Here position of Strawson, Russell, and others. According to it the principles of inductive reasoning (or some subset of them) are such that a search for justification is inappropriate. Like the fundamental rules of deduction, they can be appealed to in justifying other inferences, but cannot themselves be justified by reduction to any more elementary reasoning. In Strawson's view, these principles appear to be analytic; Russell seems to hold that they are synthetic *a priori* truths. But in either case, to sustain this line of argument, one needs at least to show that the validity of basic inductive principles is as self-evident as that of, say, *modus ponens*. This has not been done.[3] Indeed, against the background of Hume's ontology, some of the required principles become decidedly *un*intuitive.

A variety of other justifications of induction are either pragmatic (Salmon 1962-63; Burks 1977) or "local" in that they assume certain principles that are neither established *a priori*, nor entailed by any finite body of evidence (see Levi 1967). Pragmatic justifications do not supply any grounds at all for assigning likelihoods to propositions not entailed by our evidence; in addition and for this very reason, they fall prey to the same difficulty about using inductive reasoning to guide action as does Popper's view. Arguing that, say, enumerative induction gives us our best bet with respect to forming expectations about the future – competing methods being only as good or worse – they nevertheless must concede that such reasoning gives us no assurance whatever that the bet will be won.

Local theories, on the other hand, can be regarded as useful contributions to a solution of the problem. They may help us locate the minimum assumptions upon which inductive logics can be founded; and further, they develop the formal apparatus of such logics. But from the point of view of a foundationalist, they no more *solve* the fundamental problem than Hume himself solved it.

Finally, there is a different strategy which is worthy of mention, although I cannot name any philosopher who explicitly makes use of it. The Inflationist Strategy, as I shall call it, is inspired by a maneuver which is aimed at another problem, the problem of distinguishing laws from accidental generalizations. But clearly the solution of that problem might be taken to invite a solution to the problem of induction. For to ascertain that a generalization is a law, or lawlike, and not accidental, is, arguably, to ascertain that its instances stand in the sort of evidential relation to it which warrants projection.

The maneuver proceeds by attempting to subsume low-level generalizations under an ascending hierarchy of higher-level generalizations embracing wider and wider classes of instances. The inspiration for the hierarchical model is to be found in the reductive explanations employed in the sciences (e.g., biochemical explanations of biological phenomena). A candidate generalization is deemed lawlike if, roughly, it has a position in such a hierarchy of generalizations, and no member of the hierarchy has been falsified by disconfirming instances. The upshot of this maneuver is that a generalization can be regarded as accidental if it finds no home in such a hierarchy.[4] Because other members of the hierarchy must have positive instances and no negative ones, the field of phenomena among which relevant observations can be obtained is vastly broadened.

It is true enough that we think of laws of nature as joined together in a systematic way, whereas accidental generalizations ought to be only accidentally associated with one another. But there is another natural motive which undoubtedly informs this way of construing the distinction. If a generalization is merely accidental, then "the odds are" that it will at some point be violated. Still a generalization may have very few instances, and all of these positive. Here an argument from "the odds" is of little help – unless the field of relevant observable events can be broadened. This is what the Inflationist Strategy achieves. If a whole system of generalizations receives confirmation and no disconfirmation, then its members "must be" lawlike, for the odds against this are vanishingly small. Unfortunately this strategy is powerless against Humean skepticism. Hume's argument shows that any regular pattern of events, no matter how wide-ranging, may be destroyed tomorrow, and that we can have no reason for thinking that it will not be. As we shall see, however, reasoning similar to that which underlies the Inflationist Strategy can legitimately be employed by those who do not accept Hume's theory of causation.

Perhaps some radically new approach to induction, compatible with the Regularity Theory of causation, will yet emerge; but I think it is reasonable to say that the problem cannot be solved within that framework. The consequences of a failure to solve the problem may well extend far beyond its universally recognized implications for practical action and scientific theorizing. Consider the causal theory of perception, as well as other causal theories of more recent vintage (of reference, knowledge, and so forth) which have begun to receive wide attention. If such theories are coupled with a Humean account of causation, the problem of induction is of paramount importance. In order that any singular causal assertion can be known to be true, it must be established that every circumstance which has and will satisfy the antecedent conditions relevant to that assertion is followed by a similar outcome. In consequence, the truth of a singular causal claim cannot be known unless it is known either that all other instances of the law which covers that claim have been observed, or that the law can be inductively supported. Lacking a solution to the problem of induction, one has no rational grounds for belief in singular causal assertions.

Causal theories make it a necessary condition for the existence of a certain state of affairs that some appropriate causally linked chain of events has occurred. The causal theory of perception, for example, requires that in order for a perceiver P to perceive an object O, it is necessary that certain sensory experiences of P be caused, *via* a suitable causal sequence, by O. But in order for it to be the case that O's presence caused P's experience, it must be the case that in every future circumstance in which a P-like observer and O-like object are brought together under identical conditions, the observer has a qualitatively identical experience. The Humean can give no reasons whatever for expecting this condition to be satisfied. Hence if he adheres to a causal theory of perception, he has no reasons for believing – at least prior to the end of human existence – that anyone has ever perceived any object. This I take to be an intolerable consequence. Parallel consequences are entailed, *mutatis mutandis*, for other causal theories. The tentacles of the problem of induction thus reach far. Can it be solved, however, even by those philosophers willing to embrace natural necessities?

2. HUME REVISITED

It is not my intention to attempt a full solution of the problem of induction or of all the problems involved in using inductive reasoning. For example, the application of inductive reasoning requires the use of premises concerning past events. Thus justifying inductive inferences requires in part justifying other forms of nondeductive reasoning: notably, solving the problem of knowledge of the past. This amounts to the problem of justifying inferences from observed effects to unobserved causes, and I shall only touch upon that problem.

Most of what has been written about the problem of induction has been written by empiricists under the sway of Hume, and very little by philosophers who have thought that causal relations involve a kind of objective necessity.[5] Clearly this is not due to the fact that there is no problem of induction for a philosophy of the latter sort; it is due rather to the fact that advocates of such a philosophy are in short supply. For although there can be little doubt about the tremendous dialectical advantage which acquaintance with causal relations bestows, the achievement of an adequate account of inductive procedure from this perspective is by no means a trivial task.

The application of inductive reasoning can be usefully subdivided into four tasks. These are:

1. Isolating and identifying significant patterns of regular recurrence from the complex welter of actual experience.
2. Isolating all those factors which are causally relevant to what will happen in a given circumstance.
3. Justifying the prediction of single future occurrences.
4. Justifying generalizations based on finite evidence.

In some favored cases, a philosophy which accepts direct acquaintance with causal relations can accomplish these tasks in a relatively straightforward fashion. The favored cases are those in which one is directly acquainted with a causing event, and with all of the causal relations of which it constitutes a relatum. In certain such cases, I have claimed in Chapter 1 that in principle it is possible to predict, at least roughly, what the effect will be even in the absence of any relevant previous experience. Clearly where this is possible, the first problem becomes irrelevant, and the third and fourth are solved provided the second one can be. Even in the most favored cases, however, the second problem raises difficulties. What is in any case clear is that many – doubtless most – of the inductions we actually perform are not ones whose foundation rests upon such favored circumstances. Either we are not directly acquainted with the cause(s) of an event, or we are not acquainted with the causal relation(s) present, or we are acquainted with neither. In such instances, it is evident that one's inductive inferences must rely upon observed regularities – that is, upon enumerative induction, upon the method of difference, and upon the panoply of statistical procedures which science and common experience alike employ. Of what significant advantage, then, is it to have had experience of causal relation? My answer to this question will focus on three central inductive procedures: Mill's methods, enumerative induction, and Bayes' method.

Each of Mill's inductive methods assumes the truth of some general empirical propositions, namely, that the phenomenon to be explained has a cause, and that this cause can be found in some restricted domain. As an example, I shall discuss a particular one of Mill's inductive methods – the method he calls the Direct Method of Difference. This method enables one to eliminate from the antecedent circumstances of an event those which are causally irrelevant to it. It does this by varying, or eliminating, one component of those circumstances while holding the others fixed. If C is a complex event consisting of $C_1, \ldots,$ and C_n, antecedent to E, we ascertain whether C_1 is causally related to E by examining the consequences which follow an event C' similar in all respects to C, save for the absence of an event corresponding to C_1. If C' is followed by an event E' exactly similar to E, then C_1 is not causally related to E.

The application of this reasoning depends, as Mill realized (1973, Book III, Chapter 8, §3), on the assumption that on the second occasion, there is no event beyond those included in C' which is causally relevant in E'. For otherwise, the causal contribution of C_1 to E, lacking in C', might be replaced by an unknown causal influence outside of C'. To eliminate this possibility, it is at the very least necessary to rule out (significant) influence from events spatially and/or temporally distant from E'. What grounds are there for ruling out non-local causal influences? Unless these can be ruled out *a priori* – which seems doubtful – one must rely on inductive grounds. Such grounds are available – but only if enumerative or Bayesian inductive procedures can be justified. In that case, it will be possible to argue from past experience that known types of action at a distance, mediated by force-fields, have effects which can be calculated and which fall off asymptotically with increasing spatiotemporal separation. Hence it is necessary to examine enumerative induction and Bayes' method, if we are to justify applications of the Direct Method of Difference.

If there is no real causal connectedness in nature, if nature consists of nothing over and above a sequence of events, then no inductive procedure can help us achieve justified true belief. The reason is simple. No matter what patterns observation of the world has revealed to us, and no matter how striking these patterns may be, the structure of the set of as-yet unobserved events remains entirely open. There cannot be any question of *explaining* the existence of such patterns, except perhaps in the trivial sense of showing them to form parts of bigger patterns among the set of observed events. That sort of explanation, however, would have no evidential weight concerning the continuation of such patterns in the as-yet unobserved events. If we think of the universe as being constituted by a single sequence of (global) events, then by Humean lights any coherently imaginable event can occur equally well anywhere in the sequence. The Humean envisages the set of available hypotheses concerning the world to consist of, or at least to entail, a set of propositions, each of which specifies one of the logically possible event-histories which can be constructed from the totality of consistently imaginable events. Even if the set of consistently imaginable event-types were not infinite, the number of infinite event-sequences that can be constructed by permuting these events would clearly be infinite.[6] Conversely, even if cosmic history contains only finitely many events, we have good reason to believe that the number of event-types is infinite; for the possible number of determinate properties (of length, color, etc.) appears to be nondenumerably infinite.

The past history of the world has "eliminated" many of these possible event-sequences; but there are infinitely many distinct sequences whose beginnings exactly match the past history of the world, and whose future continuations diverge in every way conceivable. Each of these sequences corresponds to a world-hypothesis, and each must be accorded equal weight on Humean grounds, since each is equally well-confirmed by past events. Which is to say that the past does not confirm any of these hypotheses at all insofar as they pertain to events not yet observed; it is merely logically compatible with each of them.

These considerations suffice to show why any principle of the uniformity of nature requires justification; but they also show why the prospect of solving the problem of induction by invoking an *a priori* principle of inductive inference from past to future is a forlorn hope. Such principles have been invoked by Strawson (1952), Stove (1973), and Mackie (1979), among others. Let it be conceded, we are told, that Hume demonstrated the circularity of any justification of a principle of cosmic uniformity. Still, Hume thought such a principle to be required because he thought inferences from past to future must be deductive in form (and no such argument could be valid without some such principle as a premise). But Hume never considered the possibility that there might be cogent arguments whose premises probabilify, rather than deductively entail, their conclusions. And his arguments count not at all against this possibility, provided the principles of probabilistic inference employed by these arguments are *a priori*, logical relations which are either self-evident or are analyzable into simpler rules which are so.

We should be skeptical of this maneuver, ingenious as it is. I shall set aside the exegetical question, whether Hume ever addressed the cogency of such arguments. It seems unlikely that he ever did consider this question. Nevertheless I think he would have found such inferences unintelligible (or uncogent); and I think ample reason for this can be extracted from what Hume does say.

An initial ground for suspicion is this. Suppose we represent deductive and probabilistic argument-forms, respectively as follows:

(a) $$\frac{P}{\therefore \text{(Necessarily) } Q}$$ (b) $$\frac{P}{\therefore \text{(Probably) } Q}$$

Corresponding to every valid deductive rule of inference, there exists a truth of logic – e.g. '$P \supset Q$' in the case of (a). Since (b) embodies a rule of inference which is supposed to establish a logical relation between its premise and its conclusion, we should expect it to similarly correspond to some truth of logic. But what can this truth be? Would it be: 'Probably $(P \supset Q)$'? Or, to make the case more nearly parallel to (a), should we countenance a modality ('probability') which lies somewhere between contingency and logical necessity? Then, just as '"$P \supset Q$" is logically necessary' can be represented by '$\square_{\text{log.}} (P \supset Q)$', we would countenance 'probably' as a modal operator governing '$P \supset Q$'.

Either way, 'probably' in this context cannot denote probability psychologically or subjectively understood as degree of belief, any more than the necessity of '$P \supset Q$' in context (a) can mean subjective certainty. The validity of such arguments does not depend upon the existence of certain mental states. 'Probably' can here be interpreted in only two ways. It can mean (1) degree of support relative to the evidence.[7] Or, it could mean (2) that among the conditional propositions whose logical form is similar to that of '$P \supset Q$' in (b), more than half are true. We can set aside the elucidation of the relevant sense of similarity of form. 'Probably $(P \supset Q)$' is not *a priori* on either interpretation. Interpretation (1) relies upon the opaque notion of support relative to evidence (which in this case is nil, and so could be represented by any tautology). To introduce this unexplained notion of support here would be to beg the very question at issue. On interpretation (2), it is obvious that a justification of 'Probably $(P \supset Q)$' must appeal to some principle of cosmological uniformity. So there are good Humean reasons for refusing this ploy.[8]

Perhaps this attempt to draw a parallel between deductive and inductive inferences is misguided. The advocate of the probabilist view, as I shall call it, might reasonably refuse to accept the suggestion that an inductive inference is acceptable if and only if 'Probably $(P \supset Q)$' is true. He might insist that "'P' probabilifies 'Q'" expresses a relation between 'P' and 'Q' which is not expressable in any way which involves the material conditional. It is a relation which would hold regardless of what the empirical facts are. One might, for example, suggest that such a relation obtains between the fact that one has a certain memory and the correctness of the memory.[9] It might be, after all, that we would affirm that a memory probabilifies the remembered event even in a world in which independent checks consistently revealed that our memories were mistaken. And this might be taken to show that we do have the notion of such a relation. But what could this notion be? Is the fact that one proposition probabilifies another a truth which we acquire through reflection or through perception? Hume, in effect, denies that we come by such a notion in either way, and I concur. We must, of course, be able to explain the inductive intuitions we have. But one can do this, as Hume would, by appealing to certain natural tendencies which we have, tendencies which are merely features of our psychological makeup. Much earlier, I suggested that a Humean might respond in similar fashion if challenged to explain the intuition that a person who experienced a blow for the first time would be able to make various predictions about the ensuing events. But here, it seems to me, the probabilist and I are not on an equal footing when it comes to responding to Hume. For I can point – so I claim – to an actual element of our experience which explains the intuition about the reaction to a blow. And I do not see what comparable constituent of our experience or thought there is to which the probabilist can appeal by way of deflecting Hume's challenge.

But no matter. For it is easy enough to see that any such rule of inference which goes from past regularity to future similarity cannot be known *a priori*, and is not in the relevant sense a rule of logic. If it were, its cogency would be untouched by any empirical fact. That is, if '*Q* is probable relative to *P*' is *a priori*, then no empirical proposition *R* can be such that its truth falsifies this claim.[10] No logically possible state of affairs would be such that its possibility could undermine the inference from *P* to *Q* (provided that '*P*' expressed one's "total evidence"). But Hume's argument shows that such a state of affairs is conceivable, hence logically possible, and that whether it obtains or not cannot be known by us. (Thus if we would not be justified in saying that memories probabilify the remembered events in a world in which memories were *known* to be regularly false, we would not be justified in saying that memories probabilify the remembered events in a world in which we had no idea whether they were or not.) The state of affairs in question is one which obtains when no two distinct events are so related that any intrinsic feature of the one forces or necessitates or makes more likely than not the occurrence of the other. For then *A*, which immediately precedes *B*, is not so relevant; and neither are all the past sequences of *A*-type events which were uniformly followed by *B*-type events. We admit this much by our refusal to project what we take to be accidental regularities. Unless we have direct evidence of the existence of such intrinsic relations – so Hume's argument goes – we could have no *in*direct evidence for their existence in cases where they are unperceived; for the existence of such a relation in the objects would be, strictly speaking, unintelligible. But if we cannot hypothesize the existence of such a relation, we can have no reason to expect the future to resemble the past, *even if the past is known to have been patterned*. In this situation, we could *not* say that there was an evidential relation of support between past patterns and future-directed conclusions. So if we do not know *a priori* of the existence of a necessitation relation between events, we do not know *a priori* of any such relation of inductive support. In that case any rule of inference which purports to license expectations about the future is illegitimate.

Of course Hume might be mistaken about the nonexistence of such relations. I have argued that he is mistaken. But that is an empirical matter. No *a priori* rule of inference could be such that its cogency depends upon such empirical considerations. Thus we may conclude that this stratagem for solving Hume's problem will not pass muster.

Evidently it is necessary to begin instead, as has been done in Chapter 1, by directly addressing Hume's ontological concern. But how, then, does the supposition that a past or presently observed pattern among events may reflect the operation of a necessary causal relation help us to escape the Humean impasse?

One thing is clear. If a causal relation (in our strong sense) ever does obtain between observable events, then some sort of pattern or regularity will appear in our experience, on the assumption that we witness repeated instances of these event-types. For if causal relations connect universals, then whenever the universals which characterize the causing event are instantiated, those characterizing the effect will also be. A causal relation between universals entails the corresponding universal generalization. But the converse inference cannot be made; and thus from a finite patterned sample, or even from a total sample which encompasses every existing instance of the relevant event-types, one cannot deduce the corresponding necessary relation. Can we, then, have inductive grounds for such an inference? Can we, in other words, have inductive grounds for distinguishing between accidental generalizations and laws of nature? I think we can.

3. ENUMERATIVE INDUCTION AND BAYES' METHOD

Although enumerative induction and the Bayesian theory both founder on the seas of the regularity analysis of causation, they do so in slightly different ways. Bayesians face the problem of infinitesimal priors; enumerative induction faces the problem of showing why the future is more likely to copy the past than continue in any one of an infinitely large variety of alternative ways. Burks (1977) and Salmon (1962–3), following Reichenbach, support the fundamentality of enumerative induction. R. D. Rosenkrantz (1983), on the other side, would jettison enumerative induction in favor of a Bayesian policy. Rosenkrantz's rejection of enumerative induction leans heavily on the problems generated by the confirmation paradoxes of Hempel and Goodman. Rosenkrantz also tries to show that in cases of conflict between them, the Bayesian strategy wins out over enumerative induction.

The natural necessitarian's attitude toward these questions cannot be worked out in full detail here. Only the main outlines of a solution will be attempted. But, to anticipate a bit, we can say that this solution is essentially Bayesian in spirit: it makes use of prior probabilities. At the same time, the necessitarian uses something like enumerative induction, but in a special way. The role of "enumerative induction" is in guiding the formulation of plausible hypotheses – that is, it has a role in what is sometimes called "the logic of discovery." The role of Bayesian reasoning lies in its application to the testing and confirmation of hypotheses, that is, in the "logic of justification." As for the various paradoxes of confirmation, no explicit treatment of them will be offered. It is worth stating, therefore, that I believe the necessitarian has the resources to solve these problems in a rather intuitively natural way. It will be part of the burden of the present discussion to show that, by contrast, neither enumerative induction nor Bayesian arguments can hope to overcome Goodman-type difficulties for those who avail themselves of a Humean ontology: on this point Rosenkrantz is in error. I shall begin however with a general difficulty about enumerative induction.

A. J. Ayer (1973: 149–50) (among others) has argued that if natural laws have modal strength, they will be even harder to confirm than if they are taken to be generalizations. A generalization embraces all the actual instances of a law; but a modal law, in effect, generalizes over possible instances as well. Thus it is a stronger generalization, and hence more weakly supported by any finite observed sample of positive instances. Natural necessitarians must and do argue against Ayer that the admission of modal concepts makes the solution of the problem of induction *easier*, not more difficult. One way to show this would be to show that modal laws permit us to make use of a conception of explanation – and hence, of arguments to the best explanation – of which the Humean cannot avail himself. What is required is an explanatory hypothesis which, if true, renders an observed sequence of events more "probable" than it would be on any competing hypothesis. Indeed, natural necessitarians all make use of some form of the argument from inverse probability – that is, of a Bayesian argument. I shall present my own version of this argument, which is perhaps more general than others which have appeared.

Let us consider a possibly infinite sequence of events, a sequence which may or may not display a patterned order. By an event-sequence I shall mean, in what follows, a chronologically ordered set of event-pairs such that the antecedent event (or cause) of each pair is of the same type. The consequent events may all be similar or not. (We can think of the sequence, if we like, as being generated by all the repeated performances of some experiment: the flipping of a coin, or the colliding of two billiard balls.) Now, *any* such sequence, having occurred, is equally deserving of an explanation – if there is an explanation to be had. On the Humean view of nature (and setting aside the essentially irrelevant possibility of deriving the course of a sequence from some more general set of generalizations), the role of laws is to do nothing more than to summarize the facts; thus no such sequence is intrinsically more explainable than any other, there being no fact about the world which renders any sequence intrinsically more likely than any other one. 'Explanation' consists, essentially, of a recitation of the actual facts. If a sequence is regular, then we may give the appearance of providing something more powerful by way of an explanation by virtue of the facts being prospectively summarizable in a particularly simple and elegant form – a universal generalization. But the impression of greater explanatory power is an illusion, fostered perhaps by the fact that a universal generalization typically – and thus far unjustifiably – embraces cases which have not yet been examined. At any rate, we should agree with the Humean that *any* sequence calls equally for an explanation, if one can be found. Our point is that, by Humean lights, the sort of explanation available to explain a regular sequence is in no material sense *better* than the sort of explanation which can be given a random sequence.

Richard Fumerton (1980) has argued, correctly in my opinion, that for a consistent Humean, arguments to the best explanation are to be understood as just disguised inductive arguments. Leaving aside questions of simplicity, an explanation is "good" or plausible just in case we have inductive grounds for believing that it correctly summarizes the facts, and correctly predicts the future. We think, for example, that the molecular theory of gases gives us good explanations of gas behavior only because, on inductive grounds, we have reason to believe that small particles such as the postulated "molecules" have behaved and will behave somewhat like colliding billiard balls on a smaller scale. If we had no evidence that molecules (and billiard balls) regularly behave in the required ways, the explanation in question would have the status of empty speculation.

At this point we are in a position to state the contrast between the Humean and the necessitarian, as follows. For the Humean, *no* conceivable sequence is intrinsically more explainable, or better explainable, than any other. But for the necessitarian, regular sequences are candidates for significant explanation, whereas irreducibly chaotic sequences are not. He has available to him a much more full-blooded conception of explanation; but it is one which only admits sequences which are in some sense regular. (This is not to say that the necessitarian can never hope to explain apparently chaotic sequences. It may be possible to break up an apparently chaotic sequence into disconnected parts, and to show how each part is an element in some other regular sequence.)

The fact that, for a Humean, every conceivable sequence is "on a par" generates, as we have seen, the problem of induction. In its Bayesian form, this problem is reflected in the fact that the degree to which a piece of information confirms any hypothesis is proportional to the product of the previous degree of confirmation of that hypothesis and the degree of expectation which the hypothesis confers upon the information in question. Now because, prior to the collection of any empirical information, all the Humean hypotheses are on a par, this means that they should all receive the same initial "weight" or epistemic probability. That is, it is reasonable to make use of a Principle of Indifference: as between any two self-consistent hypotheses, when one has no more evidence for or against the one than for or against the others one must assign them equal epistemic probabilities. Secondly, if the available hypotheses are exhaustive and mutually exclusive, then the sum of their probabilities must always sum to one. That is the Normalization Principle. But for a Humean the number of conceivable event-sequences is clearly infinite. Thus, by the Principle of Indifference, and the Normalization Principle, each sequence must be assigned a prior probability of $1/\infty$, or, effectively, zero.[11] But the degree to which further information is made probable by any hypothesis is no greater than one. So the posterior epistemic probability of a Humean hypothesis can never be raised; it is always $1/\infty$. Thus inductive confirmation of a hypothesis is impossible, since initially each hypothesis, though consistent, is essentially "impossible," having a prior probability indistinguishable from zero. This is the so-called problem of the priors.[12] Hume's heirs have not laid his inductive skepticism to rest.

4. PRELUDE: INDIFFERENCE AND NORMALIZATION

The preceding paragraphs have made reference to two principles, the Principles of Indifference and Normalization. Something more must now be said about them; although they are not principles which (taken alone) sanction inferences from past to future, they have a central role in such reasoning. They are not formal principles of deductive logic. Yet both principles, I maintain, are *a priori* and self-evident.

The Normalization rule incorporates, first, a convention for quantitative probability assignments: the highest degree of probability (certainty) is given a value of 1, the lowest (certain falsehood) a value of 0. Then it says that if a set of hypotheses $\{h_1, \ldots, h_n\}$ is such that each excludes the others, and such that jointly they are known to exhaust the possibilities relative to a field F of phenomena, then the sum of their probabilities must total to 1. For their disjunction is known to be true; and the conjunction of any pair is known to be false.

Our version of the Principle of Indifference may be stated thus:

> If a given field F is covered by n hypotheses $\{h_1, \ldots, h_n\}$ which are jointly exhaustive and mutually exclusive, then relative to there being no evidence for or against any of these, each should be accorded a probability 1/n.

Though this principle seems quite intuitive, it has been subjected to a number of criticisms. Before defending it, however, I must say some things about its conceptual role in the argument which follows. One way of understanding Hume's challenge to inductive reasoning is to see that it is an attack upon the very intelligibility of the notion that one proposition should constitute evidence for another, where the first does not figure in a deductively valid argument whose conclusion is the second. Thus part of the task which any defense of induction must set itself is that of giving sense to the notion that some proposition e constitutes evidence for (or against) another proposition h.

The Principle of Indifference, as stated, makes use of the notion of evidence, but not in a way which presupposes that sense has been given to the notion of (nondeductive) positive or negative evidence.[13] The Principle applies where it is not the case that there is any such evidence – which is distinct from the case where positive and negative evidence for a hypothesis exist but balance. We can apply this principle even if we were to have no conception of what it would be for e to constitute confirming or disconfirming evidence for h.

It is of course one thing to understand what it would be to have positive but inconclusive evidence for h, and realize that one lacks evidence of that sort; and another to lack evidence by virtue of failing to understand the very notion of evidence. But we can proceed as follows. First, we have the *generic* notion of evidence, derived from that of deductively conclusive evidence. Can we in fact generalize this notion, find weaker species of it? Even if we do not initially understand the notion of weaker species, we can understand what it would mean to represent degrees of evidential support by numbers nominally ranging from zero to one. We would say that when e entails h, its degree of support for h is 1. And we would say that when e has no bearing on h, its degree of support for h is zero.[14] Now if someone does not understand at all what it would be for e to inconclusively confirm h, then he can at least understand that e provides him with no support for h, if it does not entail h. For such a one, e provides zero confirmation for h. Starting from this position, we must now develop an account of what it is for e to fractionally confirm (or disconfirm) h.

Part of the project, then, is to give content to the notion of inductive evidence. We begin with the Principle of Indifference, in terms of which prior probabilities can be generated, and with the notion that a hypothesis h can render certain observations e probable or improbable. (We shall confine attention to the deterministic case, in which h plus initial conditions entails e, in which case this relation is unproblematic.[15] Bayes' Theorem then does the rest of the work.)

A second conceptual matter concerns the notion of epistemic probability with which we are dealing. How is this to be understood? I should understand it as a normative notion:

> The epistemic probability that h is true $=$ $_{df.}$ the degree of confidence that one ought to repose in h.

"Degree of confidence (belief)" is a notion which can be understood by appeal to the phenomenology of belief. We know what it is to feel more or less certain about a proposition; and assigning numbers to such degrees is a plausible – if sometimes unrealistic – idealization. Furthermore, 'X ought to believe that P' can be explicated through appeal to cases of deductive validity and tautologousness. We use the expression 'ought' in the same univocal sense when we consider the question whether one ever ought to believe a proposition for which one lacks a sound deductive argument and which is not self-evident.

Although probability thus defined is an epistemic notion, it is not subjective in the sense of reflecting either actual or arbitrary degrees of belief. The rules which govern such epistemic probability assignments must be given objective justification. These constraints, as will become apparent, go beyond the usual minimal requirement of Bayesians, that probability assignments be consistent. And we need to go beyond. Consistency will keep the Dutch bookie at bay, but it won't satisfy the needs of science, or for that matter, build new bridges. A bridge engineer whose predictions about the behavior of his materials is guided by an arbitrary (though consistent) choice of priors would not be someone to rely upon to design bridges.

I turn now to a defense of the Principle of Indifference, which will be used to generate initial assignments of epistemic probability. The use of this principle does not, clearly, commit one to the theory that all probabilities are subjective or epistemic. However, we must address two arguments which purport to show that the principle is incoherent. The first difficulty is that the alternative hypothesis to which the principle is in a given case applied must be equally specific. For suppose $\{h_1, \ldots, h_n\}$ is a set of equispecific alternatives, so that applying the principle to the set yields, for each h_i, $P(h_i) = 1/n$. We can construct another $(n - 1)$-membered set of exhaustive, mutually exclusive hypotheses, namely, $\{h_1 \lor h_2, \ldots, h_n\}$. Applying the principle to this set, however, yields for each member a prior probability of $1/(n - 1)$. So we must require that the principle be applied only to equispecific alternatives, and this introduces the problem of deciding how, in general, to divide up the field of possibilities into such alternatives. If we count as alternative hypotheses a die's landing sixes, and it's not landing sixes, and assign each a probability of 1/2, then by parity of reasoning we must assign to each face a probability of 1/2; and this violates the requirement that the probabilities of all possible outcomes sum to 1. In practice meeting the requirement of equispecificity is often not difficult; but in any case the existence of problematic cases can for present purposes be conceded.[16] A critical step in the argument which follows concerns how to do this with respect to the alternatives confronted by the necessitarian. A second objection is this: if we know the die to be loaded, surely we shall not want to assign equal probability to each of its faces; but in that case, how are we to define a set of equiprobable alternatives among which we are indifferent – for the class of equispecific outcomes is the same whether the die is loaded or not. But this objection applies only to situations analogous to that of loaded dice; and we can for our purposes also ignore such cases. However, the objection is misguided in any case, as regards probability assignments which are strictly *a priori*. The only reasons for assigning unequal probabilities to the faces of a loaded die would perforce be inductive, and hence *a posteriori*. *A priori*, we have no reason to believe that weighting one side of the die will affect the distribution of falls: hence we ought to assign the same prior probabilities as for a fair die. Furthermore, the solution to the problem of induction does not require us to assign definite prior probabilities to each hypothesis, for in general posterior probabilities converge to the same values in a way largely independent of this. What is needed is something weaker: assurance that the priors are nonzero.

5. NECESSITARIAN INDUCTION

The inductive strategy of the necessitarian makes use, as Bayesians do, of an inverse probability argument. Schematically, the argument runs as follows. We observe an event-sequence which exhibits a regular, repetitive pattern. Intuitively, and in the absence of any auxiliary information, such a sequence is remarkable. The (*a priori*) odds are against it. Of course, the odds are equally great against any other particular sequence. But *if* (and only if) the sequence is a regular one, then there is a hypothesis, the truth of which would render the objective probability of the observed sequence very high, and the probability of any alternative sequence very low. What is this hypothesis? It is that there is a necessary connection between the constantly conjoined event-types.[17] By Bayes' Theorem, an event or event-sequence raises the probability of a hypothesis in proportion to the degree to which that hypothesis raises the expectation of its occurrence over its prior expectation. So the existence of the regular sequence enhances the chances that this hypothesis is true.

That is the heart of necessitarian reasoning. Obviously, there are a multitude of complications in its application. When an apparent regularity is violated, for example, it may yet be possible to show that regularity still obtains, only of a more complexly articulated sort. Hence talk of "other things being equal." The necessitarian strategy can also be applied in ways I shall not explore, for example, to the problem of justifying the reduction of low-level laws to deeper, more general theory.

What is more central is that the necessitarian argument involves two maneuvers which may initially appear to cancel each other. On the one hand, the strategy depends upon the fact that the prior probability of regular event-sequences is very low; it is this fact which prompts the search for an explanatory hypothesis. The longer the sequence, the more surprising its regularity, in the absence of an explanation. The longer – hence initially less probable – a regular sequence is, the stronger the case for an underlying explanation. But on the other hand, the more powerful an explanation is, the lower *its* intrinsic probability. Such, at least, is the case if explanatory power is understood in terms of degree of generality, and generality (for finite ranges) is measured by the number of instances a hypothesis covers. The more instances a hypothesis projects over, the lower its prior probability. So the more it can explain, the less it is (by Bayesian reasoning) confirmed by its positive instances. The necessitarian strategy depends *both* on the low prior probability of long regular sequences, and on the existence of explanatory hypotheses which project over infinitely long sequences of this type hypotheses whose power would appear to mandate priors of zero. How then, can the strategy succeed?

For the Humean, as has been shown, these two aspects of Bayesian strategy do indeed conflict. The prior probability of a hypothesis which postulates a specific regular sequence of event is just equal to the prior probability of any random sequence of events of the same length. This probability is effectively zero even for sequences of *finite* length (given an infinite variety of possible event-types); and it is certainly zero (or $1/\infty$) for infinite sequences. Thus the confirming power of regular sequences of increasing length is always cancelled by the decreasing prior probability of hypotheses strong enough to project over those sequences – certainly if the hypothesis projects to an infinity of cases. From the standpoint of confirmability, there is no distinction here between a hypothesis which predicts a universal regularity and a self-contradictory hypothesis. Neither is confirmable by evidence.

These considerations help to clarify what the necessitarian's strategy must be. He begins with a finite (but fairly long) sequence of events which display a patterned structure or regularity. He argues that the intrinsic probability of that sequence is, on pure chance, exceedingly small (as would be the chance probability of any particular random sequence). Next he argues that, since the sequence is regular, there is available to us a causal hypothesis which, if true, would make that sequence inevitable – give it objective probability of 1. That hypothesis can be shown to have the following features: (a) it is intelligible and consistent, provided that, as I have argued, empirical content can be given to the notion of natural necessity; (b) it is powerful enough to warrant projection over an open class of unexamined cases; (c) it is genuinely explanatory; and (d) its form enables the problem of zero priors to be outflanked. To formulate the relevant hypothesis, the necessitarian uses, in the simplest sort of case, enumerative induction. Thus one hypothesis which will explain the regular association of *A*-events with *B*-events is that there is a causal relation between *A*-hood and *B*-hood.[18] Bayesian reasoning can be used, in a manner to be explained, to gain confirmation for this hypothesis.

6. INTERLUDE ON HOW TO COUNT

The first step in the argument – and one of the most crucial – is to show that the necessitarian way of counting hypotheses is quite different from the way forced upon the Humean. For the Humean, each statement which proposes a a sequence of events, whether it is a "regular" sequence or not, counts as a distinct hypothesis; laws are but summaries of occurrences. Not so for the necessitarian. For him, each hypothesis proposes a causal structure, not (or at best derivatively) a sequence of events. And this raises the possibility that the field of independent hypotheses which vie for confirmation is finite rather than, as for the Humean, infinite. But if a finite field can be achieved, then the problem of zero priors is solved. Before attending to that detail, let us then see how to count hypotheses the necessitarian way.

What a hypothesis predicts is a set of observations or data. Its predictive "riskiness" prior to experimental confirmation is a function of the number of logically possible sequences of outcomes, confirmatory and disconfirmatory, which experimental tests of it could produce. Thus the chances that the results of a series of experimental tests will match the predicted ones becomes, *a priori*, vanishingly small as the number of tests goes to infinity. The degree of riskiness of a hypothesis, in that sense, is often infinitely high, whether it be a Humean or a necessitarian one. But its prior probability, in the sense relevant to a Bayesian calculation, is a function of the number of independent explanatory hypotheses which compete with it. (Not the number we happen to think of, but the number which could, in principle, be formulated.)[19] The Humean, because he takes hypotheses to be essentially summaries of the data, identifies the number of possible hypotheses with the number of possible sequences of test results, which is infinite. Thus, by the Principle of Indifference, he must assign each hypothesis a vanishingly small prior probability. The necessitarian does not proceed in this way. For him, a mere summary of the data does not explain that data at all; it is not a hypothesis. Putative laws, grounded in proposed structures of relations between properties, he does count. He need not, however, subscribe to an *a priori* Principle of Sufficient Reason. He need not rule out the possibility that the data literally have no explanation; but for him, this possibility amounts to just a *single* hypothesis, a hypothesis which is, by the way, compatible with any possible sequence of data. Because compatible with every data-sequence, it cannot be highly confirmed by any one of them, and hence not by one which is sufficiently "non-random" to be compatible with the predictions of some causal hypothesis. (This is so even if the causal hypothesis is one which, like the laws of quantum theory, permits some statistical latitude in the data. In that case, of course, confirmation requires longer runs of data.) For the necessitarian, then, the a-causal or random hypothesis counts as a *single* hypothesis, one compatible with any set of outcomes, and hence one which has no predictive power. It denies the existence of underlying structure.

Since this conclusion is crucial to the argument, it must be emphasized that it involves a certain conception of what an empirical hypothesis is and does. I have said that according to this conception, a hypothesis is *not* to be identified with – nor is it logically equivalent to – those states of affairs which it predicts. It is a conjecture about the existence (or nonexistence) of some stable underlying structure which necessitates what has happened and what will happen. It is only from the Humean perspective – a perspective which does not really admit this notion of explanation at all – that it seems natural to collapse the notion of a hypothesis into the notion of a proposition about a sequence of happenings. From the Humean point of view, the happenings are "all there is," so that it makes no sense to distinguish a hypothesis which predicts a given list of happenings, from a hypothesis which predicts the same list of happenings, but as non-random, grounded in some causal principle. Conversely, a Humean must distinguish one list of (random) happenings from another, as corresponding to distinct hypotheses, simply on the grounds that different event-types are listed, or that their order differs. If we discard the Humean perspective, we must still of course admit that the Humeans have a genuine hypothesis – namely, that the world is so constituted as to have *no* causal structure. From the point of view of that hypothesis, as we saw, *any* sequence of events – including any highly regular one – is equally possible; but each is also – under this hypothesis – *equally* a manifestation of what that hypothesis asserts concerning the nature of the world. Some of those sequences – the "regular" ones – are also compatible with – and predicted by – distinct, non-Humean hypotheses. The induction we want to perform is not one to predicted outcomes, though its success depends in part on the fulfillment of predicted outcomes; it is an induction to the existence of a structure which will explain those outcomes (except in the degenerate, but admissible, case of randomness). It is only *via* an induction which favors one explanatory hypothesis and disfavors competing ones, that we can justifiably move to predictions of single future events.

This view of the matter is corroborated by scientific practice. Indeed, induction does not proceed in the Humean manner in the very area of science which approximates most closely to the study of truly random phenomena. In a quantum mechanical system, many distinct sequences of events are compatible with a given hypothesis as to the mechanisms operating in that system. But here hypotheses are never individuated by counting the number of alternative conceivable event sequences compatible with the theory as a whole; nor is a hypothesis which is compatible with a statistical distribution of outcomes weighted initially in proportion to the number of event-sequences or the number of consequent event-types, with which it is compatible. Indeed, competing hypotheses may permit the *same* observed event-sequence. Arguments which select among competing quantum mechanical hypotheses are always arguments which employ reasoning from inverse probabilities, counting as *single* alternative hypotheses, laws or theories which predict a *spread* of possible experimental outcomes. Since quantum hypotheses place some non-logical constraints upon possible outcomes, and the Humean hypothesis does not, one can view the latter as a kind of limiting case. But by parity of reasoning, it is to be counted as just one hypothesis. Perhaps appeals to such facts about scientific practice should count for little in methodological debates about issues as fundamental as the problem of induction. But at the very least, the fact I have cited suggests that physicists treat their hypotheses in a way that is a natural one from the necessitarian point of view, but not from the Humean one.

Now it may be that the necessitarian still confronts an infinite number of *causal* hypotheses, *a priori*, so that the prior probability of each will be given, by the Principle of Indifference and the Normalization requirement, as vanishingly small. This is an issue to which I shall return. But if the number of causal hypotheses is initially m, and if each of these must be assigned equal weight, then the prior probability of each hypothesis (including the a-causal or no-explanation hypothesis) is $1/m+1$.

It is now apparent why Ayer is mistaken in supposing the necessitarian's inductive task to be more difficult than the Humean's. In Humean fashion, Ayer judges the prior probability of necessitarian hypotheses as an inverse function of the number of their instances – and these include not only actual, but potential instances. But the necessitarian judges prior probability in terms of the number of alternative explanations available, not in terms of (what is for the Humean, but not the necessitarian, its equivalent, namely,) the number of actual or possible instances which a hypothesis is able to explain.

7. AN ARTIFICIAL EXAMPLE AND THEN THE REAL WORLD

A simple and rather artificial example will bring out the central features of the contrasting epistemic situations in which the Humean and the necessitarian find themselves. It will also permit us to assign finite prior probabilities to the evidence e and to the hypothesis h to be confirmed or infirmed by it – thus yielding a well-defined value for the posterior probability of h. To make the case relevant to most "real world" inductive problems, we will then calculate the limiting value of the posterior probability of h relative to e, as certain parameters tend to infinity. For the purpose of this example, suppose that someone is given a large number of boxes. Each of these boxes contains n marbles, and the marbles can be of any one of m distinct colors. Each box is so rigged that each time a button on it is pushed, a marble of a given color comes out; the sequence of colors ejected when its button is pushed n times, is unique for each box. There is, in fact, one box for each possible n-membered sequence of colors. Therefore, there are m^n boxes. A box is picked *at random* by the experimenter from this set. His task is to guess, on the basis of a sample of k marbles ($k < n$), the color composition of the full sequence of n marbles for that box. Suppose that each of the k marbles drawn on a given trial is blue. What is the probability that he has chosen the box all of whose marbles are blue? Suppose the experimenter knows about the nature of the boxes; or, at least, that the uniform color of his k marbles in no way disfavors the above story about them. Then, clearly, he is in the Humean predicament. Intuitively, the probability that the next marble from his box will also be blue is $1/m$; and a Bayesian calculation easily shows that the probability of all $n-k$ of the remaining marbles being blue is $P(H_i, k\ g) = 1/m^{n-k} = m^k/m^n$, where H_i is the hypothesis that the box in question contains the all-blue sequence, and g is the condition of picking that box at random from the set of m^n boxes, constructed as specified. Obviously, this probability is exactly equal to that of any *other* box having been picked, from among that subset of m^{n-k} - membered subset of boxes whose first k marbles are all blue. A randomly colored k-membered sequence gives as much information about the future as this uniformly colored sequence does. Furthermore $\lim_{n\to\infty} P\ (H_i, k\ g) = 0$ and $\lim_{m\to\infty} P\ (H_i, k\ g) = 0$ for any fixed and finite value of k. Hence, in the real world, where the values of m and n are typically infinite, a finite sequence of k constant conjunctions does nothing to improve the posterior epistemic probability of any hypothesis.

Now the preceding Humean predicament may be contrasted with the following situation. An experimenter is given a single box, which contains, he is informed, some mechanism for ejecting marbles. This is activated by a button the experimenter can push. Prior to any such trial, the experimenter entertains the following two available hypotheses:

(i) The box is so constructed that it cannot but eject marbles of a single color; and
(ii) The box is so constructed as to pick marbles at random from m internal bins, each containing marbles of a different color.

Hypothesis (i) subdivides into the m initial hypotheses that the box is so constructed that all the marbles are blue, that all are green, etc. It might be thought that hypothesis (ii) similarly subdivides into m initial hypotheses, one corresponding to each possible sequence of n marbles, thereby plunging the necessitarian into the Humean morass. But this is not so. There is but a single hypothesis expressed by (ii) – namely, that the machine be such that its mechanism randomizes marble colors. That single hypothesis can account – in the degenerate sense of "explanation" which then applies – for any sequence such a box may actually produce in a trial; that is, it is compatible with any outcome. The necessitarian, therefore, confronts the following set of jointly exhaustive and mutually exclusive hypotheses:

h_1 : The box is so constructed as to eject only marbles of color 1.
h_2 : The box is constructed as to eject only marbles of color 2.

     ⋮

     ⋮

h_m : The box is so constructed as to eject only marbles of color m.
h_{m+1} : The box is so constructed that no constraint is placed upon the color of ejected marbles.[20]

Suppose the experimenter depresses the button one time and receives a blue marble. This automatically eliminates all but one of the sub-hypotheses of (i) – and would do so *even* if the number of subhypotheses of (i) were infinite. If *blue = color i*, the surviving hypotheses are h_i, that the box must eject only blue marbles, and h_{m+1}, that its ejection-policy is random. If this exhausts the possibilities, it is reasonable to assign each of these hypotheses a prior of $1/2$.[21] Suppose now the experimenter depresses the button $(k-1)$ times more, and each time receives a blue marble. Should he bet on h_i or on h_{m+1}? The answer here is obvious. Quantitatively, we can say that, if the colors of the marbles were determined by chance, the probability of such a sequence occurring is $1/m^k$, and (see above) the posterior probability that the first n marbles will all be blue $(n > k)$ is given by m^k/m^n. The first fraction becomes small very rapidly as either m or k increase, which is to say that the probability of a uniform "chance" sequence is very small. Conversely, the probability, on h_i, that the k marbles are all blue is 1 as indeed is the probability that the first n marbles will be blue, for any value of n. In fact, the posterior probability of h_i is given by Bayes' Theorem as

$$P(h_i, k\ g) = \frac{1}{1 + \dfrac{1}{m^{k-1}}}$$

and this tends rapidly to 1, as either m or k gets larger. Moreover, it is independent of n, the total number of marbles, past and future, ejected by the box; hence, knowledge of n is unnecessary for computation of $P(h_i, k\ g)$, and the value of $P(h_i, k\ g)$ is independent of whether n is finite or infinite. Comparison of $P(h_i, k\ g)$ and $P(H_i, k\ g)$ shows, further, that (other things being equal) the Humean probabilities decrease while the necessitarian ones increase, as m increases. This affords the necessitarian an explanation why, when m is large (as it usually is), scientists can justifiably feel confidence in laws based on only a few well-defined experimental results which agree. It has a second significant consequence: if we are insufficiently imaginative, and the set of hypotheses which we concoct is not exhaustive, then as necessitarians we shall err by calculating $P(h_i, k \, g)$ with too small a value of m. Thus our probability assignment to h_i will be lower than it ought to be. In those numerous situations in which we cannot be sure of having an exhaustive specification of the set $\{h_i\}$, we at worst get degrees of confirmation which are too conservative. Even such low figures can rapidly be brought to an acceptable level by increasing k, since $m > 2$.

Now the above example was brought forward to illustrate the difference between the epistemic situations faced by the Humean and the necessitarian. But like so many examples used by those concerned with the theory of confirmation, it is highly artificial; and this artificiality generates the worry that it may be of little help in showing us how to solve the inductive problems we face in real life. The essential shortcoming of this example, in particular, is that it is implausible to suppose that the hypotheses (i) and (ii) are really exhaustive. Thus, before we can celebrate a victory, there are difficulties to be examined. Perhaps, for example, the box we are given contains a causal mechanism, but one which is so constructed that the first k marbles ejected are blue, the second k are green, and so on. Or . . . clearly we can imagine an infinity of such hypotheses.[22] Are we not then directly back in the same boat with the Humeans? Would nature be so cruel as to present us with boxes of such prankish sorts? My response to this difficulty has several parts.

8. HOW MANY HYPOTHESES FOR THE NECESSITARIAN?

"Cruel" boxes, such as the one just envisaged, have causal mechanisms, all right; it is just that they are especially cunning mechanisms. The cunning feature of these boxes, in fact, is that they have mechanisms which enable them to measure time, or to keep track of how many times their button has been pushed.[23] The hypothesis that a box is of some such sort is as genuinely explanatory as is hypothesis (i). The trouble here is that, with respect to every box, the pushing of the button does not constitute the total cause of the ejection of a marble. There are other causally relevant features, which are internal to the box. A box which is able to count the number of times it has previously been triggered is such that its antecedent state can change, in a hidden way, during successive trials.

It seems clear that, if we are not allowed to pry into a box, we are not going to be able to eliminate, simply by collecting more marbles, any but a finite number of unwanted hypotheses. But what if we are allowed to pry apart the box, as nature evidently permits us to pry into her contents?[24] If the mechanism inside is a causal one, perhaps we shall be able to discover its workings, and thus make correct projections concerning future marble ejections. But: what does "discovering its workings" consist in – except the making of further inductions about the behavior of the components in the box, on the basis of our observation of them? Might not some of them, in turn, be little black boxes, as pernicious as – and perhaps responsible for – the perniciousness of the original box? Well, then, we must tear *them* apart. What are the prospects of an infinite regress?

Let us pause here for a moment. Thus far, we have pursued the strategy of trying to render the number of initial hypotheses finite. Perhaps, however, the threat posed by the problem just mentioned, reminiscent of Goodman's, can be overcome. But before looking further in that direction, we should examine an argument due to Ewing which may obviate the difficulty. Ewing (1962) considers the problem of zero priors from a different angle. His response to the problem is to regard the notion of a quantitative probability as meaningless unless relativized to a body of data. Hence assignments of epistemic probabilities can only be made *a posteriori*; prior probabilities are meaningless. It does not follow, according to Ewing, that the problem of induction cannot be solved at all (due to the inapplicability of Bayesian reasoning to hypotheses which have no assignable prior probability). For although the notion of quantitative priors is supposedly meaningless, Ewing believes that a qualitative notion of probability is applicable to untested hypotheses.[25] Ewing does not explain this notion, however. I should agree with Ewing that it is unrealistic to suppose that our probability estimates typically are, or can be made, quantitative. But on the other hand, I believe that the principles of Indifference and Normalization are *a priori* principles which give a reasonable, if perhaps idealized, model of rational procedure.[26] Nor can I think of any other principles which could serve (with one qualification mentioned in the preceding footnote). If initially there are infinitely many candidate hypotheses, then no restriction to qualitative probabilities can help us. Thus I believe that Ewing's tactic does not succeed.

Hence we arrive at the following position. The fundamental processes which underlie the history of the world are either random or causal.[27] That they are purely random is, we have seen, something we can have Bayesian grounds for dismissing. If we are right about the nature of causation, moreover, a *fundamental* causal process must be such as to be both time-independent and independent of the number of its previous instantiations. This follows from the fact that universals, whether they are atemporal entities or exist in time, are such that their natures are invariable. If the causal relation is a second-order relation between such relata, then its nature cannot depend upon purely temporal facts – for example, what time it is, or how many times previously it has been instantiated, or how many of its instances have previously been observed by us. Our problem, therefore, comes to this: how do we know when we have succeeded in analyzing a natural mechanism or process into its "basic" causal components?

The answer to this last question is, unfortunately, not easy to give. But there are some things which can be said about it, in the relatively short compass which I shall allow myself.

9. FUNDAMENTAL THEORIES AND ANTECEDENT CONDITIONS

Thus far I have largely ignored a fact which is of fundamental importance to the solution of the problem of induction. It is that, among the sorts of causal relations of which we are *directly* aware in experience, are ones which relate event-types whose properties are among those we count as primary properties, properties which are not only presented in sense experience but which are possessed by the objects studied by science. These properties include spatio-temporal properties (position, velocity), solidity, and mass or inertia.[28] In those cases where we directly experience a causal relation, we have non-inductive or direct grounds for asserting that properties or event-types are causally related. It makes no difference whether all instances of these event-types are observed by us or not. Since the causal relation is perceived to relate the events themselves (or their constituent properties), and not to be accompanying feelings of nisus as Hume thought, anything which instantiates those very properties will *ipso facto* instantiate the associated causal relations. If, therefore, we can have grounds for believing that some event (whether directly perceived by us or not) instantiates the properties of the antecedent of a known causal relation, we can have the required grounds for predicting what will follow. Here we have a decisive advantage over Hume. To illustrate: when we visually apprehend the collision between two billiard balls, we do not perceive the forces they exert upon each other. Nevertheless, we perceive that they instantiate certain kinematic properties – relative position and velocity; and we can discover, by colliding with them ourselves, that they possess mass and solidity. Thus we have grounds for predicting future behavior. There is, to be sure, the possibility that something will secretly cause a change in the mass or solidity of either billiard ball, or of both; so that their next collision exhibits unanticipated behavior. That is the problem of insuring that the antecedent conditions are really the same. Often enough, we cannot guarantee the absence of unknown causal factors; and sometimes, we cannot even in principle predict their arrival – for example, the arrival of a light signal into an open system. But, if we can have good grounds under such circumstances to believe that the system is suitably isolated, then we can extend our own direct experience of collision phenomena to the billiard balls.

Let me now summarize and take stock of where we are. I began by distinguishing four inductive problems. They were:

1. Isolating and identifying significant patterns of regular recurrence:
2. Isolating all those factors which are causally relevant to what will happen in a given circumstance;
3. Justifying the prediction of single future occurrences; and
4. Justifying generalizations and law-statements based on finite evidence.

Next, I contrasted the epistemic situation of the Humean and the necessitarian with respect to problem (4). I showed that, at least for certain artificial cases, the necessitarian can solve this problem whereas the Humean cannot. But these cases relied upon the fact that the causal hypotheses with which we began were particularly docile, or else finite in number. When we dropped that assumption, we were faced with an inductive problem paralleling, to all appearances, the original Humean one – for our wild hypotheses, the "Goodmanian" ones, are neither docile nor finite in number.

Nevertheless there is a fundamental difference. Goodman's own hypotheses involve performing a test (observing the color of emeralds) and obtaining one kind of result (green color) up until some future time when the same test produces what would ordinarily be regarded as an arbitrary and different result (blue color). Thus Goodman's problematic hypotheses present a challenge to inductive reasoning by embodying the possibility that the same type of antecedent condition will in the future be followed by a novel consequent condition, or at any rate one which we would ordinarily regard as novel, even though Goodman himself would consider that judgment to be a function of linguistic conventions.[29] One might describe the sequence of test/result event-pairs generated by such a hypothesis as a consequent-cruel sequence. For Humeans, the fact that the number of consequent-cruel sequences is infinite reflects the infinitude of Goodmanian hypotheses, and results in the problem of zero priors. But not for the necessitarian. For him, consequent-cruel sequences must be admitted as possible, but they all fall under a single hypothesis.

By contrast, the hypotheses I have just been considering are not consequent-cruel. There is no such thing as a genuinely causal hypothesis which generates a consequent-cruel sequence, and the behavior of the sorts of "cruel" boxes I have been considering is governed by causal laws. If novel things begin to happen, this can only be because the antecedent conditions have changed in some (perhaps undetected) way. If this change is hidden and unanticipated, we might say that the test/result sequence is antecedent-cruel. I have put the description 'Goodmanian' in scare-quotes in order to reflect this fundamental difference. It is fundamental because the problem created by "Goodmanian" hypotheses is not the problem of zero priors at all, but rather the problem of ascertaining that one set of antecedent conditions is qualitatively identical to another set.

Causal laws – fundamental causal laws, at any rate – are grounded in relations among universals. Hence the "indexical" character of our "Goodmanian" laws – the fact, for example, that they predict new behavior after some definite time-period or some determinate number of experimental trials – shows that they are not basic laws and that their antecedents do not account for all of the relevant antecedent conditions. For we are supposing that those "Goodmanian" laws do not, given the satisfaction of their antecedents, by themselves allow us to predict everything about the internal evolution of a system; and that they do not enable us to do so even when taken in conjunction with other well-established laws. Otherwise there would be no inductive problem here. Put another way: a relational property one of whose constituents is a particular time or a particular number of experiments is not a pure universal. Whether such "impure" universals characterize a system or not is on our ontology not a matter of linguistic habits. If it matters to an object what time it is, or how many times it has previously been examined, that can only be because there is some causal connection between the state of the object and the determinants of our temporal reference-frame; or a causal trace left by prior examination.

This means that the problem we are now addressing is no longer problem (4). It is instead a two-fold problem: the problem of ascertaining antecedent conditions (problem (2)), and the problem of knowing when theory has reached the level at which its laws are basic in the sense of not being further reducible.

These two problems are related, inasmuch as one way in which a dissimilarity between antecedent conditions can be hidden is if it occurs at a level of structure below that which current science has probed. In fact the problem posed by cruel boxes is just a special case of the problem of inferring causes from known effects. The observations by means of which antecedent conditions are compared may fail to register a relevant difference, for two sets of antecedent conditions may appear qualitatively identical by virtue of affecting measuring instruments identically. Yet they may produce distinct effects elsewhere – for example, in the domain of our prognostications. I shall not attempt here any general solution to the non-deductive problem of inferring causes from effects. Instead I shall confine myself to a few sketchy remarks concerning the question of whether it would be possible to ascertain whether physical investigation has reached the terminus of the reductive process. If physics ever reaches, or comes close to, a level of structure below which no further structure exists, are there signs by means of which we can determine the advent of this stage?

This is a difficult and little-investigated problem. Undoubtedly most philosophers feel that speculations as to the form of fundamental theories in physics lie outside the proper domain of philosophy. Yet, it may be that there are certain special formal or quasi-formal constraints which a theory must satisfy in order to qualify for candidacy as explanatorily fundamental. One such constraint, I believe, is that all of the laws of such a theory must be strictly exceptionless. Unlike the laws of a derivative theory, they cannot admit of exceptions or approximations due to incomplete description.[30] Unfortunately the requirement of non-defeasibility is merely a necessary condition, and not a sufficient one. Moreover, a law which is defeasible may not be known to be so, because none of the difficult cases falling under it have been encountered.

A second sort of reason for holding that the limit of structure has been reached is the discovery of particles which give evidence of being indivisible. If, for example, a particle behaves as if it were a point-mass, this would constitute grounds for holding that it cannot be composed of anything smaller. Such an argument has been suggested for the view that electrons (which behave like point-masses) are elementary. The argument seems to involve an *a priori* principle to the effect that a point cannot be subdivided. However I am not at all sure how to evaluate the strength of an argument in which that principle is applied to entities in physical space.

There is a different sort of strategy which bears mentioning. Science has delved more and more deeply into the constitution of matter. In so doing, it has revealed many complexities, but few structures which behave as mechanisms that suddenly undergo a major transformation after a certain period of time. So far, we have found few mechanisms which behave as "cruel" boxes do. Is there any inductive reasoning which justifies, on this basis, the expectation that the universe is not filled with "cruel" boxes? "Cruel" boxes are rare at the microscopic level. Molecules, atoms, and subatomic particles do not, so far as is known, contain mechanisms which would cause them to behave cruelly. Is it not unlikely that still finer levels of structure contain "cruel" boxes?

Unfortunately there does not seem to be any sound basis for this bit of inductive reasoning. For one thing, it involves reasoning from the character of entities at previously investigated levels of structure to the character of their unknown constituents. But this means reasoning from the nature of entities of one type to that of entities of (possibly) quite different types. Such reasoning is bound to be weak. It seems entirely conceivable that structures below the finest levels penetrated by current science are marking the time elapsed since the inception of the universe (the "Big Bang") and are destined to surprise us, through sudden changes in the microscopic behavior of the world, at some future date. Moreover there is no *a priori* guarantee that structure does not descend from level to level *ad infinitum*. If it does so, then the preceding argument is entirely inconclusive.

To conclude these remarks on induction, I return to two issues raised near the outset:

1. What is the correct analysis of '*e* confirms *h*,' where '*h*' is not deductively entailed by *e*?
2. How are true accidental generalization to be distinguished from the laws of nature?

The response which has developed during the course of this chapter to the first question began with an evidential relation which was assumed to be understood, namely, that between a statement and its entailments. The problem was to explain how a generalization of this notion could be formulated which extends to statements not deductively related. The first step was to introduce the generic idea of varying degrees of epistemic relevance between two statements, ranging from entailment to complete epistemic independence. The generic idea, and the negative notion of independence, do not presuppose that we understand what a positive evidential bearing (falling short of entailment) would be: but the former is empty unless we can give content to such a notion. The negative notion was used to articulate the Principle of Indifference: hypotheses which (logically) exclude one another, and concerning which we fail to have evidence, must be accorded equal degrees of belief. The Principle of Indifference gives content to the notion of prior probabilities, required for the application of Bayes' Theorem. That theorem determines when the epistemic probability of one statement is rationally raised in consequence of accepting another. Finally, then, we can say that *e* confirms *h* just in case, following Bayes' Theorem, *e* increases the rational epistemic probability of *h*.

The second question poses a problem. Although accidental generalizations are unlikely to be true, undoubtedly some of them are true. How are they to be distinguished from laws of nature? *Ontologically*, the distinction depends upon whether causal relations exist between the universals instantiated by the event-pairs which are instances of the generalization. But except in those cases where we are directly acquainted with that relation, we must rely upon Bayesian reasoning. Yet when a few positive instances and no counterexamples to a generalization are known, that reasoning appears to lead inexorably to the conclusion that some law of nature is operating. However, we clearly do recognize some generalizations as accidental, even when multiple positive instances and no counterinstances have been collected. The problem is to account for this fact.

To account for it, appeal must be made to a broader field of inductive knowledge than that provided by the instances of the generalization in question. The general idea is this. We count a generalization 'All *A*'s are *B*'s' accidental when at least some of its known positive instances are ones in which a causal account can be given of the occurrence of the *A*-event, and also an account of the occurrence of the B-event, such that (1) the two accounts square well with our other (inductively supported) causal beliefs, and (2) the two events are (a) causally "independent" of one another, or else (b) interdependent in different ways from one instance of the generalization to the next.

Independence is a vague notion. Two events A_1 and B_1 which instantiate 'All A's are B's' are causally independent if the causal sequences which produce them share no event which is a major causal determinant in the occurrence of both A_1 and B_1. But even if A_1 and B_1 are interdependent, by virtue of a shared major determinant of type C, 'All A's are B's' may still be accidental. If A_2 and B_2 provide another instance of this generalization, and A_2 and B_2 are independent, or share a major determinant which is not of kind C, then 'All A's are B's' is accidental. Our grounds for judging a generalization to be accidental therefore depend upon the nature of the causal stories which our total evidence determines to be the most plausible reconstruction of how its positive instances came about.

I have argued that the necessitarian is able to solve one major aspect of the problem of induction for which no plausible Humean solution exists. That is the problem of projectibility, our problem (4). However solutions to other aspects of the problem remain outstanding. Until the remaining work is done, even those who count themselves natural necessitarians cannot claim to have solved the problem of justifying inductive reasoning.[31]

In his book *The Logical Foundations of Probability* (1950, pp. 227–8), Carnap argued against the Straight Rule on the grounds that a uniform sequence, no matter how long, ought not to lead to perfect confidence (hence, a willingness to bet at any odds) in its uniform continuation, even to the next instance. This argument constituted, in part, his justification for permitting the weighting of prior probabilities to be affected by a "logical" factor, namely, the width[32] of the property ascribed by the uniformity. We can concur with Carnap's observation that it would be irrational to bet on the results of applying the Straight Rule at any odds (even given a large sample as evidence); but our explanation of this will be quite different from his. It lies in two facts: (a) the hypothesis of randomness can never be decisively ruled out; and (b) we do not know how, in general, to conclusively rule out the possibility of "cruel" boxes.

5 Causality and time

1. SIMULTANEOUS CAUSATION

The connection between causation and the passage of time is undoubtedly a deep one, and raises some difficult questions. One traditional issue is whether the passage of time is prior to or anterior to the occurrence of causal processes. A second issue is whether, moreover, there is some connection between the "direction" of time and the direction of causality. If there is, is the connection a necessary one, or is the temporal relation between cause and effect one which can vary?

As regards ontological priority, one view is that causal processes presuppose the passage of time, so that the temporal dimension provides one part of the independent matrix – space-time – in which events occur. If this view is right, it should be possible for time to pass in a universe in which nothing happens and nothing changes – or at least one in which events are not *causally* related. There is some difficulty about what sorts of universes would satisfy this condition. Would a universe which consisted of a single material sphere, qualitatively unchanging through time, constitute such a universe? Or should we say that even here, the state of the sphere at t and at a later time $t + \triangle t$ are causally related? Is the continuing existence of material objects dependent upon causal relations?

A second picture is one according to which causality precedes time in the order of being. According to this picture, it is the operation of causality which, by producing events, engenders the passage of time. Thus causality is a necessary condition for the passage of time, and also a sufficient condition for temporal succession.

A third possibility is that causality and time (and perhaps space) are *coeval* in that neither presupposes the other except in a symmetric sense: that they are all required for the being of a universe, and that none can obtain without the other(s).

In this chapter, however, I will focus mainly upon the second issue, the temporal relation between cause and effect. Hume accepted the asymmetry of the causal relation; for him, the only basis upon which this asymmetry could be founded is the temporal precedence of causes to their effects. Thus Hume needed to deny that causes could occur simultaneously with, or subsequent to, their effects. Thus if it could be argued that effects are sometimes or always simultaneous to their causes,[1] this ground for the asymmetry would be undermined. The necessitarian, on the other hand, must consider the possibility that the causal relation – since it is a real relation holding between pairs of events – may be intrinsically asymmetric. Such an asymmetry would not by itself suffice to establish a univocal temporal relation between causes and effects. There remains the question whether the relation is linked to the passage of time in such a way as to forbid simultaneous and/or backward causation.

There are two approaches to the problem of establishing asymmetry which are likely to recommend themselves to the necessitarian; one phenomenological, the other formal.[2] The phenomenological appeal is the more fundamental of these. It is that the causal relation – in the form of forces – is perceived to be asymmetric. We understand whether we are pushing or being pushed, pulling or being pulled; and this is not the result of any inference we make, but something directly perceived. More obscure is whether we can *perceive* that this relation is intrinsically oriented *vis-à-vis* the passage of time in some determinate way. This question I shall defer.

A formal approach to asymmetry is to distinguish cause from effect on the grounds that the (total) cause of an effect is (counterfactually) sufficient for its cause, whereas the effect is not (counterfactually) sufficient for its cause. As we know, there is a problem with whether this criterion can be so formulated as to accommodate events governed by indeterministic laws. Even setting this aside, there is a difficulty. When we say that the same (type of) event e can have different types of total causes, $c_1, \ldots, c_n$, we are in selecting e considering an event which is a common part of the total effect of c_1 through c_n. But this selection presupposes an identification of cause and effect. It is by no means clear that in no instance is the total cause of a *total* effect both sufficient and necessary for that effect. If, conversely, we consider partial causes and their total effects, we shall be likely to find cases in which a partial cause is necessary, but not sufficient, for the totality of the effects to which it is causally relevant.[3] For this reason, the phenomenological argument for asymmetry is the preferable one. It is not, however, generally applicable. Unless causes and their effects have some uniform temporal relation, we shall be pressed for a criterion for distinguishing causes from effects where the causal relation is not itself perceived.

Hume[4] presents an important argument for the claim that causes must be simultaneous with their effects. Suppose that a (perhaps complex) event c is the sole and sufficient cause for the occurrence of an event e, that c occurs during a time interval $t_0 - t_1$, and suppose that c itself undergoes no intrinsic change. Finally, suppose that event e does not commence until t_1, lasting perhaps until t_2. Now the question is: Why did not e begin at t_0? For, if nothing happens over and above c to trigger e during $t_0 - t_1$, and if c already obtains during that time and is sufficient for the production of e, then e should occur as soon as c does. There is a sufficient reason for e at t_0, and no sufficient reason for its delay until t_1.

But Hume goes on to point out that if effects did not succeed their causes, in some instances there could be no temporally extended causal chains. There are temporally extended causal sequences; hence some causes precede their effects and the principle of sufficient reason previously appealed to is false.[5] Ignoring at present the possibility of backwards causation, we are confronted here in fact with three distinct options: (1) that a cause and its effect are simultaneous occurrences, (2) that effect follows cause, but is temporally contiguous to it, or (3) that effect follows cause, but separated from it by a finite lapse of time. Furthermore, we must ask whether more than one of these is possible; and if so, whether more than one is realized by nature. The present difficulty lies, however, in the opposite direction: if Hume's two arguments are both sound, then *none* of these options is viable. Confronted by a related antinomy, Russell (1917) was pleased to conclude that the notion of causation needed to be jettisoned altogether.

Before proceeding, I make two preliminary remarks. First, we wish to entertain the hypothesis that a temporal gap may exist between a cause and its effect, with no intervening events causally linking the one to the other. Thus in what follows, I shall always have in mind the proximate cause of an effect, unless the contrary is indicated. Secondly, we must consider the temporal duration of the events in a causal chain. Initially, it appears that these can be of two sorts: events which occupy a finite span of time, and instantaneous events. That there are instantaneous events is strongly suggested by the fact that an event of finite duration has a beginning and an end; its beginning would, it seems, be itself an event, in fact an instantaneous event. We must not, however, ignore the topological possibility that time is not infinitely divisible.[6] If it is not, then there are no point-events. If time is a continuum, then (presumably) there can be.

Brand (1980) has argued that temporally extended causal chains are possible even on the supposition that cause and effect are simultaneous. Brand's argument is that many events are complex, involving internal changes and hence subevents occurring during shorter time-spans. Thus a soccer game is a complex event consisting of many plays and moves:

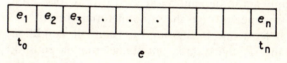

Figure 5.1

Brand then argues that (a) *simple* events, ones involving no intrinsic change, are always simultaneous with their causes and their effects, where these are also individuated as simple events; (b) that if c caused e, then there is at least one subevent of c which temporally coincides with one or more subevents of e, and it is these subevents which are causally related; and (c) that the temporally sequential subevents of an event are *not* causally related. On Brand's view, a causal chain looks like this:

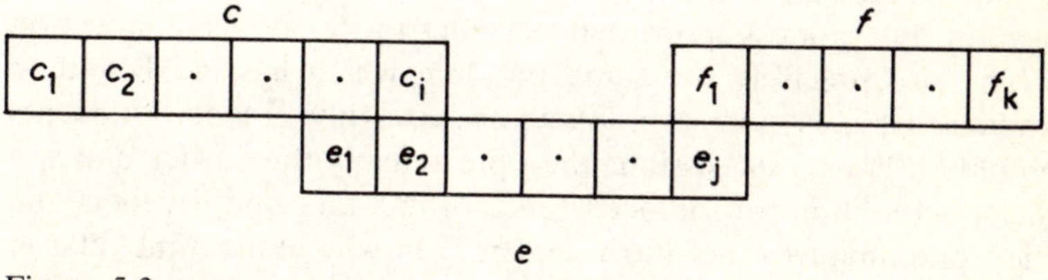

Figure 5.2

In such a case, causation strictly speaking is not transferred from *c* to *f*. To say that *c* caused *f* is to speak with the vulgar. At the same time, Brand has to allow that there are laws of succession governing sequences of subevents, so that, at least in some cases, there is a connection which is stronger than mere succession between two successive subevents, yet weaker than causation. What Brand has to say about this is of some interest. Considering a ball in free fall, Brand claims that the falling of the ball during the *i*'th temporal segment of its fall does not cause its falling during the (later) *j*'th temporal segment. Yet the relation between these two events is stronger than mere temporal sequence since their occurrence supports the counterfactual:

(i) If the ball had not fallen the *i*'th segment,
     it would not have fallen the *j*'th segment.

Brand says:

> The relationship appears to depend on at least two factors. First, the events in the sequence involve the same material objects. . . . Second, there is at least one background or standing condition, beginning before the sequence and continuing after its ends. In the case of the freely falling ball, the standing condition is the force of gravity. . . . The force of gravity . . . is necessary but not sufficient for the ball's falling the *j*'th segment. Note it follows that the force of gravity does not cause the ball's falling the *j*'th segment, since the cause, whatever it might be, is sufficient for the effect. The relationship among members in a temporally extended sequence of events can be thought of as a form of physical necessity, though with a warning not to confuse it with causal necessity. Instances of this form of physical necessity exemplify laws of succession.
>
> (Brand 1980: 150)

Brand has nothing to say, however, about the metaphysical grounding of this new species of nomic necessitation. It is hard to see, on Brand's showing, why we shouldn't call this a species of causation; but what is more, with respect to this nomic connection we can raise precisely the same problem which has led Brand to postulate that causation is simultaneous. Roughly: If a pair of events exemplify a law of succession, then presumably the earlier one is a sufficient condition for the occurrence of the later one. If, then, the earlier one involves no intrinsic change, why must time elapse between its beginning and the beginning of the other event, for whose occurrence it is sufficient? But even if the earlier event is not sufficient, it is allegedly relevant to the occurrence of the latter event. At the time, therefore, that the sufficient condition of which it is a part obtains, the next event of the series must also obtain. But this resurrects Hume's difficulty. Brand is constrained to deny that the force of gravity plays a causal role in the falling of the ball since, on his analysis, this event or state of affairs was obtaining before the falling of the ball.

In fact, Brand's example is unfortunate for his case in a number of respects. (1) Counterfactual (i) is untrue unless a *ceteris paribus* clause is added. In this respect its form is just what we would expect if the relationship between the *i*'th and *j*'th segments of the ball's fall were causal. (2) It seems perhaps odd to say that the ball's falling for the *i*'th segment caused its falling for the *j*'th segment; but this oddity may be due partly to the insufficiency of the former, and partly to the fact that the ball's motion is so imprecisely specified. It is not especially odd to say that, under the circumstances, the prior portion of the ball's fall contributed causally to its subsequent motion. I shall have more to say about this felt oddity below. (3) Brand's first condition on his new species of nomic necessity seems easily violable. Suppose the ball were to change into another physical object between the *i*'th and *j*'th segment of its fall. Then two objects are involved in the sequence, and although the production of the new object may be causal on Brand's own analysis, the *falling* of the new object admits of the same explanation as in the case where no substantial change occurred. (4) It is hard to deny that the force of gravity was a causal factor in each segment of the falling of the ball. Indeed the case of free fall, when it involves acceleration, is just one example of a wide class of causal chains which involve (or appear to involve) the continuous presence of forces, and the absence of static states of affairs which endure for a finite time.

Every one of these considerations argues for the natural view that the temporal sequences Brand has in mind are causally related. So, evidently, Brand has not provided us with a parsimonious solution to the problem regarding causation.

Hesitancy over whether it is correct to say, in the case of a free falling body, that its earlier state of motion contributes causally to a later state, is perhaps more acute when the case is instead one of uniform motion or rest. If a body is at rest and remains so, is a later state of motionlessness caused by an earlier state of motionlessness? Brand would say that it is not; but if one identifies causal relations with forces, it might also seem correct to say this. For there are, we may assume, no forces acting upon the body; and the absence of a force is not itself a cause. Since a body in uniform motion experiences no net forces, we are also forced to say about such an object that an earlier stage in its motion does not cause a later stage. Or so it seems. On the other side, it is clear that the earlier state of motion is one of the boundary conditions which, together with the laws of nature, determines the subsequent motion. This fact argues for the conclusion that the earlier state of motion causes the later.[7]

Now our everyday hesitancy as to what to say about these cases will be nicely reflected by a theory according to which forces are causal relations, if there are conflicting pressures in such a theory – a pressure to say that in these cases no causal relation obtains between earlier and later states, and a pressure to say that it does. Such is the case. The pressure to deny the existence of a causal relation comes from the fact that there is here no force acting upon the body. The contrary pressure arises in part for the reasons (1)–(3) cited above against Brand's example, but more fundamentally, from the fact that zero is just one of the values which the forces in a system may assume. A zero force is just one of a continuum of forces of different magnitudes, and as such is one which is covered by the laws which govern forces. It is one species of the genus of forces. It is, from this perspective, a "degenerate" or limiting case – but nevertheless still a case in which it is appropriate to speak of a causal link between the earlier and later states of the system. If causal laws map positive forces isomorphically onto effects – as they do – then they must also dictate the effect in the zero force condition. For if a zero force condition can sometimes yield an effect which is at other times the result of a positive force, or if conversely, a positive force sometimes achieves what otherwise a zero force would, then the necessary connection between positive forces and their effects is lost.

Thus there is some justification for Brand's claim that certain temporally extended processes are linked in a continuous, nomological, but non-causal way. But Brand's own example is not one of these; and others can easily be given in which forces are constantly present and in which change is ongoing. The propagation of an electromagnetic wave is a temporally extended event in which the causal interaction between varying electric and magnetic fields occurs at all times. It is hardly plausible to say that such an event can be analyzed into temporally extended subevents which are simple in Brand's sense and not causally connected. For these reasons, I think we must deny that Brand has found a new species of nomological necessitation, or that, even if he had, it would perspicuously describe all those temporally extended processes which are nomologically governed; or finally that, even if it did, this would solve the fundamental paradox which Hume raised.

If the causal relation were exhausted by constant conjunction, there would be no difficulty in allowing any temporal relation between cause and effect, so long as this relation was constant for every instance of a given causal law. Since the existence of constant conjunction is for the regularity theory a brute fact, no argument which seeks to demonstrate the necessity of a particular temporal relation, excluding others by means of an appeal to a principle of sufficient reason can gain a foothold. That is probably the reason why Hume did not take very seriously the argument he presents for the necessity of simultaneous causation.[8]

But that argument cannot be so easily dismissed by the necessitarian. For him, the existence of a temporal gap between the beginning of the (full) cause and the beginning of its effect constitutes a problem. According to him, the causal relation is real and its existence explains how and why the effect follows its cause; thus the question of why the effect does not begin sooner has bite. If the existence of an effect depends upon the existence of the cause for its production, but on nothing else, then how can there be such a gap? Moreover, where we have direct experience of causal relations there is no perception of such a gap; though we do experience causal processes as temporally extended. If there is a temporal gap, it lies below the threshold of perceptual discrimination.

But there is one way in which it might be thought that the incompatibility of the existence of temporal gaps with the principle of sufficient reason can be avoided. Perhaps the mere passage of time constitutes by itself a change which (as the enduring of a static state of affairs) has causal efficacy. If we interpret this to mean that the passage of time constitutes a change in an otherwise static state of affairs, then there will be a temptation to say that the passage of a certain amount of time may be required for a given state of affairs to become causally efficacious – that is, for the "full cause," to wit the enduring of that state of affairs for a certain time interval, to come into existence.

But this solution must be declined. For even static states of affairs involve internal causal relations in at least the degenerate sense which obtains when the force is zero. Moreover, this solution threatens to undermine the doctrine that nature is uniform. That doctrine entails the time invariance of causal relations; if the passage of time is itself causally efficacious, it will not be easy to justify our expectation that circumstances which occur at different times but are otherwise similar produce similar effects.[9] This being so, the necessitarian appears to be driven to the conclusion that cause and effect occur simultaneously.

To summarize, we have arrived at the result that Brand's solution is unsuccessful, for it leads to the impossibility of extended causal chains, but that the necessitarian also seems to be forced to deny the possibility of a temporal gap between cause and effect. We have not, therefore, removed the original impasse. Let us therefore examine an argument of Russell's which purports to show that a cause and its effect must each be of finite duration, and that there must exist a finite temporal gap between the end of the causing event and the beginning of the effect:

> No two instants are contiguous, since the time-series is compact; hence either the cause or the effect must . . . endure for a finite time. . . . But then we are faced with a dilemma: if the cause is a process involving change within itself, we shall require (if causality is universal) causal relations between its earlier and later parts; moreover, it would seem that only the later parts can be relevant to the effect, since the earlier parts are not contiguous to the effect, and therefore . . . cannot influence the effect. Thus we shall be led to diminish the duration of the cause without limit, and however much we may diminish it, there will still remain an earlier part which might be altered without altering the effect, so that the true cause . . . will not have been reached. . . . If, on the other hand, the cause is purely static, involving no change within itself, then . . . it seems strange – too strange to be accepted, in spite of bare logical possibility – that the cause, after existing placidly for some time, should suddenly explode into the effect. . . . This dilemma, therefore, is fatal to the view that cause and effect can be contiguous in time; if there are causes and effects, they must be separated by a finite time interval τ . . .
>
> (Russell 1917: 184–5)

This last suggestion of Russell's is surely at least as strange as the notion that a static cause should "suddenly explode" into its effect. Why should the effect suddenly explode after a finite time lapse τ? Nevertheless Russell's intention was not, in any case, to defend this view of the temporal relation between cause and effect; it was rather to destroy the philosophical respectability of the notion of cause and effect by crushing it between the twin impossibilities of temporal contiguity and temporal gap.

But Russell's attempt to show that the notion of causal connection is incoherent does not succeed. There are no fewer than three ways to escape his dilemma; and each of these three ways has the further merit of not succumbing to the other difficulties previously detailed. The first solution involves the supposition that time itself is discrete rather than continuous. If we accept this supposition, then events are not infinitely subdivisible into shorter subevents. At some stage we reach events which have no temporal parts, but which are of finite duration. In that case two events may be contiguous, but no question as to the causal relation between earlier and later parts of either of these events can arise. Thus both horns of Russell's dilemma are escaped. This solution requires the assumption that time is granular, which may seem bizarre. But there is no empirical evidence which contradicts this hypothesis, provided that the *minimum divisibilia* of time are short enough. Indeed there has been some speculation among physicists about the possibility that time is quantized. However there are two other solutions, neither of which requires this assumption.

Suppose, with Russell, that the series of temporal moments is compact. Then one possibility is that the sequence of events which make up any causal chain themselves form a compact series. The upshot of this is that we must give up the notion that an event has any proximate cause(s). If causal chains are compact, then between any two events in such a chain, there exists a third event which is an effect of the former and a cause of the latter. But giving up the existence of proximate causes does not, so far as I can see, have any unacceptable consequences.

There is, however, still a third possibility, one which requires neither the quantization of time nor the abandonment of the assumption that events have proximate causes. This solution involves our attributing to the time series more points than there are on the real number line. In particular, we allow there to be moments separated by non-zero infinitesimal durations. At the finest level of analysis, causal chains consist of events which are of infinitesimal duration and are contiguous. It is true that every infinitesimal duration can be subdivided into smaller infinitesimal durations; but it may nevertheless be the case that events themselves cannot be indefinitely subdivisible in this way. Perhaps every event needs some minimum (infinitesimal) time to constitute itself as an event. I have no argument that this is so; however, the notion of infinitesimals itself is defensible. Russell did not consider this third solution because he wrote at a time when the notion of infinitesimals was thought to be an incoherent one. In *The Principles of Mathematics*, Russell dispenses with infinitesimals and uses the methods of Cauchy and Weierstrass to provide a foundation for the calculus. Since Russell thought that infinitesimals were at best a mathematical fiction, he would not have considered our third solution a viable option. However, in the last two decades it has been shown, by Robinson and others[10] that the notion of infinitesimal numbers is one which can be made respectable after all. Hence this solution cannot be rejected on the grounds which Russell would have given.

According to the second and third solutions to our difficulty, causal processes are continuous. There is no gap between cause and effect; nor are they simultaneous. Temporally extended causal chains are possible. This accords well with both our direct experience of causal processes, and with currently favored mathematical formalizations of physics, for the causal laws of physics can be expressed as differential equations in time. Nothing which has been said rules out simultaneous causation; it merely defends the existence of nonsimultaneous causes and effects. Although it is possible that causes are sometimes simultaneous with their effects, there is no reason to suppose that this is so, and it is more parsimonious to suppose that it is not, that is, that just one of the three solutions considered above is universally correct. The standard examples which are given of simultaneous causation (the lead ball depressing the cushion, the motion of one end of a stick causing motion at the other end) turn out upon more careful analysis to be examples of the rapid propagation of compression waves – paradigm cases of nonsimultaneous causation.

2. BACKWARD CAUSATION

Thus far I have argued, first, that the necessitarian has a phenomenological justification for causal asymmetry, one which does not commit him to anthropomorphizing causes; and second, that the supposition that causes and their effects are nonsimultaneous is a coherent one. This supposition is not required by the necessitarian to ground causal asymmetry, and he can allow for the possibility of simultaneous causation, so long as this is not universal. But can the necessitarian allow backward causation?

There is no denying the fact that we find the suggestion that causes may follow their effects conceptually disturbing. It is less clear what the source of this discomfort is. To someone who argues, as I have, that asymmetry is a feature of causation of which we are directly aware, it is natural to seek also a phenomenological ground for a univocal connection between causal asymmetry and time. However, I am unable to discover any such phenomenological ground. It is doubtless true that all of the instances of causation which have been directly experienced are ones in which cause precedes effect. But this hardly suffices to rule out the possibility of reverse causation, though it may explain our psychological disposition to reject that possibility. If reverse causation is to be excluded, it must therefore be on other grounds.

What sort of empirical data can be imagined, for which a hypothesis involving backward causation would offer the most natural explanation? Short of a direct experience of backward causation, we can see that such data must have three features. First, there must be a regular conjunction between events of two kinds – call them '*A*' and '*B*' – a conjunction which is sufficiently remarkable to rule out effectively sheer coincidence as a reasonable explanation of its occurrence. Secondly, the circumstances surrounding the paired events of types *A* and *B* must be sufficiently well understood to rule out the existence of forward causal chains linking *A* to *B*. Thirdly, there must be no independent sufficient causal explanation of *A* which appeals only to events preceding it. Hence, we would be forced to choose between two alternatives: either that *B* caused *A*, or that *A* has no cause and that the correlation between *A*'s and *B*'s is entirely inexplicable. The former alternative is, allegedly, the more palatable. The claim to have satisfied these conditions is sometimes made on behalf of persons with alleged precognitive powers. For example, Helmut Schmidt has performed experiments involving a machine which is activated by a subject who presses buttons to indicate his prediction as to which one of four lights the machine will illuminate; the machine subsequently picks one of these lights by means of a randomizing process using radioactive decay. Some subjects are claimed to have made predictions over a long series of trials at a rate well above statistical expectation.[11] Can such cases be coherently described (whether correctly or incorrectly) as involving backward causation? We must guard, I think, against allowing our answer to this question to be governed by overly narrow appeals to what we "mean" when we speak of causation, or by our "concept" of causal connection. If events are connected by an objective, asymmetric relation which involves more than constant conjunction, then it may transpire that our conception of that connection is in some ways inadequate. If we wish, we can reserve the term 'cause' and its cognates for the forward-directed varieties of this relation; but that will not settle the question whether there is or is not some clearly analogous relation which is backward directed. What puzzles us about the suggested explanation in terms of backward causation is that forward directedness is, for whatever reason, such a central aspect of our causal discourse.

Like creation *ex nihilo* and clairvoyance, confrontation with a striking correlation between events in the absence of any forward causal connection leaves us with *some* of the characteristic marks of a causal relation while removing others which are so deeply entrenched that their absence leaves us baffled. Perhaps we should always insist that there must be some undiscovered forward causal connection, or that the correlation, no matter how striking, is pure coincidence.

One argument against the possibility of backward causation is that if A and B are two temporally separated events, and if A precedes B but is caused by B, then it would be possible to prevent A by preventing B, and moreover possible to prevent B by introducing some change in the causal antecedents of B, after A has already occurred. But once A has occurred, it is impossible for its occurrence to be prevented. Hence the supposition that there can be backward causes is incoherent.[12] This argument is best viewed as a modal argument, which can be more precisely expressed as follows. Let it be supposed that both A and B occur, that B is (part of) the cause of A, in the sense that B is necessary, in the circumstances, for A and causally prior to A. Let it be further supposed that B is itself the result of antecedent causes, in the sense that, at some time prior to the occurrence of B, conditions exist which are sufficient to bring it about. If B is necessary in the circumstances for A, then the prevention of B would, in the circumstances, result in the nonoccurrence of A. But if it is causally possible for B to be prevented by means of some intervention in the causal chain leading to B, which intervention postdates the occurrence of A, then it is causally possible, at a time which postdates A, for A not to occur. This contradicts the fact that A has occurred. If, alternatively, it is impossible to prevent B once A has occurred, we must conclude that the occurrence of A has some causal effect upon the conditions which produce B, and thus a causal direction from B to A is ruled out. Hence, backward causation is impossible. This argument does not rely upon its being the case that any event of the same type as A has ever actually been prevented by the subsequent prevention of an event of type B; it depends only on the claim that this must be causally possible, if B is a cause of A. But since A will have occurred in any case, whether or not B were prevented, it must follow that it is causally possible that some events of the type of A be caused, and others uncaused; the only difference between the two cases being the occurrence of something after A. This consequence is one which Max Black (1955–6) finds unacceptable.

One response to this argument, due to Scriven (1956–7), is to allow that backward causation is possible in cases in which B is produced by some indeterministic device which is triggered after the occurrence of A. To allow an interference that guarantees the nonoccurrence of B is to allow circumstances which violate the conditions under which backward causation is possible. Thus if, for example, an experimenter were to intervene in such a way as to invalidate the guesses of subjects, one would not have a case of backward causation, but instead a case in which the subjects' guesses negatively influence, via the experimenter's intervention, the outcome of the experiment. To be sure: but may we therefore say when the experimenter does not intervene and the subjects' guesses succeed, that they are caused by the machine's subsequent behavior? What is odd about this is that it makes the question of whether A is a partial cause of B, or vice versa, dependent upon some event for whose occurrence A is causally insufficient, and which follows A temporally. It is extraordinary that such an occurrence could change what would otherwise be the causal antecedents of A, without in any way changing A.

J. L. Mackie (1980, pp. 178–80) has suggested a similar circumvention of the bilking experiment, namely, the requirement that some event C which antedates A be causally sufficient for the occurrence of B, where there is of course assumed to be no causal chain linking C to A which does not first pass through B. Mackie's proposal makes use of his view that if C is causally sufficient for B, then C includes such negative conditions as are required to exclude interventions which would prevent B. Now my view is that the total cause of an event includes only those events which *do* occur and which produce forces which contribute to the effect. But in any case Mackie's notion of causal sufficiency cannot rule out the causal possibility of such intervention, that is, since indeed the initial conditions of the universe might have been different, although it rules out the actual occurrence of any contravening cause. This means that it is causally possible, without making any other changes in the causal chains which lead to A, to introduce something which will prevent B, and thereby produce a situation in which an event similar to A has no sufficient cause. Still, this is just the difficulty which Black noticed.

But all the arguments which focus upon the bilking experiment involve the use of counterfactual judgments: if B is a cause of A, then if in the circumstances B had not occurred, A would not have occurred; if someone were to intervene in a certain way after the occurrence of A, B would nevertheless be prevented. The truth conditions of such counterfactuals are notoriously difficult to specify. When we are dealing with a topic that stretches our intuitions as severely as thought about backward causation does, how sure can we be that these counterfactuals have the truth values which we have taken them to have?

The difficulty in analyzing counterfactuals stems in part from suspicions about possible worlds, but additionally from the difficulty of specifying the counterfactual situation(s) which are relevant to evaluating the truth of a (causal) counterfactual. Take the counterfactual schema: (S) 'If A had not occurred, B would not have happened.' To evaluate this, we must imagine a circumstance (a possible world if you like) in which A does not occur. But we must also, it seems, imagine this circumstance to be one which is otherwise identical to the actual circumstances preceding B. For if we do not observe this constraint, we could never have grounds for affirming that B would not, in the imagined circumstances, happen. B is causally possible, since it is actual, and there will almost always be circumstances other than the actual one, and in which A does not appear, which are nevertheless sufficient for the production of B, as well as ones which are not. Thus (S) is bound to be false, but also uninteresting, unless understood so as to require that it be evaluated with respect only to possible worlds which duplicate the actual world in all respects, or in relevant respects other than the occurrence of A. But what is the proper criterion of relevance?

There have been various attempts to address this difficulty.[13] Most of these efforts have relied upon the notion of a possible world which is as close as possible to the actual world, except that A does not occur. But in a deterministic world, this requires either that the causal chain(s) which in the actual world lead to A be modified in some way, or that the laws of nature be temporarily abrogated. The second alternative, which is the one considered by Lewis, hardly seems acceptable. According to it, our causal judgments depend upon our imagining situations in which the laws which guide those judgments are supposed to be violated, in some inexplicable way. If we take such suppositions seriously, they will undermine the grounds we have for making any judgment about what "would happen" in the imagined circumstances. In a possible (?) world in which one miracle occurs, what is there to rule out another?[14] To imagine the antecedent conditions altered is equally problematic. In a deterministic world, such an alteration cannot in general be kept temporally localized; and if adjustments have to be made indefinitely far into the past and future, it is doubtful that we shall be able to specify the relevant possible world. To suppose that under some vague specification we can judge whether B will occur in that world is to have an unrealistically inflated estimate of our powers of causal inference.

I believe, nevertheless, that an analysis of counterfactuals which invokes altered antecedent conditions can be given; it is one that probably cannot capture the sense of every causal counterfactual, but I believe it will serve to secure the counterfactual premises of the argument against backward causation. Such an analysis will, I trust, also be of interest in its own right.

I shall offer this analysis in the context of examining a specific application of it. Diagrams (I) and (II) below depict two contrasting causal processes. Here 't_1', 't_2', 't_3', and 't_4' indicate successive times, and an arrow drawn from one event to another indicates that the first is the total cause (sufficient and, in the circumstances, necessary) of the second:

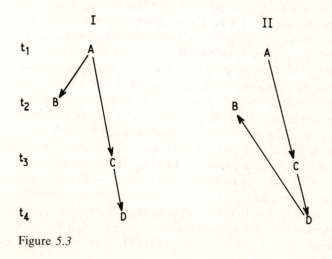

Figure 5.3

As these diagrams suggest, case (I) involves only forward causation, and D is not a cause of B. In (II), D is the cause of B, and the causal relation between them is directed backward in time. The contrast between (I) and (II) can also be expressed counterfactually, as follows:

(I) Holding the circumstances and laws of nature fixed in all other respects, B would have happened even if D had not happened.
(II) Holding the circumstances and laws of nature fixed in all other respects, if D had not happened, B would not have happened.

In other words, if (I) obtains, we suppose B cannot be prevented just by preventing D whereas in (II) it can be. The difficulty with articulating the difference between (I) and (II) in this way is that the meaning of counterfactuals such as (I) and (II) is unclear. What is it to hold fixed all the laws of nature and all the surrounding circumstances except one, which is somehow changed? I believe that a clear sense can be given to this supposition.

To show this, we need to introduce a new notion, the notion of a pair of causal chains which are (at a time) causally independent. To say that two sequences of events form a pair of causally independent causal chains (CICC's) at a time is to say that each sequence is an ordered causal sequence, and that up to the time in question, no event in either sequence has causally affected, or been affected by, any event in the other sequence. Two CICC's will be said to *merge* at a time t if at t an event in one sequence causally affects or is affected by an event in the other. At that time, of course, these sequences cease to be CICC's. So as not to beg any questions, we shall want the definition of CICC's to allow also for backward directed causal chains: if two backward-directed causal chains merge at t, we should regard them as merged for all earlier times but not at times later than t. If a forward-directed causal chain merges at t with a backward one, we must say, if the interaction is mutual, that the forward-directed chain is independent of the backward-directed one prior to t, but not after t, and that the backward-directed chain is independent of the forward-directed one after t, but not before.

Now I want to claim that what (I) asserts, properly speaking, is that if we hold all the circumstances which are in the actual world causally relevant to the occurrence of A, B, C, and D fixed, but introduce some change which prevents D without directly interfering with the causal chains that produce A, then B will still occur; whereas (II) denies this. To introduce such a change, what we need is to consider the sequence $A, \ldots, D$ as part of a causal sequence which is up to t_2 causally independent of another causal chain . . ., *E*, *F*, where the event *F* is such that its occurrence will in the presence of *C* lead to the nonoccurrence of *D*. If we imagine *F* to be such that it combines with *C* to prevent *D*, we are imagining *A*, . . ., *C* and . . ., *E*, *F* to be CICC's which merge at some time between t_3 and t_4:[15]

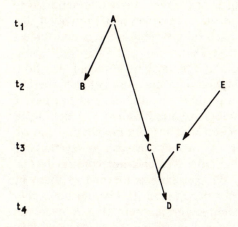

Figure 5.4

To speak of circumstances being otherwise held fixed is, then, to imagine, counterfactually, just the following change, namely, the introduction of a CICC, . . ., *E*, *F*, which is such that, in the circumstances, *F* is sufficient to prevent *D*.[16] (I) asserts that under these conditions B nevertheless occurs. (II) asserts that under these conditions B does not occur. Envisioning a sequence with the causal properties of . . ., *E*, *F* does not place any unduly demanding burden upon our powers of imagination; indeed it is not even required that we be able to specify any *particular* sequence of this sort in specifying the counterfactual situation. All we need is grounds for holding the existence of a sequence with the required features to be causally possible.

Causal independence can be made a matter of degree, for it is possible to make comparative judgments about the extent to which one event contributes to the occurrence of another. We may do this in terms of the relative strength of the forces exerted by various causal factors or, where an analysis in terms of forces is unavailable, in terms of the degree of similarity between events whose causes are identical except for the presence or absence of the causal factor in question. Armed with this, we can say that the degree of causal independence of two causal chains is a function of the strength and number of the causal interactions between their constituent events. In thinking about a counterfactual conditional, it may be admissible to specify a sequence . . ., E, F in terms of which the counterfactual situation is characterized, which has some causal interaction with the sequence A, C, D prior to the occurrence of C, provided that that interaction would not by itself be sufficient in the circumstances to prevent either C or D as described.

To illustrate how we can get CICC's, imagine a hitchhiker who is thumbing on Route 66 and stumbles on some loose pebbles, thereby kicking a pebble in such a way that it lands on, and crushes, a beetle; and also thereby causing a passing motorist to laugh at his plight and as a result to lose control of his automobile and run off the road some moments later. We would not wish to say that the killing of the beetle caused the auto accident; nor conversely that the latter caused the former. We can express the first of these by saying that if the beetle had not been killed, this would not, other things being equal, have prevented the accident. For it need not imply that the hitchhiker does not stumble: there exist possible worlds in which an incoming CICC prevents the demise of the beetle without affecting the motorist's misfortune. For example, we may imagine a larger rock interposed between the beetle and the path of the pebble in such a way as to deflect the fatal path of the latter. The causal chain which would put that rock there can be imagined to be causally independent of the surrounding events under discussion – at least to sufficient approximation. To be sure, if the rock had been there, light waves reflected from it would have impinged upon the hitchhiker and the automobile; but their effect would be negligible *vis-à-vis* the events as described.

In a deterministic world, how extensive a change from the actual world would result from the introduction of a chain such as that which introduces the envisaged life-saving rock? It has been correctly observed, by Lewis (1973) and others, that such a chain would have to be traced back to the beginning (if any) of the universe, and would thus modify its entire past history (or future history, if the incoming CICC were backward directed). True. But such modification – however extensive – is only relevant for purposes of evaluating a given counterfactual to the extent that it impinges causally upon the antecedent conditions which, in the actual world, lead to the events under discussion. And in general, though we would have difficulty in specifying the details, we can have good grounds for thinking that it is possible for there to have been a causal chain which is at all times causally isolated (to a sufficient degree) from any given actual one.

It should be remarked that counterfactuals, construed as I have construed them, cannot be offered as part of an *analysis* of '*A* causes *D*', or even of causal priority. For such an analysis would be circular; it relies upon the notion of causal chains and of causal independence, and hence presupposes that these notions are understood. But of course they are, on my view, previously understood: our understanding of these counterfactuals is dependent upon our understanding of the more primitive causal relation itself.

We may now turn to a reexamination of the bilking experiment in terms of this analysis. Counterfactual (II), which describes an alleged case of backward causation, is equivalent, under our analysis, to:

(II)* Holding the laws of nature and all other causally relevant circumstances fixed, if there exists any causal chain . . ., E, F which is a CICC relative to A, C, D up to a time t_3 later than t_2 but earlier than or identical to t_4, and which in the circumstances suffices to prevent D, then B will not have occurred.

Now we can see that there is strong reason to think that (II)* is false. For even if in the *actual* situation – that is, in the absence of . . ., E, F – the occurrence of D is deterministically fixed prior to t_2, still there is a causally possible counterfactual situation in which D does not occur – for it is causally possible that . . ., E, F have been present. But moreover, such a CICC as this will not have prevented B, since causally independent of it. That is, at t_3, when B has occurred, there will be in the actual world no incoming causal chain . . ., E, F destined to merge with A, C, . . . between t_3 and t_4. But is the existence of such a chain causally impossible? Surely not, for by hypothesis, . . ., E, F is causally independent of A, C, . . .; and this is true at t_3 whether E, F, . . . is a forward-directed causal chain or a backward-directed one in which the causal antecedents E and F of D postdate D. Given this causal independence (and assuming that the chain E, F violates no causal laws intrinsically), there is no reason to suppose that it would be causally impossible for such a chain to exist, relative to the actual situation at t_3. Thus it is false that any CICC which in the circumstances suffices to prevent D also suffices to prevent B. Hence (II)* is false. The supposition that backward causation is causally possible leads to the conclusion that a contradictory state of affairs is causally possible. But this shows that backward causation is not causally possible.

It might occur to someone to wonder whether this argument does not beg the question. The counterfactual reasoning upon which it relies can be metaphorically restated as follows: If God has created the world in such a way that a certain subset of its (causally, not temporally) initial conditions lead causally via causal chain(s) X to an event D, then, so my argument goes, God could have created an additional set of initial conditions which, in conformity to natural law, would have generated a CICC, Y, which would have merged with X just in time to prevent D. And the initial conditions which generate Y would *a fortiori* have been causally independent of those which generate X. But (an objector could say) if the additional supposition that there is backward causation leads in this case to a contradiction, perhaps what this shows is that God could not, on pain of contradiction, have created the initial conditions for Y (given that He creates those for X) after all. What is logically impossible is *a fortiori* causally impossible as well.

But this objection is certainly odd. It requires us to suppose that there can be two causally isolated states of affairs, each of which is, when taken singly, consistent with the laws of nature; and which are nevertheless such that when jointly added to the laws of nature, an inconsistency results. If we are asked to choose between the impossibility of backward causation, and the supposition that the laws of nature can constrain the initial conditions of causally isolated systems, not merely individually but also conjointly, we should prefer the former, for the latter seems unintelligible.

But perhaps the initial conditions for X and Y are not causally isolated. If they merge at some time, and if backward causation is possible, then perhaps these initial systems are joined after all by a causal chain which goes forward to the time of merger, and then loops back to the time of creation. This, however, while allowable under the hypothesis that backward causation is possible, cannot be invoked to escape the difficulty. For although such causal loops would be causally *possible*, I cannot see any reason to suppose that they would be causally *necessary* in every instance of backward causation. Presumably Y can be constructed in such a way that its initial conditions escape being "tagged" by any backward causal chain extending from the merger with X.

However, we must observe that the arguments just given do not, strictly speaking, exclude backward causation. If the argument is sound, what it excludes is forward causal chains which at some time reverse temporal direction. There is nothing in this which disallows causal chains that are *entirely* backward directed. Indeed the same arguments can be applied *mutatis mutandis* to backward-directed chains to demonstrate the impossibility of their reversing into a forward direction. This is consistent with the hypothesis that the world contains some forward causal chains and some backward ones, so long as it is guaranteed that there is no causal interaction between chains of the former type and chains of the latter.

It is tempting to think that we can exclude backward causal chains, given that we know there to be forward ones, on the ground that we do not detect any backward ones. But of course if there *were* backward chains, we *could* not (if I am right) detect them, for doing so would require causal interaction with them. One might legitimately wonder, however, why or how the world could be so arranged as to make such interaction impossible, just as we lately wondered how it could be impossible for God to create both X and Y. Really the hypothesis amounts to the supposition that there are two entirely distinct universes, one of which is, from our point of view, ontologically otiose. Nevertheless, the hypothesis raises an important conceptual point. Whether there are two such universes, or whether there is indeed only one, what sense can we attach to the claim that "our" universe is one in which causal chains are directed *forward* in time? If ours were a backward universe, how could we know this? I shall not attempt to investigate this question in any detail. Yet it seems to me that if there were two such universes, even God (whose epistemic access to them would not be causal) could have no basis for deciding that causation ran in opposite directions in them. Suppose that the laws of the first universe were not time-reversal invariant, and that the sequence of events in that universe was exactly reversed in the second. This is consistent with the supposition that the laws governing the second universe are the same (only with the direction of causation reversed); but it is equally consistent with the view that the direction of causation is unchanged, but that the laws are "mirror images" of one another. It does not follow from this that it is just a matter of convention how temporal direction and causal direction are linked, for what is meaningful to suppose (by way of alternatives) may not be actually possible. But I know of no consideration which settles the matter.

Part two
Universals

6 Nominalism reconnoitered

1. METHODOLOGICAL CONSIDERATIONS

In Part two of this essay I shall attempt to develop some of the main features of a theory of universals. Before embarking on this task, it would be well to recapitulate the epistemological viewpoint from which I proceed. The belief that there are universals has often been associated with rationalism, or more generally with epistemological positions which empiricists reject. My discussion of causation in Part one deviated in its conclusions quite radically from empiricist orthodoxy; but at least for the most part, my procedure in arriving at those conclusions was canonical. Or so I hope. Indeed my epistemological stance was that of traditional empiricism, at least with respect to knowledge of the material world. I did not allow myself a comfortable world peopled with other persons and with physical objects, but only the contents of my own experience, described in as philosophically neutral a way as possible. This was to avoid begging many of the questions which it is common enough nowadays to find begged, even among those who consider themselves good empiricists. In other words, I have taken the problem of perceptual skepticism in its classical form seriously.

My conformity to the phenomenological starting-point of radical empiricism is not merely a dialectical ploy. For I share with other empiricists the conviction that if we have any knowledge of a physical world, the factual content of that knowledge derives from sensory experience. This thesis may be generalized: our knowledge of those things which exist "in time" must be founded upon sensory experience.

What is less certain is that the world consists *only* of things which are temporal beings, only of things which can be apprehended through sense experience. It is not even an entirely easy question to

147

settle which things are the sorts of things that, if they exist, exist in time. I find it conceivable that there exist such things as: numbers, propositions, and sets. If such things do exist, it seems that they are not spatiotemporal beings, but there is a lack of agreement even here. If there are such entities and they are abstract, it is likely that some truths concerning them are apprehendable by us without the use of our sensory faculties. We must then entertain the possibility that there are synthetic *a priori* truths; truths about abstract entities may express facts which are not merely the result of linguistic convention. On the *other* hand, if there are such abstract entities, one must be cautious not to dismiss out of hand the possibility that some of the truths concerning them might be empirical, or might come to be known to us only in a way which somehow makes use of sense perception.

These reflections bear in two ways upon a discussion of universals. In the first place, there is the question whether universals (if they exist) are, one and all, transcendent beings, beings to which spatiotemporal characteristics do not apply. In the second place, there is the possibility that while some universals exist in space and time, some do not. Such a view might be tempting to someone who held that there are some particulars – for example, material objects and perhaps minds – which exist in space and/or time, and other particulars – perhaps numbers or propositions – which do not. It would be tempting to say that the properties and relations of the former, properties such as color, shape, and mass, exist in space and time. But it would hardly be plausible to say that properties and relations of the latter existed in this way (for example, being tautologous, being prime).

Among those empiricist philosophers who have adopted realism with respect to universals, it is common to find an insistence that our knowledge of universals is dependent upon sense perception. The issue is in my opinion a difficult one. I shall examine it only partly, since I intend to restrict my purview, among first-order properties, to properties of material things and some mental things, namely, sensations. Thus I shall have nothing to say about the existence of numbers, propositions, and the like, or about their properties. It is important that this restriction be borne in mind. One of the deep puzzles for realism is that there are cogent reasons for believing that properties (of material things) are abstract; and other strong reasons for concluding that they are not. To a significant degree, a resolution of this puzzle must await a consideration of what we are to say about spatial and temporal properties themselves. In what sense, if any, do these latter exist "in space" and "in time"? What – if anything – are space and time themselves?

It is my intention, once again, to rely quite heavily upon arguments whose premises are phenomenological. However, experience cannot play quite the same role in the examination of the problem of universals as it did in the investigation of causation. This is because, in a sense, no philosopher denies those basic facts of experience upon whose foundation a theory of universals must be built. No one denies that there are things which have properties. No one denies that two things may have "the same" property. It is true that this pillar-box is red; and it is true that all the pillar-boxes in London are the same color. What is under dispute is how these sorts of facts are to be analyzed. Perhaps, then, the experiences from which our knowledge of these facts derives does not of itself decide the philosophical issue. Perhaps that must be settled on dialectical grounds – that is, by constructing alternative theories and judging which one outstrips its competitors in terms of explanatory power, simplicity, comprehensiveness, coherence with other systematic aspects of our picture of the world, and the like. On the other hand, since all are agreed to the *basic* facts at issue, it might seem odd that realism is so often attacked as being an unempirical theory. Undoubtedly, that is because realists have so often held that universals are abstract. Transcendent realism does face the problem of explaining how it is that universals, if not themselves spatio-temporal beings, can enter into states of affairs which are spatiotemporal and are the objects of experience. It is obvious that the problem of how a belief in abstract universals can be empirically justified depends crucially upon how this can be explained. Both of these problems are enmeshed in the issue of what it is for a universal to have instances – since the instances of some universals would clearly be spatiotemporal in character. Whether or not universals, if they exist, are abstract beings, is a question which therefore cannot be decided in advance of our seeing how these issues might be handled. But at the very least, we can say that we need go no further than what is phenomenally given, in order to see why there is such a problem as the problem of universals.

2. PROPERTIES, PREDICATES, AND MEANINGS

There are two preliminary matters which need to be disposed of before embarking on the discussion of universals. The first is a simple terminological matter. Many philosophers distinguish between properties and relations. The term 'property' is restricted by them to the monadic case. I shall, however, use the term 'property' generically, to cover the entire class of items under discussion. When it is necessary to make the distinction, and the context would otherwise make it unclear whether I mean a monadic property or a relation, I shall use the term 'quality' to denote the former. These terms are not intended to carry with them the philosophical baggage of realism. Thus, where there is any chance of begging philosophical questions, I shall use them rather than the term 'universals'. Nominalists, therefore, can agree under this usage that particulars have properties, that is, qualities and relations.

The other matter is not terminological. It concerns the relation of certain linguistic entities – particularly predicates, adjectives, and adverbs – to the nonlinguistic entities, if any, which are universals. I believe that it is a mistake – and a bad one – to suppose realism commits one to the view that every meaningful predicate (adjective, etc.) must be isomorphically associated with a universal. On the contrary: a realist may hold that one and the same meaningful predicate (used univocally) may be "associated with" *more* than one universal; and with different universals on different occasions. Or it may be associated with none. For suppose that a predicate is used to describe things which have ostensibly the same property. Further investigation may reveal that there is no such property, or that there is no single property which warrants the application of the predicate, as it has been understood. The predicate 'schizophrenic' may be meaningfully used to describe what is supposed to be a single disease but which proves to embrace a number of quite distinct conditions. The term 'phlogisticated' may meaningfully describe what purports to be a chemical condition, when in fact that condition does not exist at all. If the correspondence between meaningful predicates and properties were required to be isomorphic, then scientific theories which used such predicates, and which were later discredited, would have been shown to have not been merely false, but meaningless. I find this consequence unacceptable. But I do not intend to embark here upon a discussion of semantics. I shall therefore assume dogmatically the view that a realist theory of meaning must accommodate the fact that what we wish to say using a predicate can sometimes be meaningfully said, even when there is no property to correspond to the predicate we use.[1] I shall, however, return briefly to this issue later. For the time being, let me, in what is once again intended to be a philosophically neutral way, refer to the semantic relation between predicate and universal (where it *does* exist) as designation: a predicate designates a universal or set of universals. Many philosophers have supposed that we can speak meaningfully "of" non-existent individuals, but only because we are able to do so by using predicates whose meaningfulness is guaranteed by the existence of their designation. That is the cornerstone of Russell's theory of (definite) descriptions. Now it *may* be that a non-designating predicate functions in the same way that Russell thought (most) names do – namely, as an abbreviated definite description whose descriptive content designates properties known to exist. In that case, a non-designating predicate would be meaningful because the complex definite description (of a property) which it abbreviated, was itself couched, ultimately, in terms of designating predicate expressions. This would mean that such a description would designate, if anything, something other than the complex of properties designated by its ultimate predicates. I do not wish to rule out such a theory, though it seems to me unlikely to be correct. Nor do I wish to rule out the more general possibility – indeed probability – that our knowledge of properties plays a major role in semantics. But I shall not begin by assuming a Russellian semantics.[2]

I shall give one illustration of the way in which a confusion of linguistic matters with metaphysical matters can lead to error. Renford Bambrough (1960–61) has offered a solution to the problem of universals which makes essential use of Wittgenstein's notion of family-resemblance. Wittgenstein observed that some meaningful predicate expressions demarcate a class of objects, the members of which seem to have no single property in common. Wittgenstein's own famous example is the predicate 'is a game'. There seems to be nothing which all games have in common, in virtue of which they are games.

Bambrough interprets Wittgenstein as having intended this point to be a general one. He claims that *all* predicates indicate at most a family resemblance among objects. To predicate 'red' of something is not to say that there is some one thing which it shares with all other red things. Thus, there is no single thing which is shared by all particulars falling under a predicate, nothing which is identical in all of them. Hence we have no need to postulate the existence of universals. This argument of Bambrough's simply misses the point. Even if all the predicates in every language shared the (alleged) semantic features of 'is red' and 'is a game', this would have no bearing upon the problem of universals. Perhaps, for some reason, languages make use only of inexact concepts, as they are sometimes called.[3] But this fact could hardly be used to show that no two particulars contain or share something which is literally identical in both of them. Nor could it be used to show even that we have no grounds for supposing that there are such shared universals. For an "inexact" language is logically quite compatible with our being able to *see* exact resemblances. Even if we have no color-words which designate *precise* shades of color, with no spread, that does not show that there are no precise color-shades, nor that we are unable to perceive that two objects share a precise shade of color. It might be odd or surprising that beings who were able to perceive something shared or universal in a multiplicity of particulars, should not possess a language whose semantic features reflected that fact. But it would be no more than odd. Once the existence of exact resemblances is admitted, it will not do to dismiss as "logically unsatisfiable" the demand for an answer to the question: Is the existence of such a resemblance an ultimate fact, or is it to be explained in terms of the existence of (one or more) universals? That is what is under dispute between realists and one type of nominalist. Bambrough has not demonstrated that the realist's answer to the question must remain incoherent.

3. NOMINALISMS

Because he denies that one and the same thing can be shared by two distinct particulars, the nominalist sees his main task as that of explaining how it is that we classify particulars. Our classificatory behavior is reflected most prominently, perhaps, in our use of language; and so it is natural that nominalists should seek to explain such facts as the fact that there are meaningful predicate expressions, and that these expressions can have multiple correct application. Because these facts appear to admit of a simple and natural explanation on the realist hypothesis, it is not surprising that they are often taken by realists to constitute central evidence for their position. But whatever connection there may be between the semantics of general terms and the existence of universals, it is not likely to be a simple one. The semantics of the general term 'game,' just mentioned, should be sufficient warning of that. But we can ignore such semantic questions, even though it may be that the existence of universals is a necessary condition for the existence of language as we know it. There are more fundamental facts to which the realist can appeal.

David Armstrong (1978a) provides a useful classification of

nominalism into five species. These he calls: predicate nominalism, concept nominalism, class nominalism, mereological nominalism, and resemblance nominalism. The classification reflects the differing ways in which nominalists have sought to give an account of what it is for two particulars to share a property – for example, what it is for two things to be spherical. According to the predicate nominalist, for two things to both be spherical consists in nothing over and above the fact that they both *fall under* the predicate 'is spherical'. To say that they are both instances of 'is spherical' is to say that they are both called, in virtue of some linguistic convention, 'spherical' by human beings. For a concept nominalist, the role of the predicate in predicate nominalism is played instead by something mental, a concept. Class nominalism is the view that an individual has sphericity by virtue of its membership in a certain class (redundantly specifiable as the class of spheres). In mereological nominalism, a spherical individual is thought of as a part or portion of the aggregate (the "heap") of all spherical things. Parts of this aggregate may be scattered throughout space. Finally, resemblance nominalism is the view that spherical things are spherical by virtue of some similarity or resemblance between them.

4. THE CASE AGAINST NOMINALISM

It is not my intention to present a full-scale discussion or refutation of the various nominalist positions. Nevertheless, fairness to those positions requires that something be said about them, enough to indicate at least why I think they should be rejected. I shall be quite selective in doing this. In this section I discuss predicate and resemblance nominalisms. Finally, in a separate section, I consider the theory of G. F. Stout.

Predicate nominalism can be classified as an "extreme" form of nominalism, in the sense that predicate nominalists hold that over and above the recurrent applicability of general words, there is nothing to be said about the facts which give rise to the problem of universals. Predicate nominalists believe that the repeatable rule-governed use of predicates is a fact about human linguistic practices which is ultimate, and does not admit of further explanation. In particular, there is nothing *outside* linguistic practice to which we can intelligibly appeal, if we desire an explanation for these practices.

Resemblance nominalism is less anthropocentric than predicate nominalism. Resemblance nominalists do appeal to facts which are independent of human experience and convention, in order to explain the multiple applicability of general words. Resemblances between particulars are, or can be, taken to be objective and not dependent upon human cognition in any sense. Thus resemblance nominalism is a moderate form of nominalism, which shares with realism an objective stance toward the reasons for human practices of classification. Indeed, some philosophers (including Armstrong) hesitate to regard resemblance nominalism as a form of nominalism.[4] At any rate, I believe that resemblance nominalism is the alternative to realism which most deserves to be taken seriously. I shall therefore indicate why I think it can be defended against some of the criticisms which have been levelled against it, and why nevertheless I believe it is not a plausible theory. But first I shall discuss predicate nominalism, a representative of the more extreme nominalistic positions.

A. Predicate nominalism

The idea that there is literally *nothing*, outside the re-applicability of general terms, which accounts for our practice of grouping individuals together in certain ways, is a difficult one to believe. Common sense certainly holds that there is something, something in the objects themselves, and something which we experience, which accounts (often, if not always) for our groupings. It may well be that, whenever we wish to appeal to the relevant non-linguistic facts in order to provide a realist explanation, we find ourselves forced to express our thesis by making use of general terms. But this fact could not be used to show that realism is a doctrine which is viciously circular.[5] For anything we wish to *say* must be said in a language; and it may be that the non-linguistic facts to which the realist wishes to appeal are themselves inescapably general, and hence not expressable except by means of those linguistic devices – general terms – which have been devised for that purpose. Does this mean that we cannot "escape from the circle of language"? It does so only if there are no *other* ways of identifying the features of the world to which non-nominalists wish to appeal, save by talking. To escape the circle it is not even necessary that it be possible to communicate about these features to another person, or to refer to them in a non-linguistic way. All that is minimally required is that each person have the capacity to recognize such features as part of the content of his own experience. Nevertheless such non-linguistic interpersonal identification is possible, using repeated ostensions.

Were it not, it is hard to conceive how a language could be learned and transmitted.

Because recurrence seems to be such a dominant fact of experience, independent of our labelling conventions, predicate nominalism is not, intuitively, a particularly attractive position. It is hardly likely that it would have much appeal for the philosophically unreflective man; though he, the plain man, might equally find realism a perplexing doctrine if it were explained to him in certain ways. What then are the motives for nominalism? In part, nominalism is encouraged by specific difficulties in the articulation of a consistent realism – for example, by the difficulty of giving a consistent, non-vacuous explanation of exemplification. In part, however, nominalism is fueled by broader philosophical concerns. These broader commitments include three which deserve mention.

1. First, rejection of abstract or transcendent entities generally, on the epistemological grounds that they are inaccessible to experience, and hence that there can be no justification for supposing their existence.
2. Second, the power of the mereological model as a model of what it is for something to have constituents. Universals, if they exist, are in some sense constituents of propertied particulars; but the mereological model does not seem to elucidate this kind of constituency. What, then, does?
3. Third, the apparent arbitrariness of systems of classification. It is well known that the objects we encounter can be grouped or classified in many distinct ways. In fact, they are classified in different cultures in ways significantly non-isomorphic to one another. The nominalist takes this as evidence that classification is an essentially arbitrary device, imposed by human beings upon the world so as to enable them to better satisfy the particular and varying purposes of their interaction with it. To back up this view, it is usual to point out that any two individuals will resemble one another in some respect or other. It is vacuous, therefore, to defend a particular classificatory distinction by pointing out that a pair of individuals belonging to the same taxon resemble one another or share something in common, while pairs whose members come from different taxons do not. That claim is true only if it is specified in what respect conspecifics resemble one another, and differ from members of other species. Once such a specification is made, the nominalist proceeds to argue that there is no fact which can be pointed to,

over and above the conventional decision to apply the term naming that respect to a certain group of individuals. Nominalism, therefore, is often associated with forms of conventionalism and cognitive relativism.

The nominalist can challenge the realist to give a noncircular account of what it is for a term to have multiple application. The way in which that challenge can be met was indicated at the beginning of this section. But the tables can also be turned against the nominalist. Circularity threatens his own account; so this line of attack against realism invites a *tu quoque*. In making his charge, the nominalist admits the "linguistic" fact that general *words* are repeatably applied. But an analysis of this fact appears to require the re-introduction of universals, or else leads to a vicious regress. What is it for a word to be multiply applicable? The word 'red', for example, is multiply applicable because one man can correctly use it to describe a setting sun, and another man can correctly use it upon another occasion to describe a tulip, and so on. It is clear here that the two men are using the *same* word in the sense that the word 'red' is a type which can have multiple tokens. Each of these tokens will have in common with the others that it is a token of the same word-type. This fact need not embarrass the nominalist, so long as he can give an adequate account of what it is for two word-tokens to belong to the same type. But this he cannot do. Clearly, one must be able to *recognize* that two tokens belong to the same type, if one is to have mastered the use of a general term. Now word-tokens must be embodied; and the manner of their embodiment cannot be entirely arbitrary. If it is to serve its purpose, the embodiment of a word-token (in a spoken sound, a written symbol, or a hand signal) must bear a certain similarity to other tokens of the same word-type; and this similarity must be one which is learnable and recognizable. It is apparent, therefore, that the problem of recurrence which originally appeared at the level of non-linguistic particulars can be generated all over again at the level of words – for word-tokens themselves are particulars which exhibit this same feature.

The obvious maneuver is for the nominalist to describe this feature of word-tokens in exactly the same manner in which he described the feature of recurrence in the non-linguistic things those word-tokens are used to describe. He will point out, first, that not all pairs of tokens of a given word can be said to "naturally resemble" each other closely (e.g., a written and a spoken token of 'red'). Secondly, he will maintain that the features which all written tokens of 'red' "have in common" is just that there is a description which correctly applies to each of them, and perhaps not to anything else. This description may, of course, be quite complex. But where is there any difficulty in this?

Consider a person who is being shown a shade of blue he has not previously experienced, and who is being taught, by associated repetition of the word, that this shade is cerulean. He eventually learns what it is for something to be cerulean. For the predicate nominalist, this means simply that he has learned when it is correct to verbally describe something as cerulean, and when it is not. But of course, this means that spoken instances of the word 'cerulean' have also come to be correctly identified and distinguished from other spoken words. Does this mean that the person in question has learned to describe in language the spoken sounds which characterize utterances of 'cerulean'? Does it mean that what spoken tokens of 'cerulean' have in common is that they (and not other things) are such that a certain description can be applied to them – and that the user of 'cerulean' has learned what that description is? Even if there is such a description, it is not plausible to maintain that a competent user of the word 'cerulean' must know what it is. He need not have learned the descriptive vocabulary in terms of which such a description could be couched. Nor is it plausible to suppose that *someone* must be able to give such a description. There is no necessity in there being linguistic resources at hand which are sufficient for the construction of such a description. This is, of course, merely a special case of the general fact that we are often able to recognize members of open classes, even when there exists no word which is used to describe them.

At this point a more sophisticated nominalist might reply that the notion of verbal behavior needs to be – and can be – generalized. Recognition of recurrence need not consist in the correct repeated use of a *word*; it may consist in the regular exhibition of any consistent pattern of behavior. Thus, even if no one is able to *describe* what all spoken tokens of 'cerulean' have in common, the fact that a certain class of speech-events constitutes the class of 'cerulean'-tokens consists in the fact that these speech-acts elicit a certain consistent pattern of recognition-behaviors. But what sort of behavior is that? It could be said that the test for recognition of 'cerulean' is that a subject is able to utter that word upon being presented with cerulean things. But that suggestion is blatantly circular. It could be said that a good test is the subject's ability to repeat the word after its utterance by someone else. But that is to admit a second use for 'cerulean', just as "correct" by nominalist lights as its application to cerulean things; in that case, what it is for something to be cerulean cannot be explained solely by the correct use of 'cerulean' in connection with it. Or perhaps, a man could signal his recognition of 'cerulean' in some arbitrary way – say, by blinking his left eye. But then, we could raise the problem once again, in the form of questions as to what constitutes recognition of token eye-blinks. Thus the predicate nominalist's explanation of the use of general terms seems to lead to an infinite regress, or else in a circle.

B. Resemblance nominalism

Resemblance nominalism is initially a much more plausible theory than predicate nominalism, for it recognizes at once that the fact of recurrence is given to experience as an objective fact which is independent of linguistic convention or stipulation. But resemblance nominalists and realists disagree over the nature of the ultimate fact which accounts for recurrence. A realist may allow that the recurrence of a quality in *a* and *b* can be said to consist in there being a resemblance between *a* and *b*. But the existence of this resemblance is not for him ontologically fundamental. Rather, the resemblance must be understood as consisting in there being something which is identically the same in both *a* and *b*. Resemblance nominalism, however, holds resemblance to be ontologically unanalyzable. The resemblance nominalist may allow that two particulars, *a* and *b*, share something "identical." But that there is an identity here is not for him ontologically fundamental. It is a limiting case of resemblance: namely, exact resemblance.

As H. H. Price (1953, p. 14) points out, one main strength of the resemblance theory is that it can account for inexact resemblance in a straightforward way. Inexact resemblance is a phenomenon of the same order as exact resemblance. If resemblance be taken as the ontologically fundamental relation, then there is no trouble in explaining inexact recurrence, for resemblance is a relation which naturally admits degrees. Identity, by contrast, does not. The sky and Paul Newman's eyes are not (contrary to what some of his fans may imagine) the same shade of blue. Hence if they share something, it is not some particular shade of blue. There is no such shade which is identically the same in both of them.

There are two strategies of which the realist can avail himself in deflecting this difficulty. The first is that he might regard properties which lead to the phenomenon of inexact resemblances as complex properties. Then a common *part* of two complex properties is shared by inexactly resembling particulars; and the degree of resemblance reflects the extent of the "overlap" between the complex properties involved. The second strategy is to introduce the distinction between *determinate* properties and determinable properties.[6] Blue is a determinable property; it has several determinate shades. Blue objects share something identical by virtue of falling under a common determinable; the resemblance is inexact by virtue of the shades being distinct shades. Hence the particulars which these shades respectively characterize are inexactly resembling. This reply places the realist under the onus of giving an account of the determinate/determinable distinction.[7]

Of course we may reflect that the problem of accounting for degrees of resemblance has not really been solved by the resemblance nominalist. After all, the different *degrees* of resemblance form a resemblance-class: *resemblance* is a determinable which admits of as many species as there are degrees of it. Thus the nominalist appears to be covertly presupposing the intelligibility of the very phenomenon he purports to explain. This, however, is the realist's way of conceiving the matter; and I think the resemblance nominalist would be right in rejecting this difficulty as misconceived. From his perspective, resemblances, whether exact or inexact, are not to be further analyzed; it is the realist from whom a further analysis of this is required.

But perhaps the nominalist could be forced to admit second-order relations of resemblance (both exact and inexact) by means of which to describe the resemblance-relation between different resemblance-classes. Suppose that two objects, a and b, resemble each other closely in that they are nearly the same shade of blue. Two other objects, c and d, resemble each other "less" closely in that one is spherical and the other ovoid. Then the pair $\langle a,b \rangle$ inexactly resembles$_2$ the pair $\langle c,d \rangle$ in that $\langle a,b \rangle$ and $\langle c,d \rangle$ each exemplify (different degrees of) *resemblance*$_1$, where *resemblance*$_1$ is first-order resemblance and *resemblance*$_2$ is second-order resemblance. Similarly, there may be third-order resemblances between second-order resemblances.

This brings us to the first serious objection I shall discuss, which is due to Russell. Russell argued that resemblance nominalists have to admit at least *one* universal, namely, *resemblance*$_1$, and went on to point out that if they admitted *resemblance*$_1$ as a universal, the nominalists might as well become fully fledged realists. For if *resemblance$_1$* is not admitted as a universal, then instances of *resemblance$_1$* must be unified in terms of the second-order relation, *resemblance$_2$*. However, the same question can be raised about instances of *resemblance$_2$* – namely, what they have in common; and so the nominalist is forced to appeal to a third-order resemblance-relation, and so on. Russell took this regress to be vicious.

But I think H. H. Price is right that the nominalist must and can resist this regress. He resists it by insisting that resemblance is not, in the ordinary sense, a *relation* at all. It is, as Price says, "too fundamental to be called so."[8] And if the realist takes umbrage at this, it can be pointed out to him that he is apparently saddled with an analogous problem, and the necessity of an analogous solution. For he – unlike the nominalist – must speak of particulars as exemplifying universals; and if asked whether *exemplification* is an ordinary relation, and whether it is in turn exemplified$_2$ by instances of exemplification$_1$, it is clear that he will stop the impending regress by means of a similar insistence upon the metaphysical specialness of *exemplification*. Thus I believe that this argument of Russell's fails.

A second argument against resemblance nominalism, however, is not so directly disposed of. This argument consists in challenging the nominalist to say what the resemblance between two particulars consists in. The resemblance between an apple and a fire engine, as we all know, is different from the resemblance between a lime and malachite. The realist can explain this difference by saying that the apple and fire engine resemble each other in both being red; whereas the lime and malachite resemble each other in virtue of both being green. The challenge to the nominalist is to tell us in *what respect* two resembling particulars resemble one another, for it seems likely that *every* pair of particulars are resembling in *some* respect or other. What is the nominalist to say? He cannot respond that the apple and fire engine resemble each other in respect of *redness*, for in so doing, he at least gives the appearance of smuggling in by the back door the very universals he refused entry by the front.

The nominalist can respond to this difficulty by making use of the notion of a set of exemplars. The exemplars for the class of red things might be: this particular sunset, this tomato, and that fire engine. These particulars resemble each other to a certain degree; and the class of red things is defined by the nominalist as the class of all those things which resemble the exemplars at least as closely as these latter resemble each other. Hence no mention need be made of redness.

How satisfactory is this definition? There are difficulties for it which are serious and which, to my knowledge, have not been answered. Suppose the nominalist defines the class of dogs as the class of all those objects which resemble Marmaduke, Fido, and Rin Tin Tin as closely or more closely than each of these resembles the other. What, first, is the status of the statement 'Marmaduke is a dog'? According to Price, this is a tautology, since it is tautological that Marmaduke resembles Marmaduke, Fido, and Rin Tin Tin at least as closely as these resemble one another. However Marmaduke is, let us say, identical to Bowser. If an agent for whom Marmaduke, Fido, and Rin Tin Tin serve as exemplars of doghood identifies Marmaduke under the name 'Marmaduke' but not under the name 'Bowser', it seems false that, for him, 'Bowser is a dog' is tautologous. Thus we must regard this class of tautologous statements to be restricted to those utilizing names or identifying descriptions known by an agent to single out exemplars for the class to which the predicate attaches. Furthermore, those things which serve as exemplars of doghood for one agent need not do so for another agent. Thus the tautologousness of 'X is P' is relative both to the referential terms which serve to identify X, and to which X's are taken as exemplars. Price recognizes this latter consequence. Neither consequence is one with which we should be happy. For if tautologousness is a function of meaning, then we are forced to say that the meaning of the predicate 'is a dog' varies from speaker to speaker, if they identify the same exemplars under different referring expressions, or if they use different sets of exemplars. Since, indeed, it is implausible to maintain that a single agent uses the *same* set of exemplars of doghood throughout his life (always checking animals against the long-departed canine companions of his youth, perhaps), we are forced to say that the meaning of 'is a dog' changes in time for a single agent.

In choosing exemplars for 'is red', it is wise policy to pick items which bear as little resemblance to each other as possible, *except* insofar as they are red. For suppose the predicate 'P' applies to a class whose exemplars (for an agent) are a, b, and c. If, as the realist would put it, a, b, and c resemble one another also with respect to some property Q, then *this* set of exemplars cannot be used to pick out the class of P's. For in that case, something which is not Q might be P, yet not resemble a, b, and c as closely or more closely than these resemble one another. At best, a, b, and c could be said to pick out the class of things which are P and Q. Now the difficulty is not merely that of having exemplars which have not in common (as the realist would put it) any additional property Q, but of finding exemplars which are *known* not to bear to one another this additional resemblance. Resemblance, after all, is an objective matter, whereas the *use* of particulars as exemplars depends upon an agent's *recognition* of the character and degree of their resemblance. If each of the exemplars, for agent A, of 'dog', is also vicious, and if one or more of these exemplars is not *known* by A to be vicious, then, paradoxically, A's use of 'dog' correctly applies only to vicious dogs, and not to all dogs. One would not have thought that an understanding of the applicability of a predicate such as 'is a dog' requires this kind of knowledge. As an account of how we *do* manage to apply predicates, it appears to be manifestly false. This objection, it may be parenthetically noted, becomes especially powerful whenever we are confronted with coextensive predicates. Were the world a place in which all and only red things were spherical, even omniscience on the part of an agent would not enable him to select a set of exemplars for 'red' which was not also at the same time a set of exemplars for 'spherical'. Yet if that is the case, the resemblance nominalist could not distinguish these two properties in such a world.

There are perhaps *some* sets of objects for which it is true that we can sensibly speak of an ordinal ranking of them, taken pair-wise, by degrees of resemblance. However it is by no means clear that the notion of degree of resemblance can be as widely applied as the resemblance nominalist's thesis requires. That thesis requires that relative degrees of resemblance can be sensibly said to obtain between *any* pair of particulars whatever, for in deciding the application of the predicate 'is red', say, one can only decide upon its application to a particular by comparing the degree to which that particular resembles exemplars of red, with the degree to which these resemble one another. If the predicate 'is red' is to be a workable one, not only must talk of degrees of resemblance be intelligibly applicable to the entire field of particulars, but it must actually be possible to *judge* degrees of resemblance for all those objects concerning which we make cognate judgments. It is doubtful whether this is in fact as easy as it is to tell whether or not something is red.

Finally, there stands against resemblance nominalism the intuition that particulars resemble one another because they share one or more properties. To say that they share these properties because they resemble one another is, according to this intuition, getting it backwards. I do not think it can be denied that most of us have this intuition. It amounts to taking resemblance to be an internal relation. If resemblance is an internal relation, then that one thing resembles another is dependent upon those things having the properties they do have. If this is so, an account of what it is to have a property cannot be given in terms of resemblance.

Is there any evidence which directly supports this "intuition"? In a way, there is. The resemblance nominalist would have it that what we primitively notice, when we classify particulars, is the feature of resemblance itself. We do not notice this feature *in virtue* of noticing anything else about the objects being classified. This however does not seem to be a plausible account of what we notice when we notice that something is, say, red. It does not seem that in judging something to be red we are making a comparative judgment at all. We may, to be sure, have had to learn the application of the term 'red' by making comparative judgments. Only in this way could we have learned to pick out that feature of experience to which the term 'red' has by custom been assigned. But it does not follow from this fact that that feature is a relational one. It is the realist who gives a more natural account of what it is to recognize that something has a property. These various objections should, then, lead one to reject resemblance nominalism.

5. ABSTRACT PARTICULARS

There is however an important variant of resemblance nominalism which has not been discussed; it is due to G. F. Stout (1923). According to Stout, each of what I have been calling the *instances* of a property is itself a particular. Stout calls these particulars *abstract particulars*, to distinguish them from concrete particulars or substances. Abstract particulars, Stout maintains, form classes. There are more general classes and less general classes. Thus instances of *crimson* fall into a class, and this is a sub-class of the class formed by all the instances of *red*. In this way, Stout accounts for the fact that some properties are more general than others. But what is it that makes it the case that instances of crimson are to be classified together into a class distinguished from the class formed by the instances of blue, or of roundness? Stout speaks of each class as possessing a "distributive unity". In what does this unity consist? If we look for Stout's answer, we find him saying in one place that it consists of abstract particulars *as such* being instances of a universal.[9] Yet he seems to deny that a universal is present in its entirety in each of its instances. Elsewhere, Stout suggests that the unity of a class of abstract particulars consists in their resembling one another.[10] Yet Stout denies that resemblance can account for the unity of classes of concrete particulars, and it is hard to see why his reasons for this denial should not apply to classes of abstract particulars as well. Thus Stout's own view appears to be ambiguous. But unless Stout's actual view is some *third* view, perhaps the exegetical question need not delay us.

Let us then examine Stoutian nominalism, according to the second interpretation suggested above. According to it, the *primary* relata of resemblance-relations are abstract, not concrete, particulars. Concrete particulars can be said to resemble one another only derivatively, by virtue of being characterized by abstract particulars which are resembling. It is perhaps even less appropriate to classify Stout's view as a variety of nominalism, than it is to so classify the form of resemblance nominalism previously examined. For, although Stout's universe contains only particulars, these particulars are of two radically different kinds. On the other hand there are no universals in this universe. One reason Stout's view is important is that it escapes the criticisms I have marshalled against the first variety of resemblance nominalism. Essentially, this is due to the fact that it compares abstract particulars rather than concrete particulars for resemblance. Since it is quite easy to see why each of the previous arguments fails against Stout, I shall not stop to spell the matter out.

The crux of the argument for Stoutian nominalism is easy to state. It is that when a property P recurs, it recurs at distinct spatiotemporal locations. But, since one and the same thing cannot be at two places at the same time, it follows that each recurrence of P is a distinct individual. In arguing thus, Stout is of course assimilating properties to concrete particulars. In particular, he is arguing that the way in which identity and difference are determined for concrete particulars applies to properties as well. Difference in spatiotemporal location is a sufficient condition of non-identity for concrete particulars; it is also a sufficient condition for non-identity among properties.

The short way with this argument, on behalf of realism, is to deny that difference in the spatiotemporal location of two instances of P shows that there is nothing which is identical in these two cases. It is to reject spatiotemporal location as a principle of individuation for properties, for example on the grounds that properties are not spatiotemporal. This is the argument G. E. Moore (1923) opposed to Stout's. If two circular figures are both round, it is one and the same *roundness* which we find in each of them. Moore, in effect, is suggesting that the same identity-criteria cannot be applied to properties as are applicable to concrete particulars. This is because properties and concrete particulars are not the same sorts of things: there is a categorical difference between them. Properties can be predicated of or ascribed to particulars; but concrete particulars cannot be predicated of or ascribed to anything. Yet, it is not clear why this categorical difference should entail a difference in identity-criteria. We must avoid facile assumptions which model one category upon another; but on the other hand, conceptual economy favors the postulation of similar structure when there are no positive reasons against doing so. Thus far, the controversy between Stout and Moore seems to end in a stalemate.

Are there then any further considerations which shed some light on the problem? I shall discuss four difficulties for Stoutian nominalism. The first three of these are perhaps not decisive. The fourth may well be decisive; but it engages difficult issues concerning the nature of space and time. It may be, therefore, that a Stoutian nominalist can escape all four difficulties. But I am not sure how he might do so.

The first difficulty concerns the existence of abstract particulars other than property-instances. Possibly there are such things as, for example, classes or propositions. At the risk of engendering some confusion, I shall call such things abstract individuals, so as to distinguish them from Stout's abstract particulars. Yet they are, purportedly, particulars – that is, they have properties but are not themselves predicable of anything. Perhaps there are no abstract individuals in this sense. Perhaps numbers, etc. either do not exist, or are analyzable in terms of concrete particulars and/or abstract particulars. But if there are abstract individuals not so analyzable, it is plain that *their* properties can both recur, and that they are not individuated by the spatiotemporal locations of their bearers: for their bearers do not have any spatiotemporal location.

There are several maneuvers available to the Stoutian nominalist with respect to this point. The simplest – and perhaps the most attractive – is to deny the existence of abstract individuals. But abstract individuals can be retained, so long as some *other* way of individuating their property-instances can be found. There are two ways in which this might be done. One is to hold that each abstract individual is a bare particular, and that it is its association with a distinct bare particular (rather than spatiotemporal location) which individuates these property-instances.[11] The other way is to hold that no two abstract individuals are qualitatively identical; what individuates each property-instance is its membership in a unique collocation of other property-instances. For abstract individuals, if not for concrete ones, this view has some plausibility.[12] Thus – if any of the above views is independently defensible – the first difficulty does not rule out Stoutian nominalism.

The second difficulty concerns relations. The question before us is whether the instances of relations are spatiotemporally individuatable. And this amounts, I suppose, to the question of whether relations are spatiotemporally localizable. We have previously encountered the difficulty of specifying "where" particular instances of relations are to be found. Once again, it seems that it is open to the Stoutian nominalist to locate relation-instances which relate concrete particulars at the spatiotemporal locations of those particulars. Yet, at least, this view of them cannot claim the kind of phenomenal support which Stout adduces for the particularity of monadic properties. Is it clear that the two instances of the relation *being father of* exemplified by a man and his twin sons are individuated by the distinct spatiotemporal locations of the twins?

Thirdly, one might challenge the use of spatiotemporal location as a criterion of individuation for concrete particulars. There are certain elementary particles, classified as bosons, which can "occupy the same place at the same time," insofar as it makes sense to ascribe spatiotemporal co-ordinates to quantum particles.[13] (If it does *not* make sense to ascribe location to such particles, Stout's criterion of individuation is inapplicable anyway.) But I shall pass over this objection, which relies upon technical issues in quantum physics.

The fourth difficulty is the most crucial one. We may begin our exposition of this difficulty with the general observation that when spatiotemporal location is ascribed to a concrete particular, it is evident that what is being ascribed to that particular is, or involves, one or more properties. The question is: how are the instances of these spatiotemporal properties individuated? To say that they are individuated by their spatiotemporal location gives every appearance of leading to a vicious regress. To assign spatiotemporal location to instances of spatiotemporal properties is, if intelligible at all, apparently to ascribe to them second-order spatiotemporal properties, whose instances must in turn be individuated, and so on. Clearly, if Stout's view is to be saved, this regress must be shown to be indicative of some error in the way in which the argument conceives what it is to have spatiotemporal location. It is therefore necessary to analyze that notion more carefully. I suggest that this requires us to examine whether the existence of space and time is independent of the existence of concrete particulars, or whether it depends upon their existence. Whichever of these opinions is adopted, the strategy for escaping the regress remains the same, for it must involve concrete particulars as the individuators of abstract particulars. However, what those particulars are, and how their association with instances of spatiotemporal relations is conceived, depends upon the question just raised. I do not, of course, pretend that Stout himself would have any sympathy for the strategy I am suggesting. But he seems to have no alternative.

Consider the view that space and time have independent existence. According to this view, spatial and temporal location could exist even if there were no (other) particulars. Each such location must itself be a particular, whose essential – indeed only – features are given by its spatial (or temporal) properties. A concrete particular – say, a material body – having a location would then consist in that body's bearing to a given spatial location (itself a particular) and a given temporal location (also a particular) the relation of coincidence. In the context of this view, the question previously raised becomes: how are distinct instances of coincidence distinguished? Clearly, it will not do to invite a regress by saying that they do not *coincide* with one another. Can we say instead that they are individuated by one of their relata – namely, the spatiotemporal location itself? Perhaps so, although Stout himself would certainly have rejected this suggestion.[14] The main difficulty with it is that it is hard to see how, in this case, *we* could individuate abstract particulars. For it is hard to see how we could identify space-time positions, apart from the qualities and relations they possess. Indeed, a similar objection can be brought against a second way of providing for the individuation of abstract particulars.

This second strategy does not rely upon spatiotemporal location for the individuation of either abstract of concrete particulars. Instead, concrete particulars themselves play the fundamental individuating role. They themselves – independently of the properties they exemplify – *are* inherently particular. Their particularity is what, in turn, individuates the property-instances which they exemplify.[15] According to this view, there are such things as bare particulars, to which we bear a cognitive relation which is such as to apprise us of their particularity. The main objection to this view arises, once again, from doubts as to the existence of such a cognitive relation, which does not depend upon any of the properties of a particular.

The only other alternative which I am able to imagine is one according to which spatiotemporal locations are identified by reference to a single spatiotemporal location and spatial direction, p and $\bar{r}$. These are themselves identified without making use of any descriptive resources. All other space-time points are then located by means of their spatial and temporal relations to p and $\bar{r}$. It might seem that p and $\bar{r}$ could themselves be identified "indexically" – for example, as "here" and "in that direction." But I do not see how this could be done without presupposing the prior identification of an individual – that is, a perceiver – which is not a space-time location.

Each of the above strategies relies upon a problematic identification procedure. I have not shown that none of these procedures is one we use; nor do I know how to prove this. And the Stoutian nominalist may think of yet another, less troublesome way of explaining how abstract particulars are individuated. Indeed, as we shall see, the realist must confront analogous problems in explaining the individuation of concrete particulars. Thus the above arguments do not enable us to conclude that Stoutian nominalism is mistaken. What they do show is that this view has not been adequately articulated by Stout.

Before leaving the topic of Stoutian nominalism, there is one further consideration which requires mention. Some realists have held that a property can exist, or have being, even when it has no instances. Whatever grounds can be offered in support of this claim – these we shall presently have occasion to discuss – must *a fortiori* be grounds for rejecting Stoutian nominalism.

6. EMPIRICISM AND REALISM

A long history of antagonism marks the relations between empiricism and realism. This is not to say that no philosopher has thought the two positions reconcilable, nor that no one has been both an empiricist and realist. Most empiricists, however, have also been nominalists. Yet empiricism is an epistemological doctrine. Realism (in the present sense) is an ontological doctrine. Why have these two doctrines so often been thought to be incompatible?

The main reason for conflict between empiricism and realism lies in the sort of account that has often been given to explain how we come by our knowledge of universals.[16] Clearly, any account will depend heavily upon what sorts of entities universals are understood to be. Thus, the traditional antagonism between empiricism and Platonic realism. Here it will be convenient to revise my use of the term 'abstract,' so as to disengage it from its preceding association with Stout's view. Henceforward, by an abstract entity I shall mean one which is not spatial or temporal. According to Platonic realism, universals are abstract entities. That there could be such entities is, for an empiricist, a hard doctrine to swallow. Or, it is at least hard to accept that the existence of entities of such a sort could be known. It has seemed obvious to most philosophers that something whose existence transcends space and time cannot come to be known through the medium of sense perception.

Plato felt forced to assign the acquisition of knowledge of universals to non-sensory faculties. But his theory of recollection was not destined to win the hearts of empiricists. Few philosphers would take this theory seriously; it may be wondered how literally and seriously Plato himself took it. His later writings suggest that the ascent of knowledge to a knowledge of forms is mediated by intellectual processes which go beyond sense perception; but it is not necessary to suppose that Plato retained the view that this ascent requires a life before or after death. Empiricists anathematize, nevertheless, the idea that there is a kind of intellectual vision which can take us beyond the evidence of the senses. Or rather, they are by and large agreed that substantive knowledge has no proper bailiwick beyond the boundaries of what can be supplied by sense perception, reinforced or extended by inductive reasoning.

I think it can fairly be said that I have adhered to the spirit (if not the letter) of the empiricist tradition. Yet in discussing the problem of induction I suggested that its solution requires a richer conception of causal explanation than empiricists have traditionally tried to get along with. Those investigations which, while carried out in an empiricist spirit, suggest that the richness and variety of scientific explanations cannot be adequately elucidated by the deductive-nomological model,[17] may help to alert us to the dangers of a too narrowly conceived view of what sorts of explanations ought to be judged admissible in metaphysics. Thus, one must be wary of dismissing Platonic realism out of hand on the ground of its supposed violation of empiricist principles. For *if* this form of realism provides the best explanation of the phenomenon of recurrence, a phenomenon which *is* observed, then we have *prima facie* grounds for adopting it. In saying this, I am, then, allowing that we have a conception of explanation – or rather, I should say, conceptions of explanation – which are richer than the thin format permitted by Humean empiricism. But one does not thereby renounce empiricism as such.

Those philosophers who have combined realism with empiricism, it must be said, have generally held some non-Platonic version of realism. The critical issue, I believe, is whether universals can exist unexemplified. For if they can, it seems necessary to conclude that they exist in a non-spatiotemporal way. I shall argue that there are, or may be, unexemplified universals. Whether we can identify *particular* universals of which this is so is a difficult question, since, obviously, our knowledge of universals ordinarily derives from knowledge of their instances. But we may have grounds for the general proposition that there are or may be such universals, without being able to identify any particular one. If unexemplified universals do exist, then there is reason to hold that universals can exist both "in" space and time – insofar as they have spatiotemporally locatable instances – and "outside" of space and time. If this be allowed, then every instantiated physical universal has both of these modes of existence. But before we can pursue this line of thought any further, it will be necessary to first discuss two topics which are central to the development of a realist treatment of the recurrence of properties. These are, first, the relation of universals to space and time, and second, the problem of giving identity-criteria for universals. These subjects are treated in the next two chapters.

7 The relation of universals to space and time

1. PHYSICAL VS. NON-PHYSICAL UNIVERSALS

The principal concern of this essay, as previously stated, is with physical universals. By 'physical universals' I shall mean universals whose instances can be located in space and time. This definition generates a difficulty similar, but not identical, to one just discussed for Stoutian nominalism. For Stout the question was: If properties are individuated by spatiotemporal location, what individuates spatial and temporal properties? The present question is: If physical properties are those whose instances are "in" space and time, how are spatial and temporal properties themselves to be classified – that is, can they themselves be in space and time? Moreover, for any universal and its instances to have such a location implies, at least, that the thing in question has spatial and temporal relations to other things. But when we say that *universals*, or their instances, are in space and time, can we mean that *they* bear spatiotemporal relations to other things, or must we mean that the particulars which they characterize do so?

However we decide to answer the preceding questions – whether by assigning spatial location to universals as such, or to their instances, or to the particulars which bear them (or to several of these) – we shall not rule out the possibility that there are particulars which are non-physical and bear non-physical properties. If such particulars exist outside of space and time, the universals they instantiate, as well as the instances themselves, will not have spatiotemporal location. Moreover if mind/body dualism is correct, then there exist particulars which exhibit temporal, but not spatial, properties; in that case mental properties may be such that they (and/or their instances) have temporal but not spatial location. I shall leave the existence non-physical particulars and properties

171

open, for I believe that nothing I have to say about physical properties depends upon resolving this question.

2. THE LOCATION OF PROPERTIES

The most straightforward way to explain what it is for the instances of a property to be "in" space and time is to say that such instances are necessarily co-instantiated with instances of (some) spatial and temporal properties. But this way leads to difficulty in understanding how, without apparent circularity or regress, it can be that spatial and temporal properties are themselves physical. If we say that co-instantiation means instantiation in the same place at the same time, then the co-instantiation of a spatial or temporal property with others cannot be explained without circularity – for spatial and temporal coincidences are themselves spatial and temporal properties, respectively, which recur. How, then, could we explain what it is for instances of coincidence to be in space and time? If we say that co-instantiation means just instantiation by the same particular, then we are driven to suppose that the individuation of particulars does not depend upon any of their properties. To say that co-instantiation is primitive and directly recognizable also yields a formal solution. But it is as mysterious as the appeal to bare particulars as ultimate individuators. Alternatively – and this is not implausible – it may be possible to hold that spatial and temporal properties are somehow "special." But then this specialness needs to be explained and its consequences brought to light.

If spatial and temporal relations themselves have location, then it follows that **these** relations characterize both particulars and instances of **universals**. Among these instances are included instances of spatial and temporal relations. To be *square*, for instance, is, or entails, the existence of certain spatial relations among the parts of a particular; if an instance of squareness is located in a particular place, then instances of these relations are located there, too. But this is just to say that these instances of spatial relations instantiate spatial relations to other things; and the latter spatial-relation instances will in turn stand in spatial relations, and so on. But surely this does not mean that every instance of a spatial property in turn instantiates some higher-order spatial properties. It merely constitutes an elliptical and rather misleading way of saying that there is a system of places in which are embedded the physical particulars which have these spatial properties. To speak, in other words, of the spatial location of property-instances is to speak elliptically of the locations of the things which possess these properties.

This, however, does not yet answer the question, what it is to be "in" space and time. I have recently mentioned two main ways of answering this question. According to one way, space and time are constituted by a system of "places" which bear to one another certain ordering relations, and whose existence is independent of the existence of material particulars. In this view, places are rather like substances, and are occupied by other (material) substances when the matter of the latter coincides with them. In this view, to be in space is to bear spatial relations to the places which constitute space.

The second view is that there are just material particulars between which spatial (and temporal) relations obtain. To speak of space and time is just to speak of these relations. In this view, which appears more parsimonious, space and time do not exist independently of the particulars which are "in" them; if the latter did not exist, neither could the former. How are we to decide between these alternatives? One possible route to an answer leads through a consideration of what it is that individuates distinct material particulars.

3. THE IDENTITY OF INDISCERNIBLES

The nature of space and time are not only relevant to the question of what it is for something to be embedded in space and time. They affect our understanding of spatial and temporal properties. And they affect the question of the individuation of spatiotemporal particulars. The latter question can be put in the form of a challenge to realists. This challenge may be expressed in terms of the incompatibility of the following principles.

(A) There is no individuating principle for particulars which is independent of the properties they possess.

(B) If *a* and *b* are particulars such that there is no qualitative difference between them, they may nevertheless be numerically distinct.

Principle (A) is adhered to by those philosophers who hold that particulars are "bundles" of properties. But it would also be accepted by anyone who held there to be substances, but denied that there was any ground for the identification of substances, apart from their possession of properties. The main arguments for (A) are epistemological: we cannot perceive bare substance (or individual-ity) as such; the only way in which quantitative distinctness is recognizable is in virtue of qualitative difference. Principle (B) is a denial of the principle of the Identity of Indiscernibles (hereafter I.I.). An evaluation of (B) will require the making of some distinctions.

Realists who accept (B) must deny (A), for if $a \neq b$, and $(\forall F)(Fa \equiv Fb)$ – where 'F' is a variable ranging over qualities – then there must be some individuating principle which underlies the nonidentity of a and b, which does not depend upon their qualities. For this reason some realists – notably Gustav Bergmann (1967) – have denied (A) and rejected the arguments in its favor, holding that the individuality of a particular has a presentational character, although this is not a question of our being presented with any quality or universal.

One way to approach the problem is to consider the intelligibility of a case suggested by Max Black (1952). We are asked to imagine a universe which contains two qualitatively identical metal spheres and nothing else. These spheres, *ex hypothesi*, do not differ in any of their non-relational properties; Black goes on to argue that they will not differ in any of their relational properties either. If one sphere, for example, has the property that its center lies 2 miles from the center of a metal sphere of such-and-such description, then *a fortiori* the other sphere will have that self-same relational property. The proposition that such a universe exists entails no contradictions; hence, Black reasons, I.I. is false.

Suppose one of the spheres is named 'a,' and the other 'b.' Then, surely, a has the property of *being 2 miles from b*, but b does not have this property. Conversely, b, but not a, has the property *being 2 miles from a*. But in order for these to be genuine properties, 'a' and 'b' must be genuine names; in order for 'a' and 'b' to be genuine names, it must be possible to refer to a and b; and in order for there to be genuine reference, it must be possible to distinguish a from b. What basis is there for such a distinction? An observer might notice that one of the spheres is to his left, and the other to his right, but Black wards off this maneuver on the grounds that to suppose a and b to be distinguishable in this way is to illegitimately import into the specimen universe a third object, namely, an observer.

Perhaps we can elude this difficulty by imagining each of the two spheres to be a percipient homunculus. Let each sphere survey its surroundings. (We can imagine the entire surface of each sphere to be photosensitive to avoid asymmetries creeping into the universe.)

Of course we shall imagine that each sphere has qualitatively identical thoughts, etc. Now it seems that each homunculus could see – hence refer to – the other. Nothing, so far as I can see, bars the logical possibility of each homunculus also referring to itself: through awareness of its own thoughts, or by virtue of proprioceptive sensations which enable it to be aware of its own body. Thus one of the homunculi could name itself 'a,' and name its sibling 'b'.[1] But then – contrary to Black's argument – it is intelligible to say (in the idiolect of either sphere) that it – but not its sibling – has the relational property *being 2 miles from b* and hence *this* universe is not a counterexample to I.I.

I am uncertain as to what should be made of the above argument. There is, on the one hand, a strong intuition that either of the sentient spheres could use indexical expressions to differentially refer to itself and to its companion. On the other hand, since no expression containing only general terms can serve to replace the identifying role of the indexicals or proper names thus introduced, it seems that the predicate expression 'being 2 miles from *b*' does not correspond to a genuine universal.[2] Another difficulty, in any case, is that the possibility of introducing names in my modification of Black's example appears to depend upon the fact that the homunculi are conscious entities. The position of each *vis-à-vis* its own thoughts and sensations differs from its position with respect to those of its siblings. Thus what is crucial here is the privacy and intentionality of conscious states. This suffices to give content to the required names and/or indexical terms. In a universe in which the two spheres were *not* conscious beings, this crucial feature would be absent. Hence, the possibility of identifying reference would be absent. Thus, even if my amended version of Black's universe is not a counterexample to I.I., it still appears that Black's own example is. And only one counterexample is required to disprove the thesis. Yet, it seems odd that the presence or absence of consciousness in such a universe would in any way be relevant to the question of whether that universe satisfied I.I.

The force of Black's counterexample to I.I. relies upon the fact that his universe appears to be quite conceivable, and that in it, there are spheres which are *in different places*. Thus the critical question is whether, and in what sense, being in different places constitutes a difference between the spheres – a difference in their properties. Do spatial relations individuate? Of course if Black is correct, the individuating function of spatial relations here is not a matter of there being distinct spatial relations instantiated by the two spheres. Rather the claim would be that the spheres are individuated by virtue of their being the relata of some antireflexive spatial relation(s), such as *being 2 miles away from*.

E. B. Allaire (1965) denies that spatial relations individuate. He argues that, in order for two particulars to stand in a relation, it must be presupposed that they are already two individuals. It cannot be the existence of the relation which *makes* them two. Against this, Meiland (1966) argues – correctly – that the instantiation by *a* and *b* of an antireflexive spatial relation (e.g., *being to the left of*) is logically sufficient for the numerical diversity of *a* and *b*. For reasons which will I hope become clear, I do not think it follows that the numerical diversity of concrete particulars *consists* (merely) *in* their occupying different locations. Nevertheless, I shall argue that spatial location plays an essential role in the individuality of physical particulars.

We may begin by noting some puzzles concerning the attribution of spatial location to a particular (at a time). We may, I have said, regard spatial location as a property of that individual, and as involving nothing more. Or, we may regard the claim that *a* occupies spatial point *P* as asserting a relation (*coinciding with*) between *a* and *P*. (The former construction suits an ontology in which space is not regarded as having any existence apart from material particulars; the latter an ontology which gives space independent status – for example, as consisting of a collection of particulars, namely, spatial points.)

In what way might an ontology which includes spatial points bear on the issue which confronts Realism? The question was: can the realist account for the individuation of particulars? And in particular, can he do so without appeal to epistemologically problematic entities? The appeal to substance, conceived as a substrate for properties, is problematic on at least two counts: first, because so conceived, it is something distinct from its properties – hence in itself unperceivable; and second, because if it is propertyless and unperceivable, it is hard to imagine how it could serve as a principle of individuation. It seems that substances, if individuated, must be individuated by being different in some way – that is by having distinct properties. Black's example counters this suggestion. A philosophically direct way of dealing with the difficulty is advocated by Bergmann (1967) and Allaire (1965): the individuating is done by a bare particular. In any particular, this is the element of distinctness, and it grounds the individuation, the distinguishability, of particulars. So, particulars *per se* are claimed to be both perceivable and not properties. Bare particulars are countable. To those who claim to be unacquainted with bare particulars, this combination of features seems strange indeed. Yet, in a sense, the phenomenological fact upon which the view is based can scarcely be denied. We *are* (sometimes) "presented with" the distinctness of concrete particulars even though we perceive no qualitative difference between them. The difficulty is to understand precisely what this distinctness consists in.

The temptation to secure the distinctness of concrete particulars in terms of the distinctness of the spatial positions they occupy draws a quick response from Allaire: an account of the distinctness of spatial points requires that we regard *them* as bare particulars – or as containing bare particulars as constituents. Thus the solution to the problem is not advanced but only deferred another step. Let us see whether this conclusion is indeed forced upon us. It may seem, initially at least, that it is. Positions in empty space are, so far as their monadic properties are concerned, indistinguishable. And, unless they can be differentially related to some independently distinguishable reference point, their relational properties are indistinguishable as well. Russell (1948, Chapter 8) suggested that the spatial positions of visual space could be distinguished in terms of their centrality in the visual field; the construction of a physical space which contains unperceived points is possible because it is plausible to assume that there is at least one position in physical space which is uniquely characterizable in terms of the monadic properties of whatever occupies it. Other points can be specified in terms of their distinct spatial relations to that one. But Russell's position depends upon what amounts to a pious hope. There is no reason to suppose that duplicate worlds to ours are logically impossible. Yet in Russell's view they are ruled out *a priori*, for in that case there would be no descriptively unique point.

Nevertheless, Russell's analysis of visual space takes note of a crucial fact. It seems plain that there is a difference between noncoinciding positions, and that this difference attaches to material particulars which occupy these respective positions. Moreover, if we see these particulars, or even if we see an empty volume of space, we perceive this difference. Thus something individuates these positions.

It might seem that the realist should hold different spatial positions to be distinct tokens of some single universal. But this he cannot do if he wishes to make use of difference of position as a criterion for the individuation of all concrete particulars. For he must be able to say what distinguishes different instances of the universal, *occupying a position*, and appeal to distinct positions here generates, as we saw, either a circle or a vicious regress. Moreover, it seems that positions themselves can exist independently of anything else; in particular, independently of being occupied by any material substance. It is perhaps true, as a matter of physical law, that all of physical space is permeated by material substance (in the form, perhaps, of energy); and more to the point, it is sometimes held to be logically impossible for space to exist if there are no material particulars. This latter view is, I think, counterintuitive but I know no way of disproving it. At the very least, an entirely empty space seems to be something we have no difficulty in conceiving. This suggests that spatial positions fall under the general category of substance, rather than under that of universals. Similar considerations apply to temporal location. In particular, I find nothing contradictory in the supposition that an empty space could endure through an interval of time. If this is so, then a natural conception of what it is for a concrete particular, namely *a*, to be in space and time is this: to say that *a* occupies a spatiotemporal position *P,t* is to say that *a* bears a certain relation (namely, *coincidence*) to another particular, namely *P,t*.

Exception may be taken to this analysis on the grounds that *being at P,t* is not a universal, relational or otherwise. For, it is commonly held that at most one particular can occupy a spatiotemporal location. But if it is a necessary truth that only one particular can occupy *P,t*, then *occupying P,t* is not a universal. It is obvious that such an objection would be misplaced on several counts. First, because even though it be allowed that only one material particular could bear the relational property *coincides with P,t*, the *relation*, *coincides with*, is multiply instantiable. Second, because, perhaps, the spatiotemporal position *P,t* itself possesses the relational property *coincides with P,t*. (I shall examine this claim below.) Third, because occupancy of *P,t* can be analyzed into *coincidence with P* and *coincidence with t*, and each of these is multiply instantiable by material particulars.

Finally, suppose it is a necessary truth that a universal can be multiply instantiated. Suppose also that, necessarily, at most one particular can instantiate *occupying P,t*. Does it follow from these two principles that *occupying P,t* is not just a relational property? How we answer this depends upon how we disambiguate an ambiguity that attends the first of these principles. Where '*U*' is a variable ranging over universals, we can express this principle as:

(1) $\Box(\forall U)(\Diamond U$ has more than one instance)

But this can be expanded either as:
(2) $\Box(\forall U)\Diamond(\exists x)(\exists y)(x \neq y \ \& \ Ux \ \& \ Uy)$

or as:

(3) $\Box(\forall U)(\exists x)(\exists y)(x \neq y \ \& \ \Diamond Ux \ \& \ \Diamond Uy)$

The objection to regarding *occupying P,t* as a universal rests upon interpretation (2) of (1). But surely (3) is the correct rendering of the principle which (1) is intended to express?[3] There may be properties which can characterize only one thing. If, however, such a property could have characterized something other than the particular it does characterize, then it is multiply instantiable, and hence a universal. Or at least I shall count it as such, if it be insisted that the choice between (2) and (3) is a matter of definition. For things which satisfy (3) but not (2) can surely belong to the same ontological category as things which satisfy (2). For example, many (perhaps all) the things which satisfy (3) without satisfying (2) are complex properties. These include *occupying P,t*; for not even a Minkowskian view of space-time should lead us to regard this property as simple and unanalyzable.[4] Yet the simpler properties into which these complex ones are analyzable are, often at least, properties which satisfy (2) as well. Thus I take (3) to be the more plausible interpretation of Principle (1).

So far I have defended the analysis of space-time occupancy which regards material particulars as bearing relations to spatio-temporal points. But there are several puzzles with the notion that spatiotemporal points are particulars.

Take, first, spatial points. For some material particular, *a*, to occupy a spatial point *P* was, on the suggested analysis, for *a* and *P* to stand in a certain relation, namely the relation of *coinciding* or *being in the same location as*. However, if point *P* is also a particular, it is evident that it must be a particular of the sort which has a location. Here is the puzzle. Either *P*'s being where it is consists in its relations to other points, or in some intrinsic feature which it has. But if the former, then the relations in question must be spatial ones. It would be by virtue of the fact that they hold that *P* would be distinguished from other points. But how can spatial relations individuate purely spatial entities which have no individual being apart from exemplifying these relations? And considered intrinsically, no point is different from any other; so *P*'s location cannot be one of its intrinsic features. Perhaps, then, we should reject the substantial view of space.

This conclusion is reinforced by a peculiar feature of locations. We have been exploring the possibility that the individuation of otherwise qualitatively identical particulars must consist in their difference of position. This suggests that the distinctness of distinct positions is prior to, or at any rate, independent of, that of material particulars. It was this idea which led to the notion that positions are themselves particulars of some sort, related to the distinct material particulars that occupy them.

The contrasting view is that there is no determining of different positions unless there were some material objects; or even, that no space could exist without such objects. Since I believe that an empty space is conceivable, I regard this position as implausible. I shall therefore proceed, provisionally, on the assumption that there could be such a space. Very well: let us imagine an empty space, infinite in extent, which lacks material objects. Since such a space is extended, it clearly contains different locations. But there is a peculiar sense in which these locations are necessarily anonymous. There is nothing which distinguishes any location from any other. The sense in which this is so can be brought out by seeing that there is no way of tracing the "same" spatial location through time – no criterion for reidentifying it which distinguishes it from other locations. It will be seen that this is not simply a trivial consequence of the fact that, *ex hypothesi*, an empty space contains no human identifiers of points. It is rather a consequence of the very nature of such a space. Not even a non-spatial deity, were he somehow *en rapport* with such a space, would be able to identify locations as temporally enduring entities. It is in this sense that all locations are the same in their "intrinsic nature." Yet, such a space contains more than one location. If continuous, it must indeed contain infinitely many.

Suppose we introduce a single, enduring object into such a universe. Let it be a metal sphere of finite radius. Clearly this sphere is somewhere, and not everywhere. At any given moment, there is a distinction between the point-locations that are on or within its surface and those which are not. No point-location can at that time be both inside and outside the sphere. The sphere thus divides the space into two sets of points. Yet, once again, there is no criterion of identity through time for each of these sets of points. If there were some independent way of deciding whether or not the sphere were moving, such a criterion would be available. Since there is no way of deciding this (short of stipulating a state of motion or rest for the sphere), the addition of the sphere in no way reduces the anonymity of spatial points, except insofar as we can specify them, at a given time, via reference to the sphere.[5] It is obvious I think that adding other objects to the imagined universe in no way improves this situation.

Nevertheless it *is* intelligible that the other objects should be – at a given time – in *different* locations than the sphere, just as the different parts of the sphere itself are differently located. Although spatial locations *per se* cannot be thought of as reidentifiable through time, material objects can be at well-defined distances from one another, and move with well-defined velocities with regard to each other. The genidentity of spatial locations is only intelligible if their identity is parasitic upon the location of some reidentifiable material object; but the distinctness of spatial locations at a given time is in no way dependent upon material objects.

What import do these observations have for the nature of space and its contribution to the individuation of material objects? First, as regards the puzzle concerning the location of spatial points: If points could be assigned "absolute" positions, there would be no problem of anonymity, nor of reidentification through time. The fact that points are anonymous is a reflection of their lack of absolute location. To say that a point coincides with itself, while true enough (indeed tautologous) neither provides that point with an identity in this strong sense, nor presupposes it. The identity of a point is exhausted in the system of relations which it bears to itself and to other points; in the fact that these are spatial relations. If any one of these points could be identified as a particular persisting through time, all the rest could as well (as long as the space containing them is connected). What can be said is that: (a) there is more than one location; (b) spatial relations are instantiated by these locations; in that sense, the latter are particulars; (c) the existence of more than one point is necessarily connected to the fact that there are instantiated antireflexive spatial relations; (d) since we can think of spatiotemporal points as particulars, it is evident that we are able to identify some of these (or small space-time volumes) indexically – that is, by reference to ourselves, provided it is true that perceptual consciousness is directed toward physical space.

Such *reference* to a spatiotemporal location logically presupposes, therefore, the existence of some object(s) within space. For conscious awareness can provide a perspective only insofar as it sees itself directed upon objects (or points in empty space) from a given spatial standpoint; only insofar as it views itself as situated within the same space as its objects. Thus, the existence of such a perspective, and of indexical reference, presupposes spatial relations. A coherent account of these facts seems possible if we allow: (1) that anonymous spatiotemporal particulars are ontologically independent of material objects; and *a fortiori*, that spatial relations can be instantiated by an empty space; (2) that the identification of spatiotemporal particulars logically presupposes the existence of material particulars, or at least of concrete individuals located in space, other than the spatial points which constitute it – spatiotemporal points therefore are particulars of a peculiarly "thin" sort, albeit not bare particulars; and (3) that spatial points do not endure through time.[6]

Second, material objects require or presuppose the existence of spatiotemporal location. They are not independent of the existence of space and time; space and time, therefore, are ontologically prior to material things.

Although positions in space-time are intrinsically anonymous, they are nevertheless capable of conferring individuation upon physical particulars which occupy them. Physical particulars confer identity upon locations; locations reciprocate by individuating physical particulars. This initially puzzling fact occasions no charge of circularity. It is a consequence of the fact that locations, even *qua* anonymous, are able to instantiate antireflexive relations, and to "confer" those relations upon physical particulars which occupy them. That is what the individuation of physical particulars ordinarily depends upon. *Being 5 miles from* is an example of such an antireflexive relation.[7] If instantiated by material objects, it must be instantiated by a pair of them. Hence the existence of this relation between two objects will distinguish them even when they resemble each other in all (other) respects. Difference in position is a difference in kind. But, because spatial points are anonymous *prior* to the introduction of material objects which can serve to fix reference on them, it is not possible to specify this difference of kind by speaking of a relational property which the one location has and the other lacks. Take Black's two spheres: we can say that sphere *a* has the property, *being 2 miles from b*, which *b* lacks – but only subsequent to the fixing of reference on *a* and *b*; that however presupposes their individuation. Granting this, there is nevertheless a difference between the spheres: they are in different places. Identifying the spheres, and identifying the places they occupy, are correlative operations, neither of which can be said to presuppose the other. But that there are two spheres rather than one, and a difference in where they are, does not presuppose the identification of either spheres or places. It is the anonymity of spatiotemporal locations which might lead us to suppose that Black's universe is a counterexample to the principle of the Identity of Indiscernibles. But the two spheres are discernible, even though this discernability rests upon a fact which cannot be specified in the way Black would require of us.

After having belabored this issue, it might seem now possible for us to conclude that it is just spatial relations which individuate physical particulars. Unfortunately, this conclusion would be too hasty. Difference of location is indeed a sufficient condition of distinctness. But it is not, in my opinion, a necessary one. The question which confronts us here is whether two physical objects, which are identical in all their (other) properties, can occupy the same place at the same time – and remain two. There is a widespread opinion that physical objects must either spatially exclude one another or, failing that, merge into a single object.

There is a kind of verificationist rationale which underlies this intuition. Suppose there were two transparent disks, one tinted pink and the other light blue. Imagine that the matter of which they are composed is of such a sort that the two disks can be made to merge completely; and suppose that the matter in each disk is spatially continuous, so that there is no question of being able (in principle) to distinguish in terms of distinct locations the matter of the one from the matter of the other after they have merged.[8] We see the disks merge into a single purple one. Then, a separation occurs: out of the purple disk emerge a pink one and a blue one. How is the case to be described? If there is any inclination to consider it a case in which two disks merged and, retaining their separate identities, moved apart again, this could be challenged by asking what criterion distinguishes it from a case in which the two initial disks are destroyed, a purple disk created from them, and finally two new disks created. There does not seem to be any way of deciding the issue experimentally. The question becomes, if anything, more acute if we imagine both disks to be qualitatively identical pink ones. In the form I have just posed it here, the question is merely one of a whole class of conceptual issues which surround the problem of identity through time for material particulars. Yet the original issue has nothing intrinsically to do with identity through time. One can just as well ask, with respect to "instantaneous" material entities, whether two of them can occupy the same place at the same time. Either way, the verificationist wants a criterion for determining that there are two entities rather than a single one.

Now unless lack of an empirical criterion renders talk of identity and distinctness unintelligible, I see no *logically* compelling reason for ruling out co-occupancy of space by material objects. On the other hand, the verificationist demand (as I have called it) for a criterion deserves to be taken seriously. Unless we can address it, we are open to the charge that the concept of a material particular which we are employing is unclear.

As it happens the challenge can be addressed. The way to address it is suggested by the previously mentioned physics of elementary particles, where cases of this controversial sort are not merely countenanced as possible, but are claimed actually to occur: the class of elementary particles known as bosons are alleged to exhibit such behavior. But the point does not in any way depend upon an appeal to the special features of quantum mechanics. Conspatial material particles are intelligible in any system which exhibits the following features: (1) matter consists of elementary particles; (2) the elementary particles fall into natural kinds; (3) being of a given kind depends upon the possession of certain monadic properties which are magnitudes having only discrete values; and (4) some of the allowed values are not whole multiples of any smaller allowed magnitude of the same property. Suppose, to take an extremely simple hypothetical case, that every particle of a given species (I shall call them penetrons) has a mass of 1 unit and an electric charge of 1 unit. Suppose that *no* elementary particles of the system have a mass of 2 units and a charge of 2 units, nor a mass and charge of less than one unit respectively (such values are forbidden by the laws that govern the system). If at a given spatiotemporal location we find something which has a mass of 2 units and a charge of 2 units, we can conclude that it is not a single particle but composite. Given the right values for its other properties, we may have to conclude that it consists of two penetrons occupying the same space. And, if a theory were to specify that penetrons of a given type cannot decay or be created, and a system which contains *n* spatially separated penetrons and nothing else at one time were observed to contain a single concentration of mass at another time, we could conclude that this object was composed of penetrons. To be sure, we could not *distinguish* the individual penetrons in such a cluster. Nor, if the cluster flew apart, could there be any question of empirically identifying individual emerging penetrons with ones which had earlier entered the the cluster. But this shows, I think, only that the *distinguishability* of material entities must be considered separately from what it is that constitutes their *particularity*. Under some circumstances we may be in a position to say that a box contains (at least) *n* particulars of a given kind, but be in no position to individually identify those particulars. Thus, distinctness of spatio-temporal location is not a necessary condition for the distinctness of particulars. Where it is absent, there may be some other criterion, supplied by theory, which enables us to determine independently the number of particulars of a kind which are present at a given location. The existence of any criterion of this kind is sufficient to enable the realist to deflect the objection that his metaphysics commits him to a principle, the Identity of Indiscernibles, which is false: it enables him to make the distinction between numerical identity and qualitative identity.

The preceding arguments serve to show, if I am not mistaken, that realists can account for the individuality of particulars without resorting either to bare particulars or to I.I. However, I think these arguments also suggest that the bundle theory is mistaken. The bundle theory cannot explain particulars simply by saying that they are bundles of universals. For the theory must tell us what the principle of unity is, which groups a set of universals into a single bundle, and what distinguishes one such bundle from another. This cannot be done simply by supplying the list of universals which constitute each particular. For we cannot think of a particular as merely a set of universals. If anything, such an object would itself be a universal.

It seems necessary to say that for a universal to be a member of a bundle is for it to enter into a certain relation with other universals. But this is not a promising direction in which to look for an explanation, if the relation in question is yet another universal. Clearly, we cannot merely *add* the relation to the universals said to constitute the bundle. For to add the relation as another constituent is merely to enlarge the set of universals; the result is another set of universals, not a genuine bundle or particular. The relation must instead be said actually to relate the universals; but the natural way to interpret this claim is to take this special relation to be a second-order one. And that cannot solve the problem: a particular does not consist in the obtaining of a second-order relation among universals, as red's being darker than pink does. Thus, in particular, we cannot analyze a particular as constituted by universals standing in spatial relations to one another: these relations are first-order relations. It is difficult to see, therefore, how the bundle theory can account for particularity at all.

I suggest that particularity cannot be reduced to universality. A particular is no mere constellation of universals as such; it is concretely in space and time in a way universals are not. The bundle theorist has two tasks which are not easily fulfilled: to explain the distinction between a universal as such and a universal insofar as it enters into a bundle; and to link this explanation to an explanation of what it is in which the unity and distinctness of a bundle consists.

A realist may be either a bundle-theorist or a substance-theorist with respect to particulars. A bundle-theorist holds that particulars are bundles of universals and nothing else (the bundling-relation itself is a metaphysically special relation which is not simply another member of any bundle). A substance-theorist may hold either the bare-particular view or a substance view. According to the former, a particular is constituted by a bare particular connected to a set of universals by a metaphysically special tie or bond of exemplification. According to the latter, particulars are bound to at least certain of their properties in a stronger sense. What this stronger sense is has been difficult to articulate. At the very least, such a view regards the identity through time of a particular as always being a matter of that particular belonging to a kind. Hence transtemporal identity is dependent upon (at least some of) the properties of a thing. But also, such views regard individuation of a particular at a time as dependent upon some of its properties – though not necessarily its essential properties.

Those arguments which centered around the principle of the Identity of Indiscernibles were designed to show that the view that individuals are individuated by their properties is defensible. They do not suffice to prove that bare-particularism is mistaken, but (in view of the problematic epistemic status of bare particulars) they serve to make it unattractive. They do not serve either to decide between the bundle theory and the substance theory. In the case of conspatial bosons, each of these positions will be equally able to avail itself of whatever theoretical justification there is for asserting that a given spatiotemporal region contains *n* particulars of a given kind. However, we have seen that the bundle theory encounters difficulties in explaining how it is that universals can be united into concrete individuals in space and time, if this is supposed to involve their standing in spatial and temporal relations. That leaves the substance view. It also leaves metaphysical problems. It requires an account of substances, and of their relation to their properties (both the individuating and the non-individuating ones, if such a distinction is viable). I regard these problems as largely beyond the compass of this work. However, the preceding discussion points in a direction which it will be worth pursuing a bit farther.

4. PHYSICAL SUBSTANCES

Having rejected both Nominalism and the Bundle Theory, we are committed to the proposition that there are both particulars and universals, and that these constitute distinct categories, neither of which is reducible to the other. Moreover I believe there are good grounds – to be discussed later – for maintaining that universals can exist even though not (ever) instantiated. When a universal is instantiated by a particular, then the fact that the universal characterizes that particular must consist in there being some relation which holds between the particular and the universal.

These three claims appear to commit one to some sort of Platonic Realism. At least, they entail that the connection between universals and particulars is loose enough to allow that the existence of universals is not strongly parasitic upon the existence of particulars. The existence of a given universal does not require there being any particular instantiating it. Nevertheless, the existence of universals may be weakly dependent upon the existence of particulars. For example, it may be that a group of universals (perhaps all universals) form a unified system; and it may be that the existence of this system of universals is not independent of the existence of particulars which instantiate at least some of the members of that group. This I believe is in fact the case.

Be that as it may, the form of Realism we have before us tends to discourage the use of such locutions as 'is in the particular' or 'is partly identical to the particular' in describing what it is for a universal to be instantiated. These locutions are associated with Immanent Realism. Yet it is not entirely easy to characterize the distinction between Immanent and Platonic Realism. Or rather, the distinction could be characterized in several independent ways. Platonic Realism might be taken, as we have taken it, to be the view that the existence of a universal does not depend upon its being instantiated. Or, it might be taken as the view that universals must be "bound" to the particulars they characterize by some relation. Or thirdly, Platonic Realism might be understood as asserting that universals are not in space and time.

Perhaps it could be shown that each of these three definitions entails the other two; but this is not at all obvious. Immanent

Realism can be variously defined as the converse of each of these three positions.

It cannot be denied that a belief in the independent existence of universals at least encourages the view that instantiation is a relation. Yet the view that instantiation is a relation faces a severe difficulty. If instantiation is a relation (whose terms are a universal and a particular), then a vicious regress is generated. Ryle (1939) put the point thus: There are many instances of this relation. If these are to be explained, it will have to be in terms of an instantiation relation which binds each of these instances to its relata. But this second instantiation-relation is also instantiated; which requires the postulation of a third such relation and so on; *ad infinitum*. Thus instantiation cannot be a relation after all.

But there are also serious difficulties for a non-relational view. Suppose there is no relation between a particular and a property in virtue of which that particular has that property. Yet there is a difference between that particular's having that property, and its not having that property. When the property is one which a particular has contingently, both the particular and the property may exist whether or not the particular has the property. Hence its having the property cannot be a matter merely of the existence of both. If there is no relation which obtains between the two when the particular has the property and lacking when it does not, in what can this difference consist?

Armstrong, who advocates an immanent realism, suggests at one point that the nature of a particular is partially identical to that particular.[9] For he says that two particulars which have a common property (i.e., which "overlap in nature") are partially identical. And he also maintains that 'partial identity' means overlap or identity of a part. Thus the nature of a particular is a part of that particular (i.e., a part of what Armstrong calls a particular in the "thick" sense). The other part is the particular taken in abstraction from its properties (i.e., a particular in the "thin" sense). Though these parts can be distinguished by the intellect, they cannot be separated. Still, if they can be distinguished (as they must be if a particular is not to be wholly identical to its nature), then it seems that they must also be related (by the intellect, if you will) in the case where a property is a constituent of a thick particular. But what is this relation of constituency? This depends upon how the notion of distinction-cum-inseparability can be understood. Perhaps indeed I have taken the notions of 'part' and 'overlap' too literally or univocally. But this solution requires further explanation; until it is supplied it is unclear whether the Immanent Realist can make out the required distinction between *a*'s being *F* and *a*'s not being *F*, or avoid Ryle's regress and thus outstrip its Platonic rival.

Is there any middle ground between the supposition that instantiation involves a relation and the supposition that it does not? The best prospect for the Realist, I believe, is to maintain that instantiation does involve a relation. But, on pain of succumbing to Ryle's infinite regress, he must hold that this is no ordinary relation. The regress must get stopped before it can start; and this means that when *a* instantiates *F*, the instantiation-relation cannot itself be said to be instantiated, if this is to be understood in terms of some further instantiation-relation. Several philosophers, among them Cook Wilson, Bergmann, and Strawson, hold that the instantiation "relation" is *sui generis*, fundamental, and not further explainable.[10] Perhaps this is correct, but there is an inevitable desire not to be reduced to silence at this crucial point. At least, it would be desirable to have some clarifying remarks, some analogy, or some explanation of how it is that no further explanation exists. There are, I believe, some observations that can be made along these lines.

By way of approach to this problem, let us first consider the third thesis associated with Platonic Realism. This thesis is that universals are not in space and time. What can this mean? Physical particulars, at least, are in space and time. The universals they instantiate are 'in' them. Does it not follow that these universals are in space and time? The *redness* of *a* is identical to the *redness* of *b*; that is, both are simply identical to *redness*. The *redness* of *a* is located where *a* is located, and it lasts for a certain time; so should we not say that *redness* is at that place and lasts for that time? Clearly, much depends upon the precise sense(s) in which 'in' was used three sentences previously. If a universal is not in a particular in the same sense in which a particular is in space and time, then matters are not advanced by the use of the term 'in.'

We do not wish to say that universals exist in space and time. If they did so exist, it would obviously be "as" their instances that they existed. Such instances can be created and destroyed; they can change their location. But these vicissitudes cannot be shared by the thing which these instances have in common; for it is precisely in respect of their temporal duration and spatial location, that instances differ. And if universals are in space and time, then spatiotemporal relations characterize universals. Moreover, it will not do to say that spatial and temporal properties exist in space and time, for if they did so, they would themselves have spatial and temporal properties. It will not do to say that the property *enduring for one second* has the property of enduring for one second, nor of enduring for any other period of time. So universals – even physical properties – are not *in themselves* in space and time. Yet physical universals other than spatiotemporal ones "enter into" space and time; for the particulars which have them are necessarily spatio-temporal. It is a necessary truth that they are coinstantiated with some system of spatial and temporal relations.[11]

I return now to the problem of elucidating the relation of instantiation. What has been said suggests that, for physical properties, instantiation is somehow connected to the fact that entities which are not themselves spatiotemporal are somehow "injected" into space and time. This "injection" and instantiation are one and the same thing.

It was argued in the preceding section that spatial and temporal locations are not properties. But neither, I held, are they full-blooded particulars. They are necessarily anonymous particulars. The existence of distinct locations does not presuppose the existence of any material particulars; but identity through time of spatial locations can only be given a sense in relation to such particulars, supposing the latter to be continuants. Thus the system of identifiable and reidentifiable locations, and of individuatable physical objects, is one whose constituents are not logically separable. The existence of physical objects logically requires a space-time framework; and the existence of such a framework logically requires physical objects. So the being-in-space and the being-in-time of a physical object is not a matter of some ordinary *relation* which objects bear to space and time. There is no such relational property as *being-at-location*-α which exists independently of physical objects; for there is no such nameable location as α which so exists. The "relation" between physical objects and space-time is therefore of a very special sort. It seems reasonable to classify it as a formal relation.

What is meant by this can best be illustrated by another example of such a relation, namely set-membership. It is not easy to explain what these relations have in common. However, in each of these cases, the identity of one or both of the relata is constituted by the identity-conditions which determine the other relatum, plus the relation itself. Neither relatum exists independently of the other, and both are then somehow bound together by the relation. Because in these cases the connection between the relata is so intimate and also so transparent, these relations form a very special class. Although they are relations, we do not require any further explanation as to what "binds" them to their relata. Indeed there is no explanation for this. We have reached the ontological bedrock.

Instantiation, I wish to suggest, is in this sense a formal relation. In fact, in the case of physical particulars, it is the very relation previously mentioned between physical universals and identifiable space-time locations. Where such a relation obtains, we have a material particular. Universals "under the aspect" of space and time – that is in union with an anonymous spatial and temporal location "become" individual, distinguishable instances or tokens. They "become" universals "in" particular things.

It is in one way misleading to use the word 'particular' in this connection. The relation of instantiation is indifferent to the distinction between material stuffs (the referents of mass-nouns) and individuals (the referents of count-nouns). The distinction between these is important, but it is metaphysically less fundamental than the distinction between universals and their instances. The stuff, *gold*, instantiates certain properties, whether or not we think of it as divided in a certain way into discrete chunks. But, whether or not it is so divided, it occupies space and time.

A second point must not be lost from view. It concerns the objection which might be raised, that the identification of *instantiation* with the relation between physical particulars and their spatiotemporal location is incompatible with the admission that more than one material particular can occupy the same spatio-temporal location. For, if the particularity of a material thing is constituted by its occupying spatial and temporal location, then does not identity of location entail the unity, in a single particular, of whatever property-instances are "in" that spot?

But this argument employs fallacious reasoning. It has already been urged that a clear distinction must be maintained between the question of what it is for something to be a particular, and what the conditions are under which a particular can be individuated from other particulars. When several bosons of a given species occupy the same location, they cannot be individuated. Nevertheless they exist in space and time; and *a fortiori* they are instantiators of universals. That there are several bosons, each instantiating the same universals, is something which can be determined on independent grounds; it does not presuppose their individuation.

Finally, it is pertinent to raise the subject of abstract or non-material particulars. What implications does the view just sketched have for the relation between non-spatiotemporal particulars and their properties? It seems clear that, if the foregoing theory is correct, and if there are abstract particulars, then their relation to their properties must be importantly different from the relation between material things and their physical properties. The former relation cannot be a matter of "injection" into space and time. If there are abstract particulars, it would be natural to seek some completely general way of describing the universal-particular relation which would embrace both abstract and concrete particulars. But I shall refrain from investigating whether this is possible.

8 The nature of universals

1. THE UBIQUITY OF DISPOSITIONAL PROPERTIES

I begin this part of the investigation with a discussion of the nature of dispositional properties. Although initially it may not seem that this is one of the more central issues to be faced at this level of discussion, it will become clear that it is of very general significance. A cryptic way of expressing this generality would be to announce that all universals are dispositional. Actually that claim is, I think, false. But I shall argue that it is true of a very broadly defined class of properties.

I think it is true that all physical properties are dispositional. However, I do not wish to imply that there are no nondispositional, or occurrent, physical properties. All physical properties are occurrent as well as dispositional. If there is an air of paradox here it can be removed. I shall argue that to speak of a property as occurrent or as dispositional is to speak of different ways in which reference to a property can be linguistically embodied. These ways do not mutually exclude one another. These two modes of reference to properties reflect aspects of their objective character. One aspect is enshrined in dispositional locutions; another in locutions which are nondispositional. But these distinct aspects are compatible. In fact, they require one another. That is why every physical property has both aspects. The dispositional aspect of physical properties reflects the fact that they form a causally interconnected structure or web: each of them confers causal powers. Instantiated properties are occurrent, on the other hand, because causal power is conferred on a particular only when it actually has the required property. When we refer to a physical property, we must make use of its associated powers; for it is only via these that we can single it out. But what we thereby refer to exists (in its instances) not merely potentially but actually. That is what I shall argue.

The cryptic remarks just made can be given substance by offering a theory of the semantics of dispositional expressions. In proposing this theory, or rather, partial theory, I shall emphasize the reference or denotation of predicate expressions – that is, their function in singling out universals. But in so doing there is no intention to minimize other aspects of the meaning of these expressions – for example, their association with general rules or criteria of use. Nor does the treatment of predicates as denoting undermine the subject/predicate distinction.

2. THE SEMANTICS OF DISPOSITION TERMS

The linguistic marks which, in English, signal that a predicate expression is dispositional include the use of certain verb endings. But there are no invariable marks of this sort. When the fact that a certain property is possessed by particulars is not observable under usual circumstances, or in some cases when a property is posited by theory, there is an inclination to regard it as dispositional. (Thus: *being fragile* and *being magnetic*.)

At the same time, it is widely supposed that, associated with every dispositional property, there is a nondispositional or enduring property whose presence explains the dispositions which a particular manifests under given conditions. Empiricists have generally been concerned to spell out the meaning of a dispositional term in terms of the way in which this manifestation takes place: the conditions required for it, and the resulting observed occurrent property. The focus of attention was therefore on two problems: spelling out the relevant antecedent conditions (in terms of observable properties) in a finite way, and explicating the semantics of the subjunctive conditionals utilized in the defining expressions. A further problem arose because many dispositional properties reveal their presence in several ways – indeed indefinitely many ways. The use of operational definitions of dispositional properties had the unhappy consequence that – assuming one property per "meaning" – each of these definitions corresponds to a distinct property, there being merely empirical correlations between them. Yet no satisfactory criterion for individuating operational procedures has ever been proposed; and an operationalist semantics multiplies properties in a manner certainly not congruent with ordinary or scientific thought. The term 'multi-track' has been used to characterize such multiply manifesting dispositions. But if correlation is what unifies "tracks" then every disposition is violently "multiple."

Our approach is different, and bears close analogies to the semantic theory of natural-kind terms which has been developed by Kripke (1972) and Putnam (1975). The fundamental suggestion (but this is a "first approximation") is that we think of dispositional terms as *denoting* the self-same enduring, underlying property which explains speculation as to the existence of that underlying property. Thus, whereas the style of an operational definition of a dispositional – say 'is soluble' would be:

(1) 'x is soluble' = $_{df}$ 'If x were placed in water, x would dissolve',

our style of semantics yields:

(2) *being soluble = having whatever (enduring) property it is which causes dissolving when immersed in water.*

The *objective* of these two semantic analyses is quite different. The first attempts to spell out the meaning of a mentioned expression by supplying a synonymous expression which conveys the rules of use for the first. The second analysis *uses* two expressions to elucidate the denotation of one of the pair. No synonymy claim is being made. This difference is reflected in the difference between '=$_{df}$' which may be read 'is synonymous to,' and '=' which means 'is identical to.'

I shall not defend (2) in detail. But a few remarks will enable me to suggest its advantages over the first analysis. The first and most important remark is that (2) makes explicit, in a way which (1) does not, that the relation between the dispositional property and the properties describing its occurrent manifestations is a causal one and not a logical or analytical one. This difference is far-reaching. It spells out the nature of the explanatory connection which is hinted at by the subjunctive form of (1). One of the implications of (2) is that

(3) If x is soluble, then if x were placed in water, it would dissolve,

expresses a causal law, not an analytic truth. (3) would, if Kripke is right, be an *a priori* truth – since dissolving behavior is used to fix the *reference* of the term 'is soluble;' but it would not be analytic. Thus the bridge-laws and correspondence-rules devised by positivists to define dispositional terms (and theoretical terms generally) represent truths which are laws of nature, not definitions. This explains why there were difficulties over regarding them as analytic.[1]

The alternative semantics I am suggesting throws into sharp relief an ambiguity which has bedeviled positivist linguistic theory since its early days. According to the verificationist theory of meaning, a term is meaningful if and only if it is possible to specify, in purely ostensive (observational) language, the necessary and/or sufficient conditions for its correct application.[2] A sentence is meaningful if and only if its truth-conditions can be similarly spelled out in terms of observation sentences. In either case, the leading idea was that it must be possible, through observation, to distinguish correct from incorrect circumstances for the use of an utterance. But possible in what sense? To this question there is but one answer available to followers of Hume, and Schlick (1932/33), for instance, is seemingly quite explicit on this point. He says that meaning is conferred upon a sentence if it is *logically* possible that observation would decide its truth or falsity. Yet, significantly, the examples Schlick uses[3] all involve something stronger than mere logical possibility. They are all cases in which the "definition" is controlled by what relevant observations are physically possible – that is, are such that making them would (presumably) not violate any causal laws.

In a way, it is not surprising that Schlick (and other positivists) chose their examples as they did. For, first, it is not clear what the requirement of logical possibility would come to. We think of logical possibility as much more clearly understood than physical possibility. But whether that is so or not, it is not so clear when a sentence fails to meet the verificationist criterion of meaning. Certainly, if a sentence asserts the existence of an object whose properties are self-contradictory, it fails to meet the criterion. But what about the exclusions typically credited to the criterion? What would show that it was *logically* impossible, for example, for any observation to count as verifying (or confirming) the existence of a deity? Or of moral goodness?

A second motivation for Schlick's choice of examples is unquestionably a desire to model them upon actual scientific practice. But actual scientific practice, it is easy to show, makes use of the requirement that scientific statements be such that it is *physically* possible to confirm or disconfirm them; and at least some of the conditions under which this is possible must be reasonably well spelled out. It is this kind of reasoning which led Einstein (1917) to his famous criterion for temporal simultaneity of spatially separated events.[4] It was similarly reflections upon what kinds of measurements are causally possible which led Heisenberg to his justification for the Uncertainty Principle, and Bohr to his arguments for the Principle of Complementarity. The success of these conceptual maneuvers in physics had a profound influence upon the thinking of the early positivists.

Yet, given the context of the positivist program, Schlick could not have appealed to the notion of physical possibility in articulating his criterion of meaningfulness. This is not simply because the notion of physical possibility, like that of physical necessity, is an unwelcome problem-child within Humean philosophy. It is, further, because Schlick took questions about meaning to be answerable *a priori*, whereas what does or does not violate the laws of physics is clearly an *a posteriori* matter. Moreover, a verificationist theory of meaning which employed a criterion requiring physical possibility would have an unfortunate consequence. It would entail that a false physical theory – even one which represented the best science of a given period – would be meaningless. For at least some of its statements would conflict with what is physically possible. Ironically, scientists themselves were influenced by the language of early positivists such as Mach. Thus Einstein, in formulating his criterion of simultaneity, speaks of it as a "definition," suggesting that the Galilean conception is physically meaningless.[5] (Einstein later repudiated verificationism, but his earlier language surely seemed to reflect the view that operational criteria were what conferred meaning upon expressions.)

It may seem that we have digressed. But if so, this digression was necessary in order to make clear the significance of the fact that the alternative semantics being proposed for dispositional terms is *not* a theory of meaning, in the same sense that Verificationism was. It does not propose a general criterion for distinguishing meaningful expressions from meaningless ones. A meaningful expression may lack a denotation; there may nevertheless exist intelligible rules for its use and application. Furthermore, the new theory is compatible with the fact that scientific practice requires quantities whose measurement-procedures conform to physical law. Measurement, after all, is a causal process. Indeed, the semantics we have offered *relies* upon this fact.

The other advantages of (2) can now be briefly spelled out. (2) recognizes that the denotative success of a dispositional term relies upon the existence of circumstances which recognizably involve the presence of some causal process. Because (2) recognizes this, and because it does not purport to construct a *synonym* for 'being soluble', it is not plagued by the difficulty of spelling out in infinite detail the relevant circumstances which shall count as proper "test conditions." We need not even know what these are – just so long as we have some grounds for thinking that, in a given range of cases, one and the same underlying property is causally implicated in the production of an observable effect.

Correlatively, (2) shows why one does not have to construe multi-track dispositional terms as ambiguous, that is, as sheltering a range of different senses corresponding to different tests, unified only by the fact that the results they give are (perhaps within partly overlapping ranges) empirically correlated. To say that different tests measure the same property or quantity is to say that the presence of that property causally affects a variety of measuring devices, in different ways, but in every case in a differential manner which makes detection of that property possible.

One of the tests which is used to detect the presence of a property may have a certain linguistic priority over the others. For it may be by means of just one such test that the property is initially picked out. Thus the predicate term whose denotation is that property will be linked in a semantically preferential way to the test in question. It will be a matter of empirical discovery that other tests are sensitive to that same property; but if there is such a property, it is true *a priori* that the test in question is sensitive to it. However, I see no *requirement* that, for any property, a particular test be uniquely singled out to play this semantic role. As long as there exist good empirical grounds for holding that each of several tests reliably signals the presence or absence of a property, there is no reason why a semantic "decision" which favors one of them must be made. There is some considerable plausibility to the view that it is usually the historically first test-procedure which leads to the detection of a property and consequent introduction of a predicate to denote it, which has this preferred status. But circumstances can be easily envisioned in which historical priority would be over-ridden. A Johnny-come-lately test procedure may prove much simpler or more reliable, and under circumstances involving disagreement as to the extension of a predicate, may usurp the reference-fixing function of the original test. And, sometimes, a predicate is introduced to denote a property whose existence has been inferred on theoretical grounds, but which has not yet been measured.[6] I shall not explore these semantic complexities further, but they suggest a more natural semantic account than the positivist one of the behavior of multi-track disposition terms. It is easy to say what principle unifies the cluster of test procedures associated with such a term. It is that the tests detect the presence of one and the same property.

It is necessary here, however, to mention one further complication. The foregoing theory was presented as an alternative to verificationist semantics. I also introduced it as a "first approximation." The reason for this qualification can now be brought forward. It seems to me that a dispositional term could acquire, under certain circumstances, a semantics which conforms more nearly to the traditional verificationist account than to the one just offered. Under what circumstances might this semantic strategy be adopted?

The introduction of a dispositional term to denote some underlying property requires the truth of a crucial presupposition. This presupposition is that the test(s) used to fix the reference of the term effectively single out a unique property. That is, there must *be* a property whose presence those tests measure; and they must measure (upon yielding a result) just *one* property. That property may be a complex one; but it must not be an instance of one property on one occasion and an instance of another one on a different occasion. The presupposition in question may be false; if it is false, the result is failure, or at least infelicity of reference.[7]

The risk that such presuppositions are false is largely associated with the fact that the very means of achieving singular reference introduce the possibility that reference will be lost. Let me explain. The primary difficulty is that the expression 'whatever property is the cause of test result x' does not ever pick out a single property. For in any measurement situation, there is no such thing as *the* cause of the measurement result. Suppose that a measurement-process measures the presence of a property F in a subject a, by yielding a test-result (say, b's becoming G). Among the causal antecedents of b's being G are many besides a's being F: a's being F is merely one state of affairs in a complex, backward-branching sequence of causally related events leading to b's becoming G; that event-tree includes the causes of a's being F, and also all of the other relevant background conditions of the test, as well as their ancestral causes. How, then, is it possible that a test should enable us to single out a particular state of affairs in this sequence, and to fix reference upon its constituent property?

The answer, I think, is that no *single* test could enable one to do this. Nor could a series of tests, in which the antecedent conditions are precisely the same. But a series of tests in which the antecedent conditions are suitably varied *can* provide a context which makes unique reference possible. I think there are two distinct ways in which the field of potential referents can be narrowed down. In order to fix ideas, take the measurement of temperature. Temperature is a determinable quality which has a range of determinate values. One way to narrow the field of causes of thermal measurements is to vary the value of the determinable property to which reference will eventually be made (temperature in this case) over a series of tests. This will require the alteration of some events in the causal tree which leads to the test-results; but others can be held fixed. One can stipulate that the set of varying conditions contains the property to which reference is to be made. Thus, we can take 'temperature' to refer to some one of the conditions which, when varied over a sequence of otherwise similar tests, yields a variation in the readings of a mercury thermometer. But this device only serves to narrow the field: one cannot *just* vary the temperature of a thing, without qualitative changes in the causal ancestry of that state, and changes in its causal descendants.

The more fundamental reference-fixing strategy relies upon the fact that every state of affairs has multiple effects, achieved via distinct causal routes. A single state of affairs, such as Matilda's having a body-temperature of 103°F, can yield a panoply of results: feverish behavior on Matilda's part, a certain reading on a mercury thermometer, a given thermocouple reading, and so on (all of which vary as Matilda's temperature varies). Now in general the causally relevant background conditions which feed into these different test procedures will be quite *different* – with (we may hope) one exception: the state of affairs of Matilda's having a temperature of 103°(and its causal ancestors). We can rule out the *ancestors* of Matilda's fever by designating the referent of 'temperature of 103°F' as the (temporally or causally) *last* state of affairs which all these test-procedures have as a common causal ancestor. Or, we can add to our reference-fixing series of tests ones which employ different objects, all heated to 103°F and yielding the same temperature-readings, but whose temperatures were produced in causally distinct ways. Now common to these tests, we may have reason to believe, there will be just one type of state of affairs (i.e., just one property) which is causally ancestral to each test in the series. It is that property which we now use the series to fix reference upon. Although these procedures may appear highly complex and artificial, I shall argue that they are the ones we actually do use.

First, however, we must return to the issue of reference-failure. We are now in a position to see how the use of a reference-fixing series of tests can fail to provide a denotation for a predicate term. In order to use such a series for this purpose, it is not necessary that we know any of the details of the causal chains which make up the ancestry of our test results (indeed if we did know all of these details, we would not need to use the series to fix reference on the common feature in the first place).[8] All that is required is that the series exhibit systematic features which provide good grounds for supposing that there *is* just one such common feature. But such grounds are fallible. Two (or more) quite distinct properties may produce, in the test-conditions used, very similar or identical symptoms. If our, in this case false, presupposition is that there is just one common feature, what shall we say about the denotation of the introduced predicate expression in this case?[9]

Take *being soluble*. As it happens, theoretical advances in physical chemistry have shown (so far as I am aware) that solubility in water is associated with a single generic property which concerns the structure of the electron-orbitals in the outer shells of an ion or molecule. Here, then, the predicate 'is soluble' can be assigned a denotation. But suppose it had been otherwise. Suppose that scientific investigation had uncovered two very distinct mechanisms underlying the disappearance of solids placed in water. The uniqueness presupposition would have proved false. After this discovery, how should we use the predicate 'is soluble'?

Clearly, there is no single right answer to this question. Roughly speaking, it will be a matter of linguistic stipulation. One could restrict the range of 'is soluble' to those cases in which one of the underlying mechanisms is at work, introducing a new predicate to handle the other. One could, in the interest of clarity and precision, abandon the predicate and introduce *two* new ones. But, finally, it seems clear that one could decide to retain the old predicate *with* its former extension – possibly because the phenomenon of disappearance in water happens to be of similar practical concern, regardless of what underlying mechanism is at work. (This is naturally compatible with the introduction of two new terms to mark the distinction for scientific or other reasons.) This last option seems to reflect a decision to assign to 'is soluble' a semantics which is the same as, or very similar to, that expressed by (1). The rule governing the use of 'is soluble' would now conform to an operationalist semantics.

The obvious question which now arises is: what semantics did 'is soluble' have (in our hypothetical example) *before* the uniqueness presupposition was discovered to be false? I am somewhat doubtful that *this* question has a "right" answer, either. Unlike universals, the meanings of terms are man-made. The semantics of a word are, in some complicated way, the conventionalized product of the intentions of the speakers of the linguistic community who use it. The difficulty is that, so long as the presupposition in question is believed to be true, the semantic intentions which would be associated with an operationalist semantics, and those associated with a referential semantics, need not come into direct conflict.[10] Hence, there may be no real semantic decision which crystallizes from general use into explicit convention. Even the use of a dispositional term on a single occasion by a single individual need not be accompanied by any clear or unambiguous intention to use the word in accordance with the one kind of semantics or the other. Nevertheless, human beings are *primarily* concerned with capturing in language the underlying structure of the world, rather then with superficial classifications based upon arbitrarily chosen phenomena or symptoms.[11] The exception, perhaps, is where the symptoms themselves are of overriding practical importance, and not the underlying causal structure. But in general, it is precisely this underlying structure which we wish to lay bare for practical purposes as well. In such felicitous cases, then, a dispositional term picks out an underlying property whose enduring instances explain the episodic manifestation of those symptoms which inspire the dispositional mode of reference.

3. THEORETICAL TERMS

The semantics outlined above for dispositional predicates can be generalized. Theoretical terms come in for the same treatment. Indeed our semantic analysis of dispositionals is essentially identical to that which has been proposed by Robert Causey (1972) and others, for theoretical terms. According to that analysis, the relation between a (relatively) observational predicate such as 'being at temperature T' and its theoretical correlate 'being composed of molecules at mean kinetic energy $K = (3/2)kt$' is one of coreference. The two non-synonymous predicate expressions, one drawn from the language descriptive of macroscopic phenomena, the other from the language of reductive micro-theory, codenote one and the same property. Similarly, on our analysis 'is soluble' denotes a property which – from the point of view of micro-theory – is to be identified with some enduring, occurrent underlying property.

Indeed, verificationist semantic proposals do not recognize any fundamental difference in kind between dispositional terms and (other) theoretical terms.[12] There may be differences in degree of complexity, or in degree of "remove" from observability, but the form of the correspondence rules is essentially the same. If our verdict upon the significance of the correspondence rules is correct, this will come as no surprise. The correspondence rules simply reflect the mistaken attempt by positivists to recast certain laws describing the causal link between tested property and test data as an analytic connection. But if that property which we identify as solubility causes the dissolving of a substance under test conditions, it is equally true that theoretical properties make themselves manifest by causing the readings and data which laboratory equipment produce. Such causal chains may be more complex or less so, but, as causal chains, they are of a kind. So the analysis we have offered for dispositionals dovetails with the reductive identification of the denotata of macro-descriptive predicates with those of micro-descriptive ones. We may think of properties denoted by theoretical terms (e.g., 'is electrically charged;' 'has mass;' 'has quantized spin') as occurrent properties; but we can also identify them in terms of the observable effects they produce under suitable conditions. The latter type of identification, via effects, is in the "dispositional mode." But this, then, is simply a matter of the style of identification. Every theoretical property is, or can be, instantiated at a time. Hence it is, or can be, an occurrent property. Every theoretical property confers causal powers upon the particulars which instantiate it. Hence it is, or can be, measured at those times and under those conditions in which such powers are suitably manifested. Each such dispositional property is identical to some occurrent theoretical property.

4. OCCURRENT OBSERVATIONAL PROPERTIES

I shall now argue that the semantic view just urged on behalf of dispositional and other theoretical predicates applies equally to everyday garden-variety predicates which have been widely regarded as denoting properties which are occurrent and observational: for example, 'is crimson,' 'is burning,' 'is too heavy to lift,' and so on. The theory/observation distinction has come under heavy attack over the past two decades. A variety of arguments have been used to show that the distinction – at least in a form required for it to perform the epistemological role for which it was introduced – is untenable. These arguments – at least those of them which I find convincing[13] – can be turned to good account here. But the fact which has central relevance to the present issue can be quite simply stated without reviewing those arguments.

Everyday properties of physical things, like those mentioned above, are properties whose presence we detect directly or indirectly, by means of our senses. No matter how "direct" the perception of a physical object may be, it occurs by means of a process involving our sense organs. That process, whether fairly simple or very complex (and it is invariably highly complex) is (or at least involves) a causal chain. Perhaps, ordinarily, that causal process is relatively less complex in cases involving the detection of "observable" properties than it is in the detection of "theoretical" ones. But it is not always so, by any plausible measure of complexity, nor is a difference in complexity a difference in kind. It is a difference of degree. Thus precisely the same kind of inferential process must underpin the identification of a property referred to via a relatively simple causal chain, as underlies the identification of one which stands at the referential terminus of a complex one. Proponents of the causal theory of perception do not – or should not – maintain that perceptual identification of a property requires a knowledge of the causal chain which effects perception. All they need be committed to is that every case of perception of the physical world necessarily involves a causal process. Thus it could not be urged that the difference between our detection of redness and our detection of electron charge – the difference which renders the former observational and the latter not – is familiarity with the causal details of the perceptual mechanism operating in the former case, but not in the latter. There is indeed *some* kind of difference between these cases, but in what does it consist?

An insistence upon such a difference was essential to the shift which occurred around 1930 from a phenomenalistic to a physicalist foundationalism. But although this shift was well motivated by the seriousness of the difficulties which phenomenalism confronted, it is telling that little was done by way of justifying the allegedly favored status of physicalistic observation-terms from the point of view of epistemology. And if there is any lesson which subsequent developments should by now have taught us, it is that we must either abandon foundationalist programs in epistemology, or else begin with something which really is "immediately given." The physicalist way of making the distinction between what is observed and what is not, however it might be formulated and refined, has no deep epistemological underpinning.

Indeed, the inferential procedure which accompanies the learning of a term like 'is white,' has the same structure as that which was suggested above as being required to fix the reference of theoretical predicates. The complexity of the procedure may be much less great, but the form is exactly the same.

The teaching of words like 'white' typically proceeds largely by means of repeated ostension. It is tempting to think that, when such ostension is successful, it focuses the pupil's attention upon something which is directly present to him in a simple act of perceptual awareness. He is directly acquainted with: whiteness. Once he has learned to associate the content of this experience with the word, he has learned the meaning of 'white.' The reason why repeated ostensions are required is that the student must, by a process of elimination, infer *which* of the possible elements of his perceptual field the ostender means to pick out. The difficulty with this attractive picture is that we are not directly acquainted in this way with physical universals such as *being white. Being white* is, as we usually use the word, one which denotes – if it denotes anything – a property of physical objects.[14] If we take it in this sense, our acquaintance with whiteness is mediated by causal chains.

Something can be white – and can be recognized as being white – even when it does not look white (as under red light). Understanding that something can be white without looking white – that how it looks depends in part upon surrounding circumstances – is part and parcel of a full mastery of the notion of what it is for something to be white. Conversely, achievement of this mastery includes recognition of the fact that something may "look white" but not be white. These facts can be neatly explained by a causal theory of perception and a correspondingly causal theory of how a denotation gets assigned to 'is white.'

Nevertheless, there is a strong urge to view matters in the following way: Although on some occasions when we see white things we are not directly *en rapport* with their whiteness, there are occasions upon which we are directly acquainted with whiteness. But what are these occasions which enable us to perceive whiteness "as it truly is"?

One might try: when we look at white things under normal conditions, we are directly acquainted with whiteness. White is the way white things look under these conditions.[15] (One might even offer this as a definition of 'white,' after replacing the expression 'white things' by names of one or more particulars which serve as exemplars of whiteness.) Let us see why this is unsatisfactory. There is, in the first place, the problem of non-circularly specifying what the "normal conditions" are. One could mean, by 'normal conditions,' simply those conditions under which, in the majority of cases, white things are seen. But – even if there *is* such a set of conditions – why should *those* conditions be ones specially required for the job of bringing us into a favored epistemic position *vis-à-vis* whiteness? Why should these conditions – as opposed to any others – be expected to give us the best access to whiteness?

It is not difficult to see how implausible this is. Imagine a planet – I shall call it 'Rubra' – which is inhabited by creatures who are biologically and psychologically identical to us. They have color vision. They have a color vocabulary: certain objects they describe as being colored etihw. These objects are just the ones which, if transported to Earth under conditions which preserve their chemical constitution, we would describe in English as white. Moreover, white Earth-objects transported to Rubra in a similar way are described by Rubrians as etihw.

Now it happens that Rubra orbits a star – Rube – which is a red giant. The light from Rube has – as we would say – a decidedly reddish cast. In fact, white objects look pink to us under "normal conditions" on Rubra. (And of course pink objects look etihw to Rubrians under normal viewing conditions on Earth.) One can imagine a terrestrial philosopher and a Rubrian one engaging in a debate over whose "normal viewing conditions" are the proper ones for experiencing whiteness (or etihwness, as you please) as it truly is. But I should not care to be a partisan in such a debate. I would maintain, however, that if 'etihw' is a physical color-word in the way 'white' is, then the correct translation into English of 'etihw' is 'white'. For the words name one and the same physical property.[16] We have no more grounds for supposing that whiteness just *is* the quality we are directly acquainted with when we perceive something white under (our) normal conditions, than the Rubrians would have for claiming that whiteness is the quality *they* are directly acquainted with when seeing something white under *their* normal conditions. Moral: the "normal conditions" ploy is a failure.

One could, to be sure, try to spell out the relevant perceptual conditions in some alternative way which makes no appeal to normalcy. But such a description will be circular or it will generate a regress. It will have to specify the viewing situation either in terms of properties it *appears* to have, or in terms of properties it *does* have. Appeal to the properties it *does* have is regress-generating, since determining what these are will once again require appeal to normal conditions or else will be open to the charge of not being empirically ascertainable. If, on the other hand, we appeal to the properties the viewing situation *seems* to exemplify, then all we are legitimately permitted to infer is what the quality of whiteness seems to us to be like under those circumstances. If we can be deceived as to the intrinsic nature of the properties characterizing the background conditions, we are equally eligible for deception concerning the intrinsic character of whiteness.

What has gone wrong here? We are imagining an empiricist who has identified whiteness with the character of a certain type of visual experience – call it 'W' – and who (in order to allow for the fact that white things do not always appear W) might offer the following definition:

(4) 'X is white' = $_{df}$ 'X would present one with a W-experience if X were perceived under such-and-such conditions'

Naturally (4) has the same structure as the operational definitions which are offered, for example, for 'is soluble' and 'is fragile.' It contains the same mistake. So far from being analytic, (4) reflects the existence of a causal law which connects *being white* and *being viewed under such-and-such conditions* with *having W-experiences*. Had our ocular apparatus been differently constructed, it might have been false that, viewed under the same (external) conditions, white things would produce W-experiences in us. But this circumstance does not require us to suppose that white things would not exist. Of course, given a new optical organ, we might well still encounter experiences of type W. But were these to occur under the specified conditions in (4), they would be produced by objects of some other color. (Though we might, under these circumstances, *call* this color 'white,' that would have no bearing on the semantics of 'white' as English-speakers now use it.)

If this is correct, then we could not appeal to (4) as giving us the *meaning* of 'X is white.' It is merely one nonprivileged member of a whole class of nomological truths of the form:

(5) X is white *iff* X would present one with a Y-experience if X were perceived under conditions Z.

What, then, is involved in mastering the notion of what it is to be white? Three facts which need to be accommodated are these. We use the predicate 'is white' to ascribe to objects a property which

(i) we take to be a single universal;
(ii) we intend to be understood to be a property of physical objects; and

(iii) we take to be such that lawlike regularities connect the whiteness of objects and the circumstances of observation to the color those objects appear to have.

Given (i), (ii), and (iii), a natural account of how the term 'is white' is learned can be modelled upon the treatment we gave theoretical predicates. The trick is to use ostension to fix reference upon the correct universal. This will be a matter of taking it to be one of the properties causally implicated in the having of a certain range of experiences, and of inferring from the pattern of those experiences the expectation that a single property may be causally implicated in all of them. Those experiences will include ones in which things "look white;" but also – at a more sophisticated stage – ones in which white things do not look white. One may speculate that the first stage serves to focus attention upon the proper element within the field of experience; and the second stage to force recognition that the desired denotatum is an "external" property whose perceptual manifestations are subject to an interlocking set of causal considerations. Both inferences are, I believe, required.

If this is so, then it can *turn out* (as a result of scientific inquiry) that *being white* is a property which is identical to one upon which reference has been fixed via some quite different causal linkages – for example, to some theoretical property describing certain microstructures of the material world. (Statements expressing such identities will be both nonanalytic and informative.) It may also turn out that there is no single physical property which is suitably linked to our application of the expression 'white.' But the consequence of most direct interest is that a property such as *being white*, while quite correctly thought of as an enduring, occurrent property of physical objects, is also "dispositional." That is, our mode of fixing the denotation of 'is white' relies upon the fact that certain causal conditionals describe the process by means of which whiteness impinges upon our senses.

It should be clear that the above arguments generalize to all physical properties of which we acquire knowledge only through sense perception. There are, however, three special categories of properties which require special consideration (and will, in due course, receive it). These are: spatial and temporal properties, the properties which characterize the contents of sense-perception itself, and the properties which characterize abstract particulars.

We may pause here, momentarily, to address a question raised earlier: What is the difference between "observational" and "theoretical" properties? On the above analysis, there is no epistemologically significant distinction between *being white* and, say, *having a quantum spin* + *1/2ℏ*. But surely there is *some* difference here? There is. But it is, I should say, entirely a matter of degree. The *form* of reasoning which leads us to recognition of quantum spin as a physical property is no different from that which leads to recognition of whiteness. It is simply much more complicated. The chains of inference are much longer and more ramified; the pattern of experiences which exhibit the existence of the property are both more diverse and more complex. But there is no point which marks an epistemological watershed in the range whose extremes are represented by these two properties. If there is such a watershed, it lies elsewhere: in the distinction between physical and phenomenal properties. Between these, there is a genuine difference. Contact with the former is mediated by causal processes; contact with the latter is not. A question which I am exploring throughout this work is: Can a foundationalist who begins with a subjective given sustain both a realist metaphysics and a realist epistemology?[17] This was the general aim of many of the early positivists. But the attempt mired in efforts to "construct" the physical world out of sense-data using fairly limited logical resources, a Humean notion of causation, and verificationist semantics. The tools I would appropriate for this task include instead a notion of natural necessity, and a "referential" semantics.

5. IDENTITY CONDITIONS FOR PHYSICAL PROPERTIES

Philosophers who hold that we are directly acquainted with physical properties have available (at least in the simpler cases) a relatively straightforward answer to questions about property-identity. For if, as realists, they maintain that one can see that two instances are exemplifications of one and the same property – that identically the same property is "in" both of these instances – then by parity of reasoning they can argue for the possibility of seeing that two instances are exemplifications of *different* properties. Complicated cases will be, in part, a matter of analyzing complex properties into simple (or simpler) ones or else a matter of distinguishing closely similar properties. The criteria for simplicity may again be perceptual.

For us, the matter is more complicated. Two property-instances may look like exemplifications of a single property, but not *be* exemplifications of a single property. Two property-instances which look to be instances of distinct properties may prove to be exemplifications of just one. We must therefore face two questions. What is it for a physical property, F, to be identical to a physical property, G? And, how can we come to know whether such identity obtains or not?

Physical universals are linked by causal relations. These causal relations play a necessary role in the perceptual process by means of which we come to identify such universals. I shall now argue that causal relations have a central role to play in the identity-conditions for first-order physical universals. I shall argue that it is via their causal relations that universals are identified or distinguished. The causal relations which connect one universal to others constitute part of its "essence." I shall then consider a thesis which bears some analogy to verificationism. Since first-order physical universals are known only through the causal relations which connect them, should we hold that they are nothing but the set of causal powers which they confer upon individuals which instantiate them? Should we adopt a kind of bundle theory for universals, holding that they are just clusters of causal powers? Or, should we maintain that physical universals, like Kantian *noumena*, cannot as such be known?

Our ability to detect the existence of the properties of physical things depends upon the fact that those properties confer some causal powers upon the particulars which exemplify them. The causal powers conferred upon particulars by virtue of their instantiating a given universal must be in every instance the same. There is nothing about the *particularity* of a particular which affects these causal powers.[18] But the conferral of these powers must be understood conditionally (that is what makes them powers). What sorts of causal sequences a particular x will participate in will depend not only upon the fact that it instantiates a universal U, but upon this fact combined with facts about what other universals x instantiates, and what properties other things related to x have. Thus the correct formula is: *Other things being equal*, the ways any particular will act and react causally by virtue of instantiating U will be the same.

There may be two universals U and U^* (or more) which confer the *same* causal power C upon any particular which instantiates them. Moreover, the background conditions under which C becomes manifest, when conferred by virtue of a particular's instantiating U, and when conferred by virtue of a particular's instantiating U^*, may also be identical. That is, U and U^* may be indistinguishable with respect to conferral of C. A rather crude example of this for one type of background condition is the basis of an old party prank: placing the tip of an ice cube on the back of someone's neck produces the same sensation as a heated knife-tip. An example in which the effect is identical, but the background conditions must differ, is easy to find. A pink surface under white light, for example, may have the same perceptual effect as a white surface under red light. More generally, this conclusion follows from the fact that a total resultant force of a given magnitude and direction can be generated in indefinitely many ways.

Consider, however, the set of all causal powers conferred by U – call it $\{C_U\}$ – and the set of all causal powers conferred by U^* – call it $\{C_U^*\}$. Suppose that $\{C_U\} = \{C_U^*\}$. What would this entail? An obvious consequence is that we could not – causally 'could not' – ever distinguish U and U^*; they would be causally interchangeable. So much the worse, perhaps, for our cognitive abilities. But one should avoid anthropomorphizing this consequence: not only would U and U^* be indistinguishable by *us* – since their respective effects upon our sense organs would be indistinguishable; they would be indistinguishable whether or not conscious observers present. That is to say, the form of the laws governing any particular x in its interactions with the rest of the universe would be precisely the same whether x exemplified U or U^*. Thus the difference between U and U^* would be a difference that doesn't make any difference. Having a separate set of laws for U and U^* would be otiose, even if we could somehow know (*via* revelation from a deity?) that there were here two properties and not one.

These considerations, together with the necessity of causal relations between universals, constitute strong grounds, in my opinion, for thinking of $\{C\}$ as a kind of individual essence of U. $\{C_U\}$ would be an individual essence, although what it individuates is a universal, not a particular. Thus each (physical) universal would have its own individual essence, its own unique "place" in the causal structure of the world. In the possible-worlds idiom: there would be no possible world in which the set of causal relations of U differed. Such a difference would not be causally impossible merely; it would be "metaphysically impossible," to employ Kripke's terminology.

However there is also a stronger result which is suggested. This suggestion is that U is *identical* to the set $\{C_U\}$, or perhaps to some "sum" of its members. This idea would *not* require one to claim that 'x is U' is synonymous with 'has the causal powers which are members of $\{C_U\}$'; it would not require ruling that

(5) $U \neq U^*$ but $\{C_U\} = \{C_U^*\}$

is either meaningless or formally self-contradictory. But both the strong thesis and the weak thesis require one to hold that (5) is necessarily false, in the same sense in which 'Cicero ≠ Tully' is (if false) necessarily false. Both the weak and strong theses lead to an identity-criterion for physical properties. It can be formally stated thus:

(6) $(\forall T_i)(\forall T_j)\{(T_i \neq T_j) \equiv$
    $(\exists C_k)(\exists C_l)(\exists B)([(B \ \& \ T_i){\rightarrow}C_k] \ \& \ [(B \ \& \ T_j){\rightarrow}C_l] \ \&$
    $[C_k \neq C_l]\}$

First, the symbols. 'T_i' and 'T_j' are variables which range over types of events or over states of affairs (individuated as an individual's having a property, or n individuals standing in an n-adic relation). 'C_k', 'C_l' and 'B' similarly range over types of states of affairs; the letter 'B' indicates, specifically, that background-conditions are meant. Finally, '$\rightarrow$' is to be read 'causally produces.'

Under the intended interpretation, what (6) says is that two event-types are nonidentical if and only if there exists at least one causal context (background condition) in which they produce some different effect. This is simply a more explicit rendering of the more succinct formula, 'Same universals, same powers.'

We may note here that, under the proposed criterion there is a very intimate relationship, both metaphysically and epistemologically, between physical universals and causal laws. The relationship is not, as Humeans would have it, purely external and accidental. In order for the identification of physical universals to be possible, there must be genuinely necessary causal connections. Otherwise there would be no telling whether any given set of property-instances represented the exemplification of a single universal or of more than one. We do not, to repeat an earlier point, have to know what these laws are in order to be able to identify the universals which determine them (or are determined by them). However it must be observed that unless we are, in some way, aware of all of the causal powers a universal confers, there is a possibility of confusing it with other universals.[19]

But there is a further problem. To identify causal powers, we shall have to identify effects – which means recognizing instances of yet other universals. A regress threatens here, with which I shall be concerned shortly. Yet even if the regress can be halted – as I believe it can – our criterion carries the implication that one can never be *sure* of having fully identified any one universal (and of having distinguished it from every other) until one has identified every universal. That is, all parts of the causal system of the world must be known before any part is fully known. For only when one knows the structure of the entire causal web of the world does one know the unique position of an element in that web; and only then will one have fully characterized both it and all its (causal) relata. This need not be as epistemologically disastrous as it may initially seem. For it does not preclude the possibility that we can have better and better grounds for identifying parts of this system, as we progressively explore more and more of it. But this is a theme to which I can return in more detail only later, in the closing chapter.

6. NEO-VERIFICATIONISM

In the preceding section I put forward two alternative views about the constitution of physical universals. According to the strong thesis, a physical universal is just a bundle of causal powers. According to the weak thesis, these powers belong to a universal's essence, but do not fully constitute it. It is evident that the reasoning used in support of both the strong and weak theses above bears strong analogies to verificationism. This may seem ironic, in view of the fundamental disagreements which separate the positions. But it is not an accident. Both verificationism and the above reasoning take as one source of inspiration concrete cases in which scientific knowledge has been advanced by taking seriously the limits to our intercourse with the world. I have in mind, as examples, Einstein's reasoning about simultaneity and certain of Bohr's and Heisenberg's analyses of the relations between complementary properties in quantum mechanics. But I believe that the principle which underlies the methodology of these historically prominent cases is quite ubiquitous – and quite correct. Because it is inspired by the same model which influenced positivists, I have (rather facetiously) labelled the new doctrine 'neo-verificationism.' As an ontological principle, this says that something which (causally) cannot make a difference to the rest of the world (hence to our senses) has no physical existence at all. Its epistemological counterpart is that every physical thing which exists must in principle be detectable by means of sense perception. Of course the differences in the positivist analysis of this methodological principle, and my own, make a great deal of difference indeed. Thus it is worthwhile to briefly enumerate both the parallels and the differences.

First, the parallels. Both verificationism and neo-verificationism view hypotheses about what exists as being constrained by considerations as to what is, in principle, accessible to experiment. Both subscribe to the principle that there is no difference that can not make a difference; which is to say that postulated entities or properties which have no connection with the rest of the world are regarded as metaphysically idle. *Having a certain absolute space-time position* is an idle property because instantiating it has no causal consequences; and supposing a particular to have one such position rather than another does not lead to any difference in causal consequences. Thus far, both philosophical views are agreed. However, what I have called the strong thesis with respect to universals pushes the principle of parsimony further than the weak position. It does not allow that a universal is constituted by anything over and above the associated set of causal powers, on the grounds that this is in principle the only epistemic access we can have to the nature of a physical universal. There is no constituent of a universal which binds this cluster of powers together: no "Dinge-an-sich."

A second parallel is that both verificationism and neo-verification-ism (strong and weak) are relevant to semantic theories of language – though they differ as to the favored theory. Finally, both can be construed as having ontological import, though some verificationists have denied this.

The differences between verificationism and neo-verificationism are several. First, the associated semantic doctrines are different. One semantics places heavy emphasis on rules of intelligible use ("meaning"); the other on ontological import ("reference"). According to the first (in its "pure" form), correspondence rules are analytic; according to the second, they express causal connections. According to the first, hypotheses which posit the existence of entities or properties not accessible to experience are meaningless. According to the second, such hypotheses are ordinarily meaning-ful, but certain terms used in expressing them suffer from reference-failure. So the Principle of Verifiability is a criterion of meaning, whereas (6) is not a criterion of meaning. It is a criterion which bears on the referential success of predicates, by providing a condition required for determining when the uniqueness-presupposition is satisfied. It clearly does not yield synonymy as a condition for co-referentiality of predicate expressions. Two non-synonymous predicates may prove, under criterion (6), to denote the same universal, and one predicate univocally used may prove to "name" several distinct universals (i.e., include their instances within its extension), or none.

Which of these methodologies more accurately reflects what scientists in fact do? I think that the more accurate theory is neo-verificationism, or what might more properly be called referentialism. The constraint that scientists place upon their descriptions of physical states of affairs is just that properties are not to be imputed where obtaining information about the presence or absence of that property would require the violation of causal laws, laws which any measuring apparatus must perforce obey. So scientific description requires the physical possibility of a confirmation-procedure. This accords with (6) above, but not with the Principle of Verifiability, for (6) says that for a universal U to play a distinct role in the economy of the universe, it must confer a distinct set of causal powers, of interaction possibilities, upon the particulars which have it. It is by virtue of this that U can be detected and distinguished by us; and it is by virtue of this that it differentially affects other, inanimate particulars.

7. UNINSTANTIATED UNIVERSALS

Universals *per se* do not have spatial or temporal existence. If they did exist in space and time, the only plausible location to assign them would be at the "where" and "when" of their instances. This leads to difficulty, as we have already seen, for spatial and temporal universals themselves. But there is more trouble in store, as the following set of sentences suggests:

(7) Universals *per se* exist in space and time;
(8) A universal exists wholly in, and at the location of, each of its instances;

and

(9) A universal is not changed, and is neither created nor destroyed, by the destruction of any of its instances or the creation of a new one.

Is it possible to consistently maintain all three of these claims? If it seems mysterious that (7), (8), and (9) should conjointly be true, perhaps that is no less mysterious than the supposition that an entity which is not itself spatiotemporal could be "in" particulars which are spatiotemporal beings. Yet if U has instances at a time t_0, and none at a later time t_1, and U has temporal existence, then it seems forced upon us to say that 'U exists at t_0' is true, whereas 'U exists at t_1' is false.[20] If so, then U ceased to exist between t_0 and t_1: presumably it was destroyed when its last instance was. So universals can go out of (and, *a fortiori*, come into) existence. But if the destruction of U's last instance, or the creation of U's first instance, have such profound implications for U's existence, why is it that, when U is multiply instantiated, the creation or destruction of a single instance carries no such implication? For "all of" U is "in" each such instance. This seems to be another good reason for taking universals to be transcendent entities.

Now if universals are transcendent, it is at least an intelligible possibility that they can exist uninstantiated. If universals can be neither created nor destroyed, and if it is intelligible that a universal may exist at one time when it has no instances, then it is intelligible that it should exist and never at any time have instances. Is there however any positive reason to believe that universals do, or can, exist uninstantiated? There are, I believe, at least two reasons. Both depend on the assumption that causal relations are relations between universals.

The first argument is one proposed by Michael Tooley (1977). Here is Tooley's argument. When a universal comes to be instantiated, there exists some cause of this event. Conceivably, there are universals which are never instantiated, but which could have been instantiated. They fail to be instantiated simply because the right causal conditions never appear. So a universal may never be instantiated, but be such that it might have had instances. Does such a universal exist? This depends upon how the expression 'might have been' is interpreted. In speaking of causal conditions, we need to make a distinction between initial or boundary conditions, and the causal laws by virtue of which those initial conditions bring about a certain effect. We can imagine a universal whose instantiation, while in itself involving no logical inconsistency, would require the violation of the laws of nature. Such universals, I shall argue below, do not exist. But one can also imagine a universal whose failure to be instantiated is not entailed by the laws of nature, but is simply due to the nonappearance of the required initial conditions. These initial conditions could be consistent with the laws of nature, and be such that if they were to appear, the universal in question would be instantiated. Such cases are entirely possible; the laws of nature by themselves do not (so far as we know) guarantee that every set of initial conditions consistent with them will sooner or later appear. So suppose it is true now that certain physically possible initial conditions which never obtain are such that, if they were to appear, a certain universal U would be instantiated. What makes this statement true? Presumably, the truth of certain causal laws. These laws would have to make mention of U. They would be true, on our account, in virtue of the fact that certain other universals (perhaps themselves instantiated) bore a causal relation R to U. But if these other universals – which we may assume are elsewise instantiated and hence exist – bear a relation R to U, then U also exists. Relation R cannot obtain between relata, one of which exists and the other not.[21]

David Armstrong, whose realism is Aristotelian, rejects this argument of Tooley's. Armstrong's (1983, Chapters 7 and 8) answer to Tooley's challenge begins with a discussion on functional laws whose antecedent conditions may, for certain values of a variable magnitude, never be instantiated. Suppose properties of the genus P are causally related to those of the genus Q in such a way that the magnitude of any Q is a function f of the magnitude of the causing property of type P. Then perhaps the law $P_0 \rightarrow Q_0$ (where P_0 and Q_0 are determinate values of P and Q) has no instances. What makes this law true? Not some relation between the universals P_0 and Q_0; for Armstrong an uninstantiated universal is a nonexisting universal, hence not related to anything at all. Rather, Armstrong suggests a counterfactual analysis: if P_0 were instantiated, then it would be causally related to Q_0. What makes this counterfactual true is a *second-order* law, to the effect that all laws expressing causal relations between determinate values of the genus P and the genus Q have a certain functional form f.

Now Tooley's case is harder, for we may imagine it to involve unrealized antecedent conditions such that no genus under which they fall is associated with laws of some general functional or extrapolable form. Tooley imagines, for example, a case in which elementary particles of two types, B and J, never interact because the proper initial conditions (e.g. spatial proximity) are never satisfied, and in which there is no basis, grounded in particle interactions which *do* take place, for saying how a B and a J *would* interact. Our intuitions seem to "tell" us that, nevertheless, there must be some law governing the unactualized interaction of B's and J's, a law connecting the relevant antecedent circumstance to some (perhaps entirely unimaginable and uninstantiated) consequent-characterizing universal U; a law which would support the truth of the counterfactual: If a B and a J were brought into proximity, then U would obtain.

To handle this kind of case, Armstrong suggests an analogy. Suppose it is an ultimately probabilistic law that whenever something is P then it is either Q or R, each with equal probability. This law supports counterfactuals such as: If a had been P then it would have been Q or R. But a would not have been both; so it is tempting to think that the counterfactual: (*)'If a had been P, then it would have been Q' must be either true or false. This temptation, Armstrong plausibly insists, should be resisted. Neither this counterfactual, nor the corresponding counterfactual involving R has any truth-value, given that a never was P. Now the situation with the counterfactual involving B, J and U is similar according to Armstrong. This counterfactual has no truth-value either. Hence no supporting law is required. The inclination to think otherwise is motivated by our tendency to think of universals as necessary beings (so that counterfactuals concerning them have definite truth-values always), whereas particulars such as a are contingent. But in Armstrong's view universals are contingent as well.

This argument is ingenious. But I think it mislocates the source of our intuition that there is an uninstantiated law governing $B-J$ interactions. Our reason for thinking (if we do think this) that the counterfactual (*) is neither true nor false, does not derive from the contingency of a's existence, nor from the fact that, given the probabilistic law, there is no way to *know* whether a would have been Q, or whether it would instead have been R. Surely it stems rather from the fact that the probabilistic character of the law relating P, Q and R is ultimate and objective. There is no fact in nature – nothing about the properties P, Q and R – which could make (*) true or false. But there need be no probabilistic element underlying Tooley's case, no probabilistic second-order law which, in a parallel way, the $B-J-U$ law would instantiate if there were a $B-J$ interaction. Thus our intuitions – or mine, at any rate – about Tooley's case remain intact. Suppose the antecedent of the $B-J-U$ law is a complex universal all of whose constituents do exist. Then surely it is something about the nature of *these* universals that requires a causal connection to another universal – U – which may happen to be simple and have no instances.

Let me expand on this a bit. We may think of the universe of physical universals as being bound together into a structure. The binding relation, the cement which determines this structure, is the causal relation. Now our view (in its weaker form) is that it is part of the essence (what Armstrong calls the 'nature') of each universal that it is causally related to other universals in just the way that it is. Because the essences of the universals to which it is related are determined by the further universals to which they in turn bear relation R, and so on, it follows that the essence of each universal is in effect a function of the entire structure. It is an all-or-nothing affair: a change in the identity (essence) of one universal would ramify throughout the entire system.[22] Hence the physical universals which are Rly connected to U – and this, directly or indirectly, includes all of them – are such that their essence would not be what it is if the relations in question did not obtain. But, once again, it seems to me that these relations could obtain between existing universals and U only if U also exists. Either U is a member of the system or it is not. If it is not, it doesn't exist; and if it is, it does. As long as this system does not, by itself, entail that every boundary condition compatible with it shall sooner or later be realized, the existence of universals does not entail their instantiation.

To recapitulate. If either the weak or the strong thesis is true, a universal cannot exist in any (logically) possible world where the relevant system of causal laws do not obtain. (These laws conjointly express the structure of causally related universals which constitute the "nature" of the physical world.) The converse also obtains: if possession of a certain set of causal powers is allowed by the laws of physics in a logically possible world, then the universal whose essence those causal powers constitute exists in that world.

We can imagine, nevertheless, that some or all of the physical laws of our world did not obtain. We can even imagine, counterfactually, there being sentient creatures like ourselves having under these circumstances sensations of kinds qualitatively indistinguishable from ours. But such a world would not contain the physical properties which our world contains.[23] Because of the systematic ramification of causal connections, it would contain *no* physical properties identical to ones in our world, and hence no identical physical laws.[24] Transworld identity of properties cannot be separated from transworld identity of laws.

8. IS THE STRONG THESIS TRUE?

It is necessary now to examine whether the strong thesis is true. According to that thesis, each universal is "nothing but" a collection of causal powers. If this is so, then in a sense every property is ultimately dispositional (that is, a cluster of causal powers). There would be no underlying occurrent property which accounted for these dispositions.

I think that the strong thesis is incoherent. At least, it is incoherent if causal relations are second-order relations between first-order properties. If that is so, it is necessary that each first-order universal have some nature over and above its associated set of causal powers. For how are these powers to be characterized? To say that U is associated with a causal power P is to say that U confers P upon any individual X which instantiates it. This in turn means (on our analysis) that if X is U, and some further set I of initial conditions is satisfied, then X's being U, together with I, causally produces a certain effect E, where P is the power to produce E. But E itself is characterized in terms of universals; and if these are identified in terms of clusters of causal powers, their identity must in turn await the characterization of certain further effects which their instantiations have the power of producing. And so on. One identifies each universal in terms of its associated set of causal powers; but each causal power must be identified in terms of an effect – that is, in terms of an event characterized in terms of universals. It is clear that we are led to either a vicious regress or a vicious circle.

The source of the difficulty, and its solution, are not hard to discern. If causal powers are to be understood, ultimately, in terms of a relation R which binds universals, then the existence of such a power entails that R be instantiated by a pair of universals. But neither of the relata of R can *itself* be a causal power. For that would lead to a circular analysis of causation. Hence, the relata of R must be thought of as distinct from causal powers. To speak of causal powers is simply a way of speaking of the causal relations in which these entities stand. Picturesquely, if a bit misleadingly, a universal is a "core" around which a set of causal powers – causal relations, really – cluster. To speak of the clusters of causal powers, without these cores, amounts to speaking of the relational structure defined by R, but devoid of the relata.

I think we must conclude, therefore, that the strong thesis is false. That leaves the weak thesis. Each universal is identified via the set of causal powers it confers. This set – the set of causal relations which obtain between it and other universals – is essential to it. It would not be that very universal if these relations did not obtain. But the universal itself is not identical to this set of relations.

9. KNOWLEDGE OF UNIVERSALS

Although we have avoided the regress which just threatened by abandoning the strong thesis, there are two closely associated regresses which still remain. One of these is, like the previous one, an ontological regress. The other is an epistemological regress.

The ontological regress can be disposed of simply. The difficulty may be stated as follows. The identity of each property depends upon the causal relations it has to other properties.[25] So its identity depends upon what other properties these are. But the identity of each of those properties, in turn, depends in a similar way upon the identity of yet further properties. And their identities depend upon the identity of the first property, which is one of their causal relata. In short, the identity of each property depends upon the identity of indefinitely many others; their identities, in turn, depend on that of the first. How, then, does the identity of any property become fixed? We are led in a circle, or a regress, or both.

Neither the circle nor the regress is vicious, however. The existence of the regress brings into prominence the systematic character of the set of universals. It is the system taken as a whole which determines the identity of each of its parts. Or, one can say that the entire system is mirrored in the nature of each constituent universal. But there is nothing paradoxical about this. In order for a man to have the characteristic of being a husband, there must be a woman who has the characteristic of being a wife. But conversely, in order for a woman to be a wife, some man must be a husband. This does not prevent the existence of married couples. The ontological regress and/or circle is no more vicious than this.

The epistemological regress is more serious. It is clear that we learn about the universe, and about its constituent universals, piecemeal. We do not grasp the entire system at once. Indeed, we may never achieve full knowledge of the system of laws which govern nature. Yet it can hardly be denied that we know some of these laws, and can identify some universals. But if the identity of each universal is a function of the character of the whole world-system, then knowledge of the identity of each universal pre-supposes knowledge of every universal. Therefore piecemeal knowledge is impossible. Let me explain more fully how this consequence is forced upon us.

We can identify each universal only in terms of the causal powers it confers upon particulars. But the identification of a causal power requires identification of the type(s) of events which possession of that power causes. Identification of these event-types involves specifying the universals which are constitutive of them. But these universals, in turn, can be identified only via their causal powers. And so on. Thus – at best – the only knowledge we can have of the world is a kind of formal or structural knowledge, devoid of content. We could know, at best, that a network of causal relations obtained, and also, perhaps, something of its structure. The laws of our physics would be formal skeletons; each predicate being merely a cipher of place-holder with no semantic content.[26] For nothing could count as identifying a property in such a system. A property could be identified, referred to, by means of its (causal) relations to other properties; but only if those other properties can themselves be identified. If recognition is unable to gain a toehold, a point of entry into this system, then knowledge of the world is impossible. But this conclusion is so strange as to seem paradoxical. How, then, can our knowledge of physical universals be accounted for?

There is but one way, I believe, that this regress can be terminated. There must, at some stage, be properties, causally related to the others, whose identities can be ascertained by us directly. There must be universals within the system with which we are acquainted in a manner that does not depend upon the mediation of causal relations. It would be essential to these universals that they stand in the causal relations they do; but it would not be in terms of this essence – their causal powers – that we identify them. We should have to be able to identify the core, not the cluster of causal powers, by acquaintance with the things themselves. Of course we can be acquainted with such universals only through their instances; but it must not be (only) via the effects those instances produce.

But are there such universals? Fortunately, there are. They are the universals which characterize the immediate content of sense-perception. It is with them that the epistemological buck stops. These universals (whether we think of them as mental properties or physical properties is irrelevant to the present concern) do occupy positions in the causal structure of the world. Their instantiation can be caused by other events, and can in turn cause other events. But it is not in terms of their causes and effects that we (ordinarily) identify them, for the very thing which makes our acquaintance with them *direct*, is that it is not in virtue of anything they cause in us that we have experience of them. Indeed one of these universals does not itself stand in causal relations to any others, and hence could not be identified in terms of a causal essence. That universal is R, the causal relation itself.

There is no inconsistency in maintaining that these universals are objects of direct acquaintance, and holding that the causal relations in which they stand constitute part of their essence, even though we may not know what these relations are. The causal relations of a property, though necessarily associated with it, need not be supposed to be such that knowledge of them follows *a priori* from a knowledge of the property itself. A few pages previously, I claimed that one could imagine a world which contained a different system of properties than ours, and yet contained sentient creatures, the contents of whose experiences qualitatively matched our own. Is there not a contradiction here? For the system of causal relations which *these* sensory qualities stand in is entirely different from the system which contains "ours." Hence their essences differ; they would not be the same properties. More formally: Let the actual world be named 'ALPHA'. In ALPHA, there are instances of a perceptual quality, F, which characterizes the contents of certain sense perceptions. F stands, in ALPHA, in a causal relation R to certain physical universals, G, H, I, J. In particular, suppose that (G R F); (H R F); (F R I); and (F R J) are true in ALPHA. These facts constitute part of the essence of F. But we can imagine a world BETA containing sentient creatures such that their sensations are qualitatively identical to our own. Hence F is a constituent of BETA. If however the physical properties of BETA do not obey the laws of ALPHA, none of the physical universals of ALPHA exist in BETA. It follows that, in BETA, $\sim(G$ R $F)$; $\sim(H$ R $F)$; $\sim(F$ R $I)$; and $\sim(F$ R $J)$. Thus, *per impossibile*, the essence of F in BETA is different from the essence of F in ALPHA. What has gone wrong? The fallacy here is not hard to uncover. BETA is not, in any sense, a possible world. There is no possible world such as BETA, of which F is a constituent. It is natural to think that BETA is possible because the state of affairs which defines it is imaginable. But the principle that imaginability entails possibility is fallacious. Suppose that (in ALPHA) Cicero $\neq$ Tully. If someone does not know that this identity obtains (or has a false semantic theory) he can easily imagine (or suppose himself to be imagining) a world in which Cicero $\neq$ Tully. But, because of familiar arguments of Kripke's, I am convinced that no such world is a possible world. Those arguments apply equally to our case. If F has an essence E in ALPHA, but is not identified by means of this essence; or if its essence is not known to be E, then a world in which F fails to have essence *E* may be easily imaginable. But nevertheless, such a world is not a possible world.

The result which emerges from this argument is interesting and perhaps surprising. If phenomenological properties are constituents of the actual world, and if they constitute part of the causal system of the world, then a world with a different physics (a world which contained a physical universal not contained in ours) would be a world in which the experiences of sentient creatures would be qualitatively different from our own. There is a further corollary, which follows from the thesis that causal relations are second-order relations between universals, the causal theory of perception, and the supposition that we are able to refer to physical universals in the way I have suggested. The corollary is that phenomenal qualities – qualia – are ineliminable. Advocates of functionalist versions of materialism characteristically eliminate the sensuous content of experience in favor of belief-states and the like (see Armstrong 1968). Belief-states are in turn identified in terms of their causal roles. It will be seen that this eliminative strategy, implausible as it may be in any case, is not admissible on our assumptions. For if we are not directly acquainted with any properties, and mental states are themselves identified in terms of causal powers, then the epistemological regress to which I drew attention at the end of Section 5 of this chapter cannot be halted, and becomes vicious.

Let us, finally, return to Davidson's criterion for event-identity (cf. Chapter 2, Section 6). According to Davidson, events *e* and *f* are identical just in case it is true that

$$(\forall x)[(x \rightarrow e) \equiv (x \rightarrow f)] \text{ and } (\forall x)[(e \rightarrow x) \equiv (f \rightarrow x)]$$

(Here the variable '*x*' ranges over events, and '→' denotes 'causally produces'). In other words, *e* and *f* are identical just in case they have identical causes and cause identical effects. But, as I have previously pointed out, the causes and effects of *e* and *f* are themselves events; to speak of their being the same or different presupposes an identity-criterion for events. Hence Davidson's criterion is either viciously circular or viciously regressive. The regress is quite analogous to the regresses which threatened the criterion of property-identity advocated here. Moreover, that criterion is, on the account I offer, implicated in the individuation of events. For our criterion of event-identity was that *e* = *f* just in case *e* involves the instantiation, at the same location and by the same particulars, of the same universals as are constitutive of *f*. Thus, our criterion of event-identity threatens – in the case of physical events –

to be similarly regressive. Each event is identified (in part) in terms of constitutive physical properties. Each of these is identified in terms of associated causal powers – that is, in terms of further events which are the causes and effects of that property being instantiated. And so on. But our regress has a terminus. Davidson does not propose any terminus to the regress which attends his criterion, though apparently he is aware of its existence. Nor do I see how that regress could be terminated, unless it be in the way suggested here.

The path inward from instantiated physical universals to phenomenal events travels along a causal sequence. It may be a long path, and it is invariably a complex one. The path outward from perception to properties is equally long and complex. It has an intentional aspect – namely, the act of fixing reference[27] – whose *modus operandi* makes crucial use of the causal sequences which effect perception. Moreover it requires the (conscious or unconscious) use of one form or another of inductive reasoning. I have sketched only the grossest outlines of how it is that the mind travels this path out into the world, how it is that the universals of physics become objects of perception and of cognition. I shall not attempt any more detailed account, although certainly there are a great many respects in which this sketch is inadequate. I shall, however, revert to further aspects of this theme in the final chapter.

9 Generic universals

1. A THEORY OF ARMSTRONG'S

A determinate shade of blue (cerulean, say) and a determinate shade of red (crimson) are both colors, and not shapes. Squareness and isosceles triangularity are both shape-properties and not colors. Cerulean and crimson bear some closer relationship to one another – a stronger resemblance – than either bears to squareness. They are "of a kind," of which squareness is not. Perhaps cerulean and squareness are also both of a kind, but if so, it is a kind of a higher order than either the class of colors or the class of shapes; and both crimson and isosceles triangularity will also be members of that kind.

We may describe these facts by saying that determinate properties can (typically) be ranged as species under one or more genera, genera which perhaps cut across one another or which may themselves be ordered hierarchically into a taxonomy. To describe matters in this way suggests, but does not commit one to, the ontological thesis that there are generic universals. That thesis provides one way of accounting for the facts just mentioned; and I shall argue that it is the correct way. But it is not the only imaginable analysis.

In (1978b, Chapter 22), David Armstrong proposed a novel version of the partial identity theory to account for these facts.[1] He also presented an argument against the view that the facts are to be explained by the existence of generic universals, or determinables. I think Armstrong's theory is mistaken, and I think his argument against the existence of generic universals is unsound.[2] But Armstrong's theory will offer a useful counterpoint against which to develop my theme. Although I believe it is mistaken, I nevertheless find it usefully suggestive in a way which will presently emerge.

It will be helpful at the outset, to list the (putative) facts which, according to Armstrong, any adequate theory of this kind of resemblance among universals must explain. These are:

(1) The members of a resemblance-class of universals all have something in common;
(2) At the same time, they differ in that very respect (e.g., two different colors differ in *color*);
(3) The members of a resemblance-class exhibit a resemblance-order based upon their intrinsic nature;
(4) The members of some resemblance-classes (e.g., shapes) form a set-of-incompatibles; and
(5) When a particular instantiates a determinable property, it necessarily instantiates some determinate property falling under that determinable.

Of these, (2), (4), and (5) require some initial comment. I shall argue presently that (2) is false, and that Armstrong's argument for it rests upon a confusion. The degree of generality of (4) is doubtful. (4) is true with respect to geometric properties (a line cannot simultaneously be two different lengths), and initially it seems to be true with respect to colors. But, on the other hand, it does not initially seem to be true with respect to odors, tastes, or sounds, as Armstrong notes. A sauce may be both sour and sweet. A bell may have a tone which is composed of both a fundamental and a number of higher overtones. Given these cases, it is tempting to speculate how our perception of colors might differ if our optical information-channel were able to Fourier-analyze light into distinct sinusoidal components in the way in which our auditory channel is able to separate complex sounds into distinct simultaneous tones. Might, in that instance, a light source which emitted both blue and yellow light waves from its entire surface appear simultaneously blue and yellow, instead of green? Is perhaps the inconceivability of such a result, to which I have appealed occasionally already, no more consequential than the inconceivability, for a blind man, of the phenomenal sensation of blue itself?[3] Certainly Armstrong, given his views concerning the nature of our perceptual relation to color-properties, could not object to this speculation on phenomenological grounds.[4]

However, there is, an objection which might be advanced to vindicate (4) not only in the case of colors, but for sounds, tastes and odors as well. This objection consists in denying that the physical properties in question (e.g. the tones of the bell) belong, in all strictness, to the object to which they are ascribed. Talk of bell-tones, it might be insisted, can be either eliminated or reduced to talk about the wave-form of sound-waves generated by the bell: the properties involved are therefore wave-forms; and the particulars are sound-waves (or, if one prefers, air molecules). But a determinate wave-form does exclude other determinate wave-forms. Analogous arguments may be cooked up for colors, tastes, and odors. One might even argue that the principle of mutual incompatibility applies to all resemblance classes, basing this upon the conviction that the fundamental laws of physics are all functional laws, and that a functional law implies the metricisability of whatever properties are involved.

On the other hand, someone who maintains the universality of this principle will have to deny that there is some resemblance-class of which both colors and shapes are members; or more generally, that all determinable properties fall under a single *summum genus*, for example, *being a property*. For in that case, crimson and triangularity would both be members of some resemblance-class. Yet they are not incompatible.

Since I am unsure how to assess the above arguments, I am uncertain about the degree of generality of (4). And (5) appears to admit of exceptions in the case of certain objects of mental acts: for example, as regards the number of spots on an imagined or a hallucinated speckled hen. The objects of acts of imagination clearly provoke other ontological puzzles of a special nature, however; and (5) does seem unproblematic outside this rather special region. I therefore suggest that the central facts confronting any account of the determinate/determinable distinction are (1), (3), and (5).

Briefly, Armstrong's theory concerning determinate universals which are grouped under some common universal was this. Armstrong denied the existence of determinable (generic) universals.[5] Determinate universals, however, can be complex, in the sense of having simpler universals as parts. In what is perhaps the simplest kind of case, a universal may be complex by being a conjunctive property; in which case the universals which are the constituent conjuncts will be parts of it. In other cases, a universal may be structurally complex. To use one of Armstrong's examples, for a thing to be one meter long is for it to consist of two adjacent (physical) parts each of which has the property of being a half-meter long. In this sense, being a half-meter long is a structural component of the property of being one meter long, although a thing which is one meter long is not also a half-meter long.[6]

Armstrong proceeds to argue that what unifies a set of determinate universals into a resemblance-class is overlap in their constituent universals – that is, partial identity. The difference between the members of a resemblance-class is explained by the incompleteness of their overlap; their resemblance-order by the relative degree of overlap, with complete identity being the limiting case. Armstrong is uncertain as to whether or not at least one universal must be a common constituent of every member of a resemblance-class.[7] Certainly this will be the case, on Armstrong's account, for his most favored case, the class of lengths.

Even if Armstrong's theory works for the case of lengths, I shall argue that we have been given no adequate reason for supposing that it will work for some of the other cases he mentions, and that we have strong grounds for denying this. But before proceeding to criticisms, let it be noted that Armstrong's theory is really no more than a theory-sketch; and this makes for uncertainty in any attempt to evaluate it.

For example, it is unclear whether Armstrong means to embrace (5), the incompatibility-condition, or not.[8] This incompatibility is accommodated, in the case of lengths (where shorter lengths are constituents of any longer one), by the fact that the structural constituents of a universal *need* not characterize the same particular as the universal they constitute. Why they *cannot* do so is not, even in the case of lengths, ever explained. Perhaps this is supposed to be self-evident. But Armstrong goes on to suggest that his solution for lengths can be extended to the case of color "and other 'secondary' qualities."[9] Would these include tastes and sounds, where the incompatibility condition does not (apparently) apply?

There is a second problem in assessing this theory. Resemblance-classes are supposed to be determined by partial identities among their members; but as we shall see one must specify further what kinds of partial identity are necessary or sufficient for co-membership in a resemblance-class. Since he leaves this moot, it is unclear what position Armstrong would take on whether there is a general hierarchy of resemblance-classes, or how he would explain this position. There is no great difficulty, once we admit Armstrong's general solution in the case of colors, with providing an explanation of the hierarchy which ascends from crimson to red to being colored. Here it is simply a question of an arbitrary segmentation of the continuous color-spectrum, together with the fact that the determinate shades of red share more common structural components than any of them share with any shade of blue (though not more than any of them shares with any shade of orange).

But there are much more difficult cases to consider. The class of lengths is a resemblance-class. So is the class of (two-dimensional) shapes. Are these both sub-classes of some larger resemblance-class (e.g., the class of geometrical properties)? If not, is this because they share no structural components? Are lengths perhaps not structural components of shapes? If, on the other hand, the members of these two resemblance-classes do share common structural components, what constitutes them as distinct sub-classes? Again, what if lengths constitute structural components of color-properties (as it seems they would on an analysis of color in terms of electromagnetic wavelength)? Are we forced, then, to admit lengths and colors as members of some single resemblance-class? Perhaps the answers here can only be given in detail for each distinct case. This makes the theory untidy, but it is not a decisive objection against it. We may suppose that these untidy details fall within the province of science, not philosophy; that it is the job of science to discover the natural classes into which universals arrange themselves. But we could perhaps expect a philosophical theory to give us some guidance as to how the relevant taxonomic principles are to be determined and justified.

Finally, it must be observed that the cogency of Armstrong's argument for the structural inclusion of shorter lengths within longer lengths suffers from a similar sketchiness. We are told that *being one meter long* is equivalent to *being two half-meters in length*, from which it is to be inferred that *being a half-meter long* is a structural constituent of *being a meter long*. But we need to know what the structure of the property *being two half-meters in length* is or what its other constituents are. Perhaps it is to be parsed as: *being composed of a part which is one-half meter long and a contiguous part which is one half-meter long along a collinear path*, or some such.[10] Again, because this analysis invokes properties other than *being one-half meter long*, there arises the question whether *being one-half meter long* falls under a number of disparate genera.

I believe that Armstrong's theory is plausible – if it is plausible at all – only in the case of lengths and other linearly metricisable qualities (e.g., temporal duration). There does not appear to be any natural way of extending the theory to shapes, for example. If Armstrong's theory is so severely limited in its application, then I think we are justified in rejecting the theory. For the phenomenon to be explained – the existence of resemblance-classes – seems to be a single, general phenomenon, one for which there ought to be a similar explanation in each case. But many of the world's properties are not linearly metricisable.

It is natural, no doubt, to suppose that Armstrong's account of the class of lengths can be incorporated into an account of the class of shapes. But reflection will show that it is by no means obvious how this may be done. It is true that the sides of a triangle of a certain size have certain lengths; as have the circumference and the radius of a circle. But in what sense *being length 1* is a structural component of triangularity or circularity remains entirely unclear. I do not mean to be denying, of course, the obvious fact that shapes form resemblance classes, or that they share various geometric universals. But Armstrong's theory requires much more than this. It requires a complete analysis of every determinate shape property into determinate components, in such a way that resemblance classes can be related to the sharing of specified determinate universals. Perhaps some improvement can be made by incorporating further structural components, such as *being n-sided* (for some determinate value of *n*) and *having vertex angles of size o, p, q*, ... But in what sense would, say, *being m-sided* be a structural component of *being n-sided* where *m* < *n*?

It will not do either, of course, to argue that isosceles triangularity is a structural component of circularity, on the grounds that an isosceles triangle can be inscribed in any circle. For a circle can also be inscribed in any isosceles triangle; and by parity of reasoning, circularity would be a structural component of triangularity. This difficulty could be circumvented by requiring a specification of dimensions (e.g., *being a circle of 1" radius*); but it is clear in any event that it would be hopeless to account for such resemblance-orderings as there are among shapes in terms of this kind of analysis. For his part, Armstrong says only that "the ordering principles of the class of shapes are obviously more complex than those of the class of lengths," but that "it should not be too difficult to apply [Armstrong's account] to more complex cases, for instance, the class of shapes."[11] Having failed to see how the extension might be effected, we may reflect further that there is no particular reason to think this strategy will succeed with tastes, odors, textures, and so on.

But if Armstrong's account is inadequate, what sort of answer can be given to the question I have posed? What accounts for the existence of resemblance-classes? I wish, in developing an answer, to dispute a point Armstrong makes regarding the observability of property-resemblances. In his treatment of colors, Armstrong denies that the required complexity of determinate colors is excluded by appeals to the phenomenological simplicity (which he grants) of color-perceptions. According to Armstrong, it is possible for us to be aware of the resemblance of colors to one another without its being the case that we are aware of the respect in which these properties resemble one another. For if we are not directly acquainted, in Russell's sense, with colors, it is possible for us to believe, on perceptual grounds, that colors are simple when in fact they are complex. And at the same time, it is possible that the partial identity of colors should be causally responsible for our believing colors to form a resemblance-order without our being aware, even unconsciously or inarticulately, of the respect(s) in which they resemble one another.

Now Armstrong says, in support of this, that we can be aware of a resemblance between two faces without being in any way aware of the respect in which they are similar. In a sense, it seems that this can happen. It may suddenly dawn on us that two people have similar faces, though we can't quite put our finger on the similarity. Do we in that case not *see* the ground of the similarity? I am not sure what should be said; but I am strongly inclined to say that we do indeed see the basis for the similarity; and I think that when we find ourselves in the predicament we are considering, we are invariably convinced that we should be able to detect what underlies the perceived resemblance *just by a more concentrated inspection of the visual information we have before us*. Detecting the basis of a perceived resemblance (whether we can produce verbal description of it or not) is somewhat like managing to focus our attention upon a hitherto unattended object which has been in our visual field for some time.

Now Armstrong's account of our awareness of the resemblance between two colors is not at all like this. Given his account of the resemblance of colors in terms of the wave structure of electro-magnetic radiation, we could never hope to discern the nature of that resemblance simply by a more concentrated visual inspection of patches of color. If, in the case of two faces, our continued efforts to discern the ground of the similarity are met with failure, we would either put this down to the great (perceived) complexity of faces, or we should be left with the perplexing feeling that we had acquired a certain belief without finding any justification in our experience for it. It would seem to us to have arisen from nowhere, to have come from "out of the blue."

When we perceive the resemblance between two shades of blue, we do not have the recourse of great perceived complexity; but neither are we at all inclined to suppose that our belief in their similarity is *unjustified*. Indeed this is just the sort of case where, if we observe a similarity, we *ipso facto* observe the basis for that similarity. We do not wonder where our belief came from – we have the source of the similarity before us: it is *in* the blues. I think that what this shows is that, contrary to the view Armstrong accepts, a determinate shade of color has an observable complexity – though to be sure, it is a complexity of a special kind.[12]

2. GENERIC UNIVERSALS RECONSIDERED

This reflection leads to the theory I wish to propose. When we observe two shades of blue, we observe both that they have something in common and that they are different. I believe an account of this can be given in terms of the notion of abstraction. The theory I shall offer, then, could be called a theory of abstract generic universals. The notion of abstraction involved is, however, of a special sort.

One traditional notion of abstraction is the one which occurs, for example, in Locke's discussion of substance, where the idea of substance, if we have it, is to be found by taking our conception of particulars and isolating in thought some component of that conception which remains when we subtract or ignore each of the simple ideas which represent the properties of things. While in Locke's case this process leaves us with a puzzle instead of a substance, we can imagine using such a process to isolate in thought any one of the properties of a thing by abstracting it from the other properties of that thing. But this kind of abstraction, though somewhat analogous to what we do when we isolate generic universals, is not the same as it. For in the sort of case mentioned, each of the properties abstracted away from a given one may be properties which are logically independent of it, and which may be instantiated in a particular which does not have that given property. But a determinate property and the determinables under which it falls are not separable, except in thought. This inseparability seems, minimally, to involve the following:

(6) It is logically necessary that any particular(s) which instan-
tiate(s) a determinate universal *U* also instantiate(s) every

determinable universal *G* under which *U* falls; and
(7) It is logically necessary that any particular(s) which instantiate(s) a determinable universal *G* instantiate(s) at least one of the determinables on any given level "below" it, and at least one determinate universal falling under it. (This is just an elaboration of (5) above.)

It is (6) and (7), as Armstrong notes, which at the very least must be incorporated into a characterization of the very intimate connection between *being crimson* and *being colored*.

Can we find elsewhere anything closely analogous to this relationship? We can, I think, accept the following pair as close parallels:

(6′) It is logically necessary that anything colored be spatially extended; and
(7′) It is logically necessary that anything which has a shape has some spatial location.

Clearly, the relationship between color and spatial extension is an intimate one indeed, even though the converse of (6′) is false. We can separate color and spatial extension (or shape and location) in thought, and we can think of colorless spatial extensions, but we cannot conceive of something that is colored and not extended.

The relationship between crimson and red is even more intimate than the connection between crimson and extension. But here, too, we can have redness without crimsonness – though, to be sure, not without some other red. So it seems clear that we can distinguish in thought between the crimsonness of a thing and its being red. The proof of this distinguishability lies precisely in our being able to distinguish different shades of red, yet recognize them all as reds. That is, we recognize something they have in common, which is not their all being crimson. Since, moreover, we are able to *observe* this similarity, to notice or be aware of it, and to name it, it seems clear that red is observable every time we observe an instance of a shade of red, even though it is not separable from that shade, but is in the shade.

One of the most widely shared opinions among philosophers is that generic properties as such cannot be imagined, or even conceived by us, let alone perceived. Almost all philosophers who have held that there are generic universals, as well as those who do not, are agreed on this. Yet I suggest that they are wrong, and wrong on all three counts. Let us leave conception to one side, for if perception of instances of determinable properties is to be had, and also images of them, that would surely bring conceivability in its train. But indeed with respect to some genera of properties, it is doubtful whether we ever perceive fully determinate instances of them. That this is so in the case of colors, tones, textures, and perhaps every determinable whose species form a continuum, is a conclusion which seems forced upon us by the fact that each member of a series of colors, etc., may be perceptually indistinguishable from its immediate neighbors but easily distinguishable from more distant members of the series. And a familiar case of indeterminateness in imagination is supplied by the imagined speckled hen which has some number of spots but no particular number of them.[13] This observation is reinforced by the great probability that there are very few persons who, when they imagine a color, can imagine even as determinate a shade as those which they perceive.

Therefore red must be a genuine, existing universal distinct from, but intimately connected to, its various shades. Corresponding to the distinctness of red from its shades, and providing evidence for it, is its distinguishability in thought by means of what I have called abstraction. But this entails that our experience of crimson is complex. If it were not, how could we account for the distinction we make in thought? For this is not merely the reflection of some conventional classification we impose upon our experience, but derives from the nature of that experience itself. What, then, of the alleged phenomenological evidence to the contrary?

Phenomenological evidence can sometimes be difficult to construe – a point which I have already covered in Chapter 1. I believe that the phenomenological appeals in this case are in fact tricky, although it is thought in some quarters that judgments of phenomenological simplicity, at least, are simplicity itself. We ought to begin by noting that this is hardly the case. Perhaps there are such things as objectively simple phenomenal properties, but deciding what they are is not an easy matter, and judgments of simplicity seem typically to be preconditioned by whatever other relevant preconceptions one has. To revert to an illustration previously mentioned, the man in the street, presented with a red circular patch on a screen, is liable to say (if he understands the philosopher's question) that what he sees is perfectly simple – until he is reminded that he sees both redness and circularity. (He might equally insist that what he sees is infinitely complex, since the patch can be subdivided.) The philosophy undergraduate, blindfolded and handed a circular disk, might insist that what he touches is perfectly simple, until reminded that it is both round and flat (not to mention hard). The philosophy graduate student whose visual field is filled with crimson will aver that, abstracting from spatial extension, what he sees is a perfectly simple property. Until, that is, he is reminded that it consists of a hue, an intensity, and a saturation. But, then, isn't the phenomenal hue itself an observable simple property? Surely this regress must somewhere come to a halt?

Before responding to this challenge, we might remind ourselves of a relevant fact – namely, that the hue, intensity and saturation of a particular shade of color seem to be no more separable from each other than that shade is from extension. Perhaps these three aspects of a color are even more intimately bound up than color and extension, although in the latter case, too, the determinate value of each can be independently varied. It is this, surely, the necessary coexistence of hue with some saturation and intensity, which largely accounts (on the one hand) for our readiness to judge a particular shade phenomenally simple; and it is their independent variability (upon the other) which accounts for our reflective ability to analyze it in thought into components.

It is evident that we can discriminate between the crimsonness of a thing and its redness, even though we can no more experience (or even imagine) crimsonness without redness than without a certain intensity and saturation. So we are justified in holding on phenomenological grounds that the crimson hue is in fact complex – though of course not complex in the same way that, say, being an *astronomical quadrilateral incandescent son of a bitch* (an epithet for which I am indebted to Mark Twain)[14] would, if instantiable, be a complex property – or even in the way that *being a red circle* is complex.

But how complex then is a hue such as crimson? There are at least two generic universals associated with *being crimson* – namely, *being red* and *being colored*. But the structure of physical color-properties – the fact that they are arranged in a continuum – implies that there are infinitely many degrees of resemblance to crimson among the colors; and hence indefinitely many resemblance-classes which contain crimson and all the other hues up to a given "distance" from crimson on the spectrum. To each of these resemblance-classes there corresponds a distinct generic universal. We should resist the natural inclination to find this profligacy unpalatable. There are, after all, infinitely many hues. And they do exhibit a structure which implies that there are infinitely many degrees of resemblance among pairs of colors. Our ontology must reflect this richness in nature. We should also remind ourselves that the generic universals in such a series, though distinct, are not logically independent of one another. It is worth remarking, parenthetically, that if phenomenal colors or color-qualia are admitted into our ontology *they* will not exhibit this same infinite complexity – since our perceptual discrimination of color-differences has a finite limit.

I have affirmed the existence of generic universals. I shall defend this conclusion by replying to two arguments with which Armstrong supports his denial of their existence.

One of the objections is this: If crimson consists in a generic universal (redness) being combined with a distinct species-generating universal (call it C-ness), then we cannot adequately represent in our ontology the fact that

(8) Crimson is a shade of red.

For our ontological analysis of (8) would have to be

(9) (Redness and C-ness) is a shade of red.

But if C-ness were logically independent of redness, then by parity of reasoning *redness and D-ness* ought also to be a shade of red, where D can be any property accidentally coextensive with C. But *redness and D-ness* is not a shade of red. Thus (9) does not reflect the intimacy of the connection between crimson and redness. With this last we should obviously agree. But (9) is not the only paraphrase available for an ontological analysis of (8). Instead, I suggest that (8) should be understood to assert that

(10) (Redness and C-ness) is a shade of red, and it is logically necessary that all things that are C are red and that all red things are C or else C′ or C″ or . . . .

It is clear that the predicate 'D' cannot be substituted into (10) for 'C' *salva veritate*.

Armstrong, however, has a prior argument against the existence of generic universals. His argument is that a generic universal must constitute the respect in which all of its species are similar, but also the respect in which they differ. Red and blue are the same in both being colors, yet they differ in being different colors. This seems to be a contradiction. But it is not. To yield a contradiction, the assertion in question would have to have some such logical form as

(11) $[F(\text{red}) \ \& \ F(\text{blue})] \ \& \ \sim[F(\text{red}) \ \& \ F(\text{blue})]$

or perhaps

(12) $[F(\text{red}) \ \& \ F(\text{blue})] \ \& \ \{[F(\text{red}) \ \& \ \sim F(\text{blue})] \ v \ [\sim F(\text{red}) \ \& \ F(\text{blue})]\}$

or conceivably

(13) $R(\text{red, blue}) \ \& \ \sim R(\text{red, blue})$

where 'F' designates some second-order monadic property, and 'R' designates some second-order relation. But on the analysis I have presented, *being colored* is *not* to be understood in terms of some second-order property or relation modifying its species. Neither red nor blue are color*ed*; they are color*s*. Although they are both colors – that is, each is identical with some color – they are not same-colored. Their similarity does not consist in there being some (second-order) property which they share; nor does their difference consist in one having a generic property which the other lacks. So there is no contradiction. Red and blue are similar in that they are both colors, but they do not differ in that respect, though they are different colors. The intrinsic component which they share is the ground of their generic similarity; the ground of their difference lies in the distinct species-generating universals which they contain.

How does the theory advanced here explain the five facts about resemblances between universals which were set out at the beginning? The members of a resemblance-class of universals do all have something in common (this was point (1) – namely some generic universal. The ground of their difference is not this universal but the constituent universals which they do not share (2). When the members of a resemblance-class do exhibit one or more resemblance-orders, based upon their intrinsic natures, we are faced with comparative degrees of similarity. If there is a linear ordering of some range of determinate universals with respect to some dimension of resemblance, then this fact will reflect the existence of a hierarchy of nested and overlapping generic universals which can be mapped in a structure-preserving way onto some set of intervals on a line. A resemblance-ordering, in other words, reflects the fact that generic universals can characterize nested hierarchies of determinate universals (3). Our theory does not explain the fact that sometimes a resemblance-class forms a set-of-incompatibles (4). But our theory is intended to provide a *general* account of resemblance among universals, and as we have seen, there is no persuasive reason to suppose that the members of every resemblance class do form a set-of-incompatibles. And what, finally, shall we say about claim (5)?

3. THE NECESSITY OF THE GENUS/SPECIES RELATION

Perhaps the necessary connection between species and genus (claim 5) is a fundamental fact which admits of no further explanation. But philosophy does not rest easy when presented with such facts; she tries to reduce their number to the fewest possible. It is natural, therefore, that we should seek an explanation for this connection; and as it happens, Armstrong's account of generic universals, though I have rejected it, suggests just such an explanation. This explanation is not identical to Armstrong's, of course; but it bears to it a certain structural resemblance.

I put forward this explanation only as a suggestion, and for the purpose of exploring a few of its systematic consequences. For I am at present far from certain that it is correct, and I have no arguments (beyond systematic coherence) to establish it. My hypothesis has two parts. The first part may be compactly stated thus: If S and S' are specific universals and G is a determinable or generic universal under which they both fall, then the causal relations between G and other universals are a subset of the causal relations between S and other universals; and also a subset of the causal relations between S' and other universals. For S and S' to be species of a common genus is for them to share some subset of causal relations, which subset can itself constitute the causal essence of a universal, such as G. For S and S' to be distinct species is for this subset to be a proper subset of the causal relations which characterize S, and also of the causal relations which characterize S': there must be some causal relation which S has, but not S', and some causal relation which S' has, but not S. More formally, if $\{R\}$, $\{R'\}$ and $\{R_G\}$ are the sets of causal relations associated with S, S', and G respectively, then $\{R\} \notin \{R'\}$, $\{R'\} \notin \{R\}$, $\{R_G\} \in \{R\}$, $\{R_G\} \in \{R'\}$, $\{R_G\} \neq \{R\}$, and $\{R_G\} \neq \{R'\}$. Since the sets $\{R\}$, $\{R'\}$, and $\{R_G\}$ are essential to their respective properties, if G is related to S and S' in the manner specified, then it is a necessary truth that it is so related. This, then, explains why, if G is a genus of S, it is so necessarily. It follows from this first part of the hypothesis that physical universals are organized into hierarchies of genera and species by virtue of the structure of their causal relations.

The first part of the hypothesis explains why the instantiation of a specific universal involves, *ipso facto*, the instantiation of the generic universals under which it falls. But it does not yet explain the fact – if it is a fact – that every instantiation of a generic universal necessarily involves the instantiation of a specific one which falls under it. Why cannot a genus – for example, color – be exhibited by an object which has no *particular* color? Or, putting the question in the terms dictated by the first part of the hypothesis, if G and S are a genus and any one of its species respectively, why cannot G, with its associated set of causal relations $\{R_G\}$, be instantiated independently of any instantiation of an S with its associated superset $\{R\}$ of causal relations?

The second part of the hypothesis accounts for this fact. Although every set of causal relations which is shared by two universals corresponds to a genus under which they fall, it does not follow that any generic universal can be separately instantiated. Presumably not every set of causal relations corresponds to a universal which can be instantiated, for these universals and their causal relations must form a coherent and integrated set of natural laws. Some sets of second-order (causal) relational properties will define no universal whatever – for example, the set which consists of the union of the sets of causal relations associated with red and with green respectively. Some sets of causal properties, although shared by universals which are instantiable, correspond to no universal which is instantiable separately from these. A generic universal will be such a universal; it will be such that its instantiation is possible only when one of its species is instantiated. In that case, the existence of the genus is parasitic upon that of its species. This would explain, then, why such universals cannot be separated from their species.

But are all generic universals parasitic? Those which are, are so necessarily. But nothing I have argued shows that there could be no independently instantiable generic universals. And there is some independent evidence for the existence of such exceptions. The visually imagined spotted hen with no definite number of spots represents one possible case of a non-parasitic generic universal.[15] Another class of examples may be indicated by the probabilistic laws of quantum mechanics. Perhaps the indeterministic characteristics of quantum systems can be partly explained by supposing them to exemplify (until a measurement "reduces" the wave-packet) certain generic properties without exemplifying any of the species falling under them. But this is, of course, speculative; it serves here to indicate that it is perhaps not an *a priori* truth that there are no non-parasitic generic properties. Thus the second part of the hypothesis is not assumed to apply universally to all generic universals.

Having stated the hypothesis, it is time to consider some of its implications within the context of the general metaphysical architecture which I have developed. I shall enumerate first some advantages of this theory, and then turn to objections and responses to those objections.

Like Armstrong's theory, this one allows for the fact that a determinate universal U may be ranged under two determinable universals G_1 and G_2, such that neither G_1 nor G_2 is a subgenus of the other. The theory accounts, in other words, for the fact that universals can and do reveal orderings which are not linearly hierarchical or taxonomic.[16] Unlike Armstrong's, this theory allows us to explain how it is that all geometric shapes, plane and solid, fall under a genus. For it is quite obvious that all such figures will share certain causal relations; and it is at least extremely plausible that the more similar two shapes are (as we would directly judge) the more causal characteristics they share. Similarly, colors as a group will be arranged in a different region of the causal web of universals than shapes, sharing among themselves more of the same causal powers than any one of them shares with any shape. And so on. Finally, the theory allows us to explain why, often, it is the case that instances of two physical properties which are similar (but not identical), appear similar (but not identical) to us. They will appear similar if the perceptual phenomena which they cause in us are suitably similar, under similar surrounding conditions. But this is just what we can expect to happen – usually – if the two physical properties in question share many causal characteristics.

There are, it seems to me, two serious objections to this explanation of the genus/species relation. First, there is the fact that we recognize the generic similarity between determinate properties "directly" in the case of phenomenal properties. We have no need to investigate their causal linkages with other properties. That (phenomenal) scarlet and vermilion are similar; and in particular that they are more similar than scarlet and green, are facts we apprehend without consideration of causes; likewise with shapes, etc. But if this is so, how can the genus/species relation consist essentially in overlap between sets of causal relations? Or are phenomenal properties to be taken as differing in this regard from physical ones?

The latter suggestion is not attractive, if we regard phenomenal properties as causally linked to physical ones, and hence not differentiated from them in the radical way that properties of abstract entities might be. And anyway the suggestion collapses if we wish to identify phenomenal geometric properties with physical ones.

It seems rather that the correct thing to say is that the genus/species relation does not (for physical and phenomenal properties) consist *merely* in the overlap of their sets of causal relations, but also in some fact about their "inner natures." But it has been maintained in any case that there is a necessary connection between the inner nature of a universal and its causal linkages. Thus the fact that two universals overlap in their causal linkages is the outward reflection, as it might be put, of their inner natures. In the case of physical properties which are non-phenomenal, the structure of causal overlaps is the only means by which we are able to ascertain the ordering of universals into genera. In the case of phenomenal properties, it is their intrinsic natures which ground such judgments. But I am unable to say anything more than I have concerning what it is about the intrinsic nature of two specific universals that makes or constitutes their co-membership in a common genus. Perhaps our recognition of this is a primitive act of recognition which cannot be further analyzed.

The second objection derives from the fact that the determinate members of a genus of universals often form a continuum; in the simplest case, they can be given a linear resemblance-ordering. So some genera of universals consist of linearly ordered infinite – in fact non-denumerable – sets of specific universals. How can this be accounted for by the theory being proposed?

The ordering among such universals would naturally be explained in terms of the way in which their associated sets of causal relations overlap. Two universals are closer in the ordering if their sets of causal relations overlap more extensively. But this explanation, when offered for a continuum of universals falling under some genus, entails that the set of causal relations associated with each specific universal must itself be a nondenumerably infinite set.[17]

Such proliferation of causal relations is bound to offend the frugal sensibilities of many a philosophical conscience. However, it is not, so far as I can see, a consequence which leads to any outright paradox. Furthermore, there is a possible reply to this objection. Suppose there are two sets of specific universals, each set isomorphic to the linear continuum, and functionally related by a causal law, $s^* = f(s)$ – where s^* and s are variables ranging over numerical values assigned to the universals in each ordered set. The universals corresponding to a given range of s fall under a unique determinable D determined by that range, and this range gets mapped onto a set of values of s^* falling under a unique determinable D^*. According to the law, a given universal S^*_1 bears a causal relation to another universal S_1. But perhaps it also bears a causal relation to the infinitely many determinables under which S_1 falls. These, then, will be the infinite causal relations required in this kind of case by the hypothesis. Moreover, S^*_1 and S^*_2 will share causal relations to just those determinables in the infinite set $\{D\}$ under which both S_1 and S_2 fall, where these are the images under f of S^* and S^*_1. This automatically ensures the proper structure of overlaps between the sets of causal relations of the properties falling in the ranges of the two variables. Thus the theory can hardly be rejected because of the second objection alone.

On the other hand, the first objection has forced the admission that generic similarity must in any case be a function of the intrinsic natures of universals. That being so, the present theory, while explaining how it is that we can *recognize* generic resemblance among non-phenomenal universals, perhaps does not achieve much by way of explaining what such resemblance fundamentally consists in. Thus my diffidence in proposing the account.

10 Relations

1. INTERNAL VS. EXTERNAL RELATIONS

Until now the focus of attention has been on first-order monadic properties, though much of what has been said is intended to apply to first-order relations as well. Now, however, it is necessary to take a closer look at first-order relations. The question I wish to answer is: Do first-order physical relations have essences consisting of causal powers?

It turns out that the answer to this question involves some complications. The principal complication is this. Sometimes the fact that two particulars, *a* and *b*, stand in a certain relation is a logical consequence of their having certain monadic properties. For example, if *a* weighs 1 kilogram, and *b* weighs 2 kilograms, then *b* weighs twice as much as *a*. The latter relational fact is entailed by the former two monadic facts. Similarly, if *a* is pink and *b* is red, then it follows that *b* is darker than a. Such relations as *weighing twice as much as* and *being darker than* are internal relations. They contrast with external relations, which are not entailed by the monadic properties of their relata. Are there any first-order external physical relations? Spatial and temporal relations might be said to fall in this class, but I shall discuss them separately. There are such external relations as *being a parent of* and *being fastened to*, but these, it is clear, are complex relations which are analyzable into monadic properties and the second-order causal relation *R*. It may be that all "pure" first-order physical external relations are either spatial or temporal.[1]

If, however, some of these relations are not spatial or temporal, then it seems safe to say that their instantiations will be caused and have causal consequences. The same arguments which led to the conclusion that monadic physical universals have an essence consisting of causal relations will aply here.

Matters stand differently with respect to internal relations. The fact that an internal relation *I* obtains between *a* and *b* is a consequence of monadic facts about *a* and *b* (say, *Fa* and *Gb*). If, therefore, *I* had a causal essence of its own, the fact that *aIb* obtained would have causal consequences over and above those attending the states *Fa* and *Gb*. But no mere consequence of *Fa* and *Gb* can imply new causally related states of affairs – states not already implied by *Fa* and *Gb*. Thus the causal implications of *aIb* must already be contained within those of (*Fa* and *Gb*). Internal relations, therefore, have no distinct causal essences.

2. REFLEXIVE NECESSARY RELATIONS

There are some relation predicates which, when each of the places for individual names is filled with the same name, yield statements which express necessary truths. Examples of such predicates are 'is identical to' and 'in the same location as.' It is doubtful whether 'is identical to' denotes any relation at all. Certainly the denoted relation would have no distinct causal powers, over and above those had by its "relatum." However, 'is in the same location as' does, I believe, denote a genuine relation. And *a* and *b*, though non-identical, may occupy the same location (recall bosons). When *a* and *b* occupy the same location, they stand in a genuine, contingent relation. But *a*'s occupying the same location as itself is not a contingent truth. It is unclear whether the relation *being in the same location as* is a distinct relation instantiated by *a* (where 'a' names some physical object). Considerations of semantic uniformity would suggest that 'is in the same location as' denotes a relation – indeed the same relation – in contingent contexts as in necessary ones. We can explain the modal difference by reflecting on the fact that *being in the same location as* relates material particulars only by proxy. Letting 'L' stand for 'is in the same location as,' 'a' and 'b' name material objects, and 'x' and 'y' be variables ranging over spatial locations, we may analyze 'aLb' as equivalent to: $(\exists x)(\exists y)(aLx$ *and bLy and x= y*). Naturally, 'aLb' is not a necessary truth, for values of *x* and *y* might have been distinct. But 'aLa' is equivalent to simply '$(\exists x)(aLx)$'; and if *a* is a material object, this latter is a necessary truth.

It is so far unclear, however, what sort of causal essence, if any, attaches to spatial location *per se* – or more generally, to all spatial and temporal relations. For it seems that an empty space-time could exist, devoid of material objects; and in such a space-time there would be no (exemplified) causal relations.

There is indeed a deeper puzzle concerning the role of spatial and temporal properties within the causally linked web of universals which exist in the the world. For I have reasoned that if every physical property has a set of essential properties which are its causal relations to other physical properties, then a change anywhere in this web would necessarily comprise a change in every first-order property constituting the web. Since all the properties in such a system are linked directly or indirectly, the substitution, deletion, or addition of a "new" property would entail different essences for all the properties directly linked to it. Thus these would also be new properties; and clearly this would ramify throughout the system. But if spatial and temporal properties were merely elements like any others in this system, it would follow that a world in which any single physical property was distinct from those in ours, would be a world which contained none of the spatial and temporal properties of this world. Spatial and temporal properties, it would seem to follow, are unique to this world. If the laws of nature were different than they are – which is logically possible – then they would describe a physical world which is not a spatiotemporal one. But this conclusion is unpalatable. It seems to be a logically (or at any rate a metaphysically) necessary truth that a physical world is a spatiotemporal world; and it also seems to be true – indeed necessarily true – that our physical world is not the only logically possible physical world. Yet, on the stated assumptions concerning causal essences, this received view can only be maintained if the causal roles of spatial and temporal properties are somehow different in kind from those of all other physical properties. How then are the causal roles of spatiotemporal properties to be understood? Can the causal realist defend the received view?

3. SPATIAL AND TEMPORAL UNIVERSALS

In this section I shall discuss spatial and temporal universals generally: that is, both monadic and relational ones. Unless it is necessary to make the distinction, I shall refer indifferently to both spatial and temporal universals as locational universals.

It seems entirely plausible to regard locational universals as physical universals. They characterize material objects. On the other hand, I have argued that space and time can exist independently of material objects. From that standpoint it seems possible to hold that locational universals belong in a distinct category. In a spatiotemporal universe which was devoid of material objects, locational universals (at least relational ones) would be instantiated. Yet such a universe would not be one in which there were any events – except in the vacuous sense that time would pass. In such a universe, no causal relations would be exemplified. Space and time, then, are not ontologically dependent upon material objects.

On the other hand, the existence of material objects requires the existence of space and time. Thus locational properties are more fundamental to the structure of the world than the other properties of material objects. And if indeed we define physical objects as ones which exist spatiotemporally, and define physical properties as properties which are instantiated only in space and time, is it not somehow redundant, or circular, to count locational universals themselves as physical properties?

On the other side, there seems to be a strong, if not conclusive, reason for counting locational properties as physical. Physical properties, we claimed, are bound together by a network of causal relations. If locational universals occupy positions in this network, then in a robust sense they are physical properties. It seems clear that locational universals do in some sense occupy such positions. Universals such as *relative velocity*, which clearly play a role in causal laws, contain locational universals as constituents. Spatial properties such as length and distance influence the causal interactions of material objects. Were it not so, we could not detect and measure these qualities as they are exemplified by material objects. We can measure them because they differentially affect our measuring instruments and sense organs.

This last argument seems at first conclusive; and it is not incompatible, after all, with the supposition that locational universals are in a sense more fundamental than some or all of the others which characterize material objects. Yet this conclusion raises, as I have shown, a difficult question. Suppose that locational universals occupy positions in the causal network of the universe. This means that each of them has an essence which is constituted by its set of causal relations to other universals. But the web of relations has a kind of systematic unity. This unity is such that a universal cannot exist except in the company of a particular set of universals. There is more than one logically possible structure of physical universals. But a universal which occupies a position in one such structure cannot occupy a position in any of the others. Any logically possible structure of physical universals, if it existed, would describe a spatiotemporal world. Such a world would instantiate locational universals, hence such universals would exist in it. Thus it seems that locational universals must occupy positions in every such structure. But this is incompatible with their having essences constituted by their causal relations to particular other universals which must, *a fortiori*, exist in the structure. For such essences would perforce differ from structure to structure. If their essences differ, the locational universals must differ as well.

Perhaps this conclusion is not as uncongenial, on closer inspection, as at first it appears. After all, we are speaking here of "real" space and time, not mere mathematical constructions. Different mathematical spaces permit the instantiation of different locational properties; and whichever of these mathematical spaces characterizes space-time need not, perhaps, instantiate locational universals which would exist in other causal structures. This suggestion seems, at least, congruent with the consequences of the General Theory of Relativity. Still, it is clear that some locational universals could be instantiated in, say, both a Euclidean space and a Riemannian space of a certain curvature. That two intersecting geodesics should subtend an angle of 1 radian is possible in both spaces. That two points are separated by a distance of 1 meter is similarly possible in both spaces. And both spaces will exemplify many of the same generic locational universals. At the very least, they will have to exemplify the generic properties *being a spatial relation* and *being a temporal relation*. In Chapter 9 I argued that generic universals are distinct from each of their species, and that generic physical universals, like their species, possess causal essences. Thus the above solution does not seem acceptable to me.

I suggest, however, that the causal role of locational universals is special in a way which allows – and indeed requires – that every logically possible world which contains material objects and is governed by natural laws, is a spatiotemporal world. This is not merely so in virtue of the fact that laws presuppose causal relations, causal relations presuppose material objects, and material objects presuppose a space-time. It is further reflected in the essential form of causal relations. I have maintained that such relations are quadratic. They conform (see Chapter 3, Section 3) to the general schema: $C(P, Q, \delta s, \delta t)$, where P and Q are first-order physical universals, and δs and δt denote a spatial and a temporal interval, respectively. I now suggest further that P and Q are always non-locational universals; that locational universals always enter into causal relations by virtue of the special role of the intervals δs and δt. This means that other locational universals – for example, shapes and finite distances and temporal intervals – enter into the causal structure of the world in a way which depends upon their being "constructed" out of the minimal intervals δs and δt.

Locational universals can exist independently of the existence of causal connections; the corollary of this is that, by themselves, they are radically "incomplete" as regards causal efficacy. A set of universals which, when instantiated, has causal consequences, must contain locational universals, but it must also contain non-locational universals. Locational universals, as one might express it, are metaphysically even more fundamental than causal relations. All other physical universals are less fundamental than causal relations. Locational universals, then, have a special place in the scheme of things. Causal relations depend upon other properties. And any causal world, whether the natural laws which governed it were those which actually obtain or not, would be a spatiotemporal world.

4. CAUSAL ESSENCES AND CAUSAL RELATIONS

We have thus far attempted to work out for first-order monadic and relational properties some of the implications of the doctrine that physical universals have causal essences. Now let us examine whether there are any higher-order universals to which the same doctrine applies. For example, first-order universals can combine in various ways to form more complex first-order universals. The various constituents of such a complex property can therefore be bound together by structural relations, as we may call them, into such a complex. Sometimes such relations are purely contingent. If Jack is a six-foot-tall man, then we may speak of Jack as having the conjunctive property, *being a six-foot-tall man*. This is simply an abbreviated way of saying of Jack that he has two properties, ones which make true the conjunctive proposition 'Jack is a man and Jack is six feet tall.' But possibly there are structurally complex properties which are not simply a matter of the contingent coinstantiation of two simpler properties. To be a man, for instance, is to have a complex property whose constituent properties are not merely conjoined but causally connected in the man. I regard it as an open question whether every structural relation between universals is either contingent, in the foregoing sense, or causal.

It is clear that contingent coinstantiation is not a relation between properties which itself has a causal essence. The causal powers conferred by a conjunctive property are simply the conjunction of the causal powers conferred by each conjunct. That some of these powers may not be manifested unless the properties are conjointly exemplified is of course true, but also irrelevant. It is tempting to suppose that conjunctive properties might confer emergent causal powers, powers not associated with either conjunct singly. But such "emergent" powers must be a function of the natures of the conjuncts; and hence ultimately reducible to their causal powers.

What about causal relations themselves? Do *they*, in turn, have causal essences? They do not have causal essences either. They do not stand in some further (third-order) causal relation to other universals. It is true, of course, that one causal process can cause – that is, initiate – another causal process. But this is just to say that one event can cause another event, which can in turn contribute causally to a third. There is no need to invoke third-order causal relations here.

Moreover there is a positive argument against the existence of such relations. Take a case in which the causal relation R is instantiated by certain first-order properties, themselves instantiated by a system of particulars. Say we have a closed system which is in a total state A at a time t_0 and in a total state B at a later time t_1. Here we can say that A is the total cause of B. During the production of B, R is instantiated. Can we say that the instantiation of R – A's causing B – itself confers any causal powers upon anything, that is, over and above the causal powers conferred upon the system by the other properties it instantiates during the interval t_0 to t_1? By hypothesis, the system is closed; hence it is the causal powers of the properties characterizing the system at t_0 that determine the physical consequences of the system's being in state A. A's causing B cannot involve causal powers over and above those already instantiated in A at t_0, for A's causing B just is the exercising of some of those causal powers. Nor is there any other state at t_1 which is caused by what transpires in the system prior to that time. Since the case is quite general, it follows that causal relations do not themselves exercise causal powers.

This conclusion has two significant consequences. One is that R is world-system neutral. Any logically possible world-structure of physical universals can be bound together by one and the same causal relation R. It was argued that none of the physical first-order universals (except locational ones) which constitute the elements of one such structure can appear in another structure. This was because the total structure affects the essence of each element by determining to what other elements it is causally related. But the causal relation itself – the glue which binds these structures together – does not itself have a causal essence. Hence there is nothing barring the existence of *R* in logically possible worlds whose natural laws differ from those of our own.

The second consequence of importance is that instances of *R* in the physical world cannot, in themselves, occupy the "outer" termini of causal chains eventuating in perception. For to occupy such a terminus is to stand in causal relations to instantiations of other properties. Causal relations themselves stand in no such relations. How then could one, even in principle, detect *R* perceptually? For we have argued that, in the case of physical first-order universals, detecting the presence of an instance of such a property consists in being causally affected by causal chains which emanate from it by virtue of the causal powers it confers. Coming to know what such a property is – insofar as we ever can know it – consists in identifying these causal powers and the correlative laws.[2] If the causal relation *R* does not confer causal powers of its own, clearly we cannot stand in *this* relation to it. But how then can it be detected that a physical event *A* has caused another, *B*?

If the preceding argument is correct, perceiving this does not consist in anything over and above detecting, and knowing enough about, the universals which are constituents of *A* and *B* themselves. That is, it consists in coming to know the causal essences of these universals. This we come to know in the rather complex way that we learn to identify physical properties, through the discovery of certain systematic regularities in our perceptual experience – and which we then come to fuller understanding of through systematic examination of further associated regularities.

Thus our perceiving *A* and *B*, and that *A* caused *B*, will involve a perceptual process which depends upon some further causal consequences of *A* and *B*. We may either perceive *A* *via* perceptual experiences caused by the intermediate event *B* or perceive *A* and *B* through independent causal "channels." But, in perceiving *A*'s causing *B*, there will not be any *separate* or *special* perceptual experiences which are the causal consequences of causal powers other than those exercised by the first-order physical universals which are constituents of *A* and *B*. There will be no distinct perceptual experience which occurs in virtue of causal powers conferred by the instantiation of *R* by those first-order universals.

It follows immediately that Hume was making an impossible and misdirected demand insofar as he was asking for, or requiring us to find, some distinct and separate element in experience which would constitute a perception of one *physical* event causing another. There cannot be any such element as that; but this is precisely because of the very nature which R is required to have in order to play the role it does play in the world's structure. For there to be such a separate element, R would have to confer causal powers over and above those conferred by the states of affairs it causally relates. On the other hand, perceptual knowledge of first-order physical universals is in part constituted by our sometimes standing in causal relations to their instances. Thus the existence of R is presupposed, or at any rate entailed by the existence of perceptual knowledge of first-order physical properties.

It does not follow from the conclusion just reached that we have no perceptual knowledge of R. What follows is that in a limited sense Hume was correct: we do not perceive instantiations of R which are themselves perceived *via* the mediation of causal chains. We do not perceive instances of R as distinct elements of the physical world, in the way in which first-order physical universals are perceived and identified. But Hume was mistaken in supposing that instances of R never are constituents of our perceptual field; or so I have devoted much of Part one in arguing. Such instances of R, however, are *immediate* constituents of experience. Thus, as with other phenomenologically given universals, R is known immediately and not identified in terms of a causal essence. We are acquainted with the thing itself. Thus it is that we acquire the concept of causal relatedness which, I have argued, is necessary in order to solve the problem of induction and which is – therefore – essential to the inferential procedure by means of which we identify first-order physical universals. For we use inductive reasoning to make the required inferences about causal relations on the basis of patterned repetitions found in experience.

Returning to other higher-order relations, I shall conclude this chapter with a more general argument which applies to all second-order universals, both relational and monadic. Do any such universals stand in (higher-order) causal relations? In my view, all universals exist atemporally. Hence they cannot undergo change. Nor can they be created or destroyed. If no first-order universal changes, then it does not acquire or lose any (second-order) properties or relations. There are no events involving just universals. Thus there is no way in which causal relations could obtain among the properties of universals. From the atemporality of universals it follows that no second-order or higher-order universals have causal essences or stand in causal relations.

5. PROPERTIES OF ABSTRACT INDIVIDUALS

Thus far, very little has been said about universals which characterize abstract individuals. I have omitted them because a discussion of them is gratuitous in the absence of arguments to show that there are abstract individuals. I am inclined to think that there are such individuals – for example, propositions – but I shall not undertake to support that belief here. However, I have argued for the existence of one kind of abstract entity – namely, universals themselves – which can in turn have properties. Thus some conditional remarks are appropriate, by way of contrasting the monadic properties and relations of abstract individuals with physical properties. The most salient contrast is that the former universals do not have causal essences. This follows from the fact that abstract individuals are (as I use the term) atemporal and non-spatial by definition. If any of these exist, they do not participate in the causal web of nature. They cannot undergo change; hence they cannot be caused to gain or lose properties. It follows that their properties are not causally related to each other.

Related to this contrast is an epistemological one. Properties of abstract individuals are not identified in terms of causal powers since they have none. Thus, unless they are immediately given in perceptual experience (as is R), they cannot be identified by means of perception. They must be apprehended through some other cognitive faculty(s) of the mind, if apprehended at all. Knowledge of them is *a priori*, which few philosophers who admit their existence would dispute. We have seen that the causal relation – which we have found it necessary to classify as a second-order property and hence not, properly speaking, as itself a physical property – is not identified via causal powers, though it is a constituent of perceptual experience. And we have seen that locational properties, to which we have assigned a special status, can be perceived as properties of physical objects via causal processes. But they can be identified and understood more directly – that is, by immediate acquaintance and geometrical reasoning. Of these matters more will be said in Part three, to which we now proceed.

Part three

Epistemological realism

11 Skepticism about the existence of the material world

1. PROLOGUE

My plan in Part three is to examine in succession four major questions which confront epistemology insofar as it seeks knowledge of a physical world. These questions are, in order:

(1) Does Time have objective (i.e., extra-mental) existence?
(2) Does Space have objective existence?
(3) Is Causation an objective relation?
(4) Do Common Sense and its sophisticated cousin, the Scientific Method, yield justified beliefs concerning material bodies, their constitution, and their laws of behavior?

The first prefatory remark I must make is that, perhaps obviously, my discussion of each issue will be incomplete and selective. This sketchiness, while leaving the argument unfinished and open to many objections, nonetheless suits my purpose well. For what I propose to do here is merely to explore, in a tentative way, whether and to what extent the metaphysical conclusions of Parts one and two hold out hope for new footings in epistemology. As in metaphysics, so also in epistemology, I shall champion realism.

But this advocacy will be at best programmatic. One of its primary goals will be to join issue with Hilary Putnam, whose apostasy from scientific realism has been both lauded and lamented. Putnam abandons realism in favor of what he hopes to be a moderate sort of relativism, or "internal realism," as he prefers to call it. But relativism of a sort it is, and it is important to see what drives realism (or Putnam at any rate) into its arms. In Chapter 12, I hope to show that the possibility of gaining an independent (that is, "non-theoretical") grip upon causation plays a critical role in the dialectic of this debate. This in turn sets the stage for a discussion of how the face of epistemology may be altered if we have – as Part one claims – such an independent grip. Failing that grip, I should be inclined to agree with Putnam that the cause of realist epistemology is a lost cause. Thus it seems to me that Putnam's treatment of the problem is both perspicacious and to my purpose in locating the nub of the issue between realists and antirealists.

My second prefatory remark concerns theories of perception. Any complete epistemology must include a theory of perception. Since it is not my intention to present a complete epistemology, I shall not attempt to argue for one theory of perception or against others. Rather, I shall presuppose a theory of perception, one which I believe approximates closely the view of reflective common sense on the matter.[1] It is necessary now to make the main outlines of that theory explicit. In the phenomenological investigations of Parts one and two, I attempted to remain as neutral as possible on this issue, but elsewhere my concern for the problems raised by a causal theory of perception have already become evident. I shall adopt here one version of that theory. Those who reject the causal theory are asked to forgive this strategy, on the grounds that the causal theory has much to recommend it, if only it can be rescued from the disgrace of leading to that most unsavory of consequences, solipsism. My purpose is to investigate whether, *if* one adopts the phenomenological and metaphysical findings of the preceding pages, such a rescue can be achieved, or at least partially achieved. I think it can; but first, a few words about the causal theory I shall adopt.

According to this theory, there is mediated perception and unmediated perception (or direct awareness). Direct awareness is awareness of what I shall call sense-data. The awareness is called direct because the relationship between the event or act of awareness and the occurrence or existence of the sense-data is not causal; at least, the latter do not cause the former. In this sense at least, sense-data are "given." Knowledge of them does not involve causal inference, whatever other uncertainties it may sometimes be subject to.[2] I take the relation between a perceptual act and its immediate objects to involve intentionality; and intentionality is a relation which may not be further analyzable but is in any case not in my view analyzable in terms of causal relations. There is the further question whether sense-data are in themselves mental or non-mental entities. On this question I shall remain neutral; but I do assume that their *esse* is *percipi*; if non-mental, at least their existence or occurrence is dependent upon their being perceived. Thus they are not ordinary physical objects.[3]

All perception of other entities is mediated perception. In particular, it is mediated by causal chains, some of which lead from the entity (more precisely, from an event or state of affairs) to a perceptual act of direct awareness. We may say that perceptual awareness of something which is not a sense-datum occurs *via* the direct awareness of some sense-datum. It is this "via" which produces the epistemological difficulties. I shall not assume that the sense-datum in general resembles the extra-conscious entity whose perception it mediates, although one can say, if one likes, that the sense-datum 'represents' the extra-conscious object. All I shall assume is that extra-conscious objects are perceivable only because their existence and structure make (under suitable conditions) some difference to the existence and structure of what we directly perceive.

Some causal theories of perception hold that the expression

X perceives *Y*

means (in part) that *Y* bears some suitable causal relation to a perceptual act of awareness on the part of *X*; or at least that it means this when '*Y*' denotes some physical object. I do not hold this. On my view, 'perceives' has the same meaning whether *Y* is an extra-conscious object or a sense-datum. Thus, so far as meaning goes, the essential feature of perception is its intentionality and the fact that it involves some kind of sensuous consciousness. But I do hold that when *Y* is not a sense-datum, it is *necessary* that *Y*, if perceived, stand in some suitable causal relation to the act of perceiving it. According to the skeptic, an act of perception can be directed toward sense-data qualitatively identical to those of which I am now directly aware (by virtue of which I take myself to be overlooking a lovely duck-pond) and there may in fact be such a duck-pond outside my window; but if no causal relation exists between that pond and my sense-data, then I am not perceiving the pond.

The necessity in question is not derived from the meaning of 'perceive.' But it is surely part of our ordinary understanding of what it is to be perceptually aware of physical things (and other minds). Of course perceptual awareness of these things, like perceptual awareness of sense-data, must involve sensuous consciousness, and it must involve a relation of intentionality between perceptual consciousness and them. But although, when we perceive something which is not a sense-datum, we *a fortiori* perceive something which is a sense-datum, consciousness is not in that case directed toward the sense-datum only, but also toward the mind-independent thing. And I believe that the existence of a causal link between a perceptual act and its mind-independent object is a necessary condition for there to obtain this required intentional relation between them. Very roughly, this is because such an intention requires that we recognize an object of thought or perception *as* external to us; and this recognition of externality or independence requires the existence and recognition of a causal schema to account for the relevant perceptual experiences. This is as much as I shall say here about the causal theory of perception, in the form which the following discussion presupposes. The last-mentioned features of the theory will receive some clarification and elaboration in Chapter 12.

It will be clear that such a theory generates an epistemological problem: perhaps one should say that it is saddled with *the* epistemological problem about perceptual evidence. We have not assumed that sense-data resemble the mind-independent objects which we ordinarily take to exist. It would be illegitimate to do so, for we have no reason to believe that effects generally resemble their causes. So while it may be true that we perceive mind-independent objects, it is apparently not true that we can know that we are doing this, or know what those objects are like, unless we can in general infer the nature of causes from the nature of their effects.

That is the problem which, schematically, Part three undertakes to address.

2. EASY FOUNDATIONALISM

We have discussed already the means by which physical properties come to be identified and their natures known. Do such identifications not entail the existence of material particulars within a spatial and temporal world? Physical properties can be identified only via their instances; and if the instantiation of a physical property requires the existence of material things, or at least of material stuffs, then the identification of a physical property appears to entail the existence of (some) matter.

But this is – alas – much too easy a route to realism. It puts no pressure on skepticism, for it begs the question against skeptical arguments. The identification-procedure we have described for physical properties presupposes the causal order of nature; and it presupposes a causal theory of perception. I have argued that we have phenomenological grounds for ascribing a causal order to the content of sense perception; but this alone does not justify our ascribing such an order to anything which may be supposed to lie outside our experience. The skeptic, to be sure, allows the possibility that perceptual experience is caused by an external world, and can proceed from that very supposition to argue that we have no grounds for inferring this. Put so as to address the present view of properties, the skeptic's argument proceeds by pointing out as usual that our sensations can be caused by something radically different from what common sense takes as their cause. In the case of *geometrical* properties, I have argued that this does not impugn our understanding of the intrinsic *nature* of such properties; but it nevertheless serves to undermine any claims as to the shapes and spatial relations of objects in physical space.

I wish to discuss three skeptical claims, each of which is made by the radical skeptic. He claims that each of the following cannot be known:

(1) that every event has a cause;
(2) that objective time, space, and matter exist;
(3) that the nature of physical causes can be determined from the nature of their effects.

These three propositions form a hierarchy, inasmuch as skepticism about (1) entails skepticism about (2); and skepticism about (2) entails skepticism about (3). Suppose that we do not know that every event has a cause. Then, even if we know that some events within experience are caused by others, we shall have no grounds for holding that there are external causes of experienced events, or of experience as a whole. For, having made the distinction between the content of experience and the things we ordinarily claim to perceive, the skeptic can proceed to say that we have no reason to posit external causes except by identifying events within experience which have no cause within experience, and invoking (1). This raises the most radical skeptical possibility – namely, that nothing whatever exists which is not experienced. Descartes' evil demon hypothesis is not meant explicitly to raise this most extreme form of skepticism,[4] but that hypothesis does raise skepticism with regard to (2). The evil demon need not be a physical being, nor need he exist in physical space in order to deceive me. However, Descartes does not ask whether the demon could deceive him about the objective passage of time. This question I shall take up shortly. The narrowest form of skepticism concerns (3). A skeptic concerning (3) can concede the existence of a material world, broadly conceived; but argue that, for all we know, our particular judgments and general theories as to the nature of this world are radically mistaken.

The realist would like to defeat all three forms of skepticism. Given only the resources of a strict Humean, there does not seem to be much prospect for his achieving this. It is time to investigate whether any headway can be made against any of these forms of skepticism, if we permit ourselves the more sanguine concept of causation I have described, our *a priori* knowledge of geometrical properties, and the doctrines here advocated regarding universals and substances.

We have seen already that modest progress can be made with the problem of induction – modest because a number of outstanding issues remain to be solved. The problem we have before us here is more difficult, since it requires us to infer causes from their effects, not effects from their causes. The problem is that a given type of effect may be produced by different types of causes; and there is no *a priori* constraint upon the kinds of causes that can produce a given effect.

I shall proceed here as follows. First, I shall argue for realism with respect to the passage of time. Next, I shall consider our knowledge of physical space and the grounds for positing such a space. Thirdly, I shall argue that we are justified in claiming the existence of events which are not the contents of any immediate experience. And finally, I shall discuss the problem of what we can know about the nature of such events.

3. THE OBJECTIVITY OF TIME

There can be no doubt that time is a feature of experience. But not all philosophers have taken it as evident that temporality is a feature of "the world." Is it an intelligible possibility that time has merely subjective existence, and no objective reality? Could the phenomenal awareness of the passage of time be entirely illusory? This seems unintelligible: our thoughts and experiences exist; however that is to be understood, to deny their temporal order is to abandon all descriptions of these experiences as events.[5] It is to abandon any hope of explaining our differential epistemic relation to one class of those events (our past) as opposed to another (our future), and it would require a denial of the experience of causal connections – and for that matter, of constant conjunctions.

That there exists a temporal order is indubitable – though this is not to claim the apodicity of any putative theory about the nature of time. Moreover, if there exist other temporal beings which enter into direct or indirect causal relations with an individual, then they must exist within the same temporal order as that individual does.[6] However, awareness of time involves something more than just the experience of an ordered series of temporal points. It involves an awareness of being "carried" from one such point to the next – an awareness of the passing of time. Could this feature be merely subjective, an illusion?

The two principal theories as to the nature of time are called the A and B theories. The names derive from McTaggart's paradox, which purports to prove the unreality of time. The B theory asserts that time consists of a linear sequence of moments ordered by an asymmetric relation, for example, *earlier than*. According to this theory, all moments exist equally. The central thesis of the A theory is often expressed succinctly, if enigmatically, as the claim that temporal becoming is real.

A number of theses, linked but not equivalent, are associated with the B theory; and a parallel set with the A theory. These associated claims serve to flesh out the dialectical force of each theory, though not every B-theorist accepts each B-claim, nor does every A-theorist accept every parallel A-claim. However, it is typical for B-theorists to assert that:

1. The predicates 'past,' 'present,' and 'future' correspond to no objective properties of moments or events;
2. The future is just as real and determinate as the past;
3. Propositions about future events have definite truth values; more generally, every genuine proposition is timelessly either true or false.

A-theorists characteristically affirm the following:

1'. The predicates 'past,' 'present,' and 'future' correspond to objective features of the world;
2'. The future is open, indeterminate, or not real;
3'. Propositions about the future have no determinate truth-values.

An A-theorist may further deny, in connection with (3'), that singular reference to future events and individuals is possible, which would be sufficient to undermine the possibility of expressing certain singular propositions about the future.

However, there is another, more fundamental observation which might lurk behind the A-theorist's claim that becoming is a real feature of the world. B-theorists tend to envision time as a dimension along which features of the world are laid out, quite analogously to the way in which the world is extended in space. Relativity theory with its associated Minkowskian space-time framework, seems to lend further complexion to this conception. The thinking of A-theorists, on the other hand, sharply contrasts spatial and temporal extension, even as regards their formal or structural features. What underlies this supposed contrast? I suggest it is this. The temporal order is not merely a linear sequence of events or moments ordered by an asymmetric relation, for in this respect it does not differ essentially from space. In two-dimensional space one can distinguish right and left-handedness, and thereby define the ordering of points on a line in accordance with an asymmetric relation (e.g. *is to the right of*). But a body moving through space (and time) can traverse such a line in either direction. There is nothing intrinsic to the structure of space which requires that the order in which a body moving along a line coincides with the points of the line satisfy any condition other than that if it moves from point *a* to point *b*, then it must pass through each intervening point at least once. The way in which bodies move "in time" is different. Changes in temporal position are, as we may put it, both inevitable and inescapably unidirectional.[7]

This claim, which I take to be A-theoretic in spirit, seems to be correct. We can, of course, imaginatively reconstruct any temporal sequence in the reverse direction, remembering or calling to mind more recent events first, less recent ones later. Via the medium of memory or imagination, we can survey a history of moments, as if we were surveying a stretch of space. But this abstraction prescinds from the distinctive feature which is at the very heart of temporality.

What of the other characteristic theses of the A theory? That we cannot refer to future individuals, or have memories of future events, is not something which B-theorists need to deny. Since B-theorists make use of an asymmetric temporal ordering relation, it could be accounted for by allowing the temporal asymmetry of the causal relation, together with causal theories of reference and memory. Such a solution will serve the B theory provided that backwards-directed causal chains are inaccessible or impossible.

More fundamental is the question whether pastness, presentness, and futurity are objective features of the world. McTaggart's paradox hinges on this question, for McTaggart takes the truth of the A theory to be essential to the existence of time, but he also held that the attribution of the indexical temporal properties pastness, presentness, and futurity was incoherent. If so, then time is not objectively real.

McTaggart's puzzle is generated by the fact that each moment of time must be both past, present, and future. This cannot be, if pastness, presentness, and futurity are monadic properties, for they are mutually exclusive. But the alternative – that they are relations – leads allegedly to a vicious regress. A moment can be both past and future, if being past means preceding some other moment (e.g., "now"), and if being future means falling after some other moment – any earlier one. But this simply eliminates the notions under review in favor of the B-theoretic account, for the B-relations *earlier than* and *later than* between moments are permanent and unchanging. To capture what the A-theorist means by the changing futurity, etc. of an event, one pays the price of re-introducing the problem: for to say that a moment is sequentially future, present, and past, but not all at once, is to say that it has these properties at past, present, and future times respectively.

McTaggart's problem is deep but based on a confusion. It is based on a confusion because it fails to recognize that the indexical character of predicates like 'present' and 'now' enable them to pick out successive moments of time in a way which is parasitic upon the fundamental fact described above: that all bodies (including agents who use these predicates) move inexorably and unidirectionally through the B-series of moments, from one to the next. It is this fact which underlies the operation of the linguistic rule according to which an (ordinary) use of the expression 'now' picks out a given (changing) moment of time, without reference to any (other) moment in the B-series, and without there being any special monadic property which that moment, and no other, timelessly possesses. We do not identify which moment is the present one in the usual way in which we identify items in the world, by attending to what distinctive properties they have, any more than we identify the referent of our own use of the personal pronoun in this manner. Reference is guaranteed, even when we have no idea, in the relational sense, what time it is. And reference is guaranteed to shift in just the right way. This much would be so, to be sure, even if, *per impossible*, we could move about at will in time (compare the indexical 'here'). But the inexorability of our movement through time guarantees that the past accumulates and the future diminishes in the uniform way in which they do. Thus there is no contradiction engendered by our use of 'present' (and hence, by our use of 'past' and 'future').

But McTaggart's puzzle is deep, because it raises a deep question: do the terms 'past,' 'present,' and 'future' refer to any feature of the world, any feature over and above what can be described in B-theoretic terms? The paradox raises this question by posing a dilemma: if there is such a feature, it is either a relational property or a monadic one. But it cannot be a relational property. And it cannot be a monadic property. Hence, there is no such feature. B-theorists disagree in this only with McTaggart's conclusion that time itself requires such a feature, and hence is unreal.

In a sense, the conclusion is correct. Presentness does not straightforwardly pick out a special property of temporal moments. (If there were such a "property" it would – like existence itself – be very special; and very fundamental.) What we should say instead is that the use to which we put the predicates 'past,' 'present,' and 'future' – and the condition of their meaning and intelligibility – is a feature of time which the B theory does not capture. It is an objective feature. It is – beyond the fact that our situation in time guarantees, given the conventions governing indexicals, the achievement of reference to the correct moment(s) – that the way in which we (and all other temporal beings) coincide with moments in the B-series is ordered in a special and "inevitable" way. This world would be very different if that were not the case.[8]

A defense of the B theory that deserves mention is D. H. Mellor's (1981). In some respects, Mellor's position is very similar to the one offered here. For one thing, Mellor insists on the fundamental distinctness of the spatial and temporal dimensions. For another, he grants both that our use of tensed expressions is unavoidable and that these expressions are not reducible to tenseless ones. Moreover, his account of the truth conditions of tensed statements in terms of their token-reflexive character parallels my account of such terms as 'now' and 'at present.' However, Mellor's token-reflexive account of the tenseless truth conditions of tensed statements (along with McTaggart's argument against the A series, which he endorses) is taken by him to show that the A series has no objective reality; whereas I give an indexical account as part of a defense of that reality. That is what makes Mellor a B-theorist and me an A-theorist.

This difference comes to the fore in Mellor's discussion of the presentness of experience. According to Mellor, there is no experience of presentness as such (or of the flow of time); whereas I hold that, in a sense, there is. When I judge that I am now having a headache, the tenseless truth condition for this is, Mellor says, that the B-series date of that token judgment coincides with the B-series date of pain in my head. And what of our knowledge of the presentness of this experience? Mellor says:

> We are concerned with token judgments to the effect that experiences we are now having possess the *A* series property of being present. Now any token which says that an event is present will be true if and only if the event occurs at the same *B* series time as the token does. Those are the undisputed token-reflexive truth conditions of all such judgments. But in this case the events to which presence is attributed are themselves picked out by the use of the present tense. Not all our experiences, past, present, and to come, are alleged to have this *A* series property, only the experiences we are having now. But these, by the same token-reflexive definition of the present tense, are among the events which *do* have the property now ascribed to them: i.e. events occurring just when the judgment itself is made. So of course these judgments are always true.
>
> (Mellor 1981: 54)

But this misses the point. An A-theorist, given the token reflexive behavior of 'now,' agrees that what is now experienced must be happening at the present time. However, it is not the presentness of experience that is at issue, but rather the experience of presentness. Even if Mellor's account of the truth conditions of 'What I am now experiencing is occurring at the present' were correct, that would not touch the question of whether there is an experience of presentness as such, and whether there is something we could not know if we lacked such an experience. The natural rejoinder to Mellor is that reference to the B-series date of the *judgment* leaves something out, namely, that this reference carries the kind of information it does *vis-à-vis* my experience only because I also know through experience that the token judgment is occurring at the present moment.

We can see this more clearly if we consider that the token judgment need not be made at all in order for the proposition it expresses to be true. And what is that proposition? That my experience occurs on such and such a date? No; for the proposition contains no B-series information concerning the date whatsoever, and has in any case a time-dependent truth-value, as a B-series proposition would not. What Mellor misses, I believe, is that we are able to single out, to identify, particular moments of time (which of course are identical to moments in a B series) in a way that involves no knowledge of, or reference to, their B-series characteristics at all; we are able, rather, to pick at least one of these (the present moment) out "directly." That is what constitutes the experience of presentness. Put another way, the difference between Mellor's token-reflexive account and my indexical account of the expressions used to describe the A series lies in his referring the truth conditions for tensed judgments to B-series facts about the making of those judgments, whereas I refer them to a direct, unmediated awareness of temporal location that requires no conception of the B series. What I have given is only a partial defense of the claims typically made by A-theorists. I have defended their thesis that temporal indexicals reflect an objective feature of the world; but I have left open here the question as to the reality and determinateness of the future, and the question whether future-tensed propositions have truth-values. Indeed, so far as systematic considerations are concerned, I could have simply adopted the B-theorist's response to McTaggart, for nothing else I say depends upon the irreducibility of time to a B series. Nevertheless, I have defended a minimal A theory because I am convinced that the B theory is mistaken.

Now there is an empirical argument which has been advanced by Adolph Grünbaum (1968), among others, against the objectivity of temporal becoming. Grünbaum's argument is that if becoming were an objective feature of the world, then it would be extraordinary if physics did not require some mention of this fact in its theoretical account of the world. But physics does not require the notion of becoming, being quite content with a B-series description of time. Hence it is unreasonable to postulate the objective existence of becoming. Opposing Grünbaum's view are philosophers and physicists who claim to have found precisely the feature of becoming embedded in some aspect of theoretical physics. But neither of these arguments should impress us. I do not wish to deny that fundamental investigations in physics may shed important light upon features of the world which were not previously understood, or not deeply understood. On such cosmological issues as the nature of time (and causation) we should be extremely cautious about drawing any sharp line of demarcation between the provinces of physics and philosophy.

Nevertheless, reliance on any argument from particular features of particular physical theories suggests that whether becoming is a feature of a universe or not depends on what the laws of physics happen to be. For such a fundamental feature of the world as temporal becoming, this is not plausible. By the same token, it should hardly be surprising if physics gives us no explicit analysis of temporal becoming, precisely *because* this is such a basic – and pervasive – feature of experience. Like the notions of causation, property, substance, and matter, the notion of becoming is so fundamental as to be presupposed by any physics which could account for experience as we know it. It is for this reason that we must look to philosophy for a general clarification of this phenomenon.

Is it then the case that we must rely totally upon philosophy for our understanding at this level of experience? Or, to state the issue somewhat differently, is it the case that there is no room for physics to correct or amend the conceptions of time, causation, etc. which are framed on the basis of our naive experience and embedded in our ordinary discourse about the world? For it is only these conceptions to which a philosophy bereft of physics has access. Here we may draw the issue in more specific terms. A common model for time sees it as isomorphic to a linear continuum. Although this model may represent an idealization, it is not terribly far removed from immediate experience. Yet, there is speculation among physicists that time may prove to be microscopically granular, or quantized. This clashes with the common model. However, nothing I have said precludes the possibility that physics may alter or correct our conception of time in important respects. No physical considerations should, I think, seriously challenge our commitment to the existence of time and of temporal becoming; to reject these would be to challenge the very possibility of physics itself. Yet it is not impossible that becoming should be jumpy or quantized at a level below that of conscious discrimination. Nor, obviously, does our acquaintance with time rule out the possibility that it possesses strange metrical or topological features on a cosmological scale. These are proper matters for scientific investigation – and for the exercise of philosophical imagination.

Time and becoming, then, are objective. No paradox undermines this conclusion, and there is nothing intrinsically subjective about the distinction between past, present, and future. Trivially, it requires conscious agents to identify past, present, and future moments, and to use a language with indexicals (or any other expressions) to describe temporal facts, for non-conscious beings cannot identify or describe anything. But the facts upon which such identification and linguistic usage depend are every bit as objective as any facts are.

4. THE OBJECTIVITY OF SPACE

We come now to a topic which is more problematic. Whereas few philosophers have seriously doubted the reality of time (however understood), a great many more have raised doubts about space. This is not so much because the notion of spatial extension generates paradoxes – though there are a few of those also – as it is a result of the fact that it seems possible to drive a wedge between perceptual space and physical space. Once the evil demon hypothesis is admitted, for example, it seems possible that there be no physical space, even though the objects of perception appear within a spatial field. Mental acts and states are not straight-forwardly spatial as they are straightforwardly temporal; and although sense-data, if they exist, clearly have a kind of spatial content, both their ontological status and their relation to physical space are matters greatly disputed.

There is, on the positive side, one epistemic advantage that we have towards space and spatial properties, as compared with most other physical properties. One may allow, as I do, that the question of the existence of physical space, and (if it exists) the question of its particular metrical and topological features, are legitimate problems for epistemology; and also maintain, as I have, that pure geometry is an *a priori* science through which we are, or can become, directly acquainted with geometrical properties as such, and their relations. As for the empirical questions, one way of proceeding is the phenomenalistic way. A classical attempt of this sort is Russell's in (1927). Russell's doctrine is that each of our sensory modes is provided with its own phenomenal space. Through the inductive process by means of which newborn children come gradually to constitute the world of common sense these spaces are merged into one. Further, the individual "unified" phenomenal spaces of any two observers are never identical, and it is only through a further constructive effort that the single public domain of physical spaces is postulated. Russell admits, of course, that we can no longer discover through introspection the inferential processes involved, which have long since been replaced by automatic habits of thought. However he claims to see the behavioral evidence for this process in young children – particularly in the learning of hand–eye co-ordination.

Now it may be that some sort of inferential process is required for the constitution of a single perceptual space for an individual: more on this in a moment. But it seems to me that an individual for whom visual, tactile, and other sensory phenomena are not merged into a single spatial framework would of necessity be an individual who did not yet possess a genuine conception of space at all. Setting aside, as irrelevant in this connection, recherché speculations in modern physics about multiple universes, our conception of space is of something which may be divisible into parts, but every part of which is spatially related to every other part. This, I should say, is an aspect of the *pure* geometry of the space which is given to us by vision (and by touch, etc.): these spaces are Euclidean; or so close to it that there is no question of their not overlapping. Whether or not our perception of space is altogether illusory, there can hardly be any question here of two or more *disjoint* spaces – one being the object of vision, another of touch, etc. Were we unable to distinguish the purely geometric qualities of these spaces from the distinctively visual features of visual perception (and tactile features of tactile perception), Russell's argument would have some force. But the *a priori* character of geometric knowledge guarantees precisely the possibility of making this distinction. Nor can the relation between these "spaces" be merely one of there being an inductive correlation of specific features within each field. Each of these spaces is, as a matter of logic, imperialistic: it insists upon gobbling up the whole world. Clearly, it would be impossible for a visual space (say) and a tactual one to exist (literally) side by side. The alternative is that they have (literally) no spatial relation to one another at all – a notion to which it is hard to attach any sense, if these spaces are real and not merely imagined. There is no choice but to merge them.

There is also a further reason for this view. A perceiver is put *en rapport* with the shape of a physical object (e.g., a table) only via the mediation of the causal sequences that suitably activate his tactile and retinal receptors; both the causal processes involved and the intrinsic character of the sensory phenomena they produce may be quite distinct in each case. But we saw that even if this is so, it cannot be that a perceiver would be led to suppose that there is something such as a visual shape, as distinct from a tactual shape.[9] Such shapes – the shapes of objects embedded in perceptual space – are qualities which we abstract away from the peculiarities of each sensory mode. They are, in that sense, abstract qualities whose intrinsic character we understand as we understand pure geometry. (Plato's picturesque suggestion in the *Meno*, that geometrical knowledge is knowledge we are "reminded of" by perceptual experience is not, if this is right, entirely off the mark.) Given the causal model, and supposing there to be external influences which account for at least some visual sensations and some tactile ones, we must suppose a common space from which these causes originate. For, first, there is nothing which justifies the imputation of an intrinsically visual character to the causes of visual sensations (to the exclusion of a tactile character); and vice versa. And, second, no induction from visual/tactual correlations could support the construction of a "common" space unless it supported the inference of causal connections between the sources of these sensations. Such connections would be a mystery unless the causally linked features shared what is in fact a common spatial matrix. If therefore we are to suppose that spatial perception in its various sensory modes is not illusory, we ought to conclude that there is just one space to which we have various modes of sensory access.[10] I shall return to this theme and expand upon it in due course. This is only a small advance, however, for it does not establish the central proposition, that we are justified in supposing the veridicality of spatial perception. The evil-demon hypothesis can still account for all the sensory phenomena in question.

Naturally we can hope to establish the veridicality of "naive" spatial perception in only a very general sense. This is obvious inasmuch as we do not wish to claim that every perception of spatial configurations is bound to be veridical. Less elementarily, this caution applies to our perception-based conception of the intrinsic nature of space. Here, as in the case of time, we need to provide room for the scientific imagination to revise or amend our naive conceptions in rather profound ways. Thus when I speak of veridicality here, I mean to pose the question of whether spatial perception justifies a belief in *some* kind of space. What are the features of this generic notion of space? Science has already given us strong reasons for doubting our naive ideas about some of the metrical, and even the topological features of space – that is, if it is able to give us reasons for anything. The naive conception of physical space which we extract from ordinary experience is, quite clearly, Euclidean. It is of a continuous, (possibly) infinitely extended, three-dimensional medium, homogeneous in its metrical properties. But this conception may be mistaken. How mistaken could our naive, empirically based conception of space be, before bringing into jeopardy the claim that even the untutored use of the senses puts us in touch with a real physical space? Probably there is no sharp answer to this question. But I should say that our senses have misled us about the existence of space unless they put us in touch with something which has, minimally, the following features: spatial extension in at least three dimensions, some definable notion of distance, and the possibility of explaining the production in us of those perceptual features which account for our naive conception of space.

My procedure in the remainder of this section will be as follows. First I shall consider the explanatory power of the hypothesis that physical space exists. The strategy will be to indicate, schematically, how pervasive our use of this hypothesis is. Secondly, I shall consider rival hypotheses which compete with it; and finally I shall inquire whether there are any arguments which defeat the competing hypotheses.

Visual and tactile perception presents us with spatial qualities. Not only this, but many nonspatial visual and tactile qualities are mutually dependent upon the presence of spatial qualities. Colors require extension; so does motion. Hardness and texture do as well, and it appears that thermal sensations require at least point-location. Pains, tickles etc. have spatial location and usually extension. It is perhaps not as obvious that all of our other sensory modes involve the presentation of spatial qualities. Strawson (1963) discusses the possibility of acquiring a spatial framework if our only mode of perception were auditory. Strawson may be right in saying that under these circumstances our conception of space would be attenuated. In the case of monaural hearing, it is clear that assignment of direction to sources of sound is at best extremely difficult. I believe that even in this extreme case, however, aural perception involves the presentation of spatial qualities. There is, for example, a qualitative difference between sounds heard as originating in the head – for example, a ringing in the ears – and sounds that are heard as originating "out there." Both involve a sense of spatial location. If we had no other sensory modes, it is doubtful whether we would be able to *assign* an ear-ringing a location "in the head," for it is not clear what sense we would have of our own bodies. Correlatively, we would (probably) be unable to characterize external sources of sound as external to our bodies. This does not entail, however, that we would be unable to perceive any qualitative difference between these two types of sounds, nor that this could not be perceived as some sort of *spatial* difference. In a similar way, it is at least arguably the case that sensations of taste and smell involve spatial location; and it is clear that our kinaesthetic sense and sense of balance involve spatial qualities. Thus it appears that spatiality pervades all, or at least most, of our sensory modes of perception.

The importance of this, as regards the explanatory power of the hypothesis that there is an objective space, is not hard to see. Although the sorts of perceptual qualities I have listed can vary independently, one of the most widespread features of experience is the many, often subtle, ways in which two or more of these qualities co-vary. The spatial orientation of a sound coincides with a visual object, and as that visual object decreases in apparent size, the sound grows fainter and the outlines and colors of the object fade or grow hazy. Tactile hardness is associated with visual resistance to deformation. And so on. The postulation of a physical space containing material objects is part of a complex, if implicit, theory of the world which enables us to explain these variations. This theory need not be scientifically sophisticated; indeed it functions largely to organize experience at the level of common sense.

The covariances between perceived spatial qualities themselves provide us with an immense wealth of data which are, on the whole, easily and naturally reduced to coherent order by means of the same hypothesis of a common spatial origin. By covariance of spatial qualities I mean all the phenomena associated with visual, tactile, and auditory perceptions of perspective. When, for example, I walk around a barking dog, the variation of sizes and shapes and sounds, color and shadow gradations, are naturally explained by supposing the existence of a three-dimensional volume the shape of a dog, with respect to which the three-dimensional volume I identify with my own body is moving in certain ways.[11] If I reach out, the tactile sensations I receive are correlated with the visual ones in a way which also receives explanation in terms of this spatial hypothesis – as does the directional quality of my auditory sensations. It is rather difficult to imagine any *simple* alternative hypothesis which can give coherence to all this data in as natural a way.

There is, finally, one more relevant feature of experience which can hardly be ignored here. It is the fact that, because of the spatial characteristics of sense perception, the world seems *given* to us as "out there," that is, as consisting largely of occurrences in a larger space. Unfortunately it is hard to assess the significance of this fact, for it is uncertain how phenomenologically primitive it is. Some students of early childhood psychology have been inclined to claim that our adult three-dimensional perceptual framework is constructed out of simpler elements early in life, and acquired as a kind of perceptual habit. The ability to form this "habit" attests to the coherence and effectiveness of the positing of space; but it calls into question the claim that this is a necessary feature of perception.

Nevertheless it is clear that, as adults, we do not have to perform intellectual labor to fit our perceptions within a spatial framework. Even though we may be ignorant about the causal mechanisms by means of which information is conveyed to us, we are able to locate items of the world within that framework "without thinking" about it (except in some bizarre cases).

Thus we have a spatial conception of the world. According to this conception, there is a physical space containing volume-occupying bodies, including our own, which exists independently of our consciousness, serves a role in individuating bodies, and accounts for all the phenomena of perceptual perspective in a unified way. Let us call this hypothesis, and the conception of space which it articulates, our spatial model of the world. The term 'model' here is intended to capture both the sense in which our conception amounts to a hypothesis or theory, and the sense in which we – rather literally – visualize the world in the terms which that theory asserts.

It would be most fortunate if we were able to argue directly that the spatial features of perception could not be illusory, as we have argued in the case of temporal features. This route is not equally open to us here, for it seems that the spatial element of perceptual experience could be otherwise accounted for – for example, by the evil-demon hypothesis, or by the hypothesis that our entire experience is a dream or hallucination.

It might be argued that, nevertheless, the spatial model provides the simplest and most *natural* explanatory hypothesis for the relevant aspects of experience. Frank Jackson (1977) for example, argues that it is as simple as any hypothesis that has been imagined to compete with it; and that no such competition has been, as it must be, articulated into a detailed alternative theory. Jackson, like most of us, has little to say about the relevant concept of simplicity, or about its probative force. What he does say is that any hypothesis which lacks predictive power must be ruled out; and that predictive alternative hypotheses, such as Berkeley's hypothesis that God directly causes our ideas according to some plan, leave us with just as difficult an epistemic task as the materialist hypothesis – namely, in Berkeley's case, figuring out the plan. But these observations, even if they are true, do not advance matters much. Let there be but *one* alternative hypothesis, such as Berkeley's, which is equally as simple as the common-sense view, and which cannot be ruled out or in on the evidence, and the skeptic has his case. And it is not clear anyhow why, for the philosophical issue at stake, competing hypotheses must be spelled out in any detail greater than that which is necessary to show that they involve no logical impossibility and that they could, in principle, provide explanations for the data we have. Descartes' evil-demon hypothesis and Berkeley's God hypothesis both meet this criterion; or at least no one has succeeded in showing apodictically that they do not.

Nevertheless, there is some content that can be given to the claim, just made, that the spatial model is the natural hypothesis. It is, to fix ideas, more natural than the Cartesian and Berkeleyian hypotheses. What does this mean? It must mean here something other than the empirical claim (which would be question-begging in any case) that as a matter of fact most people do account for their perceptual data in terms of a system of beliefs at whose center stands the spatial model. Indeed, people attach a great deal of certainty to this conviction; but that is itself the kind of fact that we would wish to have an account for.

It might be argued that the Cartesian and Berkeleyian hypotheses are at least parasitic upon the spatial model in the following sense. If God (or the demon) has any plan in terms of which he generates perceptual experiences within us, then it is impossible to imagine (given the nature of the data) that this plan could be any other than one which is designed to create in us the illusion of physical space. Thus it seems arguable that we cannot escape supposing it must be at least in terms of a conception of physical space in the mind of God (or the devil) that He (he) organizes our perceptions as they are found to be organized. This means more than simply that our perceptions are found to have spatial content. It means also that the way in which our perceptions co-vary and change with respect to both their spatial and non-spatial content, fits the hypothesis that our perceptions represent, via the usual rules of perspective, an independently existing spatial world. Those laws of perspective are a direct consequence of the simple assumption that the causal mechanisms of perception, especially of sight and touch, project into our sensorium the spatial properties of the objects from which they are taken to originate by means of straight-line paths in a Euclidean space. This assumption is corroborated (in the case of sight) to the necessary degree of precision by the laws of optics; but of course one need not know any optics or other physics to find this assumption a natural one, especially in the light of the associated tactile data.

These observations constitute no refutation of the Berkeleyian or Cartesian hypotheses; they merely exhibit the conceptual role of the spatial model in providing those hypotheses with a specific organizing principle which ties them to the actual nature of our experiences.

Although I am unable to provide any clean way to defeat the Cartesian skeptic, there are two further considerations which tell in favor of the spatial model. Both hinge upon the finding that immediate experience is not a causally closed system: there are experiences which, if they have any cause, have a cause which lies outside of experience itself.[12] This in itself is quite acceptable to the Cartesian skeptic, for the evil demon would be such a cause. But there is more to the matter.

The first consideration relies upon the reflection that any account of externally caused experience which does not posit a physical space requires that there be causal relations between two minds, of a sort unmediated by bodily interactions. Abstractly, direct intermental interactions are conceivable, for there is no contradiction in the supposition that they obtain. At the same time, we have no positive conception of such a causal relation, whereas we do have a positive conception of spatially characterized causal interactions and (at least arguably) of mind/body causal interactions. Thus the spatial model has an advantage over the Cartesian hypothesis at least as regards its degree of intelligibility. Some content can be given to the idea of direct intermental causation by means of analogy to the species of causation with which we are acquainted. But this content is attenuated by the very fact that it relies upon analogy and is necessarily incomplete. Thus if the argument of Chapters 1 and 2 is accepted, we may regard the Cartesian hypothesis as defective in intellectual transparency in a way the spatial model is not. This is the first consideration.

The first consideration is admittedly far from decisive. The second might be more decisive, but because the argument hinges upon a holistic treatment of our evidence, it is difficult to formulate in detail. In Chapter 8 it was argued that the very identity of physical and phenomenal universals is tied to the system of causal relations which necessarily bind them together. Thus it might be in principle possible to show, in the light of some sufficiently complete body of evidence, that that system of universals must include spatial ones. However, I am very far from seeing how, in terms of present evidence, this might be done. In any case such an argument would hardly serve to justify the degree of confidence which we vest in the spatial hypothesis. However, I shall return to a discussion of the role of holistic considerations in Chapter 12, and thus defer further discussion until then.

5. THE EXISTENCE OF UNPERCEIVED CAUSES

If one adopts the spatial model, and the natural auxiliary hypothesis that through perception we are causally linked to physical space and its contents, then one is thereby committed to the existence of causal relations which are themselves unperceived. For then it is apparent that the causal chains which mediate perception must contain segments which are not themselves direct objects of acquaintance. But here we may pursue the question whether, short of reasons for adopting the spatial model, there are features of experience which provide reason to posit extraconscious entities; and in particular, which provide grounds for the existence of unperceived causal relations. To establish the latter conclusion is to reinforce a claim made in Chapter 1, namely that causal relations are primary properties.

In this section, three arguments for that conclusion will be discussed. The first two of these are independent of the spatial model. The third examines in more detail the consequences of adopting that model and the associated causal view of perception.

A. The mind as patient

The first argument is a familiar one. It makes use of the fact that many of our experiences are ones which "just happen" to us. They are not voluntarily produced by ourselves; or, if they do involve some exercise of the will, it is not such as we have any reason to believe would be alone sufficient to produce the experience in question. Perceptual experiences are perhaps the most important group of experiences over which we exercise no voluntary control, or at best very incomplete control. The natural conclusion to draw is that these experiences have some (partial or sufficient) external cause.

David W. Smith (1982) is a recent example of a philosopher who uses this line of reasoning. The trouble with the argument is that it relies upon two weak and not often mooted premises. The first of these is the premise that every experience must have a cause; and the second is that if the cause is not (or is not entirely) one such that one is conscious of its causal relation to the experience, then that cause (or part of it) must itself be one of which one is not conscious. The second premise implies that if the experiences in question are caused by earlier experiences, then one will be aware of the causal relations involved. If the first of these premises is false, the argument is seriously undermined. If the first suppressed premise, but not the second, were shown to be true, then the most this argument would show is that there are some causal *relations* which lie outside of experience. This is something, but not enough to show that causal relations obtain between mind-independent entities, or between mind-independent entities and mental ones. Yet the argument has some force. It does provide some reason for supposing that there are causes external to experience. But the observation that many of our experiences cannot be in any evident way caused by mental acts is of greatest significance if it could be independently established that there are extra-experiential causes and that the spatial model is true. For taken together with these two propositions, it supports the hypothesis that a wide range of mental events have, or are likely to have, non-mental causes, causes which are physical events occurring in space. Perceptual experiences provide an obvious example of such mental events. Acts of will are in general insufficient to produce them; and as we have seen, they *can* with regularity be fitted into the spatial world-model. Thus if it can be shown that some such experiences *must* be the effects of external causes, we shall have some justification for preferring the spatial model over the Cartesian and Berkeleyian ones. But to do that would require establishing the two premises just mentioned: that every experience has a cause; and that we can sometimes determine that the cause of an experience is not another (of our) experiences.

Before considering the problem of justification, we should note that the first premise is stronger than the argument requires. The argument requires only that some experiences have causes; and that we can determine which ones among our experiences these are. The two arguments now to be presented support the second premise; and the weaker version of the first.

B. An argument of Russell's for unexperienced causes

Bertrand Russell (1926, pp. 148–52) makes an observation which shows the need to postulate causes of experience which, if they exist, themselves lie outside of experience. Russell's argument concerns color-perception. Consider three colors, *A*, *B*, and *C*, which form a series such that, for a given perceiver, instances of *A* and *B* are indistinguishable, and instances of *B* and *C* are also indistinguishable, but instances of *A* and *C* can be distinguished by careful comparison. Now qualitative identity is a transitive relation;

hence if A and B were qualitatively identical, and also B and C, then A and C would be qualitatively identical as well. They are not, although A and B (and B and C) are *perceptually* indistinguishable. This shows, Russell says, that the structure which underlies color-perception is more complex than the structure actually perceived. The only way to account for this is to suppose that the color-series, or the physical variables which account for color-phenomena, form a sequence which is either dense, or whose minimum differences fall below the threshold of perceptual discrimination. In either case, we are forced to conclude that A, B, and C are different colors, although adjacent pairs are not perceived to be different. And this means that there is *something* about colors which transcends our experience of them. It is worth noting that although Russell casts his argument in terms of a feature of the color spectrum, it extends over an extremely diverse range of sensory phenomena: over all those which appear to us to exhibit the continuous variation of some quality. Thus it applies not only to color hues, but also to chromic intensity and saturation. It applies to length, to direction, to weight, to hardness, to sounds (as regards both frequency and intensity), to tastes, and even – at least arguably – to such things as pains.[13]

Before discussing the implications of Russell's argument, I wish to consider a closely related argument of Armstrong's which uses this feature of experience to support the conclusion that there are no sense-data. I shall then look at a reply due to Frank Jackson which may seem to undermine both Armstrong's argument and Russell's. Armstrong asks us to consider three pieces of cloth, A, B, and C, and continues:

> Now consider the situation if we hold a 'sensory item' view of perception. If the pieces of cloth A and B are perceptually indistinguishable in colour, it will seem to follow that the two sensory items $A1$ and $B1$ that we have when we look at the two pieces *actually are identical in colour*. For the sensory items are what are supposed to make the perception the perception it is, and here, by hypothesis, the *perceptions* are identical. In the same way $B1$ and $C1$ will be sensory items that are identical in colour. Yet, by hypothesis, sensory items $A1$ and $C1$ are not identical in colour.
>
> (Armstrong 1968:218)

This being contradictory, Armstrong rejects the premise that there are sensory items. Armstrong's conclusion, then, is different from Russell's.

Against this, Jackson argues that it is *logically impossible* for Armstrong's description of the case to be satisfied:

> This is impossible, because, for example, if one can tell A from C but cannot tell B from C, then one can tell A from B simply by reference to the fact that one can tell A from C but cannot tell B from C.
>
> (Jackson 1977: 114)

What Jackson says here is true, but misses the point. We can bring this out as follows. Let us suppose, in order to avoid extraneous difficulties, that A, B, and C are so arranged that they can all be viewed at once. We may imagine them to be arranged as three segments of a ring, so that each has a boundary bordering upon the others:

Figure 11.1

Suppose that the labels 'A', 'B', and 'C' are removed from the cloth ring pictured above, and the ring is spun very rapidly and then stopped. Can the observer reidentify patches A, B, and C? Evidently he can: he simply locates the boundary along which there is for him a perceivable color difference; if he remembers the A was lighter, say, than C, he can correctly assign the labels 'A' and 'C' to these two adjoining patches, and assign 'B' by default. Thus, he can "tell A from B by reference to C."

But although this is true, it ignores the relevant sense of "tell A from B," the sense in which that difference is given to one phenomenally just by what is revealed by an inspection of A and B themselves in the way that the difference between A and C is revealed. Jackson is aware of this objection, and hence considers whether it is possible that B could look (just) like A and just like C to a given person at a given time, when A and C do not look the same to that person. This, too, is claimed to be incoherent, for it involves B looking to have two different colors to the same person at the same time. And of course this is not how B looks.

Jackson's argument is intended to save sense-data from Armstrong's attack. But at the same time, if successful, it vitiates Russell's argument for extra-conscious causes of sensation. For according to Jackson, the phenomenon to which Russell appeals does not really exist. Against Jackson we can only say, as we must, that it does. The challenge is to discover a coherent description of the phenomenon, and then to ask whether it does indeed sustain Russell's interpretation; namely, that it gives evidence of the existence of unperceived causes of perception.

There is in fact an alternative description which promises what we seek. It is that all colors – and in particular, those of A, B, and C, may be to some degree perceptually indeterminate to an observer at a (any) given time. What I have in mind here can be otherwise expressed by making use of the notion of what some philosophers call inexact or fuzzy concepts. It is well known that most (possibly all) color *terms* of natural languages are associated with fuzzy concepts; although some are fuzzier than others. Thus 'red' is quite fuzzy, covering a much wider range of hues than 'scarlet,' and having vaguer boundaries. But even 'scarlet,' I suppose, is the name of a fuzzy range of hues. Now let the invented term 'carlet' name the perceptual color of cloth A (the color which A *looks* to have to someone at a given time). Is '*carlet*' a fuzzy term? The possibility I wish to raise is that it is.

This possibility is rejected by both Armstrong and Jackson. Armstrong makes use of the slogan 'To be is to be determinate.' In fact, Armstrong wields this principle in a further attack on the existence of sense-data. Although the existence of sense-data is not presently under discussion, the example Armstrong uses sheds light on the present point. In this further argument, Armstrong considers the perception of a speckled hen. The actual hen has some definite number of speckles, yet one is not able to see exactly how many speckles she (or her front surface) has. Armstrong notes that this feature of indeterminacy pervades sense-experience – and hence would have to characterize (most) sense-data, whose features we postulate just to account for sensory experience. Thus, if sense-data exist, many of them are indeterminate. Nothing indeterminate exists; ergo, sense-data do not exist. It is interesting that Jackson agrees with Armstrong's ontological principle. His way out is to argue that although sense-data must *minimally* have enough characteristics to account for the facts of perception, there is no reason to suppose that they do not have *more* characteristics than are given in the content of perception. In this case, there is a metaphysical reason for requiring them to have such additional properties; it is required by their existence. Thus, one's hen-sense-data have a determinate number of speckles, although one is unaware what this number is.

Here it is necessary to insist upon a distinction, for the hen example is more complex than the case of color perception. First, it is possible to be perceptually aware of, say, fifty-seven spots on a surface, without being aware *that* the spots are fifty-seven in number. This reflects no indeterminacy in what one sees, but rather the lack of a certain kind of knowledge about what one sees. The vague knowledge, derived from looking but not counting, that the number of spots lies somewhere between ten and two hundred, for example, does not entail any vagueness in what is seen. In this respect the speckled hen is for our purposes (and for Armstrong's also) a red herring.

However, there is a second kind of vagueness which the sight of a speckled hen can produce; and this is a vagueness which characterizes the seeing itself, and not merely the knowledge of what is seen. If the spots are packed densely enough, and spread over a large enough region of the field of vision, then in general not all of them will be attended to at any one time. Some can definitely be identified as within the field of attention; others can with definiteness be affirmed (later) to have lain outside it. But there are borderline cases. The field of attention, after all, has no sharp boundaries. Should we say that the spots near the boundaries are only partially attended to? Or should we say that the visual sense datum contains an indeterminate number of spots? Is the haziness which partial awareness confers to be attributed to the object of awareness, or to the mode of awareness itself – or to both? I confess there is room for maneuver here; yet the correct answer seems to me to be the first one. The mode of awareness is not itself hazy, though it is partial. It is the object of partial awareness which is hazy – though 'hazy' is clearly an inadequate description of its character.

This aspect of the seeing of a speckled hen is more relevant to Russell's problem. Although the case of near-matches in color is not one which introduces the problem of inattention, the problem of inattention suggests that sense-data may in certain respects be determinable rather than determinate. And if we wish to insist, as I do, that the very being of sense-data is dependent upon their being objects of perceptual awareness, then this solution to Russell's problem recommends itself. However even those who reject this condition on sense-data are forced by Russell's example to admit that something exists, or has features, which are not themselves observed.[14] Moreover, these entities or features are invoked to explain, causally, the facts about color discrimination. For Jackson, these features are or might be unperceived characteristics of sense-data; for us, they must be something else. But in any case, there are grounds here for positing causal relations between what is unperceived or not cognitively accessible by direct perceptual means, and what is directly known to be perceived; hence, grounds for declaring causation to be a primary, not a secondary relation.

Moreover, Russell's example may be usefully generalized, if one of the results of Chapter 5 can be accepted. There it was suggested that any causal sequence must be dense or microscopically granular, depending on the structure of time. This means that any macroscopic causal sequence with which one is acquainted must contain microscopically short temporal parts. Parts which are of sufficiently short duration will not be individually identifiable or detectable; yet we can know that they exist. Hence experience gives us reason to posit the existence of cause-effect sequences which we do not observe.

This case bears close analogy to – and indeed depends upon – certain facts about the way we perceive space and time. Take space. Our perception of space is in a certain sense paradoxical. On the one hand, we perceive space as a continuous expanse, with no breaks, gaps, or boundaries. On the other, we are unable to discriminate points which are sufficiently close together.

This last fact leads some phenomenalists – and classically led Hume – to suppose that the structure of perceived space is essentially granular, composed of spatial atoms whose extent is the distance minimally discriminable by the perceiver. This seems to me to be a mistake. We do not see space as constructed out of minimally extended spatial atoms, as if it were a pointillist painting. Indeed we could not do so; for either each atom would have no perceived extension – in which case neither could a space wholly constructed of these atoms – or else it would – in which case it must be possible to discriminate one boundary from the other, after all.

We find no such boundaries. Instead, we find the kind of phenomenon Russell pointed to in the case of colors. Points *A* and *B* may be perceptually indiscriminable; so may points *B* and *C* – yet difference of location between *A* and *C* may be detectable. Conclusion: the structure of perceived space requires constituents which cannot themselves be perceived by virtue of their smallness. The extension of this reasoning to perceived time and causal sequences will be immediately obvious.

C. The third argument

A third argument for unperceived causes is related to this second one. It is a commonplace feature of experience that it contains events which have no apparent cause, no cause which is itself an experienced event. Call such an event *E*. There are five possibilities: (1) *E* has no cause; (2) the cause of *E* is an unexperienced event; (3) the cause of *E* is an event *C* which is experienced, but the causal relation between them is unexperienced, and so *C*'s causal role remains undetected; (4) neither *C* nor its causal relation to *E* are experienced, but *E* is known to be of a kind which always has a cause; or (5) *E*, *C*, and the causal relation between them are unnoticed or not attended to. Of these, case (2) is the one I shall consider. To establish that a case is of this kind, it is necessary to eliminate possibilities (1), (2), (4), and (5). The cases which are of interest in this connection would be ones in which *E* is experienced as being caused; but *C* itself is not experienced. In that case, (1), (3), (4) and (5) are all clearly eliminated as correct descriptions. Could *C* nevertheless have been experienced but not attended to? If so, we could go about looking, on analogous occasions, for a suitable *C*; we know that there must be such an event temporally prior to, and spatiotemporally contiguous to, *E* itself.

Are there events which we experience, which we know to be caused (because we experience them as caused), and which have no experiential cause? It seems that any case in which we experience a force, and consequent bodily motion or resistance, could be a case of this kind, provided we do not perceive what produces the force. Cases of gravitational attraction appear to be of this kind. For either we do not perceive the object which produces the gravitational force at all, or if we do see it, we do not see the force "emanating" from it. Yet we know that something is pulling us. So gravitational attraction, and its effects upon us, present us with a case in which something evidently outside our experience is able to affect what we experience. This means that causal relations can obtain between elements of experience and events external to experience.

I argued in Part one that when we are acquainted with one

instance of a causal relation between two sorts of events, we can infer a general law. However, I have not argued that when we know one event of a certain kind to have a cause, we can infer that all similar events are caused. If this could be shown; and if it could be shown that there are event-kinds, some of which have experienced causes and some of which do not have causes that are experienced, then condition (4) above would be satisfied. This would provide a further argument for unexperienced causes. But I shall not attempt to establish the required premises.

12 Scientific realism

1. INTERNAL REALISM AND COHERENCE EPISTEMOLOGIES

The principal task of this book has been to defend realism with respect to certain broad and fundamental ontological categories. I have defended the realist view of properties as universals. I have advocated a realist conception of causality which understands it as a primary quality, a second-order relation between first-order universals. Also, I have suggested that there is an intimate connection between the identity of any first-order physical property and its causal connections to other properties. In the first chapter of Part three, I have attempted to defend the existence of time and space, and of extra-experiential causes of (some of) our experiences.

However, these objectives constitute only a part of the project which a realist is likely to set himself. All of us have – and tend to confidently cling to – many empirical beliefs which are much more specific than the general belief that there is a spatio-temporal world containing causally connected events. We believe in the existence of any number of specific material objects and physical events, and of determinate causal relations between them. We believe we know, in many cases, what properties some physical object has, and what properties it does not have. In a more sophisticated mode, we hold a number of scientific theories, more or less elaborate, that we regard as true, or approximately true, or at least as representing progressive steps along the path to knowledge of a correct theory – a path whose terminus is at least "in principle" within reach.

The philosophical defense of some or all of these theses is a task assumed by those who call themselves scientific realists. However, scientific realism can be understood in a variety of (connected) ways, and a discussion of the topic requires some anterior reflection on the nature of the claims being defended. Thus we can distinguish the following claims that are associated with scientific realism:

(i)   a thesis about the *meaning* of statements concerning some empirical domain – namely, that their meaning is dependent on their truth-conditions or on the denotation of their terms (as opposed to conditions of confirmation, or of warranted assertibility, or the like);

(ii) a theory of truth and/or reference for a domain – specifically, the correspondence theory of truth and/or a theory of reference which posits a real relation (e.g., causal) between words and the world;

(iii) a thesis concerning the *existence* of objects in some empirical domain (e.g., "theoretical entities");

(iv) a thesis to the effect that *if* objects in a given domain exist, then we can know (or justifiably believe) that this is the case;

(v)   a thesis to the effect that one can coherently entertain the thought that there exist objects whose existence we could not, in principle, ever come to know.

There are some connections between these claims. (ii) specifies the sense in which the truth-conditions mentioned in (i) are to be understood: if truth were a matter of coherence or warranted assertibility, then (i) would lack its intended realist interpretation. For any putative domain of objects, (iv) is, obviously, a necessary condition for the (justified) assertibility of (iii). (iii) is stronger than (i), for it asserts not merely that we can understand assertions as being (if true) about the world independently of our epistemic condition, but that some such assertions *are* true. (v) appears to be entailed by (i): if we can distinguish between truth-conditions and confirmation-conditions, it is an open possibility that there are hypotheses which are true but non-confirmable. Indeed we seem to have encountered two such hypotheses: the evil-demon hypothesis of Descartes and the idealistic hypothesis of Berkeley. These hypotheses, or rather minor variants of them, remain eligible (for the realist) even if he succeeds in establishing the existence of space, time, and extra-phenomenal causal relations. A spirit or demon – or a sufficiently expert mad scientist – could manipulate one's experiences so that, even if one is justified in inferring the existence of space and of external influences upon one's sensory field, one may be radically misled as to the nature of one's spatial environment, and the nature of the influences upon one.

Hilary Putnam (1981), in a recent examination of realism, uses (v) to characterize the distinction between what he calls metaphysical realism, and what he calls internal realism. Metaphysical realists take seriously the view that our theories make claims about a mind-independent reality to which those claims may – or may fail – to correspond. Thus, Putnam holds, they are committed to the following thesis:

> (M) The theory that is "ideal" from the point of view of operational utility, inner beauty and elegance, "plausibility," "simplicity," conservatism," etc. *might be false.*
>
> (Putnam 1978: 125)

The internal realist, as Putnam depicts him, can make use of all the semantic devices associated with realism – that is, those mentioned in (ii); only these devices are now to be understood only in relation to some background *theory* that we have about the world, and not *de novo*. Putnam's version of realism – a realism "internal" to some theory or other – is anti-foundationalist, and represents a rejection of the correspondence theory of truth and of the causal theory of reference if these are construed as giving us linguistic access to a reality independent of our conceptual apparatus. Putnam in fact considers an analogue to the skeptical hypotheses I have mentioned. He asks whether we might be brains in vats; and he wishes to show, by means of a transcendental argument, that this must be false. That argument is supposed to show not only that if it were true we could never know it – but, furthermore, that we could never assert or entertain it. What the metaphysical realist erroneously supposes is both that we *can* entertain this hypothesis, and that it might be *true*. He thereby makes a fatal concession to the skeptic. As I examine Putnam's argument, it will be important to recognize, however, that (v) can be divided into two theses, namely, (v1) that it is intelligible to entertain the possibility of the existence of objects independent of ourselves; and (v2) that such objects might in principle lie outside the domain of the knowable.

I intend to defend "metaphysical realism," though in an important respect I shall differ with Putnam over how this position ought to be characterized. Of course I shall not attempt a full-fledged defense of metaphysical or of scientific realism in this chapter. What follows is rather a series of reflections prompted by issues raised in the writings of Richard Boyd, Putnam, Hartry Field, and some others. What I hope will emerge from these reflections is a programmatic sketch of the kind of strategy the realist ought to follow in his dialogue with idealism (or with relativism, or with "internal realism"). In pursuing these reflections, I shall be making (at least) two major unargued assumptions: (a) that the problem of justifying memory can be solved; and (b) that a single individual can in principle pick out elements within his experience, recognize and compare them, and invent and use words to denote them and their types, prior to any learning of a "public" language. Thus, I shall regard Wittgenstein's skepticism with regard to the possibility of a. private language, on this interpretation, to be mistaken.

Before I return to metaphysical realism and brains in vats, I shall briefly discuss one argument for scientific realism that fails, and then, in a highly sketchy fashion, consider the question of how we are able to identify, think about, and refer to objects in the physical world.

Thesis (iv) is the realist doctrine most directly challenged by traditional skepticism. With respect to knowledge of the physical world, the skeptic's strategy is to argue that no amount of empirical data will select a single theory as the most favorable one. For any set of data and any proposed theory, the skeptic can always fashion a conflicting theory that explains the same data equally well. Richard Boyd (1973) has argued that the realist can block this strategy.

In order to apply a proposed theory T to produce confirmable predictions, the use of auxiliary background hypotheses – call their conjunction B – is required. Similarly, auxiliary hypotheses B^* must be employed in conjunction with any competing theory T^*. If 'T and B' predicts the same experimental results as 'T^* and B^*,' how are we to justify a choice among them? Boyd's response is that the evidence can make one theory – say T – more plausible than the other, on the grounds that T is a more natural extension of theories and causal principles we already accept (on the basis of evidence). But what can justify our acceptance of these theories? The answer is that the (frequent and/or approximate) truth of these theories is the only thing that will explain the success of the following methodological principle:

(P) A proposed theory T must be experimentally tested under situations representative of those in which, in the light of collateral information, it is most likely that T will fail, if it is going to fail at all.

Boyd's claim is that the only explanation of the reliability of (P), as a guide to when a new theory is likely to fail, requires the assumption that our collateral or background information is (approximately) *true*. For if that information were incorrect, it would be a matter of extraordinary luck that (P) should be effective as a principle for eliminating theories.

This argument is unfortunately defective. It assumes that (P) *is* a successful methodological principle; and it claims that only realism can provide an explanation of this fact. But is (P) reliable? The mere fact that (P) is an accepted principle of scientific research cannot decide this question. If the success of a theory is not understood in instrumental terms, then it appears that the only way one could evaluate (P) is by comparing the number of proposed theories that are in *fact* false with the number that the use of (P) succeeds in eliminating. But how – independently of realistic presuppositions – could we come to know the former of these statistics? If, indeed, there *were* some way of obtaining information as to what theories are false, independently of the use of (P), then the use of (P) would be rendered gratuitous. But if – as Boyd would have it[1] – success is instrumentally construed, then what is to prevent a thoroughgoing antirealist from also construing instrument- ally the (realist's) theory that explains that success by making appeal to such (theoretical) notions as correspondence truth? That move gives us Putnam's internal realist; and it would seem to stalemate the contest.

In any case, it is false that only realism can explain the success of (P), assuming that (P) is successful. For suppose the evil-demon hypothesis were true. It is noteworthy that a skeptical opponent is free to postulate essentially any sorts of causal processes he likes, to explain how the demon produces in us the sensations we experience. He can cheerfully accept (though in strictness he need not) a principle of sufficient reason that requires him to oppose our favored explanations of our sensations with alternative causal explanations, rather than simply propose that they may have no explanation at all. It seems obvious that a clever demon could deceive us about the reliability of (P), by arranging it so that our theories "fail" more often when tested in putatively falsifying circumstances than when not so tested, and that a small number of such theories "survive" repeated tests. Moreover, the *apparent* reliability of (P) can be explained *equally well* on the demon hypothesis as on the realist view that the theories we *do* accept are approximately true. For it accounts for all the facts, and it is elegant: singularly elegant, as cosmologies go. This argument fails to refute skepticism. Any attempt to rule out the evil-demon hypothesis as implausible in the light of current theory is bound to be question-begging. Once we have conceded the eligibility of the skeptic's hypothesis, we will find that the only way to defeat him is to argue that we can obtain evidence that, if obtained, would independently defeat that hypothesis.[2]

Boyd, to be sure, explicitly disavows the project of defending realism against radical skepticism.[3] The limited objective of Boyd's defense of scientific realism is perhaps justified by the fact that his opponents concede realism with respect to a certain class of statements, namely, those they are prepared to classify observational. But the reasonableness of framing the issue in this limited way should not conceal the powerful dialectical role that skepticism plays in the debate. Realists – and Boyd is no exception – try to defeat antirealism by exposing its inherent instability. Since the physicalist observation statements of contemporary antirealists are themselves already "theory-laden," there is nothing in principle that should bar their acceptance of full-fledged realism. When they reject that invitation, the realist suggests that their caution, consistently applied, cripples empiricism by driving them into the waiting arms of the skeptic.

Antirealists, on the other hand, are prone to argue that the very same anti-foundationalism that characterizes realist epistemology (certainly Boyd's), as well as their own, cannot be sustained except by conceding some form of coherentism and thereby abandoning the fundamental commitments of realism. But this stalemate shows that skepticism is the specter that haunts realist and antirealist alike. A consequence of this dialectic, as I see it, is that the only hope for defending realism requires a return to a foundationalist theory of knowledge. Thus it will not be amiss to frame the problem in such stark and uncompromising terms. In my concluding remarks I shall make some further observations about anti-foundationalism itself.

2. REFERENCE

Suppose we were controlled by an evil demon. Could we, in that case, ever be in a position to think about, or refer to, the evil demon in question? Or – what is quite different – could we be in a position to entertain the evil-demon hypothesis? That the latter question is different from the former is due to the fact that the evil-demon hypothesis can be construed as a general hypothesis; it need not involve making singular reference to any *particular* evil demon. All that would be required is the possibility of specifying a sufficient number of the characteristics of such a demon to make the hypothesis an intelligible and explanatory one. The following section addresses these questions.

However, I shall begin this section, not with the exotic problem of how we can speak of demons, but of how to achieve singular reference to physical particulars. How does such reference occur? Here I shall adopt the perspective of the causal, or historical, theory of reference, various versions of which have been proposed by Putnam, Kripke, Donellan, and Devitt among others. Such a theory fits rather naturally with a causal theory of perception. In that context, however, it does render problematical the notion of direct acquaintance, at least insofar as physical objects are taken to be objects of direct acquaintance. On the causal theory, one's use of a name must be linked by a suitable (but possibly unknown) causal history to the use of that name to name physical object O, and similarly the initial use of the name must be linked by means of a suitable (possibly unknown) causal chain to O itself. One consequence of this is that, in an epistemologically fundamental sense, it is extremely difficult – perhaps impossible – to articulate in a philosophically interesting way what it is for someone to know who or what it is that he refers to, in a manner that distinguishes identification of physical objects actually perceived by an observer from identification of those he knows merely "by description." For in both cases knowledge is mediated by causal processes. In any case, I have restricted the notion of direct acquaintance so that it has application only to sense-data.

Among the many difficulties that beset the causal theory of reference, one requires attention here, for it sheds special light on the realist's program. It concerns the use of definite descriptions to fix the reference of a term, and the role of associated beliefs in determining whether the term has a referent. As we shall see, the causal theorist ought to allow that the main opposing theory of reference – what Kripke calls the Frege-Russell view – *does* contain a genuine insight which needs to be preserved.

The difficulty is this. Kripke and Putnam have given powerful arguments to show that one can succeed in using a name to refer even when one has many false beliefs about the referent, no true uniquely identifying description, and little or no knowledge of the causal history which connects the referent to one's use of the name. But does this lack of constraint on descriptive knowledge go so far that nothing whatever must be known about a putative referent in order for reference to succeed? I think a consideration of actual and hypothetical cases shows that it does not. At the same time, because reference is a human activity tailored to the needs of linguistic communication, it is highly unlikely that there are formal rules that can be universally applied to determine when reference has been achieved and when not. Our judgments about this are conditioned by considerations of interpretive charity and congruence with the needs of efficient information transfer which are too variable and context dependent for that. Nevertheless it seems that such considerations generally militate against counting the use of a name successful if misapprehension about the nature of anything which could be taken as the referent is sufficiently drastic. If all a man believed about the referent of 'Bourbaki' was that it was a topologically complex space, when in fact the use of this name as a pseudonym by a group of mathematicians was causally responsible for the acquisition of the name, then in most imaginable circumstances we would count that man as unable to refer when he uses this name. And consideration of historical cases within science, such as the Epicureans' use of 'atom,' and the more recent use of 'phlogiston' and 'electric fluid' can serve to display the range of considerations (and perplexities) which surround our willingness to accord or deny referential success in the face of false beliefs – even when the users of those terms had *some* correct "reference-fixing" definite descriptions available to them.

What has been said obviously applies to reference to natural kinds as well as to reference to physical particulars. Indeed the examples I used make this clear. What these considerations are intended to show is that however the causal theorist may wish to characterize reference-establishing causal links, the existence of such a link is not *in general* sufficient to guarantee reference. Some kind of (correct) descriptive backing is also required – although such descriptions may be far from uniquely identifying.[4]

This is true, I now want to suggest, even for reference to ordinary "observable" physical objects with respect to which we are placed in favorable perceptual circumstances. On the one hand, one need not have any perceptually-based uniquely identifying description of an object in order to be said to be thinking about it, attending to it, or referring to it. One need not know where the object is, for example, even in relation to oneself and other objects in one's sensory field; nor need one have any unique description of it. On the other hand, sufficiently erroneous perceptual beliefs can undermine even ostensive reference. The most plausible cases of this are provided by deceptive optical illusions (e.g., the "oasis" in the desert) and hallucinations. Of course something is the cause here of our perceptual experiences and consequent beliefs; but nothing in the causal account sufficiently satisfies those beliefs to qualify as a referent. It might be argued that the reason for reference failure here is that the causal chain is deviant. But – particularly in the case of illusions – it is difficult to see why the causal chain should count as deviant.

If this is so, if some descriptive beliefs typically play a role in the achievement of reference to particulars and natural kinds, then the problem of reference is in part pushed back onto the problem of how predicates pick out properties. Unless this can be accounted for, the usefulness of descriptive backing cannot be explained. For a thing to satisfy a description is for it to actually have properties properly denoted by the descriptive predicates. Moreover, we cannot always explain reference to properties in terms of *further* backing descriptions, on pain of infinite regress. Some predicates can be handled by means of definition in terms of other predicates. But there will be a class of predicates whose semantics cannot be further specified through language, on pain of eventual circularity. How is the reference of these accomplished?

How is it, for example, that 'white' picks out the property *white*? It is the physical property that concerns us here, the property that some physical things have, independently of any observers, but that causes those objects to look white under suitable conditions. This look, whose content is subjective white ('white$_s$,' I shall call it) can be picked out, referred to, without further ado. Referential success here depends upon neither backing descriptions nor problematic causal chains.[5] The first attempt a causal theorist might make to give semantic content to a predicate intended to denote physical or objective white (let this predicate be 'white$_o$') would be to fix its reference by means of the definite description 'that property of spatial objects which causes, under normal conditions, perceptual experiences of white$_s$.' The predicates 'spatial,' 'causes,' 'perceptual experiences' and 'white$_s$' can all be directly given semantic content. The problem is with 'normal conditions,' and phenomenally based attempts to spell this out have not been blessed with success. A quite different strategy is called for. This strategy is suggested by the observation that white$_o$ things sometimes do not look white$_s$, and non-white$_o$ things sometimes do. Now abandoning all talk of normal conditions,[6] I suggest that what we do in assigning 'white$_o$' a denotation is to first notice that the ways in which our color-experiences vary are sufficiently regular (albeit very complex) to make reasonable the hypothesis that a single property causally contributes in some salient way to a certain range of experiences (not only of white$_s$ but also of other subjective colors: for example, of pink$_s$ when objects are experienced as being illuminated$_s$ by red$_s$ illumination.) Our denotative strategy is to take 'white$_o$' to pick out that unique property whose instances play a causal role (possibly further specified in terms, for example, of spatiotemporal coordinates) in each of the experiences of some suitably diverse set of color-experiences. (This means that someone will not have mastered the use of the term 'white$_o$' until he is prepared to say that things that look pink under red$_s$ light, and also look blue under blue$_s$ light, green under green$_s$ light, and so forth, are objects which are (probably) 'white$_o$'.) The hope is that just one property will be such that its instances play this causal role in the production of each of these experiences. But it might turn out that no single property has instances common to all these causal sequences; alternatively, that more than one does. The sorts of cases which can crop up are rather analogous to ones discussed by Kripke and others in connection with reference to natural kinds. A reference-fixing sample – for instance a sample consisting of several pieces of metal – may serve to determine the denotation of the natural-kind term 'gold.' But the presupposition that underlies this reference-fixing strategy might of course turn out to have been frustrated: some members of the sample might be of a metallic element with an atomic number of 79; others might be brass or iron pyrite. Such eventualities can jeopardize reference; so, to, in the case of 'white$_o$.' If no single property is such that its instances play a (sufficiently similar) causal role in producing the reference-establishing class of perceptual experiences, or if more than one property does, then reference is jeopardized.[7] So reference to physical properties is necessarily tentative – at least when scientific understanding is at stake. It does not follow, however, that we cannot hope to improve matters; nor that revisions of referential practice in the light of further experience cannot be regarded as increasing the likelihood of success. Our worries are (1) that more than one candidate property is present in all of the causal chains associated with the reference-class, or (2) that no property is common to all of these causal chains that is not also common to many reference-fixing causal chains for other properties. Problem (1) can arise in two ways. Instances of two properties P and Q may be present in all the causal chains which are intended to fix the reference of a single property-term (say 'P'). This may occur by accident, or because the presence of P entails the presence of Q. If P entails Q (as, for example, *being red* entails *being colored*), Q can be eliminated by stipulating that P *not* be a property common to all the causal chains of some other reference-class(es). This strategy will also help in the former case, where it is accidental that P and Q occur together in the original reference-class; as will enlarging the class. On the other hand, suppose that P and Q are nomologically equivalent. That is to say, suppose their instances occur together in space and time, as a matter of nomological necessity. Then no reference-class can include one and exclude the other. But also, in that case, P and Q will be causally indistinguishable, no matter what experimental situation we envisage. They will play a single ("joint") causal role in the causal structure of the world. And in that case, as I have previously argued, "they" must be regarded to be a single property. We can imagine such a case of two distinct properties only because we ignore the identity-conditions that govern what it is to be a physical property.

This last observation bears on problem (2). With respect to any finite reference-class, it is possible that the perceptual effects of two different properties may be indistinguishable. Two properties may largely mimic one another in their observed effects, so that our reference-class contains some causal chains that instantiate only the one, and some that instantiate only the other. Just as a reference-class for 'gold' may contain samples of gold and others of fool's-gold, so a reference-class for 'red_o' may contain chains which instantiate red_o, and others which instantiate $fool's\text{-}red_o$. The only way to overcome this difficulty is to subject putatively red_o things to as many causal environments as possible: if red_o and $fool's\text{-}red_o$ are distinct properties, then there will be some situation, in principle discoverable, in which their instances behave differently. This is, to be sure, a "holistic" enterprise: identifying distinct causal environments forces us to rely upon our identification of instances of *other* physical properties. However, what we can say is that our picture of the physical world (that is, what properties it has) is not "in principle" underdetermined by the data – in the ideal limit in which all relevant data are available. I shall return to this point in my concluding remarks.

3. EVIL DEMONS AND BRAINS IN VATS

We are now in a position to see why internal realism, in Putnam's sense, does not offer a defense against skepticism. To see that this defense fails is to reaffirm a transcendent, or correspondence, conception of truth. We are also in a position, I think, to see how the metaphysical realist's defense against skepticism can be fashioned. First let us return to Putnam's transcendental deduction of the falsity of 'We are brains in vats.' Putnam's crucial claim is that if we *were* brains in vats, we could not speculate about the question, for we would not be able to *refer* to our brains (or to the vats). This is because the brains and vats would be implicated in every causal chain eventuating in perceptual experience, and not differentially in such a way that causal chains could be used to pick out these items. We could not say: Let the reference of 'vat' be fixed by 'whatever is the cause of such-and-such experiences,' for no such reference-fixing device could single out the vat. *That* would have a causal role in *all* our experiences. Moreover, merely having an "intention to refer" and a mental image – even a vat-like image – is not sufficient for referring to a vat, for such an image is not a representation *of* a vat unless it itself stands in some suitable (i.e., reference-fixing) relation to a vat. Furthermore, we cannot specify the reference-fixing relation (putatively involving causation) itself without the question-begging supposition that we have a way of referring to *it*; that is, that 'reference,' as used by us, picks out some determinate relation, or, if defined in terms of causation, that 'causation' does so.

Indeed, Putnam (1981) gives a quite general model-theoretic argument to the effect that there are many (perhaps infinitely many) semantic mappings from the sentences of a theory T to THE WORLD that serve to make those sentences true – even if T is a global theory satisfying constraints of simplicity, empirical adequacy, etc. This plethora of interpretations undermines realism by making truth *too easy* to come by in particular; it refutes thesis (M), the thesis that an ideal theory might be false. It is useless for the realist to react by pointing out that only *one* interpretation is the *intended* one; and that what is at stake is whether T is true or not on *that* interpretation. Specifying how the intended interpretation is to be determined will require making use of such notions as reference and truth; but this is just "more theory," and can itself be multiply interpreted.

To this argument G. H. Merrill (1980) makes the reply, seconded by Lewis (1984), that Putnam makes the mistake of assuming that it is the intentions, or linguistic stipulations, of the formulators of T that are held by the realist to determine whether T "matches" the world, or not. Putnam thinks of THE WORLD as a domain over which theoretical predicates can be arbitrarily assigned extensions;

but the realist thinks of it as a *structured* domain; that is, one in which particulars fall into natural classes determined by their properties and relations. Getting the sentences of *T* to map onto this structure will be by no means as easy as a mapping that permits the assignment of any consistent set of extensions to the predicates of *T*. Nor is this constraint one placed upon *T* by our referential intentions; it is a constraint that comes from the side of THE WORLD.

Clearly, there is something right and important about this objection of Merrill's, from the perspective of a realist of my ilk – one happy to traffic in universals. But it is also, I think (and Merrill hints), inadequate as it stands. It shows, perhaps, that the *metaphysics* of 'metaphysical realism' survives Putnam's attack. But the realist, after all, wants more: he wants our theorizing to reflect a grip on THE WORLD that is not merely a matter of a lucky correspondence in structure between theory and reality. Put in "referential" terms, the point is a familiar one and one wielded by Putnam. A painting (here is the analogy) may depict a wonderful likeness of Winston Churchill; but it will nevertheless not be a picture of Churchill unless it bears a suitable (causal) relation to Churchill himself. Similarly, THE WORLD may supply strong constraints on interpretation that make it an entirely non-trivial matter whether an interpretation exists on which *T* is true; but the existence of those constraints, whether they make THE WORLD a model of *T* under some interpretation or not, in no way suffices to show that *T* is *about* (i.e., true, or false, *of*) THE WORLD. Nor will adding to *T* further stipulations about reference turn the trick; after all, such stipulations may or may not be satisfied by any real relation between language and the world; and even if satisfied, that *too* may be an accident. (If the stipulations are not satisfiable, then 'reference' – and hence 'truth' – are "undefined"!) Thus the question remains: what ensures that the term 'reference' picks out a determinate word/WORLD relation? What – if reference is understood as involving causal relations – ensures that 'causation' does so?

To this last point I make the reply that the causal relation is an object of *direct acquaintance*. Thus, if the notion of private reference is coherent (second assumption), there is no danger of begging the question at this stage. This is of considerable importance. It gives reason to expect – making allowances for the fact that an adequate causal theory of reference has yet to be articulated – that content can be given to a notion of reference that is not theory-dependent or "internal" to some "circle of ideas."

But this reply to Putnam might not seem convincing, *even* if it were conceded that a causal relation is "given" to us in experience. For it could be said that all realities – even those which are "given" – must be conceptualized in the process of forming any judgments concerning them. If conceptualization is a necessary feature of every cognitive utilization of experience, then in what way has Putnam's difficulty been overcome? All judgments are mediated by concepts, and concepts are "in the mind." Hence their relation to the reality we can hope to grasp only through them is inescapably problematic.

This objection can and must be resisted. We should admit that all making of judgments presupposes some conceptualization of that which the judgments concern. But this does not mean that concepts must "get in the way of" or distort that which our judgments are about. Perhaps our concepts of external realities are problematic in that way. But it must be demonstrated that, even in the case of the "given," we can have no assurance that our concepts are adequate to their objects. Indeed the very opposite of this can be shown. For conceptualization itself presupposes the act of recognition. We cannot form an idea of that which we cannot identify and in principle reidentify. The given is precisely that which, most primitively, we recognize. It is the soil from which conceptual activity grows; this soil must contain already the element of recognizability.

Whatever conceptual distinctions we later impose as we theorize in order to assemble our experiences into a coherent or unified picture, we must begin here, with the experiences themselves, and with conceptualizations that can be brought into agreement with them. It is on this plane that I claim we anchor the notion of causal relation. And of course such relations are recognized, indeed utilized in our conceptual grasping of much else long before we learn to *speak* of causation, or, at a much more advanced stage, to theorize or reflect philosophically upon its nature. As Plato saw, there is a large difference between being able to recognize something – justice, for example – and being able to say what it is.

What then about truth? If it makes sense to say that we are brains in vats, or are controlled by an evil demon, then the notion of truth must be similarly independent of the theories in terms of which we comprehend the world. Let us pursue this question also within the context of the vat-brain hypothesis.

It is important to distinguish between the hypothesis that I am (or that my body is) a certain particular brain in a particular vat, and the *general* hypothesis that I am some brain, or tissue-mass, in some vat.[8] The former requires singular reference to particular material objects; and aside from the fact that any putative reference will fail in the event that the alleged item does not exist, such a reference is a considerably more complex affair than being able to speak of vats, brains, or demons in general. For to deploy the general hypothesis, it is sufficient to be able to describe things of these sorts – and that requires only giving semantic content to certain predicates. Even if demons form a natural kind and even if reference to natural kinds requires reference to some actual *members* of that kind, we will not, given a suitable repertoire of predicates, be blocked from formulating a hypothesis that could be satisfied by beings of *some* natural kind with demonesque properties. There is no need to single out any particular natural kind of this sort. The intelligibility of such a general hypothesis (indeed of *any* general hypothesis) of the brain-in-the-vat type will serve to arm the skeptic against Putnam's refutation: and as well, to reinstate the traditional conception of truth.

An advocate of a causal theory of reference might be tempted to give semantic content to a singular referring expression – here I choose 'that demon' – as follows: "Let the reference of 'that demon' be fixed as the satisfier of the description 'whatever thing (or things) is (are) causing my current sensations.'" Then by Kripke's lights (and mine), the sentence 'That demon caused my current sensations,' uttered by the causal theorist, will express a proposition that he knows *a priori* to be true, and yet which is contingent. At the same time, knowledge of such a proposition represents a singular lack of progress from an epistemological point of view. It is not an empty or vacuous proposition in the way tautologies are sometimes said to be empty, for its truth depends at least upon there being sensations of his at the time in question and a cause of these. At the same time, it is clear that it achieves no gain in empirical knowledge: it goes beyond the data only in *assuming* a cause for whatever sensations are being appealed to.

Intuitively, given what we take ordinary perceptual claims to mean, such reports are *false* if it turns out that the cause of the relevant perceptual experiences is a demon. If a man says "I see a desk," he is wrong, whether or not he is facing a desk, if a demon, not the desk, is responsible for his desk-like experiences. Again, if a man says, "A demon is causing this desk-like experience," we shall want our semantics to reflect the fact that what he says is wrong if the cause is not a demon but a desk. An adequate semantics must allow us to express the fact that a person whose beliefs are naively derived from experience may be always mistaken. In particular, such a semantics must make intelligible the possibility that the demon hypothesis is true. How can this be done, while giving the hypothesis a substantive content that distinguishes it from the *a priori* proposition considered above? Only if we can do this can we say that 'A demon is not causing these experiences' is a thesis with substantive cognitive content.

Neither 'demon' nor 'desk' is a term whose semantic behavior conforms to that of pure, proper-name-like rigid designators. Each term has enough connotative content associated with it that there are *a priori* limits to what *could* turn out to be a demon or a desk. Neither an atom nor a star could be a desk. Nor could either be a demon. These claims do not turn on whether demons or desks are natural kinds. It is evident that, for similar reasons, dogs could not turn out to be kidneys, or puddles of water, or cosmic dust-clouds. This is not because we could not be *that* mistaken when we see dogs; it is because we have a certain conception of doghood which is too far transgressed by kidneys, even if it need not be too far transgressed by robot dogs. If we *were* that mistaken – if what we identified as dogs proved actually to be kidneys, then we should retract the claim that there are dogs. Such a discovery would show that there were no dogs, not that dogs were really kidneys, just as the discovery of oxygen showed (indirectly) that there was no phlogiston.

What I need to show is that the notion of a demon, or of a brain in a vat, can be given *enough* conceptual content to serve the skeptic's purpose: enough content so that the hypothesis that our experiences are controlled by a demon, or that we are brains in vats, are substantive suppositions with truth-values; enough content so that if either supposition is true, then most of our ordinary empirical beliefs are false.

It is tempting to insist that "Dogs are not kidneys" is analytic. I shall not so insist; undoubtedly this is an oversimplification. Probably what should be said is that any evidence that would force us to redescribe the things we take to be dogs as kidneys, would be evidence that would also force such a radical shakeup of our picture of the world that we would cease to consider that the term 'dog' has any application. In any event, I shall not attempt to provide a theory of analyticity.

But the conceptual limits we place on the notions we have of dogs and demons are not to be understood solely in terms of the meanings of associated reference-fixing definite descriptions of the sort, 'the cause of such-and-such experiences.' For they involve tighter constraints than this. If kidneys proved to be the systematic cause of our doggish experiences, they would not thereby have been successfully referred to by our use of the term 'dog.' On the other hand, there is no question here of resurrecting the Frege/Russell theory of reference. No uniquely identifying description is required for reference to succeed, nor even some looser stereotypical characterization of what it is to be a dog or demon.

This much Kripke's arguments can teach us. But as those arguments do not show that a suitable causal chain is the only necessary condition for successful reference, they do not entail the claim that no backing description whatever is ever required if an attempted reference is to count as succeeding. The considerations just mentioned show that (at least sometimes) *some*thing true must be known about the nonrelational properties of the referent. So a "pure" causal theory of reference gives too simple a picture.

What does the need for descriptions imply? It means that the predicates in terms of which the description would be expressed must denote genuine properties. Giving these *predicates* their semantic content is something that *may* in turn be achieved solely by means of the reference-fixing strategy that makes use of causal chains, without further descriptive constraints; that is, a predicate may be taken to denote whatever is the (common) causal property in the causal chains generating a certain specified range of experiences. However, not even this is always required: it is not required for secondary properties and for certain primary properties such as the causal relation itself and spatial and temporal properties. For we can fix the reference of the predicates we use to refer to such properties directly, through acquaintance.

It is significant that that part of the evil-demon hypothesis that is required to give it its skeptical implications can be articulated entirely in terms of predicates that can be given *direct* reference. With the term 'demon' we can associate the description 'a being, distinct from ourselves, who is non-spatial and who thinks;' our hypothesis is that such a being alone causes all our perceptual experiences. The brain-in-the-vat hypothesis is more complex and less elegant. But one can do the job in this case also with the resources at our command. Let us associate with 'material object' the conceptual content 'spatial and temporal being with causal powers.' Instead of fixing the reference of 'my brain' via some causal chain, I shall require only that my brain satisfy the description 'a material object that sustains certain activities that are causally necessary and sufficient for my thoughts to occur.' Let vats be understood to be (at least) material objects capable of supplying causally sufficient conditions for the operation of brains. One could easily imagine a vat as having a certain shape; but obviously this is unnecessary. Nor is it required for the skeptic's purpose that a detailed account be given of the causal interactions between vat and brain. However, something more must be involved in the brain-in-vat hypothesis, to avoid trivialization. As it stands, a "vat" could turn out to be a normal living human body (minus its brain). What is demanded is the supposition that the causal structure of the vat be such that our visual impressions are not produced by objects of the proper shapes and sizes in the proper positions in our environment, and that similar correlations are lacking for our other sensory modalities between what exists around us and what, on the basis of experience, we take to exist. But to explain the brain-in-vat hypothesis in sufficient detail to give it skeptical content, it is once again sufficient to make use only of properties to which direct reference is possible. I conclude that if we are the dupes of demons, or are brains in vats, these are hypotheses we can intelligibly entertain. They are hypotheses that are not trivial, hypotheses concerning whose truth value one might care a great deal. But having entertained them, how can we ever hope to show that they are true or false?

Skeptical hypotheses rely upon the fact that more than one set of conditions can be causally sufficient for the production of a certain type of effect (in this case, a sensation). The strongest reply to skepticism that I believe it is possible to construct makes use of the fact that distinct properties are "in principle" distinguishable by virtue of there being *some* differential condition(s) under which an outcome will depend upon whether it is the one property or the other that is instantiated.[9] This means that someone who was in a position of having "total evidence" with respect to the outcomes of the indefinitely many possible collocations of conditions that the physical universe might generate, *in principle*, would be able to sort out the structure of the world. The 'in principle' in the preceding sentence carries a highly theoretical sense. Clearly the obtaining of total evidence is not a goal that any human being – or even the species as a whole – can expect to achieve.[10] Certainly we can continue to collect more and more evidence. But it is extremely unlikely that the degree of verisimilitude of our world-picture will be a smoothly increasing function of the amount of evidence we have. Is it possible, falling short of total evidence, to make significant progress toward a correct picture of the world – enough, for example, to eliminate the demon hypothesis? This is a question I shall not attempt to answer. Indeed, I do not know the answer. Intuitively, everyone feels that substantial progress of this sort is entirely within reach. A full defense of epistemological realism would, I think, have to justify this feeling. To do this would require showing that the scientific enterprise was not so radically holistic as to demand, in effect, that we must know everything before we can know anything. It would require showing that it is unnecessary to amass data on the result of every possible combination of physical circumstances (or, more precisely, perceptual circumstances), before any part of the system could with some assurance be constructed. For science does not in fact work that way, nor could it. Work by Glymour (1980), however, suggests that confirmation is indeed a piecemeal process rather than a radically holistic one.[11] It is along these lines that the best promise for a rational reconstruction of scientific knowledge seems to lie.

4. TRUTH AND WARRANTED ASSERTIBILITY

Although I cannot further explore here the large question just raised, the argument I have given does have implications for the relationship between truth and warranted assertibility. More specifically, it has implications for the relation between truth and warranted assertibility in the Peircean limit of ideal and total evidence about the world.

According to Putnam's internal realist, the latter two notions are identical. There *is* no intelligible conception of truth which places it outside the bounds of what is rationally assertable in the Peircean limit. But internal realism involves more than this identification. It understands truth *in terms* of rational assertibility. It is the latter which is the fundamental notion, the notion upon which we can get an independent grip.

On the realism I have argued for, it is likewise the case that a proposition will be true if and only if, in the Peircean limit, it is rationally warranted. For the metaphysical realist, however it is the notion of truth which is the more fundamental. Our conception of (theoretical, as opposed to practical) rationality is dependent upon it.

This can initially be brought out by considering a concept that plays a central role in our chief paradigm of reasoning, the notion of deductive validity. For deductive validity is understood in terms of truth-preservation; that is why the conclusion of a deductive argument known to be valid is at least as warranted as the conjunction of its premises. Nor does there seem to be any way to understand truth in terms of deductive validity: validity cannot play the role of truth. Can truth be dispensed with in favor of coherence or warranted assertibility? Warranted assertibility involves minimally the requirement of coherence with some body of background beliefs, which brings us back to coherence; and coherence involves minimally the requirement of logical consistency, which brings us back to truth.

Of course deductive reasoning does not exhaust scientific rationality. Can we articulate a conception of non-deductive reasoning that does not presuppose the correspondence notion of truth? The traditional conception of non-deductive modes of reasoning has been that their *telos* is truth; a method of inference is reasonable just in case, and only insofar as, it conduces to true belief, in the correspondence sense. But perhaps such a conception of rationality collapses; perhaps it must be replaced with a conception formulated in terms of such criteria as coherence, simplicity, past success at predicting future experience, and the like.

Although various attempts at such replacement have been made, they cannot serve the functions that the notion of truth serves. If coherence means mere logical consistency, then we must agree that this is a necessary constraint upon any set of rational beliefs. But it is a constraint that can be passed by all but the most extreme fantasies. If coherence means more than consistency, then this additional content must be made clear. Simplicity is a criterion that also has not been given any articulation sufficiently general in application, or sufficiently precise, to offer an adequate criterion of choice between competing theories. In any case, short of stipulation, there can be two reasons for adopting such a criterion. One reason rests on the belief that, other things being equal, the simpler of two theories is more likely to be the true one. This imports the notion of truth. The other reason is that a simpler theory is easier to work with, learn, etc. But that is a practical matter; and to speak of rationality here is to speak of criteria relevant only to practical reason.[12] The past history of success of a theory in making predictions can hardly constitute grounds for our now believing the theory, unless we have grounds for believing that past success portends future success. But that is the problem of induction.

There is an argument that demonstrates more forcefully the

discrepancy between such conceptions of rationality and a conception that uses correspondence truth as the controlling notion. There is no reason inherent in internal realism to suppose that, in the Peircean limit, there will not be two or more competing theories that meet equally well the desiderata of coherence, simplicity, and instrumental success. Unless the internal realist can show that this is not so, it is clear that he cannot understand truth as warranted belief in the Peircean limit. For in that case, equally warranted, mutually contradictory beliefs will have to be regarded as true. Michael Dummett (1978) has explored the possibility of suspending the principle of bivalence in such cases. But this means that truth, understood as warranted acceptability, can only be applied in cases where such a situation does not arise. When undecidable global theories can oppose each other, it appears that *all* our empirical beliefs concerning the physical world may be such that the notion of truth (understood as warranted acceptability) is not applicable to them.

5. CORRESPONDENCE AND REFERENCE

The concept of truth has been a difficult one to give an empiricist account of because, like other highly abstract notions, it is hard to understand the role it plays in terms accessible to empirical analysis. The notion of correspondence is problematic not merely because it is difficult to define a suitable mapping from words to world, but because, more deeply, such a mapping introduces the suspect notion of a world given to us independently of what is on the side of the mind. Since the verification conditions for " '*P*' is true" are indistinguishable from those for '*P*' itself, it is tempting to conclude that, semantically, the predicate 'is true' is otiose, though its use may serve some pragmatic purpose such as emphasis. Under these circumstances a theory of truth such as Tarski's is welcome.

But Hartry Field (1972) has argued that Tarski's explication of the notion of truth is fundamentally inadequate. Tarski requires that the predicate 'is true' in a metalanguage satisfy the criterion (Criterion T) that:

'*P*' is true iff *P*

be a theorem of the metalanguage for every object-language statement '*P*.' Field insists that, although this is a necessary condition on truth, it cannot serve as an *explanation* of that notion. No one who did not already understand the object language in question – hence, understand what it is for '*P*' to be true – could understand Tarski's criterion. To be sure, any philosophical explanation of the concept of truth must be expressed in a language; and so to understand such an explanation one must already have the concept of truth. But the job that we want such an explanation to perform is to tie the notion of truth to general considerations in epistemology and ontology, in such a way as to advance our understanding of what it is to have a language. As Putnam has pointed out, Tarski's theory is neutral between philosophically distinct substantive conceptions of truth – for example, the correspondence theory, the coherence theory, and pragmatic theories.

A philosophically adequate explanation of the notion of truth ought as well to figure in theories of language-learning. It ought in particular to figure in such a way as to satisfy what was after all one of the chief motivations for verificationism: it ought to figure in such a way as to make it possible to explain how the concept of truth can itself be acquired.

Kripke has similarly criticized theories of reference whose defect parallels that of Tarski's Criterion T *vis-à-vis* truth. A particularly crude version of such a theory, which can be found in Kneale (1962), is that 'Socrates' means 'the man who was called "Socrates";' more generally,

'*N*' means 'the object called "*N*"'

Kripke's objection is that this, as an explanation of reference, is circular. It does not enable anyone to pick out the referent of '*N*' who does not already know what that referent is.

Putnam's own earlier development of a causal theory of reference was closely linked to his advocacy of realism – metaphysical realism, as he now calls it. His subsequent apostasy and challenge to metaphysical realism in *Reason, Truth and History* (1981) is not only striking but also dialectically useful because Putnam has seen so clearly and deeply into the heart of the problem. I take the crucial insight that precipitated his apostasy to be this: the causal theory of reference *does* provide (setting aside "technical difficulties") a realist way of linking words to the world (just as a causal theory of perception provides a way of linking experience to the world – that is, a way of articulating the notion that physical objects are sometimes objects of perceptual acts). *But* this linkage can be given realist credentials only if the notion of causation itself can be fixed in a language- and theory-independent way. For if reference to that notion is itself controlled by, say, global theorizing about the world, then there will be no non-circular way of anchoring our talk about the world to the world; and moreover no non-circular way of introducing the crucial metalinguistic notions of reference and truth that we need to express the idea that we have such anchoring.

Now Hume's analysis of causation, stripped of its psychological components, is free of circularity-inducing dependence upon physical theory. But of course Hume's causal relation is too weak to establish the kind of correspondence the realist needs on behalf of reference. It might accidentally be true that there exists a constant conjunction between the tokening of a word by the users of a language, and some external state of affairs. But it could not be independently ascertained by those speakers what that state of affairs is. If one does not strengthen Hume's notion, one will be confined to think about reference at best in terms of some internally coherent global theory that situates human beings in a world and is consistent with experience. A realist answer to Putnam therefore must (a) strengthen Hume's conception of the causal relation; and (b) demonstrate that we have theory-independent access to a relation of that sort. In Part one, I attempted to establish these two claims. Let me summarize in the briefest way how they would bear on constructing a realist theory of language.

The fundamental elements of such a theory are a causal theory of perception and a causal theory of reference. Physical properties are identified perceptually by discriminating between them on the basis of their differential causal relations. Predicate terms denoting physical properties that are not given in experience are to be understood as rigid designators whose reference is fixed via direct reference to experience; that is, as 'the causally unique feature in the production of such-and-such experiences.' Talk of individuals can proceed by way of description, by the use of reference-fixing causal chains or, more commonly, by some hybrid of these strategies, as I have previously suggested.

The tools used by someone who employs such a strategy are not colored by any theory, nor are they internal to any conceptual scheme. They are linguistic intentions (a subject I have not discussed), deductive and inductive logic, and direct, naive experience, in particular the direct experience of causal, spatial, and temporal relations. These form the basis on which we construct our conception of a world that exists independently of our own experiences, and to which we have indirect access through experience. Reference to the particulars and properties of that physical world is always problematic, or theoretical. If, however, the identity of physical properties is tied to their causal relations, then the causal structure of the world is in principle accessible.

Such a conception gives us an independent way of formulating what it is to have reached the ideal, or Peircean limit of investigation. This limit will have been reached when the causal powers of each thing are known as a function of the complex of properties that it possesses. In a reductively ordered hierarchy of theories, this means that the causal powers of the most elementary physical particles (if such there be) are known; the rest, in principle, can be calculated.

Is there any way in which, if one were to reach the Peircean limit, one could know that it had been reached? Perhaps not. However, one necessary condition of one's having reached this limit would be that one's theory of the world would not be underdetermined by the data. To see why this is so it is necessary to return for a moment to the characterization given in Chapter 8 of the identity conditions for physical properties. When realism is combined with the view that causation is a relation between universals that orders those universals into a uniquely determined system, the identifiability of the components of the system is assured. If the system of causal relations in which a universal stands is essential to it and unique, so that different universals necessarily stand in different relations; and if our perceptual access to the world is itself causal, then it must in principle be possible to acquire information that will distinguish all distinct universals and, in so doing, to organize them *vis-à-vis* their causal relations. But to have achieved this is to have achieved an ultimate theoretical understanding of the physical world. The data (in the ideal limit) can warrant only one theory, for to say that two eligible theories remain is to say that two ways of reconstructing the system of universals are experimentally – that is causally – indistinguishable. But this would violate the ontological (not verificationist) precept that a difference that makes no (causal) difference is no difference at all. This feature of metaphysical realism is one that the internal realist and the instrumentalist have not shown that they can match, even in the Peircean limit.

In that limit, moreover, rational belief and truth become one. This, however, is not because truth collapses into warranted belief. It is because, in that limit, only the truth can be warrantedly believed.

How does the form of realism developed here stack up against the five realist claims presented at the beginning of this chapter? Let us summarize our results by means of a quick comparison. I shall refer to my version of realism as 'R' for convenience.

(i)   *R* does not commit one to any detailed theory of meaning. It is compatible with the thought that "meaning" covers a variety of distinct features of language. But it does allow at least some component of meaning to be divorced from conditions of confirmation, for terms used to describe the physical world. And it insists upon giving a central semantic role to truth-conditions and reference.

(ii) *R* affirms a correspondence theory of truth, and a causal theory of reference.

(iii) *R* is not as such committed to the existence of material objects of any particular sort. It is not even committed as such to the existence of any material objects. But when *R* is combined with the experiences we do have, it can reasonably be hoped to yield the conclusion that there are such objects.

(iv) *R* further asserts that scientific investigation (and even the ordinary use of "common sense") can tell us about these material objects, in the sense of being able in principle to justify beliefs about them. (However it must be admitted that *R* has not been spelled out in sufficient detail to address all the skeptical objections to this claim and the previous one. So these assertions are only programmatic.)

(v)   This thesis, used by Putnam to characterize metaphysical realism, is one that *R* rejects. For *R* yields the conclusion that the world is, "in principle," fully accessible to empirical investigation. As such, *R* does not postulate any impenetrable reality. It asserts that the evil demon, if he exists, would come to light under the onslaught of sufficiently persistent scientific scrutiny.[13] Thus *R* rejects the doctrine I earlier called v2. Yet *R* accepts v1, for it also asserts that we can coherently entertain the hypothesis of an evil demon long before we have any evidence that could be decisive in deciding whether the external world confirms Cartesian demonology, or whether it confirms the common-sense picture which we all know and love.

We come to philosophical reflection with the aboriginal conviction that sensation is reliable. If the picture I have drawn in these pages is correct, the information with which sense experience affords us is bound to be always partial and often seriously defective. Nevertheless, the way in which experience and environment are connected cannot be arbitrary or capricious. It is not enough of course for sensory processes to be reliable, if partial. We must know that they are so.[14] Reliabilists often seem to deny this. They maintain that if a belief is obtained by reliable means, and is true, then it is known to be true. But if we do not know that the means are reliable, then reflective doubts about these beliefs are not merely hyperbolic. So reflection puts us in a position in which we find that we are no longer sure that we know what we formerly believed. Perhaps we do still know what we now find subject to doubt; but we do not know that we have this knowledge. We are in the paradoxical situation of being epistemically alienated from our own knowledge. It is this situation that a foundationalist finds unintelligible. A reliabilist who understands knowledge as reliably acquired true belief must either absolve us of the responsibility of knowing that we know, or face the further task of certifying the means.

But reliabilism can take two forms. An external reliabilist holds that the processes that underwrite reliable belief-acquisition include ones like the physical operation of bodily sense-receptors, whose operation we understand, if at all, only at the end of a chain of scientific inferences. An externalist recognizes that our epistemic relation to such processes is on a par with our epistemic relation to the external world generally. An internal reliabilist, on the other hand, would seek to characterize the epistemic states and processes that underwrite knowledge as ones of whose reliability we are immediately aware.

Nevertheless a consistent externalist could hold that we do know that our sense-organs are reliable.[15] He could defend this by maintaining that we correctly believe these processes to be reliable, and that this belief is itself acquired by reliable means.[16] But surely this move is more clever than convincing. It does not differ in kind from a familiar proof of Biblical infallibility. That proof uses the Pauline passages which say that God cannot lie (Titus 1:2 and that all scripture is inspired (2 Timothy 3:16) to draw the desired conclusion. If the problem of skepticism has any bite at all, if it can get an initial foothold, then such a maneuver can only be seen to be question-begging. And it is skepticism, after all, that drove us to philosophy – or anyway to epistemology.

We must somewhere stop the regresses that such theories of knowledge invite. I have argued that an initial and crucial step in the reconstruction of the process through which we gain the world is one which requires that we focus attention once more upon the natural starting-point: experience itself. I have tried to show that we need to recognize among the items that experience gives to us one that Hume drove from view – namely, the relation of causal necessity. That is the Archimedean point upon which the world can be and is raised to consciousness.

Notes

1 Natural necessity

1 For example, John Barker (1969); David Lewis (1973); John Pollock (1976); Robert Stalnaker (1981); Ernest Adams (1975); and Donald Nute (1980). Most of these writers rely upon the notion of possible worlds, and upon the even more problematic notion of degrees of similarity between possible worlds. Pollock and Adams, and also J. L. Mackie (1980), have analyses of conditionals which rely upon there being a solution to the problem of induction. I shall say little about the complex issues raised by conditionals, although I believe that where a conditional is motivated by or associated with the existence of a causal relation, it is the latter which is fundamental and mention of which will somewhere have to appear in the analysis of the former.

2 Actually the situation is rather complicated. There are laws that are neither causal nor derived from causal laws, which are nevertheless necessary; and there are counterfactuals that are true but not in virtue of any causal facts. So these categories cut across one another, and there are no simple definitional connections. I shall discuss these connections presently.

3 But some remarks on these matters are made in Chapters 5 and 8 respectively.

4 I shall have very little to say about the sources of *a priori* knowledge.

5 Hume's own attitude toward phenomenological investigation does not appear to be inimical to this stance. Confessing an inability to detect any element of experience which could underwrite causal reasoning, he nevertheless stops short of categorical rejection, begging to be informed of what it might be (1963), Section IV, Part II, pp. 48 and 52–3. With respect to phenomenological matters in general, Hume says:

> But the finer sentiments of the mind, the operations of the understanding, the various agitations of the passions, though really in themselves distinct, easily escape us when surveyed by reflection, nor is it in our power to recall the original object as often as we have occasion to contemplate it. Ambiguity, by this means, is gradually introduced into our reasonings: similar objects are readily taken to be

the same, and the conclusion becomes at last very wide of the premises.

(Hume 1963: 72)

By contrast, respecting simple sensory impressions, we have:

These impressions are all strong and sensible. They admit not of ambiguity.

(Hume 1963: 74)

Indeed, Hume considers it very unlikely, in view of his inability to find any rational principle governing causal reasoning, that there be such a principle. For even small children reason causally – hence comprehend this principle, if such there be. Hume is here mistaking implicit knowledge, or perhaps knowing how, for (explicit) knowledge that.

6 A variant of this view which has slight affinities to my discussion in Section 3 below is found in Searle (1983, Chapter 4).

7 Brand Blanshard (1962), Chapter II.

8 An act-object analysis of rational thought which denies the causal thesis is developed in Fales (1984).

9 Rom Harré and E. H. Madden (1975); see also E. H. Madden (1969).

10 William James (1968), Chapter XIII, and (1971), pp. 95–8; and A. N. Whitehead (1959), pp. 30–59.

11 Near the end of his life Pavlov articulated some inchoate hints to the effect that certain kinds of external processes are directly observed to be causal. But these hints in no way add to Michotte's findings. See Asratyan (1973). Current experimental work in psychology on the awareness of causal relations focuses almost entirely on our ability to make causal judgments when presented with information about constant or partial conjunctions. See Alloy and Tabachnik (1984) for a review and bibliography of the literature.

12 An attack on Hume which appeals to these experiences is of course not novel. For some philosophers – for example, Reid, Whitehead, Keynes, Stout, and James – the primary experience of causation is of a psychophysical relation, since it involves an agent's willing his body to move. See also Searle (1983). The psychologists Biran de Maine and Piaget held similar views. Although such instances of psychophysical causation may well afford us some of our primary experiences of causal relations, they involve complexities which are best avoided. I shall therefore emphasize sensations of physical force, an approach more closely resembling that of A. C. Ewing, (1935). One can also experience one's body as causally effective in this sense, for one's body can push against something without one's having decided or willed to do any pushing. Armstrong (1968, 1978b) also defends this view.

13 N. K. Smith claims that this notion is first to be found in the appendix of the *Treatise* (1888, pp. 632–3), but I do not find it there. What Hume there considers is whether our idea of power derives from a perceived necessary connection between the will and mental or bodily activity.

14 Hume (1963), Section VII, Part I, footnote 7; pp. 78–9. It is of some

interest that Hume omitted the last sentence of this footnote from editions K and L of the *Inquiry*. One cannot help but wonder, speculatively, whether this omission points to some uneasiness Hume may have felt over the conceptual role which he assigned to this sensation. The sentence is not so much an argument against the philosophical importance of sensations of force, as an admission that the intuitive relevance of these sensations needs to be explained away.

15 Hume (1963), Section VII, Part II, footnote 1; p. 88. Bertrand Russell is even more dismissive of an appeal to these sensations as justification for a belief in necessary connection:

> . . . the objection to action at a distance seems to have been little more than a prejudice. The source of the prejudice was, I think, twofold: first, that the notion of "force," which was the dynamical form of "cause," was derived from the sensations of pushing and pulling; secondly, that people falsely supposed themselves in contact with things when they pushed or pulled them, or were pushed or pulled by them. I do not mean that such crude notions would have been explicitly defended, but they dominated the imaginative picture of the physical world, and made Newtonian dynamics seem what is absurdly called "intelligible." Apart from such mistakes, it should have been regarded as a purely empirical question whether there is action at a distance or not. . . . Not wholly unconnected with the question of action at a distance was the question of the role of "force" in dynamics. In Newton, "force" plays a great part, and there seems no doubt that he regarded it as a *vera causa*. If there was action at a distance, the use of the words "central forces" seemed to make it somehow more "intelligible." But gradually it was recognized that "force" is merely a connecting link between configurations and accelerations . . . "force" is by no means necessary . . .
>
> (Russell 1927: 18–19)

16 Of course I am not here committing myself as to whether each of these conceptions is satisfied, precisely or even roughly, by a distinct real relation.

17 What is "essential" to the notion is a matter which I shall take up presently.

18 Armstrong (1968, pp. 96–98), as I was pleased to discover after writing this, gives a description of pressure sensations which, although more terse, is strikingly similar to the one provided here in a number of important respects.

19 The force of gravity is experienced as pervading our bodies; but that experience is not one of tactile sensation.

20 Russell (1938, p. 474) seems to have denied this, for he thought that the components of a vector sum are not parts of that sum, and hence do not exist even where the resultant vector quantity does exist.

21 See, for example, Mario Bunge (1959), Chapter 2.

22 The problem of how to explain this identification involves one in

theories of perception, a subject on which I have for the time being promised to remain neutral. However, the phenomenon itself is a genuine one, and must be explained on whatever theory of perception we choose to adopt.

23 This may be why Hume thought that force just *is* the tactile sensation, as pain might be the sensation of sharp or hot objects. For a discussion of the relation between tactual perception of force and of motion, cf. Perkins (1983), p. 248.

24 See Michael Tooley (1977), David M. Armstrong, (1978b, Chapter 24) and (1983), and Dretske (1977).

25 Thus from this point of view there is no significant ontological distinction between those components of a total cause which are singled out as "the" cause and those viewed as standing conditions. At most, we can say that static elements of the total cause are commonly viewed as standing conditions, and dynamic elements as causes.

26 Arthur Burks makes the mistake of arguing that because we are not familiar with the total causally sufficient condition for an event, we cannot be aware of the relation of natural necessitation between that event and its antecedents. This is correct, but it does not follow, as Burks assumes, that we are therefore unaware of any causal relation between that event and some antecedent(s). See Burks (1975), pp. 614–15.

27 See also Albert Casullo (1979).

28 Kneale, to be sure, finds room for the supposition that causal laws are principles of necessitation by insisting that the objects of physics are such that perception can give us only a very partial knowledge of them. Thus we have no perceptual basis for forming a clear and distinct idea of them; and it is between them that causal interactions occur. These interactions may derive their necessity from characteristics which are not perceptually accessible to us and of which, therefore, what we can or cannot conceive cannot provide any understanding. But in that case, we confront the question of what it can mean (to us) to say that such causal principles obtain, beyond analogical appeals to other kinds of necessity.

29 A simple parallel should convince one of this. We are shown for the first time a roulette wheel; let us suppose we have no information concerning whether the wheel is fair or whether its behavior is non-random. Given this background information, the result of a single trial cannot significantly influence the probability we assign to the possible outcomes of a second trial, nor can it provide significant information which confirms or disconfirms the randomness hypothesis. For, whether the wheel is fair or not, the first trial is bound to give *some* result. Here it would be completely irrational to apply the straight rule of enumerative induction. The small degree to which we ought to prefer the prediction that the second trial will agree with the first is given by Bayes' Theorem (see Chapter 4) and is inversely proportional to the number of possible outcomes. On an infinite roulette wheel, the first trial provides no clue to the future at all. Certainly, *Hume's* psychology could not hope to

explain any inclination we might feel to apply the straight rule to this evidential base. But for all one knows on Humean grounds, encounters between hand and head are infinitely fickle in their effects.

30 Let me remind the reader that when I speak here of the head and of movement, I mean to be speaking of sensory contents, not of physical objects and their properties. So, for example, the possibility of a hallucinated blow to one's (physical) head in no way undercuts the argument.

31 J. L. Mackie (1980) comes close to admitting these conclusions, in spite of his refusal to allow that felt forces forge a "necessary connection" between events. In describing causal processes as involving some sort of continuity, he says that causes "produce" their effects, and (following d'Alembert) that deviations from continuity require reasons – reasons such as the presence of a force can supply. The explanatory power of microreductions derives in large measure, according to Mackie, from the exhibition of continuities which are not macroscopically apparent. However, Mackie's criteria for continuity, and his implicit appeal to a principle of sufficient reason, are indefensible once a Humean ontology is accepted. The explanatory power of microreduction arises not, I believe, from the uncovering of "continuities," but from the demonstration that otherwise mysterious causal connections are constituted by causal chains involving the impression of forces upon bodies, something of which we have direct understanding, but not always direct experience.

32 So far as the available empirical data go, there is some indirect evidence for the view I am defending. Experiments with preschool children and infants as young as eighteen weeks suggest that causal inferences in some situations depend more strongly on cues which enable a subject to regard events as connected by the transfer of some kind of force or continuity of motion than upon constant conjunction (see Bullock *et al.* (1982), Shultz (1982), Leslie (1982), and Leslie and Keeble (1987)). Nevertheless, a Humean could respond that even four-month-old infants are not totally naive subjects. Shultz performed experiments with children from a primitive tribe who had never encountered the artifacts he used as "energy transmitters" (tuning forks and flashlights); however, this precaution does not rule out the possibility that his subjects reasoned analogically from prior experience. At the same time, conditioning experiments with humans and animals, including such primitive organisms as nudibranch mollusks, strongly suggest that Hume (1963, p. 68) was entirely right in arguing that nature has provided us with an essentially mechanical tendency to learn from repeated experience. This does not preclude, needless to say, the possibility that there are also other bases, in experience and reasoning from it, which generate and can justify causal judgments. Fales and Wasserman (in preparation) review the psychological evidence.

33 I shall put the argument as if the tactile sensation of force were the only candidate for our claim to have discovered in experience a causal

relation. Presumably the same objection would apply, *mutatis mutandis*, for other candidates.

34 E.g. Bergson (1944) and James (1968).

35 *Vide*, for example, Alec Burkill (1941). What Hume says is:

> . . . as all distinct ideas are separable from each other, and as the ideas of cause and effect are evidently distinct, 'twill be easy for us to conceive any object to be nonexistent this moment, and existent the next, without conjoining to it the distinct idea of a cause or productive principle.
>
> (Hume 1988: Book I, Pt. III, Section III, 79)

36 E.g. resemblance and temporal relations.

37 I regard it an open question whether all causal relations require contact, or whether, at the microscopic level, even any of them do. But insofar as we speak only of what is phenomenologically apparent, it seems correct to say that certain forces are exerted through contact, whereas with others (e.g. gravitational attraction), this is at least an open question.

38 Since I shall take the relata of causation to be events (see below), this requires me to furnish a criterion for contact between events. I hold that two events are in contact at a given time just in case some of their constituent concrete particulars are in spatial contact at that time.

39 Failure to distinguish force and solidity as objects of tactile awareness leads Ducasse to suppose that this sort of case is one in which there is no experience of a cause. See Ducasse (1968), pp. 115–16.

40 Chapter 5 treats the question of what this temporal relation is.

41 One can at least agree with Dretske and Snyder that Mr *A* did enough to kill the cat in the sense that he did everything that could be done in the way of killing the cat by that means; and the cat *was* killed in that way.

42 See Section 4 of this chapter (pp. 21–2).

43 I ignore the fact that Hume himself rejects the distinction on quite different grounds.

44 Hume (1888), Book I, Part IV, Section II, p. 142.

45 Hume (1888), pp. 192–3.

46 We may be aware of a slight motion in the right hand, but such motion may be, or in principle could be, too slight to enter perceptual awareness.

2 An ontological analysis of causation

1 Cf. H. J. McCloskey (1963–4) for another taxonomy.

2 I have argued in Fales (1984) that we are distinctly aware of relations of type (2), and that they form a distinct genus not reducible to any other.

3 Hume (1888, Book I, Part III, Sections I and II) of course maintains that there is no distinction between our knowledge of these relations and our knowledge of the "body–body" type. I shall not discuss these other relations further.

4 I shall discuss in Chapter 3 the analysis of laws of nature in terms of causal relations.

5 That something directly experienced can imply as "theoretical" a result as the existence of invariant conjunction in the absence of disturbing forces might seem an anomalous result. But it is not. Part of our perception of forces is an awareness of what they do; another part is an awareness of how forces are prevented from doing by other forces. A crude analogy is this: if a box contains numbers on slips of paper, and one sees just the numbers 3 and 5, then one knows that the numbers in the box add to 8 (and so for any such box), provided that there are no further numbers.

6 See, for example, Dretske and Snyder (1972), Downing (1970), Anscombe (1971) and Moyal (1949).

7 See Mario Bunge (1959) and W. R. Dennes (1932).

8 These discussions focussed on laws of nature. But their realistic analysis of laws implies a realist understanding of causation itself. Armstrong is quite explicit about this, as is Tooley in his more recent book (1987).

9 Tooley (1984) and (1987) holds that causal relations between events involve a further relation in addition to that which obtains between the relevant universals. He has an argument which shows, perhaps, that the specification of a spatiotemporal interval does not suffice in general to pick out the effect of an event. The key to the argument is the claim (with which I am inclined to agree) that the spatial distance between temporally separated locations is itself parasitic upon the existence of causal sequences – sequences which determine the genidentity of bodies. Tooley considers a very simple rotationally symmetric universe, for example one consisting entirely of two neutrons approaching one another. Consider a time t, prior to which there are two neutron-stages, A and A^*, and subsequent to which there are two neutron-stages B and B^*. What makes it the case that B, rather than B^*, is the continuation of A? Tooley's point is that spatiotemporal contiguity cannot serve as a criterion, since there is no way to determine whether it is the beginning of B or of B^* which is contiguous with the terminus of A. Thus, unless something else determines genidentity, it must be the existence of a causal relation between A and B, rather than between A and B^*, which determines this. But then the existence of a causal connection between two events is not merely a matter of their existing in a certain spatiotemporal relation, together with the existence of a second-order causal relation connecting the (other) properties they instantiate. Perhaps, then, the present analysis is incomplete.

10 In my terminology, to say that an event (or state of affairs) *occurs* during a time interval $t_1 - t_0$ is to say that some property or set of properties is instantiated by a particular or set of particulars during that period of time.

11 The criterion for this, I shall argue, is causal. If causes are understood to be events, and identity of events requires a principle of identity for properties, a vicious circle threatens: the identity of events presupposes

the identity of properties, and vice versa. I shall argue that this generates a regress, but not an infinite one. The regress ends because certain properties can be identified without appeal to their causal implications (see Chapter 8, Section 9).

12 Davidson (1969) has argued that singular sentences are not used to pick out events. They merely assert the existence, during some period of time, of an event of a certain type. Thus, 'Doris capsized the canoe yesterday' is true whether one or a dozen such capsizings occurred yesterday, and refers to no specific capsizing. Davidson's position parallels the analysis given by Russell of indefinite descriptions. Now oftentimes Russell's analysis of the indefinite descriptions is correct. If a woman were to say, "A man kissed me yesterday," she might mean just "$(\exists x)(x$ is a male and x kissed me yesterday.$)$" But on the other hand, she might not: she might be referring (obliquely) to a *particular* man; compare: "A man, the handsomest in the world, . . ." As with indefinite descriptions, so with singular sentences. These can be used in a nonspecific way; they can also be used to specify some particular event which the speaker has in mind. (This ambiguity is reflected in judgments about truth value. Suppose Doris did tip over the canoe yesterday, but that on the occasion which the speaker witnessed and had in mind, it was really Roger's fault. Then on one reading what the speaker asserted is false. This reading is the one to which (E) and (I) below apply).

13 But this criterion suffers from apparent counterexamples: witness 'Socrates believes he saw Hesperus' and 'Socrates believes he saw Phosphorus,' which can be used to specify distinct events. (I am indebted to Panayot Butchvarov for this point.) I shall not pursue the problem, for it would take the discussion too far afield into difficult and tangential matters.

14 Cf. Strawson (1950) and Donnellan (1966).

15 My discussion of these difficulties leans heavily upon Jaegwon Kim, (1969) and (1973).

16 J. Kim (1969), p. 210 and footnote 21.

17 Davidson (1967) proposes a more complex analysis of the logical form of laws of nature. This, however, does not affect the present point.

18 I shall presently say more about the distinction between a property and its instances.

3 Causation and laws of nature

1 Mackie (1980, Chapter 6) makes a similar argument against Russell.

2 My response to Hochberg bears some resemblance to Armstrong's solution to this problem. Armstrong (1983, pp. 85–93) holds that P's causally necessitating Q is a second-order state of affairs, but also a *first order* universal, instantiated in every instance of the law it grounds. My argument here avoids the problematic identification of laws as universals.

3 Armstrong (1983, Chapter 11) offers several additional arguments in

defense of the contingent-relation view. Since every one of these arguments is deflected, I believe, by the necessitarian view I shall develop, I shall not labor these arguments here. Suffice it to anticipate three aspects of that view: (1) that the existence of physical universals is causally necessary; (2) that physical universals can exist uninstantiated; and (3) that there are no causal laws whose antecedents are physically impossible. Armstrong (personal communication) has indicated that the fundamental grounds for his view are best expressed in terms derived from Hume: if two universals are separate existences, then there is no necessary connection between them. Whether two physical universals are "distinct existences" is, Armstrong and I would agree, a complex matter not to be settled on *a priori* grounds. Various aspects of the distinctness of physical universals are discussed in Chapters 8, 9, and 10. On my view, as will emerge, the identity of every such universal is bound to the identity of every other. Armstrong's views are further developed in Armstrong (1983, pp. 88–98). Since he there accepts the existence of a primitive relation of natural necessitation, and since I agree that causation is not a species of logical necessitation, it is not clear to me how divergent our view are. Tooley (1987, pp. 110–112 and 123–9) also supports the thesis that nomological relations are contingent.

4 E.g. by Kripke (1972). Kaplan (1977), argues for the view that some truths of logic, though *a priori*, are contingent.

5 Swoyer (1982) similarly argues that if laws are grounded in a contingent relation between universals, then they cannot sustain counterfactuals.

4   Causation and induction

1 E.g. A. C. Ewing (1951), p. 473.

2 The most recent and sophisticated version of Popper's approach appears in Watkins (1984). Watkins attempts – unsuccessfully in my opinion – to evade the second and third difficulties.

3 See Wesley Salmon (1962–3). An argument of J. L. Mackie's can perhaps be classified as belonging to the Strawsonian camp: see Mackie (1979). Mackie begins with an inductive inference which seems to be both valid and *a priori*. One hundred balls, identical except that one is white and the rest black, are placed in an urn and well mixed. The inference is that one which has been drawn at random will be black. Mackie says, correctly, that his inference does not depend upon previous urn-drawings; it depends rather upon an epistemic Principle of Indifference which, I should agree, is *a priori* (see below). But Hume would rightly attack Mackie's attempt to use the Principle of Indifference, coupled to a Bayesian argument, to justify a principle of uniformity of nature. I shall discuss below the problem of assigning prior probabilities, which it seems to me Mackie does not succeed in solving. (Mackie's solution relies upon the assignment of finite priors to hypotheses predicting long runs of orderly events, but I do not think Mackie has managed to justify this move.) See in this connection the criticism of Mackie by Millikan (1982).

4 R. B. Braithwaite has been a prominent exponent of this account of laws although his attempt to solve the problem of induction does not follow the line suggested here. See Richard Braithwaite (1963). Similar proposals have been made by Mill (1973), Ramsey (1931), pp. 237–55; and Lewis (1973), pp. 72–7.

5 Relatively recent attempts of the latter sort have been presented by A. C. Ewing (1962), reprinted in Ewing (1968); John Foster (1982–3); Michael Tooley (1977); Fred Dretske (1977), and D. M. Armstrong (1983, pp. 104–6). Foster and Armstrong rely upon arguments to the best explanation: causal laws best explain regularities. I avoid this strategy for two reasons. First, it requires an elucidation of the notion of the goodness of an explanation which is not inductively grounded, and I am doubtful about the possibility of providing such an elucidation. Second, it commits us to an *a priori* bias in favor of a principle of sufficient reason, that is, against the existence of regularities which have *no* explanation. My argument avoids such a bias.

6 I shall follow the spirit of Hume's way of posing the problem of induction: different event-*sequences* correspond to distinct hypotheses. Perhaps this is too strong. Laws, even statistical laws, commit us only to relative frequencies, not to an actual order of events or experimental outcomes. One strategy which Hume's way of putting the problem suggests is that it may be a mistake not to lump together as in some sense equivalent certain distinct sequences for the purpose of counting up genuinely distinguishable hypotheses and assigning prior probabilities. Both Carnap (1950, 1952) and Hintikka (1965, 1968), for example, resort to this kind of strategy in their attempts to make the problem tractable. But Carnap's structure-descriptions merely state whether or not a given predicate is instantiated in a possible world, not with what relative frequency it is instantiated. For criticisms of Carnap and Hintikka, see Watkins (1984). I shall tackle the problem in its austere Humean form, for Keynes (1921, Chapter 4) has shown that distinct sequences (or constitutions, in Keynes's terminology) must be taken, rather than ratios of event-types, as comparable Humean hypotheses. (In essence, Keynes argues that alternative hypotheses are equiprobable under the Principle of Indifference only if the evidence relevant to one has exactly the same form as that relevant to the other. Suppose we are given a set of objects O and two hypotheses about the frequency of black items in that population. Suppose h says that half the O's are black; h^* says that one-fourth of them are. There are more ways in which black color can be distributed among the members of O which will satisfy h than ways which will satisfy h^*. So the form of the evidence relevant to h is distinguishable from that relevant to h^*. Hence the Principle of Indifference cannot be used to assign them equal prior probabilities.)

7 See Section 4 and footnote 12 on this type of probability.

8 Michael Tooley has pointed out to me a purely formal reason for rejecting this representation of the *a priorist* position. If 'R' entails 'S', then 'Probably R' entails 'Probably S.' But '$\sim P$' entails '$P \supset Q$', so

'Probably $(\sim P)$' entails 'Probably $(P \supset Q)$'; i.e., the probable falsity of P would suffice to make any proposition 'Q' probable relative to 'P.'

9   I am grateful to Richard Fumerton for this example and for discussion of the larger issue.

10   I am not here appealing to the distinct (and false) general claim that if Q were not probable relative to P and R, then it would not be probable relative to R.

11   This is not quite right, for the degree of confirmation of a hypothesis h is also inversely proportional to the prior probability of the evidence for it; and by a similar argument, this prior is also $1/\infty$. So it appears that the expression for the posterior probability of h contains the fraction $0/0$. But not so; for the ratio of the prior of h to the prior of the confirming evidence e is a function of the ratio of the informational content of h and that of e, and this, however measured, tends to zero in the limit as h becomes infinitely more informative than e. But any strictly general hypothesis is infinitely more informative than any finite set of singular confirming statements. Our goal, in any case, is that of taming this fraction.

12   Here lies the fallacy of D. C. Stove's alleged "disproof" of Hume's argument for inductive skepticism. Stove (1973), pp. 68–9, claims that the prior probability of every empirical hypothesis must be less than 1. But this is mistaken. If h is an empirical hypothesis which entails a specific event sequence, then its prior probability (its probability relative to any tautology t is essentially zero: $P(h,t) \approx 0$. But if h *is empirical, then so is* $\sim h$ and thus $P(\sim h, t) \approx 1$, even though $\sim h$ is not a tautology. A main argument in Stove (1986) commits the same fallacy; see his Chapter V.

13   The principle is usually given a more general form which does presuppose the notion of assignable degrees of confirming and disconfirming evidence. In this latter form it is subject to serious difficulties to which our version is invulnerable: see Keynes (1921), Chapters 3 and 4.

14   Here an analogy may help. Suppose someone understands what it is for a geometric object to be one-dimensional, and what it is for an object to have zero dimension, but cannot form any conception of what it would be for an object to have a dimensionality between zero and one. Such a person can nevertheless understand in a kind of generic or promissory way what we say if we say that there are such objects. He at least knows what *kind* of claim we are making; if we try to give him a positive conception of such an object, he has grounds for deciding whether our construction could be plausibly classified in this way.

15   When h is a statistical hypothesis, the probability assigned to e relative to h plus initial conditions must be given some objective interpretation – for example, in terms of frequencies or propensities.

16   I do not mean to minimize the seriousness of this difficulty. To deal adequately with it, we need to be assured that none of the relevant hypotheses can be split into two more specific hypotheses; and that atomic hypotheses are "equally specific." But if we cannot determine

whether our hypotheses are equispecific we can make do with the weaker principle: assign each hypothesis in the set an arbitrary nonzero prior probability, in such a way that the priors add up to one.

17 I ignore for the moment the complication that this hypothesis may in turn split up into a number of alternate sub-hypotheses.

18 Clearly this is not the *only* sort of causal hypothesis available. It may be that an event of type *C* regularly causes both *A*-type and *B*-type events. More complex inductive procedures must be employed to discriminate between such causal alternatives. But that complication need not concern us here.

19 This dissociates the assignment of prior probabilities from purely subjective or psychological determinants. For the operative Principles of Indifference and Normalization have, it seems to me, the same epistemic status as the truths of pure mathematics. And our inability to think of an explanatory hypothesis in no way affects its initial candidacy. Thus I view prior probabilities, though epistemic, as objective in a sense. They are not the actual probabilities of the alternative hypotheses, of course, but neither are they the degree of confidence which any agent might happen to assign to them. We can think of them as the degrees of confidence which are dictated by the Principles of Indifference and Normalization under circumstances in which there is no relevant empirical data to be utilized, and in which all of the logically consistent hypotheses which could explain some set of outcomes of an as-yet-to-be-performed experiment have been enumerated. That nothing less will do is illustrated by Pascal's famous wager concerning God's existence. Supposing the evidence to be indecisive or nonexistent, Pascal considers but two hypotheses, namely, that the Christian god exists, and that no god exists. This wager is defeated by the observation that there are indefinitely many other theistic hypotheses with radically different outcomes for the Christian. Following William James (1897), a subjectivist might exclude these other hypotheses because they are not "living options" (James's phrase). This exclusion may offer him solace and comfort. Clearly that it does so in no way diminishes the infinite peril which confronts his immortal (if such it be) soul. In this situation, ironically, the subjectivist can do no better than to choose to be a Christian; but it is also true that he can do no worse.

20 I have for simplicity omitted statistical hypotheses, and also hypotheses which employ Goodmanized predicates. The latter would spell trouble, but are ruled out on other grounds (see footnote 26).

21 This assignment is "*slightly*" posterior, since one marble has already been ejected, but obviously if the experiment can be carried out at all, it can be carried out *this* far. This eliminates the difficulty that, where the number of colors *m* is infinite, the priors of each of the sub-hypothesis of (i) becomes infinitely small. In other words, a single experiment is sufficient to obviate that difficulty. The (very real) worry that the set of hypotheses {(i), (ii)} is artificially restricted and not exhaustive will be discussed below.

22 A similar objection, raised by Peter Urbach (private communication), is

that the property, *being a pushing of the button* might be lawfully connected to some disjunctive property (e.g. *being a red or green marble*) or to some generic property (e.g. *being a colored marble*) – both of which hypotheses are compatible with the ejection by the box of *k* red marbles; and neither of which warrant confidence as to the color of future marbles. My response to the first supposition is that I reject disjunctive properties (see Chapter 8), and hence basic laws which would involve them. (Perhaps Urbach's hypothesis can be construed as postulating a device that chooses randomly either a red marble or a green one, but never any other color. But hypotheses of this sort can be eliminated by the same strategy applied to hypothesis (ii).) I accept the existence of generic properties, on the other hand (see Chapter 9); still the hypothesis in question involves the instantiation not *merely* of the generic property (*being colored*) but of some one or more species of it and it is then an eligible question whether there is not some further hypothesis which would supply a reason why one of these colors rather than any other was the one which had so far been exemplified. This returns us to our original set of hypotheses, if we exclude indeterministic laws.

23 These perverse examples come courtesy of Nelson Goodman; but with a twist: the patterns exhibited by the behavior of "cruel" boxes have a causal explanation. Thus, no refutation of them on the grounds that their description involves improperly gerrymandered predicates such as 'grue' will meet the case. Any such sequence could be produced by a randomizing box; but the supposition that the box is genuinely random is a distinct hypothesis and has already been discussed. The distinction is an important one; see below.

24 It does so, at least, if we can solve the problem of inferring causes from their effects – the problem of perception, given a causal theory of perception.

25 This does not exclude the possibility of making quantitative estimates of *a posteriori* probabilities for hypotheses, in virtue of the fact that in many cases the value of the prior probability is swamped by the effect of confirming or disconfirming evidence.

26 Perhaps a certain class of *a priori* criteria of which relative simplicity is an example ought to temper the application of the Principle of Indifference. More generally, it may be that some kinds of explanations – especially at the level of reductively fundamental explanations (if such a level there be) are intrinsically more satisfying, more illuminating, than competing candidate explanations. This topic deserves closer investigation than it has yet received: it is a necessary propaedeutic to the articulation of an adequate theory of the nature of arguments to the best explanation. Such maneuvers may legitimate assignment of uneven *a priori* weights to hypotheses. In the present context however this is of secondary importance.

27 Twentieth-century developments in physics make us aware of a third possibility: limited randomness underlying an appearance of rigid order.

I shall not pursue here the complexities which this possibility introduces into the inductive project.

28 I am setting aside the problem of predicting behaviour in open systems. This is a problem which cannot be solved inductively or in any other way. According to Special Relativity, for example, electromagnetic radiation may arrive from a distant source and influence a system at any time. There is in principle no way to predict when this will happen.

29 As Goodman would characterize the 'grue' hypothesis, there is no change in the character of emeralds at any future time. Uniformly grue in the past, they continue to be grue in the future. Thus an answer to Goodman's challenge must address the question of the identity-conditions for properties, a question which will be investigated in Chapter 8. For the nominalist this question is generally linked to whether a given predicate expression is meaningful or whether some class of objects can be specified; but not so for the realist. The realist is not committed to the view that every meaningful predicate denotes a property; nor to supposing that every specifiable class corresponds to some property. Thus he will not assume without argument, that that 'grue' denotes any universal; and indeed he has reasons for denying this. First, he has good grounds for the view that green and blue are monadic properties, grounds which rest on the way in which we detect these properties. What about grue? It appears to be a relational property of a peculiar sort, for whether something is grue or not depends upon its relation to some arbitrarily chosen coordinate system for time. But if *being grue* is to figure in causal laws, it cannot be arbitrary in this way. The laws of nature must be expressable in a language which does not mention spatiotemporal coordinates. Of course, if the universe has a beginning, one could assign times to events in a way which was, in a sense, non-arbitrary. It could be that the behavior of objects is dependent upon the age of the universe. But this fact would not generate Goodman's problem – at least not if we can assume (see Chapter 5) that causal influences cannot jump across temporal gaps. If causal chains must be temporally continuous, then the age of the universe can be reflected in local behavior only via a chain of influence which alters proximate antecedent conditions. Such changes can, once again, be expressed in terms of laws which are themselves time-invariant. The upshot is that if being grue involves being subject to influences which are a function of the age of the universe, then whether something is grue or not can in principle be detected prior to the time t mentioned in its definition. And of course time itself does not figure as a causal influence, for if it did, it would be possible to detect time independently of any marker-events occurring "in" time.

Against these arguments Goodman would point out that, just as

being grue $=_{df}$ being first examined before t and being green, or being examined on or after t and being blue,

so too

being green $=_{df}$ being first examined before t and being grue, or being examined on or after t and being bleen.

But for the realist, such verbal symmetry is no criterion of ontological symmetry. The ways in which we are able to identify greenness do not encourage the supposition that this is a temporally indexed property. Compare Shoemaker (1980a), for a similar argument.

30　For a fuller exposition of the relation between fundamentality and non-defeasibility, see Fales (1978). Further discussions of the formal requirements of fundamental theory appear in Fales (1979), and in Harré and Madden (1975), Chapter 9; and other works by Harré.

31　A promising advance on one of these further aspects, I am persuaded, has been made by Glymour (1980). Glymour's "bootstrap" theory of confirmation has the virtue of showing how evidence for a theory can bear selectively upon the constituent hypotheses of that theory, and how some hypotheses play a role in the computation of their own confirming instances or those of other hypotheses, where the former are themselves confirmed by *other* computations. There is no vicious regress; but that is just because the argument makes implicit use of Bayesian reasoning: when independent computations agree in yielding a predicted quantity, and when a variety of evidence supplies the basis for confirmatory computations of instances of the various hypotheses which are both being used to generate computations testing other hypotheses, and being themselves in turn tested, then a likely explanation for this concilience is that these hypotheses are true, or approximately true. Glymour himself disavows Bayesianism, but it is the subjective Bayesians he targets; most of his objections have little force against the objective Bayesianism advocated here. Moreover Glymour's theory does not address the fundamental question why an instance of a generalization confirms it; that is the primary question addressed here. Thus I see the two discussions as supplementing each other. See also Rosenkrantz, "Why Glymour *Is* a Bayesian," in Earman (1983), pp. 69-97.

32　The width of a property is a function of the number of primitive predicates in one's language which name properties compatible with its ascription.

5　Causality and time

1　See Brand (1980); also Mackie (1980) and Rosenberg (1975).

2　A third approach is advocated by Tooley (1987, Chapter 8). Tooley understands causation as a relation that involves the transmission of logical probability from cause to effect, but not vice versa. There is something right in the idea that a cause probabilifies its effect but not vice versa, but in my view this probabilification is a relation parasitic on the more fundamental notion of causation itself. Tooley relies upon the notion of a logical probability, or degree of confirmation that one state of affairs confers upon another. I find such a notion mysterious, for reasons already given, and Tooley does not explicate it. Tooley's discussion of other analyses of causal asymmetry is very illuminating, however.

3 See Mackie (1965).

4 Hume (1888), Book I, Part III, Section II, p. 76.

5 See also Richard Taylor (1966), p. 38. Hume argues for the stronger conclusion that every cause precedes its effect.

6 This hypothesis has been seriously entertained by some physicists.

7 See also A. David Kline (1982). Kline reaches similar conclusions to mine.

8 Nor, it seems, the opposed argument that (at least some) effects succeed their causes. "The affair," he says, "is of no great importance" (1888, Book I, Part III, Section II).

9 Michael Tooley has pointed out to me that this conclusion can be avoided if temporal relations, rather than the passage of time as such, play a causal role. Tooley's suggestion is that the duration of a causing event, or of a time interval after all other requisite changes have occurred, can be causally efficacious. To be sure, this view can be characterized as one on which the effect is temporally contiguous to the cause, for the full cause includes the passage of a certain period of time, after which the effect takes place. A fuller insight into this question requires a deeper discussion of the relationship between temporal properties and causation (see Chapter 10, Sections 2 and 3). For the present, I shall rule such gaps inadmissible.

10 An elegant elementary treatment of the theory of infinitesimals is given by James M. Henle and Eugene M. Kleinberg (1979). More technical discussions may be found in A. Robinson (1974), and Keith Stroyan and W. A. J. Luxemburg (1976). I have benefited from conversations with Stroyan concerning these developments.

11 Helmut Schmidt (1969). Schmidt's experiment was conducted with an indeterministic device, but one can equally imagine an experiment in which the light to be illuminated is predetermined by conditions which are fixed prior to the subject's prediction. This would make it more difficult to rule out the possibility that the subject has access to the state of the machine prior to making his prediction, and makes his prediction on the basis of that information. But one feels that it should be possible, by means of suitable precautions, to rule this out. The two alternatives will be further discussed below. For a critical evaluation of Schmidt's work, see C. E. M. Hansel (1980), pp. 217–36, and Druckman and Swets (1988), Chapter 9.

12 The thought experiment upon which this argument relies is called the "bilking experiment" by A. Flew. The debate on this topic includes the following: Dummett (1964); Flew (1954, 1955–6); Black (1955–6); Scriven (1956–7); and Pears (1956–7).

13 See, for example, David Lewis (1973); John Pollock (1976); Robert Stalnaker (1981); John Barker (1969); Donald Nute (1980).

14 See also Jonathan Bennett's (1984) arguments against Lewis.

15 One should keep in mind that . . ., E, F may be a backward-directed chain merging with A, . . ., C at t_4.

16 This assumes what I have previously asserted, namely, that the *absence* of the sequence . . ., E, F in the actual world is not a causal factor in that world.

6   Nominalism reconnoitered

1 For further arguments in support of this view, see Armstrong (1978b), Chapter 13.
2 Presently I shall advocate a view which explains designation for most (not all) physical predicates in terms of a causal theory of reference.
3 Though I do not think this is the case. 'Is square' is not as geometers speak an inexact predicate and is not associated with an inexact concept.
4 See also Butchvarov (1966), who classifies nominalism and the resemblance theory as distinct theories.
5 As D. F. Pears argues it is (1951).
6 For D. M. Armstrong (1978b), who analyses the determinate/determinable distinction in terms of the overlap of complex universals, these two strategies collapse into a single one.
7 See Chapter 10.
8 Price (1953), p. 25.
9 Stout (1923), p. 116.
10 Stout (1923), p. 122.
11 This would involve a significant departure from the way in which bare particulars are conceived by their chief advocate, Gustav Bergmann. But I let the suggestion stand.
12 It is reminiscent of Aquinas's doctrine concerning the individuation of angels.
13 See Barenette (1978), Cortes (1981), Ginsberg (1981), and Teller (1983). Teller's argument that two bosons occupying the same region of space-time may be regarded as a single indivisible particle ignores the classificatory constraints in elementary particle physics which militate against adding such new species of particles to our ontology.
14 Stout's view is that the individuation of concrete particulars is dependent upon the individuation of abstract particulars. If space-time points are concrete particulars, by means of which abstract particulars are individuated, Stout's position is reversed.
15 Once again, this reverses Stout's view.
16 Another common motive for nominalism is a desire for ontological parsimony. But that is an intellectual desideratum which might weigh as heavily with non-empiricists as with empiricists. It poses the question: which ontological categories are dispensable? In deciding this, epistemological considerations have often played a major role.
17 I have in mind particularly studies in the nature of reductive and teleological explanations; and in the semantics of theoretical terms.

7 The relation of universals to space and time

1 The sibling, in turn, will symmetrically name *itself* 'a,' and use 'b' to designate the other. Thus their naming conventions disagree. But this in no way affects the fact that each can distinguish itself from the other.

2 Multiple predicability is neither a necessary nor a sufficient condition. Not sufficient, because 'is self-identical' is multiply predicable, but corresponds to no universal. Not necessary, because, for example, 'being omnipotent' is not multiply predicable but does designate a universal.

3 For example, *being omnipotent* satisfies (3) but not (2).

4 I rely here upon what I trust is a general intuition. No criteria have so far been offered for simplicity or complexity as regards properties. I do not think it is an easy matter to formulate such a criterion but more will be said on the subject presently.

5 The point I am making about anonymity does not depend upon the supposition that locations are enduring entities. Suppose they are momentary; then their anonymity can be brought out by observing that there is nothing about such entities which enables us to establish the spatial relations between an earlier one and a later one.

6 We do not here commit ourselves as to whether material objects are continuants.

7 Except in certain spaces with closed geodesics. But in any curved space there will always be some antireflexive spatial relations.

8 As might be possible if the disks were composed of atoms separated by empty space.

9 Armstrong (1978a, p. 112). Armstrong denies that identity is a relation.

10 They have, however, difficulty in stating what the difference is between a property and a particular which stand in this "relation", and a property and a particular which do not. See Butchvarov (1974).

11 This is a direct consequence of two facts. One of these has already been introduced; the other has not. The first fact is that causal relations necessarily involve spatial and temporal relations; the second is that physical universals have causal essences. Of this more will be said presently.

8 The nature of universals

1 See Schaffner (1969).

2 Syncategorematic terms were, by various devices, excluded from this requirement.

3 See for example Schlick (1936, pp. 342–3).

4 It is not logically impossible that light, or some other information-bearing signal, should travel faster than 3×10^8 km/sec. Even instantaneous signal transmission is not in any obvious way a logical impossibility; nor would the inconstancy of luminal velocities be, notwithstanding Einstein's (1917, Chapter VIII) suggestion that the

denial of the latter is a "stipulation." But, these things are (so far as is known) physically impossible. See also Bowman (1976).

5 Einstein (1917, Chapter VIII).

6 Analogous cases complicate the picture given by Kripke and Putnam for the semantics of proper names and natural-kind nouns.

7 There are different types of reference-failure; and again analogues can usually be constructed to the ways in which reference can fail for proper names and natural kind terms according to the causal-chain model of Kripke and Putnam. One can defend the use of a dispositional term against this kind of failure by allowing it to denote a disjunctive property. But I shall argue that there are no disjunctive properties; and in any event such a rescue would ordinarily do violence to the intention with which a property term is introduced.

8 Compare Kripke's analogous arguments in (1972) concerning knowledge of the causal chains which back up the reference made by the use of proper names.

9 A parallel case involving proper names would be this. Two identical twins move to a strange town. They undertake to fool the local population into believing that they are but one person. Both appear in public, but never simultaneously. Both use the same name: 'Charlie Twinkle.' One day, the ruse is discovered. The semantic question is: Has 'Charlie Twinkle', as used by the townsfolk, been used to refer to the aggregate of both twins, to neither (i.e., to no one), or perhaps on some occasions to the one twin and on others to his brother?

10 At least for single-track dispositional terms.

11 The important exception concerns what Locke called mixed modes: names for human artifacts or conventions (e.g., legal attributes) which clearly have practical efficacy as their leading goal.

12 Latter-day attempts to broaden the empiricist criterion of meaning included attempts to distinguish between disposition terms and more deeply theoretical terms; but those analyses help to confirm the present point. See Hempel (1952) and Pap (1962, Chapter 3), for examples.

13 See Achinstein (1963) and (1965); Maxwell (1962); and Spector (1961).

14 I believe, more precisely, that as we ordinarily and unreflectively use 'white,' it denotes ambiguously a phenomenal property and a physical one, which we do not distinguish. In the present discussion I examine what follows from our having an intention to use the predicate to describe physical objects.

15 It is obviously true that, at least during the early stages of teaching the word 'white,' it is situations of this sort which are primarily sought and used.

16 We do sometimes say that a white object illuminated with red light has (transiently) "turned pink." But *this* is a Pickwickian use of the term 'pink.' Standardly used, color terms are used to ascribe to objects or their surfaces monadic properties which are (usually) stable under changes in lighting.

17 Part three of this essay takes as its main theme the defense of epistemological realism.

18 I suspect that every truth about relations among universals is a necessary truth; but I know of no way of proving this. However, the fact that every instance of a universal confers the same powers follows from the claim that causal relations connect the universals themselves, not merely individual instances.

19 The identity criterion I propose here for universals is similar to that offered in Shoemaker (1980b). Since, however, I do not identify metaphysical necessity with logical necessity, I reject Shoemaker's conclusion that causal laws are logically necessary.

20 At least, a refusal to allow tensed predication when the entities in question are supposed to be temporal requires some special justification.

21 It may be that there are certain intentional relations which relate existing to nonexisting things. This is problematic, but in any case it is clear that R is not a relation of this sort.

22 This assumes that there is no universal or set of universals which is causally isolated from all the rest. If this were the case, there would be two universes, neither of which could causally interact with the other. But it follows from our neo-verificationism that we can have no reason to postulate the existence of such disconnected universes.

23 This claim will be defended in Section 9 below.

24 This claim must be qualified; it does not apply to spatial and temporal properties. For a discussion of this exemption, see Chapter 9, Section 3.

25 By 'depends on' I mean here simply that a property would not be the property that it is, if it did not have the set of causal relations it has. I do not mean that the identity of the universal is "generated" by these relations; perhaps it is the other way around.

26 For somewhat different reasons, a similar conclusion seemed to Schlick to be entailed by the early positivism for which sense data were epistemologically foundational. See Schlick (1932/33).

27 This need not be a linguistic act; it may be simply the act of intending (attending to, calling to mind) that property.

9 Generic universals

1 See Blanshard (1962) for another defense of the partial identity theory.

2 Armstrong himself (1983, Chapter 7) has tentatively given up this earlier theory in favour of admitting generic universals selectively for the purpose of grounding functional laws of nature. This might be seen as rather *ad hoc*; but at any rate I shall argue for a much more general account of determinables.

3 Perhaps we should have to say of someone whose visual experiences were of the sort mentioned that he did not have the same color-perceptions we have, or that he could not possess the same color-concepts. All this would not, on Armstrong's view or mine, touch the question of whether such a man perceived the same physical colors we perceive.

4 It is Armstrong's view, and also my own, that we are not directly

acquainted with most physical universals, and that it is the task of science to discover their number and true natures.

5 Armstrong cautiously admitted (1978b, p. 119) the bare possibility that science will discover universals of which there are no perfectly determinate instances. But even in this case Armstrong would, I think, admit only one "level" of indeterminacy: there could be no higher determinables under which those of greatest specificity were subsumed.

6 Armstrong has perhaps overlooked a possibility here; namely that two complex universals could be diverse not by virtue of any difference in their constituent universals, but by virtue of a difference in how these constituents are structured.

7 Armstrong speaks (1978b, pp. 127–9) of a homogeneous class of universals as one whose members are united by a "single, topic-neutral formula." It is not fully clear what this expression means, or whether it entails that the members of a homogeneous class will have a common constituent.

8 Compare Armstrong (1978b), pp. 112 and 116.

9 Armstrong (1978b), p. 124.

10 This suggestion is derived from a comment of Armstrong's (personal communication).

11 Armstrong (1978b), p. 123.

12 Unlike Armstrong, I believe that there are phenomenal color-properties, or color-qualia. It is clear that Armstrong's theory would not work for such universals as these.

13 For further discussion of these cases, see Chapter 11, Section 5B.

14 Mark Twain, letter to William Dean Howells, 13 February 1903; in Twain (1946), pp. 782–4.

15 But the universal in question would have to be one which could characterize only imaginary hens, not real ones.

16 Here are two examples. (1) To be square is a determinate way of being a plane figure, and of being a regular geometric shape. But the latter does not fall under the former, for regular solids are not plane figures; nor does the former fall under the latter, for many plane figures are not regular. (2) To carry a negative electric charge of 1 e.s.u. is a determinate way of being electrically charged, and of being attractive to protons. But being a proton-attracter is not a subgenus of being electrically charged, for neutral bodies with mass also attract protons. Conversely, being electrically charged is not a subgenus of being proton-attractive, for positively charged bodies are electrically charged but proton-repellent.

17 There are further issues, which I shall ignore, concerning how to measure degree of overlap between nondenumerable sets of causal relations.

10 Relations

1 This view was advocated by Armstrong in *Universals and Scientific Realism*, vol. II (1978b).

2 The reader should recall that some properties – and some instances of the relation *R* between them – are phenomenally given. But here we are speaking of universals and instances of *R* not so given.

11 Skepticism about the existence of the material world

1 The view of unreflective common sense perhaps resembles most closely that of naive or direct realism. But even unreflective common sense admits a causal relation between perceiver and perceived; and reflection shows that this meshes naturally with the facts of perceptual relativity and scientific realism, whereas naive realism does not.

2 See Chapter 1, Section 1.

3 I am not convinced that the sense-datum theory is correct, although I adopt (one version of) it here. There is something right about it, and that something is not captured by competing theories, such as the adverbial theory. But I suspect that, in the end, all the current alternatives are wrong.

4 In one of his arguments for the existence of God, Descartes appeals to the principle that at least one of his thoughts (his conception of God) must, because of its intrinsic nature, have been caused by something independent of him. The evil demon hypothesis does, on the other hand, call into question the truths of pure reason. That form of skepticism is not under consideration here, nor are doubts about memory.

5 Although some attacks on the reality of time – most notably McTaggart's (1927) – have levelled the specific charge that our conception or experience of time somehow hosts contradictions, most philosophical hostility toward time is motivated by the more general view that experience itself (especially empirical or perceptual experience) cannot be known or has a degraded ontological status, as compared to that of some Absolute or transcendent reality. About ontologies of this sort I have nothing to say here, except that they are hard to take seriously unless backed by some powerful argument (such as McTaggart's purports to be) that exerts pressure on the apparently ineluctable reality of experience itself.

6 I do not wish to rule out *a priori* other "universes," causally isolated from ours and with their own space-times. I doubt that we can form any clear conception of this possibility, but I know of no real argument against it.

7 The temporal direction along which bodies move we shall call, adopting the usual convention, the forward direction.

8 The feature I have been attempting to describe, so far as I can see, would not fail to be present in relativistic space-times in which the topology of time is altered in strange ways – for example, in which the temporal continuum is a closed loop. Such topologies, however, *would* force an alteration in our use of the expressions 'past' and 'future' in important ways.

9 One may come to different conclusions concerning the shape of a particular table through the use of one's visual and tactile sensations; but there is no such thing as visual, as opposed to tactile, squareness or roundness.

10 Thus it seems to me that the correct answer to Molyneux's question is that a blind man who acquires sight should, using his visual sensations, his tactile experience, and his analytic abilities alone, be able to discriminate cubes from spheres.

11 Naturally this explanation, were it explicitly formulated, would require, in addition to geometrical theorems, auxiliary hypotheses about the rectilinear transmission of shape images from object to observer. Doubtless this assumption is tacit for the ordinary man, though buttressed by tactile data. It seems clear that we can develop this kind of cognitive scheme without explicit reasoning through all the required steps; and of course without their linguistic formulation.

12 This claim will be discussed in Section 5 below.

13 Consider a machine which produces pains of continuously variable and reproducible intensity (as judged by subjects) through administration of electric shock. Consider three dial settings on the machine, A, B, and C . . .

14 Could it be that the distinct colors of patch A and patch B are observed, but that there is a failure to observe *that* they are different? Inattention (as previously noted) can lead to a failure to judge that something which has been observed is the case. No doubt, so can circumstances in which the data are so shifting, complex, or otherwise unfamiliar or bizarre, that even concerted efforts to form a definite judgment end in confusion. But the three-color case is nothing like this. To say *here* that we observe distinct colors but, try as we might, fail to be able to judge *that* they are distinct, is to eviscerate the very concept of what it is to observe something.

12 Scientific realism

1 See Boyd (1985), p. 4.

2 For other doubts about abductive defenses of realism, see Fine (1986); also Fine (1984) and Laudan (1984). Boyd is aware of these difficulties, but tries to outflank them by means of a holistic and naturalized epistemology (see Boyd 1984). My concluding remarks will make clear why I do not think that strategy can succeed either.

3 See Boyd (1985), p. 4.

4 Nor are these two conditions jointly sufficient. I am indeed skeptical about formulating any general set of necessary and sufficient conditions, though not prepared to abandon hope for a *theory* of reference. In most cases, an additional necessary condition is an intention to *use* a term referringly. The suggestion that we need a hybrid causal/descriptive theory has been similarly made, on the descriptivist side, by Lewis (1984), and, on the causal side, by Devitt and Sterelny (1987, Chapters 4 and 5).

5 This I take to be a consequence of the fact that this "look" is phenomenally given. Reference via causal chains and descriptions can fail; reference to subjective white cannot fail – or at least not for the same reasons.

6 That the invocation of "normal conditions" is unhelpful can be supported by the following parable. Twin-Earth is a world just like ours in all respects except that it is a planet of a star which is a red giant (suppose this is physically possible). Twin-English-speakers even use the word 'white' to describe the color of things like Twin-milk, Twin-chalk, and Twin-Taj Mahal. An Earth-Englishman transported to Twin-Earth would also say that these objects were white; he would insist, though, that under conditions of illumination which normally prevailed on Twin-Earth these items all *looked* pink.

7 This story about how we give physical property terms denotation is naturally an idealization. We do not need to have some *definite* remembered set of perceptual experiences in mind to serve as our reference-fixing class, any more than some definite set of gold objects needs to be assumed to have played that role in establishing the semantics of 'gold.' Moreover, we can improve the prospects of referential success by loosening the requirement that *all* the members of the reference class be instances of the same property (natural kind). Perhaps only a "sufficient number" of them need to be. This is vague, but I do not see that it undermines the strategy.

8 Similarly, it is important to distinguish between speculation about a particular evil demon and speculation about the existence of *some* evil demon.

9 This follows from the identity condition for physical properties. See Chapter 8. Section 5.

10 However, the causal connections that constitute the scaffolding of the world's structure give assurance that no particular piece of evidence is such that it would be causally impossible for an individual to acquire. Sensory limitations can be overcome by transducers (devices that convert one sort of causal influence to another in such a way that output is a function of input) that give us access to the features of the world that our bare senses are not sensitive to. In this way, even a person possessed of only one sensory modality could gain identifying information about physical properties to which we regard normal humans to have a more "direct" perceptual route. Every measuring device – but also every sense organ – is just a transducer; and the use of devices that aid the senses only introduces a bit more complexity into what is in any case an enormously complex causal process, even in the case of "direct" perception of physical objects; so our science tells us. Whether mechanical measuring devices (or, for that matter, our sense organs and central nervous system) are physically "real" or not is of course irrelevant, for the point is that we are able to manipulate, indefinitely and informatively, our sensory input. The limitations on our access to evidence, daunting as they are, are of a more practical nature.

11 I discussed Glymour's view briefly in Chapter 5, Section 6, footnote 23.

See also Rosenkrantz (1983), who argues that Glymour is a closet Bayesian who uses objective rather than subjective prior probabilities.

12 Maintaining the separation between theoretical reason and practical reason is sufficiently central to our conception of rationality that it should not lightly be given up. I may, for example, have strong practical grounds for acting on a proposition (acting as if it were true) even when I have no grounds, or weak grounds, for believing that it is. Pragmatism attempts to reduce theoretical reason to practical reason. But utility calculations are blind unless guided by factual beliefs about the future; and unless there is reason to suppose that those beliefs correspond to what is the case, they can hardly serve to guide the man who is rational and serious about his actions.

13 I have not explicitly argued that mental properties must, like physical ones, be included in a causal web. But considerations similar to those I have given suggest this must be so, at least for those properties of a demon by virtue of which he would be able to cause our experiences.

14 And we must know when to suspect error and how to correct for it.

15 I am indebted to Richard Fumerton for pointing this out to me.

16 By so arguing, he threatens to undermine the distinction between his position and that of the internalist. For now he can agree – or appear to agree – with the internalist that it is necessary to justify the reliability claim, necessary to back up a claim to know that P with the further claim to know that belief in P was acquired by reliable means. But that is not the central issue for us.

Bibliography

Achinstein, Peter (1963) "Theoretical Terms and Partial Interpretation," *British Journal for the Philosophy of Science* 14: 89–105.

—— (1965) "The Problem of Theoretical Terms," *American Philosophical Quarterly* 2: 193–203.

—— (1974) "The Identity of Properties," *American Philosophical Quarterly* 11: 257–75.

Adams, Ernest (1975) *The Logic of Conditionals*, Boston: D. Reidel.

Allaire, E. B. (1965) "Another Look at Bare Particulars," *Philosophical Studies* 16: 16–21, reprinted in Michael Loux (1970): 250–7.

Alloy, Lauren B. and Naomi Tabachnik (1984) "Assessment of Covariation by Humans and Animals: The Joint Influence of Prior Expectations and Current Situational Information," *Psychological Review* 91: 112–49.

Anscombe, G. E. M. (1971) "Causality and Determination," reprinted in Ernest Sosa (1975): 63–81.

Armstrong, David M. (1968) *A Materialist Theory of the Mind*, London: Routledge & Kegan Paul.

—— (1978a) *Nominalism and Realism*. Vol. I of *Universals and Scientific Realism*, Cambridge: Cambridge University Press.

—— (1978b) *A Theory of Universals*. Vol. II of *Universals and Scientific Realism*, Cambridge: Cambridge University Press.

—— (1983) *What is a Law of Nature?*, Cambridge: Cambridge University Press.

Asratyan, E. A. (1973) "The Causal Conditioned Reflex," *Soviet Psychology* 11: 112–29.

Bambrough, Renford (1960–1) "Universals and Family Resemblance," *Proceedings of the Aristotelian Society* 61: 207–22.

Barenette, R. L. (1978) "Does Quantum Mechanics Disprove the Principle of Indiscernibles?," *Philosophy of Science* 45: 466–70.

Barker, John (1969) *A Formal Analysis of Conditionals*, Carbondale, Ill.: Southern Illinois University Press.

Beauchamp, Thomas and Alexander Rosenburg (1981) *Hume and the Problem of Causation*, New York: Oxford University Press.

Bennett, Jonathan (1984) "Counterfactuals and Temporal Direction," *The Philosophical Review* 93: 57–91.

Bergmann, Gustav (1967) *Realism: A Critique of Brentano and Meinong*, Madison: The University of Wisconsin Press.

Bergson, Henri (1944) *Creative Evolution*. Arthur Mitchell (transl.), New York: Random House, Inc.

Black, Max (1952) "The Identity of Indiscernibles," *Mind* 61: 153–64.

—— (1955–6) "Why Cannot an Effect Precede Its Cause?," *Analysis* 16: 49–58.

Blanshard, Brand (1962) *Reason and Analysis*, LaSalle, Ill.: Open Court Publishing Company.

Bowman, Peter A. (1976) "Einstein's Second Treatment of Simultaneity," in Fredrick Suppe and Peter D. Asquith (eds), *PSA 1976: Proceedings of the 1976 Biennial Meeting of the Philosophy of Science Association*, Vol. 1, East Lansing, Mich.: Philosophy of Science Association: 71–81.

Boyd, Richard (1973) "Realism, Underdetermination, and a Causal Theory of Evidence," *Nous* 7: 1–12.

—— (1984) "The Current Status of Scientific Realism," in Jarrett Leplin (ed.), *Scientific Realism*, Berkeley: The University of California Press: 41–82.

—— (1985) "Lex Orandi est Lex Credendi," in Paul M. Churchland and Clifford A. Hooker (eds), *Images of Science: Essays in Realism and Empiricism*, Chicago: The University of Chicago Press.

Braithwaite, R. B. (1963) *Scientific Explanation: A Study of the Function of Theory, Probability and Law in Science*, London: Cambridge University Press.

Brand, Myles (1980) "Simultaneous Causation," in Peter van Inwagen (ed.) (1980): 137–54.

Bullock, M., R. Gelman, and R. Baillargeon (1982) "The Development of Causal Reasoning," in William J. Friedman (ed.), *The Developmental Psychology of Time*, New York: Academic Press: 209–54.

Bunge, Mario (1959) *Causality*, Cambridge: Harvard University Press.

Burkill, Alec (1941) "Modes of Causality," *Philosophy* 16: 185–97.

Burks, Arthur W. (1977) *Cause, Chance, Reason: An Inquiry Into the Nature of Scientific Evidence*, Chicago: University of Chicago Press.

Butchvarov, Panayot (1966) *Resemblance and Identity: An Examination of the Problem of Universals*, Bloomington, Ind.: Indiana University Press.

—— (1974) "The Limits of Ontological Analysis," in M. S. Gram and E. D. Klemke (eds), *The Ontological Turn*, Iowa City: The University of Iowa Press: 3–37.

Carnap, Rudolf (1950) *The Logical Foundations of Probability*, London: Routledge & Kegan Paul.

—— (1952) *The Continuum of Inductive Methods*, Chicago: The University of Chicago Press.

Casullo, Albert (1979) "Reid and Mill on Hume's Maxim of Conceivability," *Analysis* 39: 212–19.

Causey, Robert (1972) "Attribute Identities on Microreductions," *The Journal of Philosophy* 69: 407–22.

Chisholm, Roderick (1976) "The Agent as Cause," in Myles Brand and Douglas Walton (eds), *Action Theory*, Dordrecht: D. Reidel: 199–211.

Cortes, A. (1981) "Leibniz's Principle of the Identity of Indiscernibles: A False Principle," *Philosophy of Science* 43: 491–505.

Davidson, Donald (1967) "Causal Relations," *The Journal of Philosophy* 64: 691–703.

—— (1969) "The Individuation of Events," in Nicholas Rescher (ed.), *Essays in Honor of Carl G. Hempel*, Dordrecht: D. Reidel: 216–34.

Dennes, W. R. (1932) "Causation as Continuity and Production," *University of California Publications in Philosophy*.

Devitt, Michael and Kim Sterelny (1987) *Language and Reality: An Introduction to the Philosophy of Language*, Oxford: Basil Blackwell.

Donnellan, Keith (1966) "Reference and Definite Descriptions," *The Philosophical Review* 75: 281–304.

Downing, P. (1970) "Are Causal Laws Purely General?," *Proceedings of the Aristotelian Society*, Supplementary Volume 44: 37–49.

Dretske, Fred (1977) "Laws of Nature," *Philosophy of Science* 44: 248–68.

Dretske, Fred and Aaron Snyder (1972) "Causal Irregularity," *Philosophy of Science* 39: 69–71.

Druckman, Daniel and John A. Swets (1988) *Enhancing Human Performance: Issues, Theories, and Techniques*, Washington, D.C.: National Academy Press.

Ducasse, C. J. (1968) "Objectivity, Objective Reference, and Perception," in Ducasse (ed.), *Truth, Knowledge and Causation*, New York: Humanities Press: 90–131.

Dummett, Michael (1954) "Can an Effect Precede Its Cause?," *Proceedings of the Aristotelian Society*, Supplementary Volume 28: 27–44.

—— (1964) "Bringing About the Past," *Philosophical Review* 73: 338–59.

—— (1978) *Truth and Other Enigmas*, Cambridge: Harvard University Press.

Earman, John (1983) *Testing Scientific Theories: Minnesota Studies in the Philosophy of Science*, Vol. X, Minneapolis: University of Minnesota Press.

Einstein, Albert (1917) *Relativity: The Special and General Theory*. Robert W. Lawson, transl. 15th Ed. 1961, New York: Crown Publishers. (First German edition, 1917.)

Ewing, A. C. (1935) "Mechanical and Teleological Causation," *Proceedings of the Aristotelian Society*, Supplementary Volume 14: 67–82.

—— (1962) "Causality and Induction," *Philosophy and Phenomenological Research* 12: 465–85.

—— (1968) *Nonlinguistic Philosophy*, London: George Allen & Unwin Ltd.

Fales, Evan M. (1978) "Theoretical Simplicity and Defeasibility," *Philosophy of Science* 45: 273–88.

—— (1979) "Relative Essentialism," *British Journal for the Philosophy of Science* 30: 349–70.

—— (1984) "Davidson's Compatibilism," *Philosophy and Phenomenological Research* 45: 227–46.

In prep. "Causal Knowledge: What Can Psychology Teach Philosophers?"

Field, Hartry (1972) "Tarski's Theory of Truth," *The Journal of Philosophy* 69: 347–75.

Fine, Arthur (1984) "The Natural Ontological Attitude," in Jarrett Leplin (ed.), *Scientific Realism*, Berkeley: The University of California Press: 83–107.

—— (1986) "Unnatural Attitudes: Realist and Instrumentalist Attachments to Science," *Mind* XCV: 149–79.

Fisk, Milton (1965) "Causation and Action," *The Review of Metaphysics* 19: 235–47.

Flew, Anthony (1954) "Can an Effect Precede Its Cause?," *Proceedings of the Aristotelian Society*, Supplementary Volume 28: 45–62.

—— (1955–6) "Effects Before Their Causes? – Addenda and Corrigenda," *Analysis* 16: 104–10.

Foster, John (1982–3) "Induction, Explanation and Natural Necessity," *Proceedings of the Aristotelian Society* New Series, Vol. 83: 87–101.

Fumerton, Richard (1980) "Induction and Reasoning to the Best Explanation," *Philosophy of Science* 47: 589–600.

Gale, Richard (1968) *The Language of Time*, London: Routledge & Kegan Paul.

Geach, Peter T. (1957) *Mental Acts*, London: Routledge & Kegan Paul.

Ginsberg, A. (1981) "Quantum Theory and the Identity of Indiscernibles Revisited," *Philosophy of Science* 48: 487–91.

Glymour, Clark (1980) *Theory and Evidence*. Princeton, N.J.: Princeton University Press.

Goldman, Alvin I. (1970) *A Theory of Human Action*. Englewood Cliffs, N.J.: Prentice-Hall.

Grünbaum, Adolf (1968) "The Status of Temporal Becoming," in Richard Gale (ed.), *The Philosophy of Time*, London: Macmillan & Co.: 322–33.

Hansel, C. E. M. (1980) *ESP and Parapsychology: A Critical Reevaluation*, Buffalo, N.Y.: Prometheus Books.

Harré, Rom and Edward H. Madden (1973) "In Defense of Natural Agents," *Philosophical Quarterly* 23: 117–32.

—— (1975) *Causal Powers*. Totowa, N.J.: Rowan & Littlefield.

Hempel, Carl (1952) "Methods of Concept Formation in Science," in Hempel, *Fundamentals of Concept Formation in Empirical Science*, *International Encyclopedia of Unified Science*, vol. 2, no. 7, Chicago: University of Chicago Press: 20–50.

Henle, James M. and Eugene M. Kleinberg (1979) *Infinitesimal Calculus*, Cambridge, Ma.: M.I.T. Press.

Hintikka, Jaakko (1965) "Towards a Theory of Inductive Generalization," in Yehoshua Bar-Hillel (ed.) *Logic, Methodology and Philosophy of Science* (Proceedings of the 1964 International Congress for Logic, Methodology, and Philosophy of Science), Amsterdam: North Holland: 274–88.

—— (1968) "Induction by Enumeration and Induction by Elimination," in Imre Lakatos (ed.) *The Problem of Inductive Logic*, Amsterdam: North Holland: 191–216.

Hochberg, Herbert (1981) "Natural Necessity and Laws of Nature," *Philosophy of Science* 48: 386–99.

Hume, David (1888) *A Treatise of Human Nature*. L. A. Selby-Bigge (ed.)
London: Oxford University Press.
—— (1963) *An Inquiry Concerning Human Understanding*, Lasalle, Ill.:
Open Court Publishing Co.
Inwagen, Peter van (1980) *Time and Cause: Essays Presented to Richard
Taylor*, Dordrecht: D. Reidel.
Jackson, Frank (1977) *Perception*, Cambridge: Cambridge University Press.
James, William (1968) *Some Problems of Philosophy*, New York:
Greenwood Press.
—— (1971) *Essays in Radical Empiricism and a Pluralistic Universe*, New
York: E. P. Dutton.
—— (1974) "The Will to Believe," reprinted in Baruch A. Brody (ed.),
Readings in the Philosophy of Religion: An Analytic Approach.
Englewood Cliffs, N.J.: Prentice Hall: 247–64.
Kaplan, David (1977) *Demonstratives*, Unpublished manuscript, second
draft.
Keynes, John Maynard (1921) *A Treatise on Probability*, London:
Macmillan & Co.
Kim, Jaegwon (1969) "Events and Their Descriptions: Some
Considerations," in Nicholas Rescher (ed.), *Essays in Honor of Carl G.
Hempel*, Dordrecht: D. Reidel: 198–215.
—— (1973a) "Causation, Nomic Subsumption and the Concept of Event,"
The Journal of Philosophy 70: 217–36.
—— (1973b) "Causes and Counterfactuals," *The Journal of Philosophy* 70:
570–2.
Kline, A. David (1982) "The Established Maxim and Causal Chains," in
Peter Asquith and Thomas Nickles (eds), *PSA 1982: Proceedings of the
Biennial Meeting of the Philosophy of Science Association* 1: 65–76.
Kneale, William (1949) *Probability and Induction*, Oxford: Oxford
University Press.
—— (1962) "Modality, De Dicto and De Re," in Ernest Nagel, Patrick
Suppes, and Alfred Tarski (eds), *Logic, Methodology and the Philosophy
of Science: Proceedings of the 1960 International Congress*, Stanford:
Stanford University Press: 622–33.
Kripke, Saul A. (1972) *Naming and Necessity*, Cambridge, Ma.: Harvard
University Press.
Lamprecht, Sterling P. (1929) "Causality," in *Essays in Honor of John
Dewey*, New York: Holt, Rinehart & Winston, Inc.: 191–205.
Laudan, Larry (1984) "A Confutation of Convergent Realism," in Jarrett
Leplin (ed.), *Scientific Realism*, Berkeley: The University of California
Press: 218–49.
Leslie, Alan M. (1982) "The Perception of Causality in Infants," *Perception*
11: 173–86
Leslie, Alan M. and Stephanie Keeble (1987) "Do Six-Month-Old Infants
Perceive Causality?," *Cognition* 25: 265–88.
Levi, I. (1967) *Gambling With Truth*, New York: Knopf.
Lewis, David K. (1973) *Counterfactuals*, Cambridge: Harvard University
Press.

—— (1984) "Putnam's Paradox," *The Australasian Journal of Philosophy* 62: 221–36.

Loux, Michael J. (ed.) (1970) *Universals and Particulars: Readings in Ontology*, New York: Doubleday and Company.

—— (1978) *Substance and Attribute: A Study in Ontology*, Dordrecht: D. Reidel.

McCloskey, H. J. (1963–4) "Some Concepts of Cause," *The Review of Metaphysics* 17: 586–607.

Mackie, J. L. (1965) "Causes and Conditions," *American Philosophical Quarterly* 2: 245–64.

—— (1979) "A Defense of Induction," in Graham F. MacDonald (ed.), *Perception and Identity: Essays Presented to A. J. Ayer with His Replies*, Ithaca, N.Y.: Cornell University Press: 113–30.

—— (1980) *The Cement of the Universe: A Study of Causation*, Oxford: Oxford University Press.

McTaggart, J. M. E. (1927) *The Nature of Existence*, vol. 2, Cambridge: Cambridge University Press.

Madden, E. H. (1969) "A Third View of Causality," *The Review of Metaphysics* 23: 67–84.

Maxwell, Grover (1962) "The Ontological Status of Theoretical Entities," in Herbert Feigl and Grover Maxwell (eds), *Minnesota Studies in the Philosophy of Science*, Vol. 3, Minneapolis: University of Minnesota Press: 3–27.

Meiland, J. W. (1966) "Do Relations Individuate?," *Philosophical Studies* 17: 65–9. Reprinted in Michael J. Loux (ed.) (1970): 258–63.

Mellor, D. H. (1981) *Real Time*, Cambridge: Cambridge University Press.

Merrill, D. H. (1980) "The Model-Theoretic Argument Against Realism," *Philosophy of Science* 47: 69–81.

Michotte, Albert (1963) *The Perception of Causality*. T. R. Miles and Elaine Miles (transl.), London: Methuen.

Mill, John Stuart (1973) *A System of Logic, Ratiocinative and Inductive, in the Collected Works of John Stuart Mill*, Vol. VII, J. M. Robinson (ed.), Toronto: University of Toronto Press.

Millikan, P. J. R. (1982) "Mackie's Defense of Induction," *Analysis* 42: 19–24.

Moore, G. E. (1923) "Are Characteristics Universal or Particular?," in *Relativity, Logic, and Mysticism*, *Proceedings of the Aristotelian Society*, Supplementary volume 3: 95–113.

Moyal, J. E. (1949) "Causality, Determinism, and Probability," *Philosophy* 24: 310–17.

Nute, Donald (1980) *Topics in Conditional Logic*, Boston: D. Reidel.

Pap, Arthur (1962) *An Introduction to the Philosophy of Science*, New York: The Free Press of Glencoe (Macmillan).

Pears, David F. (1951) "Universals," *Philosophical Quarterly* 1: 218–27; reprinted in Loux (1970): 35–49.

—— (1956–7) "The Priority of Causes," *Analysis* 17: 54–63.

Perkins, Moreland (1983) *Sensing the World*, Indianapolis, Ind.: Hackett Publishing Company.

Pollock, John (1976) *Subjunctive Reasoning*, Boston: D. Reidel.

Price, H. H. (1953) *Thinking and Experience*. New York: Hutchinson's University Library.

Putnam, Hilary (1975) "How Not to Talk About Meaning," "Is Semantics Possible?," and "The Meaning of 'Meaning'," all reprinted in Putnam, *Mind, Language and Reality: Philosophical Papers*, Vol. 2, Cambridge: Cambridge University Press.

—— (1981) *Reason, Truth and History*, Cambridge: Cambridge University Press.

Ramsey, Frank P. (1931) "Theories" and "General Propositions and Causality" in Ramsey, *The Foundations of Mathematics, and Other Logical Essays*, London: Kegan Paul: 212–36, 237–55.

Robinson, Abraham (1974) *Non-Standard Analysis*, Revised ed, Amsterdam: North Holland.

Rosenberg, Alexander (1975) "Propter Hoc, Ergo Post Hoc," *American Philosophical Quarterly* 12: 245–54.

Rosenberg, R. D. (1982) "Does the Philosophy of Induction Rest Upon a Mistake?," *Journal of Philosophy* 79: 78–97.

Rosenkrantz, Roger (1983) "Why Glymour *Is* a Bayesian," in John Earman (ed.), *Testing Scientific Theories, Minnesota Studies in the Philosophy of Science*, Vol. 10, Minneapolis: University of Minnesota Press: 69–97.

Russell, Bertrand (1917) "On the Notion of Cause," in Russell, *Mysticism and Logic*, Totowa, N.J.: Barnes & Noble: 132–51.

—— (1926) *Our Knowledge of the External World*, 2nd ed, London: George Allen & Unwin.

—— (1927) *The Analysis of Matter*, New York: Harcourt Brace & Co.

—— (1938) *Principles of Mathematics*, 2nd ed, New York: W. W. Norton & Co.

—— (1948) *Human Knowledge: Its Scope and Limits*, New York: Simon & Schuster.

Ryle, Gilbert (1939) "Plato's Parmenides," *Mind* 48: 129–51, 302–25.

Salmon, Wesley (1962–3) "Inductive Inference," in Bernard Baumrin (ed.), *Philosophy of Science: The Delaware Seminar II*, New York: John Wiley & Sons: 341–70.

Schaffner, K. F. (1969) "Correspondence Rules," *Philosophy of Science* 36: 280–90.

Schlick, Moritz (1932–33) "Positivism and Realism," *Erkenntnis* 3: 1–31; reprinted in Schlick 1979, *Collected Papers*, Henk L. Mulder and Barbara F. B. van de Velde-Schlick (eds), Peter Heath (transl.), Dordrecht: D. Reidel: 259–84.

—— (1936) "Meaning and Verification," *Philosophical Review* 45: 339–69.

Schmidt, Helmut (1969) "Precognition of a Quantum Process," *Journal of Parapsychology* 33: 106.

Scriven, Michael (1956–7) "Randomness and the Causal Order," *Analysis* 17: 5–9.

Searle, John R. (1983) *Intentionality*, Cambridge: Cambridge University Press.

Shoemaker, Sydney (1975) "On Projecting the Unprojectible,"

Philosophical Review 84: 178–219.

—— (1980a) "Properties, Causation and Projectibility," in L. Jonathan Cohen and Mary Hesse (eds), *Applications of Inductive Logic*, Oxford: Oxford University Press: 291–312.

—— (1980b) "Causality and Properties," in Peter Van Inwagen (ed.), *Time and Cause: Essays Presented to Richard Taylor*, Dordrecht: D. Reidel: 109–35.

Shultz, Thomas R. (1982) "Rules of Causal Attribution," *Monographs of the Society for Research in Child Development* 47: 1–51.

Smith, David W. (1982) "The Realism in Perception," *Nous* 16: 42–55.

Smith, Norman Kemp (1941) *The Philosophy of David Hume: A Critical Study of Its Origins and Central Doctrines*, London: Macmillan Company.

Sosa, Ernest (1975) *Causation and Conditionals*, London: Oxford University Press.

Spector, Marshall (1966) "Theory and Observation," *British Journal for the Philosophy of Science*, 17: 1–20, 89–104.

Stalnaker, Robert (1981) "A Theory of Conditionals," in William Harper, Robert Stalnaker, and G. Pearce (eds), *Ifs: Conditionals, Beliefs, Chance and Time*, Boston: D. Reidel: 41–56.

Stout, G. F. (1923) "Are Characteristics Universal or Particular?," in *Relativity, Logic and Mysticism: Proceedings of the Aristotelian Society*, Supplementary volume 3: 114–22.

—— (1931) *Mind and Matter*, Cambridge: Cambridge University Press.

—— (1935) "Mechanical and Teleological Causation," *Proceedings of the Aristotelian Society*, Supplementary volume 14: 46–65.

Stove, David C. (1973) *Probability and Hume's Inductive Skepticism*, Oxford: Oxford University Press.

—— (1986) *The Rationality of Induction*. Oxford: The Clarendon Press.

Strawson, Peter (1950) "On Referring," *Mind* 59: 320–44.

—— (1952) *Introduction to Logical Theory*, New York: Wiley & Son.

—— (1963) *Individuals: An Essay in Descriptive Metaphysics*, Garden City, New York: Doubleday & Co.

Stroyan, Keith D. and W. A. J. Luxemburg (1976) *Introduction to the Theory of Infinitesimals*, New York: Academic Press.

Swinburne, Richard G. (1980) "Properties, Causation and Projectibility: Reply to Shoemaker," in L. Jonathan Cohen and Mary Hesse (eds), *Applications of Inductive Logic*, Oxford: Oxford University Press: 313–20.

Swoyer, Chris (1982) "The Nature of Natural Laws," *Australasian Journal of Philosophy* 60: 203–23.

Taylor, Richard (1966) *Action and Purpose*, Englewood Cliffs, N. J.: Prentice-Hall.

Teller, Paul (1983) "Quantum Physics, The Identity of Indiscernibles, and Some Unanswered Questions," *Philosophy of Science* 50: 309–19.

Tooley, Michael (1977) "The Nature of Laws," *Canadian Journal of Philosophy* 7: 667–98.

—— (1984) "Laws and Causal Relations," in Peter French, Theodore Uehling, and Howard Wettstein (eds), *Midwest Studies in Philosophy IX:*

Causation and Causal Theories, Minneapolis: The University of Minnesota Press: 93–112.

—— (1987) *Causation: A Realist Approach*, Oxford: Oxford University Press.

Twain, Mark (1946) *The Portable Mark Twain*, Bernard De Voto (ed.), New York: The Viking Press.

Watkins, John (1984) *Science and Scepticism*, Princeton: Princeton University Press.

Whitehead, Alfred North (1959) *Symbolism: Its Meaning and Effect*, New York: Capricorn Books.

Index